DIANA MOSLEY

DIANA MOSLEY
– *A Life* –

JAN DALLEY

faber and faber

First published in 1999
by Faber and Faber Limited
3 Queen Square London WC1N 3AU

Photoset by Parker Typesetting Service, Leicester
Printed in England by Clays Ltd, St Ives plc

© Jan Dalley, 1999

Jan Dalley is hereby identified as author
of this work in accordance with Section 77
of the Copyright, Designs and Patents Act 1988

A CIP record for this book
is available from the British Library

ISBN 0-571-14448-9

2 4 6 8 10 9 7 5 3 1

Contents

Illustrations

14 Diana and Mosley at the Shaven Crown, 1944; Crowood House, Wiltshire; Mosley on the Lido in Venice (Hulton Getty); Diana on the *Alianora*.

15 Diana and Mosley with Alexander and Max at Crowood House; the Temple de la Gloire at Orsay, Diana's home until 1999; Mosley with supporters in an East End pub in the 1950s (Hulton Getty); Diana and Mosley arriving at London airport in the 1950s (Hulton Getty).

16 Diana at a Union movement meeting in the 1950s; Nancy, Debo, Pam and Diana with Cecil Beaton and the Duke of Devonshire at Chatsworth; Diana, Pam and Debo at Nancy's funeral, 1973 (David Newell-Smith, *Observer*); the Mosleys with Christina Foyle in 1977.

All photographs not credited have been supplied by the author with the kind permission of Lady Mosley.

Acknowledgements

My first acknowledgement must be to my subject, Lady Mosley, who was generous with her time, her hospitality and her memories in many interviews and conversations over the course of several years. This book would not have been possible without her help, and I am very appreciative of her kindness and patience, and of her help with the factual accuracy of the text. However, the book does not reflect her views, either of herself or of the past, nor does she endorse its contents or opinions. Furthermore, Lady Mosley did not want me to read her unpublished letters and diaries, or those of her husband and immediate family, during her lifetime, so any information contained in those is beyond the scope of this book. I am grateful to her, and to her sister the Duchess of Devonshire, for permission to use published sources relating to the family, and for many of the photographs.

It is to Roland Phillips that I owe the initial idea, and without the kind help of Selina Hastings it would never have progressed further than an idea, nor have been completed. Nothing at all would have been achieved without the constant support of my husband, Andrew Motion. My agent Carol Heaton, and my editors Chuck Elliott at Knopf and Jon Riley at Faber have been encouraging and patient. Nicholas Mosley was unstintingly generous with his reminiscences, and Alexander Mosley took great trouble over the reading of the text and with many thoughtful and thought-provoking comments. Roy Foster was an unfailingly encouraging friend and reader who saved me from many pitfalls. David Gilmour knows how much I owe him.

Lady Mosley's family and friends showed kindness and patience in answering my questions, and I am grateful to all those who talked to me about the project. A number of people were understandably reticent about contributing to a biography whose subject was still alive, and of those who declined to participate, I remember particularly the courtesy and good humour of the late Lord Moyne and the late Lady Alexandra Metcalfe.

My thanks are due to: Lady Abdy, the late Sir Harold Acton, Mrs Rosemary Bailey, David Cannadine, the Duchess of Devonshire, Lord

Dulverton, Jonathan Guinness, Vivien Guinness, the late Jeffrey Hamm, the governor and staff of HM Prison Holloway, the governor of HM Prison Brixton, Mrs Louise Irving, the late Pamela Jackson, the late James Lees-Milne, Jerry and Emily Lehane, Lord Longford, Denis Mack Smith, Lady Mersea, Anthony Powell, David Pryce-Jones, the late Sir Peter Quennell, Lord Skidelsky, Robert Swann, the late Jessica Truehaft.

Introduction

In the F block of Holloway prison, it was just possible to see out of the high windows, peering between the studded iron bars, by standing on a table or chair pushed against the wall. During the cold nights of the winter of 1940, a group of women was usually there, craning towards the firework display of the Blitz.

It was pitch dark – while the black-out was in force the prison lights were switched off at the mains at 4.30 in the afternoon, as the sun set. Fifteen hours of complete darkness stretched ahead, the only flickering illumination provided by the German planes which arrived punctually every night. The distant whizz and boom of falling bombs was sometimes varied by the cacophony of an anti-aircraft gun in the prison grounds. Locked in their cells, some of the women became hysterical or suicidal, so the authorities decided that the cell doors should be unlocked as the lights went off. The women could roam the prison corridors, or huddle together for talk and comfort.

There was a special urgency about the watching at the grimy windows, since many of the prisoners came from the narrow streets of the East End of London, which took the brunt of the bombardment. Each night brought an agonising wait: when the East End burned in the air raids, the women had no way of getting immediate news of their children, some of whom had been removed to orphanages, others farmed out to family or neighbours. Most of these women were fascists, or presumed to be: members or wives of members of Sir Oswald Mosley's British Union of Fascists, locked up in Holloway prison in 1940 under Defence Regulation 18b.

This regulation allowed the British government to imprison suspects with no charge, no trial and no time limit. Its powers were hastily expanded in May 1940, as Winston Churchill took over from Neville Chamberlain, Hitler's armies marched across France, and the 'phoney war' came to an abrupt end. For the first time, invasion by Germany became a serious possibility, and the rumours about 'Fifth Columnists', or enemies within, seemed a real threat. The suspension of habeas corpus and the loss of some of the most dearly held tenets of British law apparently troubled only a few liberals – apart from the fascists themselves. On the day after Oswald Mosley's arrest on 23 May 1940, survey teams from Mass Observation conducted a snap opinion poll. Although some people objected to the idea of imprisoning a man for what he might do, rather than for what he had done, a huge majority approved the arrest – and most added that it should have been done long before.

It was a raggle-taggle bunch of women who made up that group in Holloway. Those from fascist groups or families had been arrested when their husbands were sent to prison at Brixton or Liverpool, or to the newly devised internment camp on the Isle of Man. But there were also German and Italian women with no political affiliations, who were married to British men or who simply happened to be in the country at the outbreak of war. There was an Italian madam from Shepherd's Market, with flamboyant tastes in clothes and music, and a number of 'girls' in the same profession. There was the wife of Admiral Sir Barry Domvile, a former head of British Naval Intelligence, who had founded an extreme right-wing organization called the Link, with the aim of 'encouraging friendship' between Britain and Germany in the 1930s. There were women whose poverty, in their life outside, was so extreme that the prison's filth, repulsive food and thin damp mattresses constituted the best living conditions they had ever known.

The prisoners' records at Holloway, brief as they are, tell bitter stories of the kind that wars produce. One woman who spoke no English ('Nationality: Unknown') had been picked up half-dead from exposure and exhaustion on the east coast of England, having crossed the Channel alone in a tiny boat; another was a German who had been in the concentration camp at Dachau before the war for her left-wing views: fleeing Hitler to England, she was locked up in Holloway as an 'enemy alien'. She thought Holloway much dirtier than Dachau.

Among them, but a creature apart, was Diana Mosley, wife of the fascist leader. She was thirty, a brilliant blonde with porcelain skin and bright blue eyes, and an acknowledged society beauty. She seemed to have lived a whole life already. Married at eighteen to Bryan Guinness, one of the richest young men in England, she had become the centre of an artistic and social set that included writers, painters and thinkers as well as pleasure-seekers. But in 1933, contravening all the dictates of the time, she had left her husband for Oswald Mosley, who had a wife, a family, and a risky political future. Like everything she did, she made this scandalous move with apparently unshakeable self-confidence.

Diana was arrested suddenly on 29 June 1940, and obliged to leave behind her ten-week-old baby – whom she was breastfeeding – and a toddler of eighteen months, as well as her two older boys. She was told that it was 'for the weekend'; in fact, she did not see her baby again for ten months, and it was to be three and a half years before she was properly reunited with her children. For anybody in that position, let alone a fashionable young woman used to a pampered life, that first cell – it had no bed or chair, just a thin mattress on a flooded stone floor – would have seemed hard.

Diana quickly became the leader of that small pack of prisoners, taking her place at the head of the table at which the British Union women ate their meals, acting as an organizer and comforter to the others. Although these women were wives of her husband's supporters and lieutenants, or members of the BU's Women's Section, none of them knew her. While Mosley was building his movement, she had stood back from his day-to-day political activities, well protected from the rough-house, choosing to spend a good deal of time in Germany, enjoying her friendship with Hitler and Goebbels and other senior Nazis, and working on a commercial project that was supposed to secure Mosley's political funding. For many of her fellow prisoners, in the fiercer, class divisions of those days, she was a figure from a world they had only dreamt about. One devoted supporter said simply, 'I had never seen anyone like her.'

She made herself popular in prison. When Winston Churchill tried to intervene to improve her conditions, asking that she should be allowed a bath every day, Diana declined this special treatment – there was only enough water in the whole prison system for four baths a day, and each prisoner was lucky to bathe once a week. She felt protective about her fellow inmates, some of them pitifully young, with shabby clothes; she remembered the piebald hair of the convicted woman, with brown roots growing through the crude bleach. In the bleak atmosphere there was at least laughter and talk, and those were Diana's strengths: she remembered that during the freezing nights of the Blitz they would huddle round while the prostitutes entertained them with stories of their customers and the goings-on inside their various establishments. Many years after Diana's release, an acquaintance of hers visited Holloway, where a Miss Davies, a warder who had worked there since the war, told her, 'Oh, we've never had such laughs since Lady Mosley left.'

The Honourable Diana Freeman-Mitford was born on 10 June 1910, the fourth child of Sydney and David Mitford, who succeeded to his father's title and became Lord Redesdale in 1916. There were seven children in the family.

Nancy was born six years before Diana; then came Pam in 1907; and the only boy, Tom, was Diana's senior by a year. After this first foursome came three more daughters: Unity, born in 1914, followed by Jessica (1917) and Deborah (1920). Diana thought her place in the family was 'inconspicuous': 'my very existence was of interest only to Nanny and to Tom, who was almost my twin,' she wrote. The family might easily have remained inconspicuous, leading the predictable country life of many families like them, with 'Farve' dedicated to his field sports, looking after his land and occasionally making the journey to London to sit in the House of Lords, 'Muv' presiding vaguely over her brood, with their governesses, pets and ponies, until the day when she brought her many girls out and saw them respectably married.

Instead, the Mitfords became famous, or infamous, through the various talents and adventures of their children. The least known of the seven was Pamela, the 'quiet' one, devoted to country life after her fifteen-year marriage to Derek Jackson, a brilliant physicist, until her death in 1996. Tom was also less disposed to make headlines than most of his sisters. He was a barrister and a musician, a Germanophile and fascist sympathizer who was killed fighting in Burma in 1945 at the age of thirty-six. The other five, however, each found the limelight early, and each in her own way. Nancy (who died in 1973) was a prolific author and wit who wrote one of the best-known and best-loved comic novels of English life, *The Pursuit of Love*. Unity aroused persistent press attention during her short life, as a convinced Nazi and a member of Hitler's close circle; in Germany at the outbreak of war she shot herself, unsuccessfully, but lived on until 1948. Jessica became a committed communist, ran away to Spain at eighteen with her first husband, Esmond Romilly, and later settled in America where, until her death in 1997, she was a well-known writer, journalist and civil-rights activist. Deborah, now the Duchess of Devonshire, runs her house and farms at Chatsworth as well as writing books on the house, the garden and the family history.

Their contemporaries recognized how unusual they were. John Betjeman, a friend of Diana and her first husband Bryan Guinness, and an admirer of Pam, is credited with the first use of the phrase 'the Mitford Girls' in 1931. In a piece of verse made up for a friend's album, he wrote:

> The Mitford Girls, the Mitford Girls
> I love them for their sins,
> The younger ones like *Cavalcade*,
> The old like Maskelyn's.*

* Maskelyn was a popular conjuror.

Sophistication, blessed Dame,
Sure they have heard thy call,
Yes, even gentle Pamela,
Most rural of them all.

Though the first few years of Diana's childhood were relatively uneventful, the Mitfords soon became well known in their own circle and then beyond it, through society pages and gossip columns, and the publication of Nancy's early novels. No less than her brother and sisters, Diana had heard the call of sophistication, as Betjeman put it, and by the end of her teens she was already used to the glare of flashbulbs. She called her memoirs *A Life of Contrasts*, and it was an apt title. The backdrop to her teenage years was a counterpoint between the traditional rhythms of the landed gentry and the shrill iconoclasm of the Roaring Twenties: a defining theme of that decade. Her next ten years were lived in the cross-currents which ran between the artistic, intellectual and social élites and the dark creed of fascism – a defining element, again, in that era. Hers was a life of the times.

She was also a traditional woman of her time, in that she chose to make her impact on the world through her men, her family and her circle. Nobody who knew her doubted the strength of her personality or her intellect, but after she joined her life to Mosley it is impossible to separate exactly which were her own achievements, which entirely his, and which were fuelled by their mutually reinforcing partnership. How much did she influence him? What part did she play in his ambitions, the development of his thinking, the course of his fate? These things cannot be quantified with precision, but the logic of their joint story suggests a number of answers. It also determines the need for including here much about Mosley's life, about the strong impulses of Diana's family and forebears, and about the significant political and social currents that moved around them all.

Diana was one of very few people who knew both Churchill and Hitler well. As a link between Britain and Germany in the 1930s she occupied a strange and perhaps unique position; she was a sharp-eyed onlooker, and sometimes a participant, at a crucial historical moment. Her life spanned what Eric Hobsbawm called the 'Age of Ideology' – roughly speaking, from the First World War to the fall of the Berlin Wall. In the chaos after 1918, unemployment and poverty became so acute that many people believed capitalism had collapsed and democracy was failing. They looked for alternatives, searching for belief, direction and certainty in one global theory or another. Communism was the most durable and, to many intellectuals, the most attractive; another, apparently viable, alternative was fascism.

Since the Holocaust the very word has been indissolubly linked with genocide, but in the early 1930s that shadow had not yet descended on fascism. It offered a rapid cure for intractable social ills, and the early successes of Hitler and Mussolini seemed to show that it worked. It was a radical ideology, and at the time an individual with a social conscience, tired of entrenched values, could turn to fascism for radical solutions. To realize that requires an imaginative leap for post-war generations looking back to the 1930s, Auden's 'low, dishonest decade', across this century's great divide – the Holocaust.

This book does not touch on that huge subject. Diana's life brought her close to the process which produced the tragedy, and close to some of the people who determined its course. The backdrop to her life invokes notions of absolute good and evil, and the many shades of human compromise which lie between. But in her personal story there is an almost eerie absence of the horrors that underlie all our thinking about fascism, Nazism and the Second World War. Whether this was pure luck or wilful disassociation, historical irony or culpable failure to make the essential connections – these are things the reader can decide. When a biographer wants to examine a life, and what that life says about its times, she must seek out the reasons for her subject's behaviour, predilections and choices. But there is an essential difference between reasons and excuses. This book tries to provide reasons, but offers no excuses.

1 *Forebears*

Believers in heredity, or genetic explanations for the emergence of certain traits, will find plenty of fuel for such beliefs in the Mitford children's two grandfathers. Between them, these two eminent and contrasting Victorians embodied most of the characteristics associated with the British in that era, for good and not so good. Certainly they had all the energy and vitality, the formidable self-confidence, the application, canny intelligence, class certainties and bloody-mindedness that manifested themselves again in their singular brood of grandchildren.

Algernon Bertram Mitford (1837–1916), known as Bertie (it was usually pronounced 'Barty' in those days), came from an old landed Northumberland family. He was a traveller, diplomat, linguist, author and collector. He rebuilt Batsford Park, in Gloucestershire, demolishing the fine Georgian manor house he had inherited and replacing it with a rambling mock-medieval monster. He had nine children; he was created first Baron Redesdale, a hereditary title.

Through the House of Commons, where both men sat as Conservative members of Parliament, Bertie made the acquaintance of Thomas Gibson Bowles (1841–1921), who was known even to his children as Tap. Bowles's origins reflect another facet of the Victorian world. Born illegitimate, he was accepted into the solid, upper-middle-class family of his natural father. He became a passionate yachtsman, entrepreneurial magazine owner, fiery parliamentary orator.

Tap Bowles seems a storybook figure, almost too picturesque to be real: handsome, dynamic, successful, eccentric, and with odd beginnings. Out of the blue one day in 1844, a radical Liberal politician called Thomas Milner-Gibson, a Suffolk landowner, brought home a little surprise: a three-year-old boy called Thomas, whom he introduced to his wife, Susannah, as his natural son. The child's mother was a Susan Bowles, about whom almost nothing is known, although Tap Bowles always carried her surname. If he remembered anything of his very early life, he never spoke of it; he did not even know the exact date of his birth. Susannah Milner-Gibson had been unaware of the child's existence, but she was obviously a woman of grit: she accepted him straight away into her family of two daughters (she later had four sons as well), loved him as if he were her own child, and quickly adopted the habit (according to family legend) of brushing away visitors' inquisitive questions with: 'This is Tom Bowles. Be civil to him, or leave my house.'

It was a potentially scandalous arrangement, but both the Milner-Gibsons were firm in their stance. Tap Bowles certainly loved Susannah as a real mother, although his father's attitude to him was more ambivalent. Milner-Gibson took his son into his family, but did not give him his surname. The young Thomas was close to his father, but when the time came for schooling he was not sent to a famous English public school, like his step-brothers, but to an establishment in France.

Milner-Gibson continued to look after Thomas, however, finding him his first job as a clerk at Somerset House when he himself was President of the Board of Trade. But Tap was not of a disposition to remain a clerk for long, and the work bored him. He was extremely good-looking, dandyish and highly sociable; he loved sport (especially rackets, running and riding), and caught from his father a passion for sailing that was to last all his life. He enjoyed the theatre and even more enthusiastically enjoyed some of the actresses. This lifestyle required more than a clerk's wages, even if they were topped up by his father, and Tap Bowles took to freelance journalism, with all his habitual flair – by the time he was twenty-five he was publishing an article on politics or current affairs in the *Morning Post* almost daily. He had apparently superhuman energy, and the self-belief to go with it.

If this success went to his head, at least his next gamble paid off. He was now well established as a writer, and at twenty-six he left his civil-service job and – with very little money and few backers – determined to start a new weekly magazine, which he called *Vanity Fair*. The first issue, which came out in November 1868, sold just over 600 copies, and the new venture teetered on the edge of failure until Bowles hit on the idea of the celebrity cartoons which became its trademark. When its controversial tone began to annoy many establishment figures, its success was assured. Another venture was *The Lady*, established in 1885, a vastly successful genteel women's magazine that still remains in the ownership of Bowles's descendants.

Tap's happy marriage to a woman he loved, Jessica Evans-Gordon, produced four children: two boys, George and Geoffrey, then Sydney (who became Lady Redesdale) and another daughter, Dorothy (always known as Weenie). He was an active and participating father – somewhat against the fashion of the times – and he had firm views about the children's regime. They were to have no medicine of any sort. They were never to eat between meals, and never to eat pork, rabbit, hare or shellfish. (This respect for Mosaic law was based on Tap's idea that Jewish children were the healthiest in London, and that Jews never got cancer.) Other rules, which were printed and hung on the nursery wall for the nurses to follow, included always having the window open, even at night (this was very much against current practice) and always rinsing the children in clean water before they got out of the bath. His own curious daily routine – rising at 6.00 a.m., a cooked *déjeuner* at 11.30, then dinner at 8.00 p.m., and nothing else – was one he stuck to until his death at the age of eighty, with a blithe disregard for any inconvenience it caused his family or hosts.

Sydney later told her own children that most of Tap's rules were ignored in the nursery, but two at least stuck with her throughout her own life: the dietary prohibitions and the injunction against medicine. All the Mitford children were brought up on Tap's view that 'the Good Body' would heal itself, if it were just left alone, and although the doctor was sometimes called, his medicaments usually went straight into the dustbin. When Pamela was three she caught polio, in those days an untreatable disease that often left the sufferer badly crippled, with little that conventional medicine could do. Sydney called in Tap's osteopath for a regime of massage and exercises (still considered unusual) which succeeded where half a dozen doctors had failed, and Pam's recovery was almost complete. Even 'normal' medicine could be strangely administered in this family. Diana, at seven, had her appendix removed on a table in one of the spare bedrooms at Batsford. 'I awoke from the anaesthetic in a huge red brocade bed,' she remembered. 'I suppose nowadays the surgeon would insist on a clinic. Personally I prefer . . . beautiful unhygienic surroundings which (if one cares about such things) hasten recovery.'

Another rule of Tap's which Sydney applied to her own brood was that no child should ever be made to eat anything they didn't want – quite normal now, but considered bizarre, even wicked, in those days of puritanical nursery regimes. Hare and rabbit were never eaten in the Mitford household, although her husband shot them so often that he had a large 'hare pocket' tailored into even his town suits. David reserved the right to eat bacon for breakfast, pork chops and so on, but the children were never allowed these forbidden delights. When Tom first went away to boarding school, his sisters were wild with envy at his letters describing the wonder of 'sossages', and when Diana was first married she asked her cook, every single night, for dressed crab.

With his large, comfortable Kensington house, a growing family and a wife who loved him, it seemed as if Tap's domestic life was to be as charmed as his business and political affairs. But in 1887 the complications of a fifth pregnancy proved too much for the delicate Jessica to survive. Sydney was only seven when her mother died, and life changed dramatically.

Tap responded to the pain of his wife's death in a characteristically eccentric way. He bought a yacht, the *Nereid*, and loaded up his family for a cruise lasting a year – despite the fact that little Weenie was only three. From now on he always kept his daughters with him, even when the boys went away to school, discussing his plans with them as if they were grown up. Invariably dressed in matching sailor suits specially made in the thickest navy serge (which they detested), with stockings of thick undyed wool and black leather shoes, Sydney and Weenie went everywhere with their strange, charismatic father, at sea and on land. By the age of fourteen, Sydney was running her father's new London household, in Lowndes Square, where he settled in some style. She had to deal with quite a number of servants, and her unease with menservants dates from this time: later, in the Mitford households, she never employed men.

This unconventional life meant that Sydney – a motherless child – was effectively allowed no childhood at all after her mother's death. Small wonder that she, in her turn, became a vague and distant mother to her seven children, rarely hugging them or even giving them the impression that she was more than mildly interested in their doings. But the respect for convention that often goes with an insecure background she certainly had, together with a good deal of Tap's dottiness.

Sydney was still wearing a sailor suit when, accompanying her father on a visit to Batsford Park in 1894, at the age of fourteen, she first met the young David Mitford.

David's father, Bertie Mitford, was not yet Lord Redesdale: the peerage was granted in 1906. The invitation to Tap Bowles had come about through political affiliations, because Bertie wanted Tap to speak at a local meeting. Although the two men had had a very different start in life, they held similar views, and seemed to enjoy each other's company – even if the very proper Lady Clementine, Bertie's wife and Diana's future grandmother, the daughter of the Earl of Airlie, was less than enthusiastic about Tap's famously rough and ready manners.

Bertie, too, had begun his career as a clerk, at the Foreign Office, and like Tap had enjoyed the social opportunities the unarduous job allowed. Bertie was also energetic and rumbustious: his sporting passion, though, was not for sailing but for bare-knuckle fighting, which had long been illegal. He rose quickly, getting a posting to Russia in the winter of 1863–4; this, like all his travels, is vividly documented in his two-volume *Memories* (which Jessica dubbed 'Grandfather's depressingly huge autobiography'). In the next ten years he managed to span the continents, relishing dangerous ventures into the unknown as much as foreign fleshpots. After a trip to Turkey he volunteered for a posting to Peking, which marked the beginning of his expertise on the Far East, and he became a collector of beautiful and rare Oriental objects. From China he was posted directly to Japan, in 1866.

After more than 200 years of deliberate isolation, Japan's ruling shoguns had opened the country to outsiders a few years before. The diplomatic task, as foreigners saw it, was to make the country ready for potentially lucrative trade. Even though Bertie's writing shows a relentlessly imperialist way of thinking (he never questioned the right of foreign powers like Britain to 'teach the Chinese a lesson', for instance, or entertained a moment's doubt about the justice of the Opium Wars), in Japan he found a culture he deeply appreciated. His arch-conservatism, his courtly diplomacy, his passion for heraldry and chivalry, and what was obviously an enormous talent for languages, all served him well. Within a short time he was fluent enough to translate for visiting foreigners, even from the elaborate language of the court; when called upon to witness the ceremonial seppuku of a samurai warrior, he was appalled but profoundly moved and affected. Everything about the samurai, from their exquisite weaponry and elaborate and beautiful garb to their codes of honour and self-sacrifice, found an echo in Bertie's solid English soul. The huge success of his book *Tales of Old Japan*, which was published in 1871, is probably attributable not only to the fact that all this knowledge about Japan was quite new, but also to the deep feeling that fuelled the book. Bertie only made one serious mistake – one which was typical of his financial acumen. He sold the book to Macmillan for a flat fee of £240, with no royalty rights: it has never been out of print.

Before the book was even published, Bertie was off to the Middle East to join his old friend, the orientalist Richard Burton, then consul in Damascus. Soon afterwards another old friend, the Duke of Sutherland, suggested they should both board the first train to be allowed into Paris after the end of the revolutionary Paris Commune; they witnessed the terrible aftermath of that defeat. The Duke's next plan was to take Bertie with him to see Garibaldi, the champion of Italian unification, whom Bertie described as 'a King among men'. After that it was the United States, where Bertie landed in New York in the spring of 1873 and headed west to the frontier. He hunted buffalo, hiked across the Rockies, admired the pioneers, was (perhaps surprisingly) fiercely critical of the treatment of the Indians; he travelled to Salt Lake City to meet Brigham Young, founder of the Mormon faith, then headed west again to Nevada and California. From San Francisco he took a ship across to his beloved Japan, rode around the country on horseback for several weeks, then sailed back again to San Francisco and retraced his steps eastwards.

The following year, 1874, he got a job, a wife, a house in London, and settled down. If he was bored, after all his adventures, he hardly gave himself time to feel it. His job as Secretary to the Board of Works (it was one of the first civil-service appointments Disraeli made) meant responsibility for London's parks and monuments, and Bertie set to work on huge refurbishments at Windsor Castle and the Tower of London, both of which had been badly neglected, as well as on the redesign and planting of London's major parks. The restoration of old buildings allowed him to exercise his love of the Gothic and the Tudor, as well as his odd contempt for Georgian style, which was later to prove a family disaster at Batsford Park. His marriage to Lady Clementine Ogilvie, produced six children in a dozen years: David Mitford was the third child and second son. Their house in Cheyne Walk, on the river in Chelsea, made them close neighbours of the American painter James McNeill Whistler – whose house, by coincidence, Diana was later to buy during her first marriage – and the painter became one of many eminent figures in Bertie and Clementine's social circle. They seem to have been thoroughly happy, although there were already money problems.

Bertie, this prototype of the successful Victorian – Eton in the 1840s, Oxford in the 1850s, travel, scholarship and wild adventure, then London society and public service – now entered his next phase. In 1886 he inherited from an elderly cousin a large Georgian house at Batsford Park in Gloucestershire, with big estates and heavy responsibilities. So he at once became country squire, magistrate, farmer, horse breeder and deputy lord lieutenant of the county. He also went into Parliament – late in life, like Tap Bowles – as the Conservative member for Stratford-upon-Avon, although he only spent three years in the House of Commons.

Not content with pulling down the Georgian manor and replacing it with a huge new house, Bertie set to work on his gardens. He replanted, landscaped, and imported exotic plants to make settings for some of his collection of Oriental statuary. To this day the gardens at Batsford contain immense buddhas and Japanese bird fountains.

How could he afford all this? No one knew, and it is likely that Bertie spent far too much capital on these building projects, laying up difficulties for his heir. Meanwhile, he remained highly respected (he was sent back to Japan, to his delight, on a mission to present the Order of the Garter to the emperor), intellectually versatile (he took up photography and became President of the Royal Photographic Society), and prolific in his output and enthusiasms. One of his more extreme intellectual interests, just before the First World War, connects strangely with the life of his granddaughter Diana. This was his interest in the writings of Houston Stewart Chamberlain.

Houston Stewart Chamberlain was an Englishman by birth and a German by choice. He had been educated in France and Germany, and had conceived a passion for German culture; he took German nationality in 1916, during the First World War. He venerated Wagner, and by the time Bertie knew him, in the early years of the century, he was living at Haus Wahnfried in Bayreuth as friend and acolyte of Wagner's son Siegfried and his widow Cosima; he eventually married Eva Wagner, one of the great man's daughters. He had produced books on Kant and Goethe, but it was his *Life of Wagner* that had made him a well-known, if controversial figure.

The book which earned Chamberlain a place in one of history's most bitter footnotes is his massive tome *Gründlagen des Neunzehnten Jahrhunderts*, or *The Foundations of the Nineteenth Century*, which was published in Germany in 1899 to huge success. When it came to an English edition – Chamberlain wrote in German, naturally – the author himself asked Bertie Redesdale to contribute an Introduction, perhaps because Bertie had corresponded with Chamberlain about his work. The Introduction was duly written, and signed from Batsford Park on 8 January 1909 – some time before the translation of the work, by John Lees, was complete; so we must assume that Bertie's German was adequate to the job of absorbing its thousand-odd densely and bizarrely argued pages. The book was published in Britain and America in 1911.

The Foundations of the Nineteenth Century can best be described as a mighty hymn to the innate superiority of the Teutonic people. It is a rambling, ranting meditation which calls up anthropological and 'scientific' evidence (from the new discipline of eugenics), as well as historical, cultural, theological, philosophical and purely personal facts and theories to prove its case – its case being that cultural achievement is determined by racial characteristics (which are inescapable and constant), and that the achievements of the Indo-European ('Aryan') language groups are demonstrably superior to those of other racial groups. Within that wider category, moreover, the Teutonic or Germanic people are markedly superior to all the rest. Thus Chamberlain's real point: that a racially pure German empire should, obviously, rule the world.

Laced through this argument is a detailed discussion of the nature and role of the Jewish peoples. Chamberlain was an anti-Semite of the most elaborate kind – that is, an apparently learned and 'expert' cultural historian (he takes issue, for instance, with a Professor Delitzsch on the knotty question of monotheism among the Semitic tribes of Canaan) but simultaneously a victim of crude and visceral prejudice. Like many racists, he tried to wrap these prejudices up in fancy intellectual ribbons in order to validate them. He pays tribute to the 'greatness' of the Jews in their refusal to intermarry, and flips this round to use the Jewish people's insistence on their own racial and cultural purity as further justification for the Teutonic people to do the same. He believed Jewish thought would impart a sense of sin to the Teutonic, and therefore weaken it, and so impair its magnificent resolve to build the future.

Why was Bertie Redesdale sufficiently impressed by this book to write an admiring Introduction to its English edition, and to describe it as being 'adorned with brilliant passages of the loftiest eloquence'? Bertie had travelled the world, he admired and respected widely differing cultures: despite this, he, too, believed that racial origins determined almost everything. His Introduction begins with a brief biography of Houston Stewart Chamberlain, explaining his brilliance by his 'illustrious ancestors', making him 'an instance of atavism, or, to use the hideous word coined by Galton, "eugenics".' Bertie, too, was a great admirer of Wagner, and through Chamberlain came to be a friend of Siegfried Wagner and a regular guest at Haus Wahnfried; the effect of performances at Bayreuth he described in quasi-religious terms. In common with many educated English people at the time, he regarded German culture as highly superior.

As to the racial question, David Pryce-Jones, in his biography of Unity Mitford, considers Bertie an out-and-out anti-Semite; though Bertie's great-grandson Jonathan Guinness mounts a spirited defence, not of Chamberlain's book but of Bertie's interest in it, pointing out that acceptable modes of thinking about race have altered completely since the beginning of the century. He insists that high respect for the Nordic races was widespread: quotas of immigrants to America, for instance, were heavily weighted in their favour. He quotes Bertie taking issue, in the Introduction, with some of Chamberlain's comments about the Ashkenazim – 'of the treasure which they have laid up they have given freely. The charities of the great cities of Europe would be in a sad plight were the support of the Jews to be withdrawn . . . Politically too they have rendered great services . . .' The last remark is a respectful nod to Bertie's hero and patron, Disraeli. It might also be seen as the 'some of my best friends' syndrome.

Whatever the arguments, there is no hiding the real nature of this book. Chamberlain's chapter called 'Jews Enter into Western History' is subtitled 'Consciousness of Sin against Race', and contains the following: 'It is very proper to lay strong emphasis on this; for such a process, however unconsciously it may go on, is an incestuous crime against nature; it can only be followed by a miserable and tragic fate.' For all his hundreds of pages ranging across world history, his arguments in the end rely on concepts such as 'an incestuous crime against nature' and (above all) 'fate'.

And there is no hiding the real tragedy of this book – its own 'fate'. If there had been no afterlife for this work and others like it, we might regard it, and its absurd little drawings of caricatured facial types (labelled 'Hittite', 'Amoritish Israelite', 'Amorite', etc.), with distant dispassion – like a belief in leeches, or phrenology, or possession by the devil. But Chamberlain's book gave high-octane fuel to the growth of the Nazi creed, providing for Hitler's theories in *Mein Kampf* just the right mixture of intellectual justification and high emotionalism.

Hitler finally met his hero Houston Stewart Chamberlain at Haus Wahnfried in September 1923 – the Wagner household was staunchly pro-Hitler, both at this date and later, when Siegfried's widow Winifred presided over Wahnfried after both Cosima and her son died in 1930 – and the admiration was mutual. A letter from Chamberlain to Hitler a few weeks later, shortly before the disastrous November *putsch* of that year, proclaimed, 'That Germany in the hour of her deepest need should have given birth to a Hitler bears witness to its living strength.'

When, a dozen years later, Hitler first met Unity and Diana Mitford, their descent from Bertie the Germanophile, friend of Wagner's son and supporter of one of Hitler's great mentors, was of huge importance to him. He used to mention it constantly. To him it was no mere chance. He was extremely superstitious, and believed in predestination of all kinds: these two big shining blonde angels, or Angles, seemed to him touched by the mighty, magical Aryan heritage. They not only looked like moon-goddesses, they not only came from a good family, they not only followed him devotedly, but they were the living embodiment of his racial theories. Their presence may even have allowed him to think that England was somehow, deep down in the genes, already his. This was a view which Unity certainly encouraged, and Hitler himself was aware of the strange coincidence of English people clustered about the precious Wagnerian heritage: Winifred Wagner, one of only a handful of women whom Hitler ever considered as anywhere near an equal, was also English by birth. Those around Hitler – and there were many – who were puzzled, resentful or outraged by his allowing two young Englishwomen into his intimate circle, even when policy was being discussed, had failed to understand what these adoring beauties represented to the mind of a fanatic.

2 An English Childhood

The Mitford family childhood has been written about so much that some of its exploits have passed into legend; it is hard now to separate mythology from truth. Nancy Mitford drew a highly caricatured picture of her father in her first novel, *Highland Fling*, in 1931. In that book 'Farve' appears as General Murgatroyd, a terrifying joke figure of the old guard, but the most famous fictionalized account of the whole family, the 'Radletts', was in her fourth novel, *The Pursuit of Love*, published in 1945. It is hilarious but poignant, giving a picture of a large, lively, isolated upper-class country family in a big rambling house, where a huge brood of children and their peculiar, adored pets are presided over by the irascible Uncle Matthew, always shouting and shooting and cursing foreigners, and his mild-mannered wife Aunt Sadie.

In 1945, on the publication of Evelyn Waugh's *Brideshead Revisited* (a novel that is loosely based on the Lygon family, whom they all knew), Nancy wrote to her close friend Evelyn that she was writing a book about her own family, 'a very different cup of tea, not grand and far madder'. Her next remark – 'Did I begin it before reading B.head or after I can't remember' – seems quite casual, but shows that she knew the two books sprang from a similar source of feeling. Like *Brideshead Revisited*, *The Pursuit of Love* (it was Waugh who suggested the title) came to be seen as a paean to a vanished way of life, affectionately mocked for its eccentricities, but revealed as all the more precious for that. Uncle Matthew may have been absurd and extreme, but everyone felt they knew someone like him: if they didn't, they wished they had. The Radlett family might have been slightly barmy, but many people would happily have exchanged their own humdrum childhood for this highly coloured, close and vivid family life. And because it is about a peer's family, who moan about poverty but drive about in a Daimler, it played to the snob in everyone.

The Second World War was just over, and heart-of-England stories were popular. Yet the Radlett's highly charged emotional tone (their 'shrieks' of laughter and 'floods' of tears) is very unlike the stereotype of English behaviour – although their way of pouring more feeling into animals than people is typical. Partly in order to refute the cosiness and established values of Nancy's account, Jessica decided to publish her own autobiography, *Hons and Rebels*, in 1960. Its tone is more critical, more challenging to the class certainties of the family, more scathing about the neglect of the children's education and the deficiencies of their quaint upbringing. Although Nancy's book is supposed to be a novel, and Jessica's was published as autobiography, many of the family considered that the fictional element, or distortion of the family's true nature, was about equal in each. Diana pointed out that when *Hons and Rebels* was written, 'Decca had been away from all of us for twenty-five years' and referred disparagingly to 'the gross injustice' of the book.

Neither of these accounts is quite a true reflection of Diana's childhood experience. There was a large age gap between her and Jessica, and the structure of their childhoods was so formalized – leading a life apart in the nursery with Nanny until the age of about eight – that they barely shared a childhood at all. There were only a few years between the time Jessica left the nursery, which meant meals downstairs with the rest of the family, and the moment when Diana left home to get married. They were in different 'halves' of the family: the group consisting of Nancy, Pam, Tom and Diana was quite separate from the three younger girls. So Diana had more in common with Nancy's version, but again her experience was different – as the reality of life for each child within the same family is always different. Diana's own autobiography, *A Life of Contrasts*, reinforces some of the family legends and places her childhood world firmly in her own perspective. But when she called her own place in the family 'inconspicuous' she was right: it was not during her childhood that she made her distinctive mark. In these early years she was carried along on the wave of a large family dominated by strong personalities: her father, her mother, her sister Nancy, her brother Tom. As soon as she could – when she was only eighteen – she escaped her family into marriage, and her individual character emerged strongly from then onwards.

An outsider's more balanced view comes from James Lees-Milne, Tom Mitford's close friend, in *Another Self*, one of his volumes of autobiography:

> Readers of Nancy and Jessica Mitford's books have probably
> concluded that their home life was a sort of nether world ruled by their
> parents, Lord and Lady Redesdale, in the guise of Hades ('fierce,
> inexorable and of all the gods the most hated by mortals,' according to
> Dr Smith's Classical Dictionary, 'whose diet was black sheep and his

own children') and his wife Persephone, Queen of the Shades. This was by no means my impression. On the contrary, Swinbrook Manor, where this large and united family lived, was to me Elysium. Lady Redesdale did perhaps resemble Persephone in her statuesque, melancholy beauty and her capacity to endow her surroundings 'with beautiful views, flowery meadows and limpid streams' (Dr Smith again), for her taste in gardens, houses, decoration, furniture and food was impeccable. She presided, for that is the word, over her beautiful and eccentric brood with unruffled sweetness, amusement and no little bewilderment. Lord Redesdale was admittedly a dual personality. I cannot see that his children had in him much to complain about. Towards them he was Dr Jekyll, indulgent and even docile. Although not a cultivated man he tolerated their intellectual pursuits and allowed them to say and do whatever they liked. He submitted placidly to their ceaseless teasing, particularly Nancy's with its sharp little barb, barely concealed like the hook of an angler's fly beneath a riot of gay feathers.

This is an attempt to portray the truth behind the myths, and a necessary one. Turning childhood experiences into fiction usually happens some time afterwards, and with hindsight, but the fictionalizing of the Mitford family had begun while that family life was still in progress. When *Highland Fling* was published, the three younger girls were still in the schoolroom, Nancy still lived chiefly at home, and Tom stayed regularly for long periods. Lord Redesdale therefore had to react to himself portrayed, as Jessica described, 'as . . . a man of violent temper, terror of housemaids and gamekeepers, who spent most of his time inveighing against the Huns and growling at various languid, aesthetic young men in pastel shirts who kept popping up at unexpected moments . . . [His] particular argot – "Damn sewer!" "Stinks to merry hell!" – his loathing of anything or anyone who smacked of the literary or the artistic, were drawn to the life.'

Within the family, the publication of Nancy's first novel had two results (not counting the inevitable row). 'Farve became – almost overnight – more a character of fiction than of real life,' Jessica said, 'an almost legendary figure, even to us.' His 'Murgatroydish aspects' began to lose some of their terror, and he started to mellow: the childhood fireworks suffered by Nancy, Pam, Tom and Diana receded into anecdote. More surprisingly, Jessica reported that Farve 'rather loved being General Murgatroyd', and the angry friends and relations parodied here for the first of several times by Nancy grew proud of having an author in the family and enjoyed playing up to their stereotype.

So much for the fiction. What of the facts? The real David Mitford, the original of 'General Murgatroyd' and 'Uncle Matthew', was born in 1878, the second son of Bertie Mitford, later Lord Redesdale, who had nine children in all. The Mitfords were descended from a long line of landed gentlemen, and the Northumberland estates belonging to the fourteenth-century Sir John Mitford, as well as land in Oxfordshire and in Gloucestershire around Batsford Park, were still in the family. The eldest son, Clement, was due to inherit the title, as well as the family properties; David, a younger son, had to earn his own living.

When David married Sydney Bowles in 1904, money was short. After a spell on a tea-plantation in Ceylon David had fought in the Royal Northumberland Fusiliers during the Boer War, and in 1902 had been invalided home, one lung shot away. He had no profession. To supplement their allowance from Sydney's father, Tap Bowles, David went to work for his father-in-law at *The Lady*. It is bizarre to think of David, a bluff, country-loving ex-soldier who hated being indoors and loathed the written word, who knew nothing of accountancy or of ladies' magazines, as 'business manager' of this flourishing enterprise. Family legend has it that he consoled himself by acquiring a mongoose and setting the creature to hunt rats in *The Lady*'s offices in Covent Garden.

Although he hated his work, David was extremely happy in his marriage and with his growing family. At their first, modest London house at 1 Graham Street (now Graham Terrace, close to Eaton Square), a succession of nannies looked after the increasing brood. It was just after Diana's birth in June 1910 that Nancy, then six, heard 'a confrontation in the nursery as of two mastodons' – David giving the sack to the latest of the line, known as the 'Unkind Nanny', who had been discovered hitting Nancy's head against a bedpost. After that there arrived a person who became very significant to the family: Laura Dicks, always known as Blor, who stayed with the Mitfords all her life and was to be at Diana's side into her adulthood. This remarkable woman not only managed to cope with a family that many others found impossible, but to remain universally loved by them all. The daughter of a Nonconformist blacksmith from Surrey, she followed her principles in everything and ruled the nursery with a strong sense of natural justice. She had a characteristic hiccupping sniff (because of it, Jessica and Debo nicknamed her M'Hinket) which could put headstrong children in their place. Nancy once said that Blor controlled her by making her feel ashamed of herself. Even the caustic Nancy, who could seldom refrain from being sharp, had nothing critical to say about Blor.

In 1910 the family moved into a larger London house at 49 Victoria Road, in Kensington. It is a tall house of cream stucco in a quiet tree-lined cul-de-sac close to Hyde Park, not grand but thoroughly respectable, emanating a sense of settled prosperity. Daily life followed a predictable routine for the children, one that was probably more or less identical in any household of the same kind. Their existence centred on Nanny in the nursery, where they lived, ate and slept. Twice a day they would all troop off to Kensington Gardens nearby. After tea, they would change into clean frocks and be taken down to the drawing room to see their mother for an hour. For such a family at the time, the Mitfords were not particularly formal; Muv and Farve were quite accessible to their children, and sometimes played with them in the evenings. But the boredom of life in the conventional English nursery is conveyed by a letter Nancy wrote to her mother (downstairs) in the autumn of 1913: 'Dear Muv,' it ran, 'It is a horrid afternoon, it is raining, this morning it was foggy. The little ones have been singing, but I have been reading Little Folks. Pam is creaking the rocking-horse.'

As well as their four children and Blor, the Mitfords' household at this point contained Ada the nursery-maid, a cook, a housemaid, two parlour-maids and Willie Dawkins the 'hound-boy'. Among his tasks was the care of the animals – two bloodhounds and a dachshund, various mice and birds, David's mongoose and a very small pony named Brownie. David had bought the pony on impulse in the street one day, brought it home in a cab and installed it in an unused boxroom on the first floor of the house. This menagerie, although large enough for a London house, was nothing compared to the proliferation of Mitford animals later in their childhood. The next year, the family acquired Old Mill Cottage, near High Wycombe in Buckinghamshire, for weekends and holidays in the country. Two small cottages knocked into one, it was set in a garden the children loved and backed on to the old mill itself, whose machinery fascinated them. In summer the whole family moved out of London and the Victoria Road house was let, usually to someone doing 'the season'. It was a financial remedy they used repeatedly over the years.

In 1912, when Diana was two, David hit on a scheme that was of double interest to him: it might solve his always pressing financial worries, and it would get him out of doors and away from the city, at least for a little. He staked a claim to forty acres of rough country on a new gold field in northern Ontario, where he planned to prospect for gold himself. A family story has it that he and Sydney were supposed to sail the Atlantic that spring, but were obliged to cancel: luckily, since the ship on which their passage was booked was the *Titanic*. In the event their first visit to Canada was in 1913. The couple went alone, leaving the children and animals with the staff, and lived in a simple log cabin, Sydney cooking and doing the chores, David prospecting for gold. There are photographs of him in heavy working clothes, looking rugged and intent, part of the landscape. This simple outdoor life, far from the responsibilities of office, home and family, was a perfect refuge for him, and the couple continued to travel to Canada every few years. Although it was one of many hare-brained money-making schemes which attracted David, it was not a hopeless dream: the neighbouring land had been staked and mined by Sir Harry Oakes, who struck it rich and made millions. (He was later the victim of murder in the Bahamas, during the Duke of Windsor's wartime governorship, in a case that made headlines round the world.)

The Mitfords never found gold, but these were happy times. Sydney makes it clear in her unpublished biography of her next daughter, Unity, that Unity was conceived on that first visit. It is ironic, or perhaps appropriate, given Unity's later Nazi sympathies, that the name of the place was Swastika.

Unity was born a few days after the beginning of the First World War, in August 1914 – another girl, bad news for a couple who longed for a second son. At the outbreak of war. David – who had been on the point of sailing again for Canada and dreams of gold – re-enlisted in the Royal Northumberland Fusiliers, although he was well past the age when he was required to do so. He served as a dispatch rider at the front: a dangerous job for a man with one lung and five children. Despite fairly frequent periods of leave and invalidity, it was a huge strain on him, and family tragedy made it worse. In May 1915 David's elder brother Clement was killed fighting in France, and when their father, Bertie Redesdale, died a year later, David was the one who succeeded to the title, the land and the ownership of the unwieldy mansion Bertie had built himself at Batsford Park. It was a severe psychological shock for David. Clement had been the adored and clever son; David the unruly, awkward low-achiever. Clement had been sent to Eton; David to Radley College (considered a lesser establishment) in case his wild behaviour spoiled his brother's school career. Now David had all the responsibilities of houses and lands – but without the money to keep them up, or the means to earn it.

By the time he inherited Batsford Park, David had already been obliged to move his family into one of the houses on the estate, Malcolm House. It is a three-storey square brick house, rather formal in appearance, more like a Georgian town house than a typical English village house, standing close to the medieval church at Batsford. The move was for reasons of economy:

Sydney's father had reduced her allowance, because of the war, and David's army pay was less than he had been earning at *The Lady*, and Bertie had offered them Malcolm House so that they could let both Victoria Road and Old Mill Cottage. The Mitford children knew they were 'hard up'. It was a relative term, of course: David inherited a house with five staircases, but after they made the move from Malcolm House the family could afford to live in only a few rooms. Diana remembered that during the war Muv went to visit Farve when he was on leave in Paris, and came back with yards of the heavy blue material from which French officers' uniforms were made. It was quickly turned into winter coats for the three eldest girls – Nancy, Pam and Diana – and these garments (first her own, then Pam's and Nancy's hand-me-downs) lasted Diana for six winters, from the age of five to the age of ten.

To modern eyes, Batsford is hardly a beautiful house, an enormous mock-medieval affair complete with decorated Gothic windows. As well as the five staircases, great hall, library, drawing rooms and countless bedrooms, there is a ballroom which is served by a small railway, hidden behind panelling, used for bringing food and drink from the distant kitchens. Perhaps our modern judgement of it is coloured by the knowledge that to build it Bertie Redesdale demolished a gem – a Georgian manor, unfashionable in his day, but the epitome of perfect taste in ours. When the Mitfords moved in during the First World War, Batsford was cold and uncomfortable, half the rooms shrouded in dust-sheets. A family of London neighbours, the Normans, came to lodge there for the duration of the war, adding two more children to the growing pack, and Jessica, the last but one of Diana's siblings, was born at Batsford in 1917. Another girl. The same year, Tom went away to board at his prep school, Lockers Park, for the first time, and Diana lost her closest ally in the family.

David was invalided out of the army in 1917, but did not return to Batsford immediately. He was given the post of Provost Marshall at Christ Church College in Oxford, and happily took up residence there. His visits home, Diana remembered, were an occasion for enormous games of hide and seek all over the dark echoing house, with scuffles and screams and their father's bellows of triumph. They all knew that as soon as the war was over Batsford would have to be sold: for the time being, though, it was a giant playground. It was also the scene of the first of the summer fêtes – in 1918 it was to raise money for wounded soldiers – that were a later fixture in the Mitford household. Batsford and its magnificent gardens were full of Oriental treasures brought back by Bertie Redesdale from his travels, and Sydney became so desperate for the success of her fête that she rushed about the house grabbing objects and putting them on the white-elephant stall, which became 'a treasure house', according to Diana, 'for any Orientalist'. Farve was just in time to buy back a Japanese buddha for sixpence; after that, 'we soon learned to hide our possessions when a fête loomed up'.

Batsford was sold at the end of 1918, together with the substantial acreage around it, many of the *objets d'art* and some of the furniture. So, too, was much of Grandfather Redesdale's large and famous library. Later commentators have taken this sale as evidence of Farve's philistinism and hatred of books. (He read one book in his life, his children claimed. It was Jack London's *White Fang*; he thought it magnificent and saw no reason to read another.) In fact, Farve consulted his bookish children carefully – Tom and Nancy, at ten and fourteen, were already voracious and sophisticated readers – and kept enough volumes to cause the building of a whole new library at Asthall Manor, the family's next home.

Asthall Manor stands on the outskirts of the village of Asthall Leigh, two miles from Swinbrook in Oxfordshire. For Diana and the older children it was the real focus of their childhood and the place they loved best. It is easy to see why. It is a long manor house of old and weathered Cotswold stone, dating from the 1620s, with high gables, a slate roof and mullioned windows. It sits nestled into the woody hillside of the Windrush valley, its back windows looking into the graveyard of the ancient Asthall church and on over the water meadows stretching either side of the winding river. Even now, it breathes peace and stability, the picture of traditional English heartland. All around are clues to ancient inhabitants – a Saxon barrow on a hill, Roman mosaics at the tiny church nearby at Widford, which still has its box pews and candle sconces, and to which there is no road. Like Asthall Leigh, the village of Swinbrook has hardly changed in the last decades, its church set on high ground beside the narrow road which winds down into the heart of the place, with thatched cottages, a doll-sized post office, and usually a duck waddling slowly across the road from the mill stream.

Diana's memories of Asthall Manor combine the conventional – the long hall running almost the width of the house, with a great fireplace at each end; Muv's drawing room with its Louis XVI furniture – and the slightly absurd: the ancestors' portraits in the dining room augmented by one of Farve, commissioned by him from a 'Belgian camouflage expert'. Sydney loved the house as much as the children did, but for David it was only a temporary home. The land he had inherited encompassed a hill above the neighbouring village of Swinbrook, and he wanted to build a house there. David and his father were quite unalike in almost all other ways, but they shared a longing to build, and suffered similar financial consequences, since they each had as little financial acumen as the other. Bertie had depleted his capital severely by building the vast new house at Batsford; David had sold it just when property prices were at rock bottom, at the end of the First World War. Two years later David launched a six-year project to build his own new house, when labour and building costs were at their height.

His finances, always a mystery to his family and, as Diana remarked, to himself, were a cause of recurrent crises, when the grown-ups would closet themselves in David's business room and emerge hours later with plans for some irrelevant household economy, like changing the brand of lavatory paper or dispensing with napkins at meals. The mine at Swastika was only one of the quirky money-making schemes that attracted David. Another was a project to set up a company that made decorative papier-mâché cases for wireless sets, on which he embarked in partnership with a dubious South American marquis: it ended badly, with considerable losses, and when David unwisely made a remark that suggested he thought his partner's title was bogus, the South American sued him for slander. David won the case, however.

Despite his money worries, David could not resist building, even at Asthall. To house Bertie's books he converted a barn that stood close to the house, making a large library-cum-ballroom below and four extra bedrooms above, with a long and strange covered passage, known as the Cloisters, to attach the outlying building to the main house. It is an addition that still sits very oddly with the grace and beauty of the old manor, but it was typically practical. For the older children the library was a delight, 'all the world to Tom and me', according to Diana. She, Tom and Nancy had free run of the place (as long as they put all the leather-bound books back in order), and all three became serious bookworms. There were deep armchairs. There was a piano, where Tom could play to his heart's content. Best of all, it was separated from the main part of the house, so there was a sense of refuge in a private world. Farve's rages, at least, never reached the library: in fact he hardly set foot there.

Although Diana was nearly nine by the time they moved to Asthall, the family was still not complete: yet another girl, Deborah, was born the following year. For the first time since the war began Farve was at home permanently. Dressed in corduroy jacket and breeches, moleskin waistcoat and gaiters, often with a cigarette in hand, he dominated the household from early morning. He always rose at five, at his most energetic – roaming the house, bossing the maids about their work, playing his favourite records loudly on a wind-up in the business room. His tyrannical side included demanding absolute punctuality at meals and perfect table manners from the children, on pain of his wrath; his softer side included a love of fancy-dress parties, wild uproarious games, romping jokes. More than anything, he lived for the sporting pleasures of the countryside. Although an accident soon after moving to Asthall left him unable to ride, he shot the pheasants he carefully nurtured up on the hill, fished for trout in the Windrush that wound through the field below the house, and every Sunday in winter went coursing for hares with his brother Tommy, who lived nearby. The children loved these outings with their father, who was at his best then: they walked behind the guns on a shoot, or followed on foot through muddy fields and watched as David's lurcher and whippet streaked away after the hare. A great treat was the child-hunt, when the children would run off across the fields to be tracked by Farve with his bloodhound and a mongrel terrier called Luncheon Tom – animals that would do no worse than lick them lavishly as soon as they were caught – although this incident has turned into a mildly horrifying one in the re-telling by Jessica and Nancy in their books.

For the children there was riding every day with Hooper ('Choops'), the groom, and often hunting in the winter. In the traditional way, blood sports and great sentimentality about animals existed side by side without contradictions, and the children grew up intensely fond of animals. They all had animals and pets galore – not just the usual range of small dogs, rabbits or guinea pigs, but also chickens and pigs, kept in an effort to raise money. Later on, the younger girls' pets became more esoteric – among the creatures they would try to smuggle into the family baggage when they went to London were a large earthworm, a lamb, a goat and a snake. (Jessica, incidentally, provides a telling detail. Enid the grass snake, instead of originating in one of the grassy open fields down by the river at Swinbrook, was purchased in the pet department of Harrods – as was Ratular, the pet rat with which Unity would thrill the company at débutante dances. These country girls were more metropolitan than they liked to make out.)

Although it was a conventional upbringing, the atmosphere in the house was by no means placid. The family fictions cast David as a perpetually stormy character, and he could be very fierce and volatile. The children lived under threat of his fury at quite small transgressions, or at none at all. He was in the habit of choosing one of the children, for no reason anyone could discern, to victimize: they called it Rat Week. If you were on Rat Week, you could do nothing right for Farve; but it would end just as suddenly as it began, and some other unlucky girl would be singled out for the treatment –

Tom, who could do nothing wrong in his father's eyes, escaped. As they got older, epic rows, followed by days of tense silence, could be provoked by such momentous events as Nancy having her hair cut fashionably short. But in fact Lord Redesdale's rages were probably the bewildered response of a simple personality to his large, outspoken family and the complicated personalities of his daughters. 'To Tom, whose straightforward nature he understood better, he was touchingly devoted,' according to James Lees-Milne. 'The devotion was returned and they were like brothers, sharing each other's confidences.' Diana remembered how terrifying his apoplectic fury could be, but also the charm of his jokes, which made them all scream with laughter, and his affection. 'Certainly he had a quick temper, and would often rage, but we were never punished. The worst that ever happened was to be sent early to bed.'

Both Redesdales were dutiful. David was a conscientious landlord, a local magistrate, a member of the County Council and a dedicated church-goer; Sydney was a supporter of the local Conservative Party, always ready to do her bit for the village and the church. In fact, neither had any real religion or any real politics, beyond what was conventionally expected of them: their political fervour came later. Going to church on Sundays was part and parcel of their place in the village. Farve had three churches on his land; as well as Asthall and Swinbrook, the ancient church at Widford, where only one service a year was ever held, stands a mile away along the river. He never went to church anywhere but Swinbrook, always for matins, although Asthall church was only ten yards from his back door – the living at Asthall was not in his gift, and he took no interest in it. But when she was fourteen Diana found a way of avoiding the ritual of matins with her father. She began to play the organ every Sunday evening in Asthall church, where a village boy pumped a wooden handle for the wheezy instrument and Diana learnt how to make any tune, even 'Swanee' or 'Ramona', sound holy if it was played slowly enough.

In contrast to David's time-bomb personality was Sydney's ever-increasing vagueness. She was efficient as a housekeeper and kept meticulous household accounts; she had a talent for making her houses beautiful and her food was always delicious. But towards her children Sydney was detached. Although she had her father's firm and slightly eccentric views about child-rearing, and although she taught each of the children herself until they were old enough for the governess, at eight or nine, they all felt her to be a very distant mother. She rarely hugged or kissed any of them. She seemed affectionately interested in the doings of her brood, but absent-mindedly.

When Diana came home from staying with cousins or friends, 'Muv was not much interested. "Oh, did you, darling?" or "Oh, was it? H'm," was about as much as one could hope for, and she stretched her arms and yawned.' Of course, there were jokes about this, as about everything else, in the family repertoire: Unity once rushed into a room where Muv was calmly writing letters and yelled that Jessica was on the roof and about to jump. 'Oh, poor duck,' Muv replied, 'I do hope she won't do anything so silly,' and went on with her letters. Yet Muv, too, was a disciplinarian, and could strike out with a cold irony which was as much to be feared as Farve's rages. As a child Diana never loved her mother; she respected her, and appreciated much about her, and came to love her in old age, but there was very little maternal warmth in Lady Redesdale. The deep visceral love that children have for the person who cares about them, Diana had for Blor, her nanny.

Sydney took little part in the family's high jinks, the boyish games of David or the needling teases of Nancy. By the time they moved to Asthall, Nancy was a lively fourteen-year-old, sharp-witted and sharp-tongued, and a dominant personality. Her high spirits, imagination and cruel teasing did more than anything to set the tone for the rest. Scared of her acid remarks but always entertained by her funny comments, her parents as well as the other children alternately rocked with laughter or cringed from her barbs. When she sparred with Farve, usually at mealtimes, the sniping would go on and on until one or the other would snap: either Nancy would dissolve into tears and run out of the room, or Farve would suddenly bellow in anger because Nancy had 'gone too far'. Pam, nearest to her in age but a slower, gentler character, was miserably tormented by Nancy, although the more robust Diana would often join in on Pam's side. Tom, when he was at home from school, managed to preserve a certain lofty calm, but the three younger girls could easily be reduced to tears by almost nothing. To torment Deborah, especially, Nancy made up a nonsense rhyme about a match – 'A little, houseless match/It has no roof, it has no thatch/If it's alone, it makes no moan/That little houseless match' – which could make her youngest sister sob. Forbidden this chant under threat of dire punishment by Muv, Nancy reduced the taunt to its essentials – she would simply pick up a box of matches and give Deborah a significant look, which produced the same effect.

Nancy admitted her 'vile behaviour to the others', but was never apologetic. Her vivid personality affected the family in ways that were creative as well as destructive. She invented games. She read hungrily; Diana was always trying to keep up with her. She was inquisitive about the world outside their sleepy village. It was impossible to be complacent or indifferent about her, and it was probably because of Nancy that the sisters became highly competitive, despite their closeness, and remained so through their lives. Since none of the girls went to school, except for short periods, their world was each other, and they fought for attention in the enclosed family circle.

Nancy was also the pioneer, fighting every battle on behalf of the others, and they all remembered the storms of parental disapproval she faced when she first shingled her hair, wore trousers, smoked a cigarette, or had tea with a male friend in Oxford. Her intellectual loneliness was accentuated by the fact that her closest sister, Pam, was no match for her quick wits. Jessica undoubtedly suffered from arriving late in a large family, overshadowed by the already successful elder siblings, her world distorted by the fact that Unity was becoming a child whose boisterousness and naughtiness verged on delinquency. Diana, although she had many grievances of her own, was perhaps in a prime position: she had the companionship of Tom, to whom she was so close in age that they felt almost like twins, and she was the baby of the first half of this family which divided so clearly into two.

In another way, too, Nancy exemplified a family characteristic. Bored and restless and under-stretched, she longed for a grown-up world and school-friends of her own age. According to her biographer, Selina Hastings, she learned to hide her emotions under a 'highly polished veneer': 'Everything, however sad, painful or dispiriting, had instantly to be turned by Nancy into a joke. The only acceptable response to misfortune was to "shriek" with laughter – an ugly word with its underlying implication of distress.' In Diana, too, the tendency to turn everything into a joke became ingrained, and a laconic irony – always cool-headed, effective both in attack and in defence – seemed bred in the bone.

3 The Voice

Asthall was a tightly enclosed world. The older girls were all educated at home, apart from Nancy in her late teens. There were visiting cousins and a few other friends and relations, but Sydney was content with little social life and David's peculiarities hardly encouraged a wide range of friends. When Nancy and the others reached their late teens, their social world became busy, but in the Asthall years the family circle mattered most. In this atmosphere, the Mitfords evolved elaborate names for each other and distinctive ways of speaking that set the family apart from outsiders, and drew them closer together. It is not unusual. Close siblings like twins often have a semi-secret language. Families thrown on their own resources sometimes make up games so intricate that they become a form of communication, like the Brontës'. The younger Mitford girls specialized in such games and rituals, often quite incomprehensible to others. The whole Mitford family was unusual, though, in keeping the speech and vocabulary of their childish world alive into their adulthood.

'My voice! It was too awful. Even loyal Debo had to complain. Still, it's too late to change it now.' This was Diana's reaction to hearing herself on the soundtrack of a television film about Nancy made in the 1960s. The languid Mitford drawl became famous: partly a matter of pronunciation, partly of exaggerated emphasis and intonation, partly made up of special words and locutions. To some extent it came from having preserved the upper-class pronunciation that was current when they were young and lasted into the 1960s, but which is now rare except in the elderly ('girl', for instance, rhymed with 'fell' and never with 'curl'; 'off' was pronounced 'orf'). Uncle George, Sydney's brother, once tried to amuse David by making up an epitaph for the writer Edmund Gosse, a hated figure because he had made an 'insolent' remark about the family in his preface to one of Bertie Redesdale's books. It ran, 'Here lies Gosse / No great loss,' but Diana said the joke was rather spoilt because they all pronounced 'loss' to rhyme with 'horse' (though Uncle George obviously did not).

Apart from pronunciation, the Mitfords' characteristic voice relied on emphasis. The drawn-out stress on quite ordinary words is reminiscent of modern-day camp, and indeed it was also typical of homosexuals at the time – though this would have had nothing to do with the Mitfords' evolution of the style. But it was as distant as could be from the clipped, militaristic speech of many of their class, or the rapid, brittle chatter of the 1920s flappers and Bright Young Things. Within the family, it was especially characteristic of Tom, Diana and later Debo. As a small boy Tom evolved what he called his Artful Scheme of Happiness, a remarkably effective ruse to persuade somebody to give him something he wanted. Diana described how he made his voice 'positively sag with desire' as he 'looked long and lovingly at the desired object, and when this had been noticed he began to speak. "Oh, what a lovely box, I don't think I've ever seen such a lovely little box in all my life. Oh, how I wish I could find one like it! Do you think I ever could! Oh, you *are* lucky!"' In adulthood, such exaggeration became self-parodying, almost a performance. In the late 1990s Debo good-naturedly broke the ice with a guest at lunch in Diana's house (a short and simple railway journey from the centre of Paris) with 'Did you come by train? Oh, you *are* clever!' – the stressed verb lasting a full three seconds.

The Mitford exaggerations imply that the speakers are fluffy-headed creatures: miss the irony at your peril. But outsiders often did. Early on, Nanny warned Tom when he was about to go away to school that eight-year-old boys rarely used the word 'amusing' with a drawling emphasis: she knew well enough how the Artful Scheme of Happiness might sound to others, and what might be the outcome for Tom as a new boy in a pack of critical peers. Many years later, a publisher's reader reporting on Nancy's novel *The Pursuit of Love* tactfully picked up on one point: 'p252 – re Dunkirk. I know exactly what Linda [the heroine] means and I think she would probably have said it, but I have a hunch that Miss Mitford ought to tone down line 6. There are just too many people who didn't think it *Heaven*.'

When the Mitfords were children, nicknames were given to everyone and everything. It says something about the various factions and shifting alliances within the family that each person had several nicknames. There was usually an 'official' one that everyone used, and another that was exclusive to one other sibling: everyone called Jessica Decca, for instance, within the family and outside it, and it was a name that lasted all her life, but her special relationships with some of her sisters were reflected in a closed circle of mutual nicknaming: Nancy and Jessica called each other Susan; Deborah and Jessica called each other Henderson; Unity and Jessica called each other Boud. There was no such reciprocity between Jessica and Diana.

The nicknames became so complicated that they were almost a secret language, like the two languages made up by the younger girls. These were Boudledidge, a nonsense-speak used by Unity and Jessica which elongated words out of all recognition and had always to be enunciated with an elaborately miserable sideways grimace and a hangdog expression. In Boudledidge, for instance, the word 'fascist' became 'veedjist' and was written thus – somehow making it comic, harmless, domestic. The other language was Honnish, a creation of Jessica and Deborah, which was based on local Oxfordshire country speech. The Hons' Cupboard, the large warm linen cupboard in Swinbrook House where the children used to congregate (and which found its way intact into *The Pursuit of Love*), was for those who spoke Honnish. (The Hons in question had nothing to do with the girls' titles – as the children of a peer, they all had 'The Honourable' before their names – but was the Honnish word for 'hen'. The 'H' is pronounced.)

Not surprisingly, Nancy was the originator of the family habit of nicknaming, as well as its most enthusiastic practitioner. In addition to calling their parents Farve and Muv, the children referred to them as the Birds (the Nesting Ones) or TPOM (The Poor Old Male) and TPOF (The Poor Old Female). Nancy liked this formula, and when Oswald Mosley came on the scene, she led the younger girls (to Diana's irritation) in dubbing him TPOL (The Poor Old Leader) or TPOF (The Poor Old Führer).

Nancy's parents had called her Koko when she was little, but all her life Diana, Tom and Pam called her Naunce. Deborah called her Natch, and later the French Lady Writer or the Old French Lady.

Pam was Woman, to everyone, sometimes shortened to Wo or Wooms; Tom was Tud or Tuddemy. Diana was never called Diana unless she was in serious trouble; 'the very word Diana was in itself sinister'. Dina to her father, Dana to her mother, Bodley (because of her big head) to Nancy, she was Honks to Deborah, Cord (from Corduroy) to Jessica, Nard or Nardy to Pam, Tom and Unity. These names moved into the next generation, too: Deborah's children called Nancy Aunt Natch, Diana Aunt Honks.

Unity was Bobo, from the time she was tiny, to everyone. Jessica and Unity called each other (the) Boud, which meant friend in Boudledidge. There were variations on this: Diana sometimes called her Birdie, Nancy called her Bowd, or later (usually in letters) Stoney-Heart, or Head of Bone and Heart of Stone. Jonathan Guinness points out that the only person who ever called her Unity was Hitler. Deborah has always been Debo, although Nancy sometimes called her Nine or Nine-year-old (supposedly her mental age) or Miss.

There were countless variations. The Mitfords' letters to each other elaborate the nicknames as much as their cod ways of speaking, or rocket off into an exaggerated self-parody. A letter from Debo to Diana, thanking her for Christmas presents in 1943, begins: 'Darling Honks, oh Honks, oh Honks the gifts, I am completely o'ercome by their glory I can't think what to thank for first. The underclothes Honks, the stockings, all the Honnish things for Em, well I must say I never saw such a parcel. The coupons Honks, you must have spent so many I can hardly bear to think of you going quite naked which is what you'll surely have to do . . .'

The Mitford voice was remarkably durable. Diana and Jessica, because of their political differences, did not speak to each other for several decades, and Jessica lived most of her life in America with her American husband. Yet at the end of their lives they still sounded alike. The voice was part of their self-image – which became stronger as the fictions grew – and part of their bonding. It was also a shield. Nancy's letters, noticeably, verge more into private language when she has something difficult to say, and when she is at her most ironic or defensive. A letter to Diana in 1933, after Nancy had attended a meeting of Oswald Mosley's in Oxford, read: 'Darling Bodley, TPOL's meeting was fascinating, but awful for him as the hall was full of Oxfordshire Conservatives who sat in hostile & phlegmatic silence . . . I think he is a wonderful speaker & of course I expect he is better still with a more interesting audience. There were several fascinating fights, as he brought a few Neanderthal men along with him & they fell tooth & (literally) nail on anyone who shifted his chair or coughed.'

During the 1930s, as Unity embraced Nazism and the political rifts between the sisters became increasingly wide and painful, Nancy's response was to resort to sheer (but significant) nonsense. In early August 1938 Unity was seriously ill with pneumonia in Bayreuth, where she had been Hitler's guest at the Festspielhaus. Hitler sent flowers; Nancy sent a chatty, 'sisterly' letter: 'I am getting on well with my German. I know Herrschaft Tish and pfui Pfennig, gemutlicht and rashenshender, six words that would get one a long way if made good use of . . .' ['Rashenshender' was Nancy's version of *Rassenschände*, literally racial disgrace, or under the Nazi regime the crime of inter-racial sex.] Nancy included a cheery little ditty that ended:

> And rashenshender we do all day
> (Tish, Tish and a merry go round)
> For my lover he is a geboren Malay.

Although Diana's barbs were never as skittish and oblique as this,

Nancy's influence was strong. Mockery was useful for both attack and defence, and chimed with an aristocratic quality she admired – namely, disdain for public opinion. Throughout her life, making light of the serious remained a significant weapon in Diana's arsenal.

4 *Learning to Read*

How was a family of such extraordinary children produced by such conventional parents: the blimpish Farve who had only ever read one book, the vague Muv with her faddy food notions and resistance to schools? Nancy, in *The Pursuit of Love*, would have us believe they were a tribe of inspired ignoramuses who somehow dragged themselves out of the Oxfordshire mud by native brilliance and cunning. Jessica equated their lack of schooling with outright neglect. Much of this is overheated family mythologizing. Their nephew Jonathan believes that 'Decca's writings, like Nancy's, proclaim that her education was bad but prove that it was good', and their schooling was deficient by modern standards only in that they missed the formative experience of school itself. The curriculum they covered, and their general education – their cultural life and influences – were fuller than in many equivalent families. Alexander Mosley, Diana's third son, challenges the idea that Sydney was a negative influence. He describes her as 'interesting and intelligent', and, despite her unconventional notions, she had an able mind. When Nancy was searching for a title for her first novel, Sydney reminded her that an aunt of theirs had produced a quaint volume called *Our Village*, and suggested, for Nancy's story of modern manners, the title *Our Vile Age*. The idea was overtaken by Evelyn Waugh's *Vile Bodies*, and Nancy's work was eventually published as *Highland Fling*, but Sydney's suggestion shows that she was perceptive and quick.

Sydney also taught each child in turn to read and write, and supervised their lessons until they were eight and ready for the governess and the schoolroom: no small task, with seven children. Despite this, though, all the girls were to some extent autodidacts. Diana said, 'I think all the talk about no education was partly to tease Muv . . . it really depends, ultimately, on oneself whether one is educated or not.'

Diana herself made sure of her education. She became very widely read, a zealous consumer of books and later a book reviewer, knowledgeable about music and art, multilingual. Other people were a vital part of this process:

she was always attracted to seriousness of mind, and even in her teens the fashionable silliness and hedonism of the Bright Young Things never suited her. Though she had a voracious social appetite, she did not value fun for its own sake, like Nancy; from childhood onwards clever conversation pleased her more than mere partying. She chose her friends differently, always drawn to talent and purpose, and that is what brought her into contact with personalities as different as Lytton Strachey, Evelyn Waugh, Lord Berners. But for all these rich influences, she had the tenacity of mind that characterizes most autodidacts: if you have found something out for yourself, it remains an unshakeable, permanent truth. Other people's views only get in the way. Oswald Mosley, too, set little store by his formal education, and went to great lengths to school himself in the political, philosophical and cultural areas he valued.

The planning of the Mitford girls' education was not abnormal; what was unusual was the way they reacted to it. Nancy had been at day school in London when she was younger, but the other girls were taught at home, to Diana's relief. She dreaded the idea of being sent away from home to school ('for one thing, I cannot abide the zoo-like smell'). It was an aversion so strong that one of Nancy's most successful teases, with Diana, was to pretend she had heard their parents discussing sending her to school. Pam did not particularly care one way or the other; but Nancy longed for boarding school. As a halfway measure, when she was sixteen she was allowed to go for a year to Hatherop Castle, not far away in Gloucestershire, where Mrs Cadogan assembled a dozen girls from neighbouring families to live in and do their lessons together. There Diana and Pam joined her once a week for dancing classes, driven over from Asthall by Turner, the chauffeur, with Nanny as companion. Stuffed into the open dickey seat of the Morris Cowley in their dancing frocks, they usually arrived stiff with cold. Later on, Unity was sent off, with disastrous results, to various establishments, but Diana never set foot in a school until the age of sixteen.

Tom was destined for the traditional pattern of education for boys of his class: away to prep school at seven or eight, Eton at thirteen, university afterwards. But it was still common in those days for girls of such families to be taught at home by governesses. What was not common was for the governesses to be subjected to the pranks and well-orchestrated resistance that the Mitford children contrived. The unfortunate women arrived and left with bewildering speed. Diana reckoned that, including the French governesses who came in the holidays, there were no fewer than fifteen in all. Some stayed no more than a few weeks, and Diana cited four school terms as being 'about the limit of time any governess could abide us for'.

The first of the long stream of governesses, and perhaps the best loved and most successful, was Miss Mirams, who arrived at Batsford Park in January 1917 to take on the teaching of four children of assorted ages, needs and abilities. Nancy, at twelve, was clever and avid; Pam was a slow learner; Tom had to be coached in Latin and mathematics (subjects which the girls were not supposed to require) in preparation for going off to school later that year. Diana, at six and a half, was extremely quick-witted, but what she needed could hardly interest a smart sister six years older than herself. Miss Mirams had a difficult job.

But it was perhaps only when Unity graduated to the schoolroom from the nursery that the going got really tough for Mitford governesses. Unity's relentless naughtiness was more than a match for most of them. Judging by accounts of Unity's behaviour, she had already established the furiously anti-authoritarian ways that always characterized her (even though the Nazi creed she later embraced with such passion was the most authoritarian of all). She was not only wild and wilful but deliberately destructive (yet often hilarious, too), and she turned her prankster's talents against the unfortunate young women employed to teach her. Yet many of the well-known tales are, according to Diana, completely fictitious. Jessica tells the story of poor Miss Whitney, who was afraid of snakes; on discovering this, Unity wrapped her pet grass snake, Enid, around the lavatory chain one morning. She waited. After some loud screams, and a heavy thud, the door had to be broken open so that the unconscious governess could be carried out. Pure invention, Diana said.

Jessica could see only the negative side of these frequent changes, and wrote bitterly that each governess stayed just long enough to impart certain pieces of information, though not long enough to explain them. The variety, though, could have been an advantage: one drawback of a governess system was that children came under only one influence, instead of experiencing different teachers' personalities, as at school. But the Mitford governesses came in all shapes and guises, and Diana mentions one, a Miss Price (she managed the full four terms), who was a fervent Anglo-Catholic and took Diana into an intense religious phase when she was about thirteen. It didn't last, but it was an important experience. Jessica remembered other influences. One was Miss Bunting, 'whose main contribution to our education was to teach a little mild shop-lifting': in particular 'the shopping-bag method', which involved an accomplice to distract the shop assistant, and the 'dropped-hanky' method, suitable for smaller items. Once again, Diana dismissed this story as one of Jessica's outlandish fictions – although the fact remains that both she and Unity were very mischievous and discontented in the schoolroom.

Perhaps the governesses found their employer as tricky as their charges. Lady Redesdale – again, despite the family myths – took more interest than many mothers in what actually went on in the schoolroom. Rather than leaving the governesses to their own devices, she insisted they follow a particular programme, and one which was of unusually good quality. The PNEU (Parents' National Education Union) system was essentially a correspondence-course curriculum, devised for British children being educated in the colonies, so that there could be some continuity even if they moved or had a fragmented education in different countries.

The Mitfords also had language training from the French *assistantes* who arrived every holidays, when French was supposed to be spoken at mealtimes. In Miss Miram's day, the visiting French teacher was Zella (short for Mademoiselle), and well liked by the older children. Both Muv and Farve spoke excellent French, and the household was far more open to cultural influence from France than is implied by Nancy's picture of Uncle Matthew with his hatred of foreigners and his abomination of abroad. Because of Nancy's invention, it is a surprise when Diana mentions that her father referred to bishops as 'les touche à tout' (meaning meddlers: he disapproved of their presence in the House of Lords), or his fondness for his old tutor, Monsieur Cuvelier, who had taught him at home at Batsford when he was a young boy. 'Douze Temps' was this old tutor's nickname, from the twelve-step rifle drill he had learnt while a soldier in the Franco-Prussian war, and his miming of it, which had enthralled David and his brothers as boys. Douze Temps would come to stay in the summer holidays and transform Farve's mood into one of nostalgic, boyish delight.

That David's earliest lessons had been in French hardly squares with the picture of him as a mindless xenophobe, but Diana guessed that it might account for his extreme difficulty in writing and spelling English. It seems more likely, with hindsight, that Lord Redesdale's disinclination to read, his difficulty in writing and angry frustration when he was forced to do so – as well as his rebelliousness about lessons as a child, and failure to learn much at his public school – stemmed from undiagnosed dyslexia.

Both sides of his complicated relationship with the written word are illustrated by letters he sent from the front between 1915 and 1917 to Nancy. One consisted, in toto, of the following: 'Dearest Koko, Many thanks for your last letter. Much love Farv.' But when she wrote a letter to show off her progress in French ('Il y a un nid de rouge-gorge dans un arbre. J'ai écouté le coucou ce matin. Votre chien est très sage il est dans la maison. De la part de votre affectionée Nancy (blob)'), he came up with this reply: 'A robin in a tree has built! / The cuckoo has not changed its lilt! /And I have no desire to quench / My child's desire for learning French.'

The new library at Asthall certainly did not quench his children's desire for learning. It was the focal point of Diana's life there, and, despite the sale during the move from Batsford, it held a fine collection of books. The children were allowed free run of the place, but still they depended very much on each other, and here Diana was lucky. Nancy was an extremely precocious reader. Her biographer tells the story of how when Blor first arrived in the London nursery, Nancy, aged six, refused to look up from her book: she was deep in *Ivanhoe*. (The family always related this incident as an example of Blor's perfect tact, without comment on the fact that a six-year-old should have been immersed in a novel by Sir Walter Scott.) Throughout her childhood, Diana would try out Nancy's favourite books, peering in secret into *King Solomon's Mines* when Nancy once declared it her favourite, then retreating to something easier until she felt she could manage it.

And there was Tom. It may have been that the best educational opportunity for girls at that time was to have a brother like him, and this was certainly true for the older Mitfords. At Eton he enjoyed the full glory of the traditional training of the English gentleman, and emerged just as he was intended to, and just as his own considerable talents allowed him to: cultured, well-informed, questioning (though with predictable political affiliations), sexually experienced and with a wide range of equally polished friends. But even before he went to Eton, Tom used to bring home friends from his prep school. Already an accomplished musician, he would drag them off to the library the moment they arrived and play to them on the piano. 'He must have picked his guests with care,' Diana noted, 'for it is not every ten-year-old boy who would want to sit indoors all day listening to classical music.' Similarly, not every nine-year-old girl would appreciate friends such as James Lees-Milne, whom she loved because he hated games as much as they did, and who 'made us read Byron, Shelley, Keats and Coleridge'. They agreed that 'when we were grown up we would scorn material things and live on a handful of grapes near the sea in Greece'. Years later, in 1963, Diana wrote to Jim Lees-Milne, a life-long friend, that he had been a defining influence on her and her brother, 'the source of our ideas and enthusiasms'.

Tom helped to educate Diana, not only because they were close, and because he was precociously clever, but because, as a boy, he was allowed to do all sorts of things that were thought irrelevant for girls. Time and again the cry would go up, 'It's different for Tom, he's a boy,' as when Diana at sixteen was forbidden by Farve to learn German, as Tom was doing. So it is hardly surprising that Diana found schoolroom life humdrum, but the holidays, when Tom was at home, exhilarating. They went to tennis parties in summer, and dancing parties in winter; there were constant visits between Asthall and their Bailey cousins, the children of Sydney's sister Weenie, who lived not far away at Stow-on-the-Wold. Diana and Tom were as good-looking, vivacious and pleasure-loving as each other, and were welcome guests when they went further afield. Diana's trips away were her great interest, especially the visits to the Churchills at Chartwell. The families were cousins (Clementine Churchill was David Redesdale's first cousin) and Diana Churchill, though a year older, became Diana Mitford's greatest friend, while her younger brother Randolph was Tom's. At Chartwell Diana felt in touch with a wider and more sophisticated world. Winston Churchill was often away, or too busy to talk to the children, but when he did appear he paid great attention to 'Dinamite'.

Despite the occasional outburst from Farve, most visiting children seem to have relished staying with the Redesdales, although apparently the experience of the younger three girls differed from the older ones'. Whereas Nancy's *The Pursuit of Love* makes the Mitfords' childhood sound intellectually starved but amusing, companionable and full of activity, Jessica's *Hons and Rebels* sets up an equally exaggerated picture of a childhood that was eccentric and isolated. As so often, Jessica's sense of the ridiculous takes over: 'At an age when other children would be occupied with dolls, group sports, piano lessons and ballet,' she wrote, 'Debo spent silent hours in the chicken house learning to do an exact imitation of the look of pained concentration that comes over a hen's face when it is laying an egg.' These conflicting accounts only underline the fact that the realities of childhood are vividly different even for different children within the same family. By the time the three youngest children were of schoolroom age, perhaps the Redesdales' parental energy had run out, or been diverted entirely on to the older ones. This seems the only explanation for Jessica's assertion that 'except for rare visits from cousins, the three of us were brought up in complete isolation from our contemporaries. My mother thought the company of other children unnecessary and over-stimulating.' She speaks of 'rare' birthday parties or Easter egg hunts at the homes of neighbouring county families. Yet one cousin, Clementine Beit, remembers 'a very jolly household'. Another cousin, Rosemary Bailey, describes the house as 'always full of people, always something going on: to us it seemed lovely, their childhood'.

The children's life had other diversions. There were the dancing lessons at Hatherop Castle. There were expeditions to Stratford-upon-Avon three or four times a year, where the whole family watched productions of Shakespeare and Shaw. Like other large families in small villages, if the Redesdales wanted something for their children, they usually organized it themselves. The episode of the Girl Guides represented utter misery for the teenage Diana, whose fear of school extended to a loathing for all kinds of group activity. The company of Girl Guides was set up by Nancy, who declared herself its Captain, after she got the idea from a similar troop at Hatherop Castle. Ten girls from the village were informed that they had to join; Pam and Diana – the most reluctant recruit – were patrol leaders. For Nancy, according to Diana, the scheme 'combined the advantages of achieving an all-time high as a tease for me with gratification of her will to power'. Luckily, the project petered out after a year: Nancy's social life in London became a much more consuming interest.

The winter of 1922, when Diana was twelve, marked a change at Asthall. Nancy was eighteen, and at long last old enough to come out. Her parents decided to give a dance at Asthall for her, an event she ruthlessly lampooned in *The Pursuit of Love*, when Linda and her family know so pitifully few young men that Uncle Matthew has to go up to London to round up elderly dancing partners in the House of Lords. In reality it was not quite that bad, but it was hardly the stuff of dreams; Diana, of course, was too young to be included. But from the dance onwards, Nancy's life, and therefore life at Asthall, was very different. Nancy was launched into society, and she took an immediate liking to débutante balls. 'She was extremely popular,' according to Diana, 'and I think had more success than any of us except Debo. In the winter she loved hunt balls and stayed away all over the place for them.' She began to bring friends home for weekends, running the gauntlet of Farve's displeasure, and Diana was suddenly able to meet new people.

For the next couple of years, 'nothing on earth would stop [Nancy] going to London for the season. Muv and Farve really dreaded it, but they did it year after year, leaving Asthall at the loveliest moment and spending more than they could afford. Sometimes they took a house and sometimes lived with Naunce (and after three years of it, Woman as well) in literal *lodgings*.'

Nancy's first full London season, in the summer of 1923, coincided with the brightest moments of the Bright Young Things, a time of rollicking and frivolity, fancy-dress parties and all kinds of hedonistic nonsense. In fact Nancy was only ever on the fringes of these groups – she was very young for her age, still forbidden to wear make-up, although she did crop her hair fashionably. But her enthusiasm for childish pranks and for parties was insatiable.

Such a social appetite paid dividends for Diana. After three years of the débutante round Nancy turned to a much more intellectual and artistic group of people, whom she had met through a Scottish friend, Nina Seafield, and her cousin, Mark Ogilvie-Grant, an Oxford undergraduate in the 'aesthetes' camp, who became a life-long friend. His fellow aesthetes – Brian Howard, John Sutro, Robert Byron – were brainy, opinionated, mildly anti-establishment, mostly homosexual. It was the kind of male company Nancy relished, for with them she could enjoy a playful relationship that was uninvolved both emotionally and sexually. They appreciated her straight away. Harold Acton was astonished by a letter from his old Eton crony, Brian Howard, a flamboyant homosexual, describing Nancy as 'a delicious creature, quite pyrotechnical my dear, and sometimes even profound, and would you believe it, she's hidden among the cabbages of the Cotswolds'. Acton added: 'He was so scornful of feminine intellect among contemporaries that I felt it was more than a special compliment.' Nancy bravely brought these butterflies home to stay for the weekend, and Diana met them while she was still in the schoolroom. They coloured her teenage years more brightly and within a few years became some of her closest friends.

The stage was set for the kind of life and the kind of people Diana aspired to. And in 1926, when she was almost sixteen, the influence of politics, too, made itself felt – even in the sleepy village atmosphere at Asthall. The General Strike which erupted in May of that year had a galvanizing effect on the middle and upper classes of Britain, in rural areas as well as in towns and cities. Well-to-do volunteers were quick to meet the national emergency, and break the resolve of the striking workers, by driving buses and trains, providing staff for essential services, even working in factories. The strike only lasted a matter of days, and the work was treated as rather a laugh. Pam organized a canteen on the main road to Oxford for the volunteers who were driving lorries, erratically helped by her sisters. Nancy performed true to style for the occasion, disguising herself as a foul and smelly tramp who wandered up to Pam's counter and demanded a cup of tea, and proceeded to terrorize her sister until she ruined the disguise by bursting out laughing. Beyond the Mitford jokes, though, the impressionable Diana's more sober conscience was struck by reports of the conditions of the workers, especially the miners and their families. Years later, she remembered it as a defining moment. With all the crusading indignation of a teenager, she hated the Conservative Party and the smug hypocrisy of the ruling class from which she came, for allowing such poverty and hunger to exist, and for crushing the miners and workers in their attempts at change. From now on, she declared herself a Liberal and follower of Lloyd George; even when she had a vote, Diana never supported a Tory. There was a long way to go, but the seeds of a political consciousness had been sown in her.

Later that summer came the blow the family were dreading: Asthall was to be sold, and they had to move to 'Builder Redesdale's' new house at Swinbrook, for no good reason except that it was the fulfilment of David's long-held ambition. Perhaps he wanted to build on land he had inherited; perhaps he believed – as some people did – that Asthall was haunted; perhaps he was simply too inflexible to accept that a home which he had seen as temporary could become permanent. Whatever the real reasons, he was the only member of the family who had the least enthusiasm for the move, and Sydney was so reluctant to leave the house she loved that she did whatever she could to delay the moment.

5 *Paris*

By the autumn of 1926, Asthall Manor had been sold, but the new house at South Lawn, a mile outside the village of Swinbrook, was not yet complete. Until the new house was ready, Lady Redesdale and all the girls, accompanied by Blor, the governess and a family of pale yellow desert rats, went to spend a few months in Paris. Tom was away at Eton, and Lord Redesdale stayed behind to oversee the progress of his building works, content to turn up in Paris from time to time bearing a brace of pheasants.

The point of the stay abroad was, according to Diana, 'to economize' – the exchange rate made France very cheap for English people between the wars, and a modest hotel in Paris was cheaper for the family than staying at home. Lord Redesdale had every reason to try to save money: although Asthall was sold, the work on the new house was proving extremely expensive, and in addition the Redesdales had just bought a large London house at 26 Rutland Gate in Knightsbridge. For Muv this was some compensation for the loss of Asthall, which she had loved; they also had four more daughters to bring out and were tired of renting London houses for the season.

The arrangements for the Mitfords' stay in France had been made by the artist Paul-César Helleu and his wife. Sydney had known Helleu, now in his mid-sixties, since her girlhood when, during the summer recess of Parliament, her father used to take his family on their annual cruise in his yacht the *Hoyden* to the newly fashionable Normandy resorts of Trouville and Deauville. It was on a boat moored in Trouville harbour that Helleu liked to spend his summers, together with his wife and two children, and before long the two yachtsmen became friends. The eccentricities of Tap Bowles and the flamboyant, *beau monde* bohemianism of Helleu made a successful combination.

Helleu is almost forgotten as an artist these days, but in his lifetime he was highly regarded as a society portraitist and dry-point etcher. Robert de Montesquiou, his patron, had introduced him to Marcel Proust in the 1890s, beginning a long friendship. The character of Elstir in *A la recherche du temps perdu* is partly based on Helleu (and partly on Monet); according to Jacques-Emile Blanche, a society painter of the day and close friend of Proust, the Elstir paintings that the narrator sees on his first visit to the Guermantes' house were Helleus (Helleu, like Elstir, often painted flowers and seascapes). Proust wrote about Helleu's painting of the rose window at Rouen cathedral: 'I know of none to equal [it] in beauty.' In 1922 Helleu made a dry-point etching of Proust on his death-bed. He completed more than 1,500 etchings in his life, including several of Sydney as a girl; as he worked, he enveloped her in a cloud of flirtatious compliments, and he adopted the same technique when he saw the sixteen-year-old Diana.

Madame Helleu had found them a modest hotel in the avenue Victor Hugo, the Villa St Honoré d'Eylau, and there they installed themselves, complete with wildlife. A move across the Channel could not stem the family obsession with animals: as pigs and chickens were out of the question, even for Mitfords, and dogs and cats would have been liable to quarantine for rabies on return to England, the sisters had had to content themselves with the yellow desert rats – 'adorable', according to Diana, 'with lustrous black eyes'. As usual, the Mitfords' pet-life was elaborate, time-consuming and crisis-ridden. The rats, poor things, could not possibly be left cooped up all day in horrible cages, but as soon as they were let out they bored a hole in the corner of one room and disappeared into it. Terrified of the murderous propensities of French chambermaids, and even more afraid of their mother's wrath, the girls set up a shift-system, taking it in turns to wait by the hole, 'making loving sounds', Diana said, 'to coax them to come out again'.

The older Mitford girls did not take much part in rat-watching. For Nancy and Pam, parties at the British Embassy (Middy O'Neill, granddaughter of the Ambassador, Lord Crewe, was a friend of Nancy), or at the fine old Parisian house of the military attaché, General Clive, or with other friends, began to take up a good deal of their time and interest; Diana was sometimes allowed to go too. They all had a lot to learn – Paulette Helleu, the artist's daughter, a year younger than Nancy but much more sophisticated, later described the Mitford girls as very 'strictly brought up and plainly dressed' in comparison to the young girls of the Parisian *gratin*. Because Nancy and Pam's move to Paris brought many more social opportunities than at home, Diana's life also changed dramatically. It was her first taste of a city that came to be her home; her first, heady sense of the power of her beauty. For the first time, too, she went to school.

Madame Helleu had found the school for Diana, the Cours Fénélon in the nearby rue de la Pompe. It was very small, with only about a dozen pupils in the morning sessions, which were overseen by an elderly governess. Most girls only came for the afternoons, after lessons at home in the mornings, and at these fuller sessions they were lectured to by 'bearded professors from the Sorbonne'. Thanks to the French governesses of childhood summer holidays, Diana's French was already good. She found herself unexpectedly happy – 'I learned more at the Cours Fénélon in six months than I had learnt at Asthall in six years.' The group behaviour of school life, of which she had no experience, was less fearsome than she had expected. In the games in the yard during morning break she showed she was very far from being sporty, but since it was a family axiom that Mitfords were hopeless at games, she hardly cared. Most of the pupils were accompanied by their governess, who would sit with them in the Cours, or by a footman who would lounge among the overcoats in the vestibule, but for Diana the chaperonage was less strict. Although in London she was not allowed even to walk to Harrods from Rutland Gate (a distance of a few hundred yards) without Nanny or a sister to accompany her, in Paris she walked alone to and from the nearby hotel: it was a small but significant freedom.

For a young woman with a brain as good as Diana's, even this limited schooling was like pouring water on to the desert. Her intellectual life began in earnest, although it was never a conventional one – her schooling was short-lived, and there was no question of university. In fact, apart from a few German language courses later on, she had no more formal tuition of any kind, but her friends, social contacts and the influence of Tom, together with her habit of ploughing through any books she could get her hands on, were enough to ensure that she emerged unusually well-read.

Paris provided an education in other ways, too – just as that city is supposed to do. At home, Nanny's routine chant, designed to deflate girlish egos, was 'Nobody's going to look at *you*, darling'; but as Diana sat increasingly often for her portrait to Helleu, she discovered what male admiration can feel like. Helleu loved women and horses, and deplored motor cars; he was 'really a relic of the Belle Epoque who disliked everything modern, including short hair and the fashions of the twenties', and his elaborate charm worked as well with favourite sitters like Consuelo, Duchess of Marlborough, as with sixteen-year-old girls. Helleu also had a passion for nicknames and an eye for a classical reference. (He called himself the 'grandson' of Ingres, because Ingres had taught the man who taught him.) When Sydney was a young woman he had celebrated her rather severe facial bone-structure by dubbing her 'La Loi'; Unity, at this time, became 'La

République', perhaps rather unkindly likened to the classic statue of the French Republic on coins and stamps; to Diana, though, he awarded the ultimate accolade, the whole panoply of the classical ideal of beauty – she was 'La Grèce'.

At Christmas 1926 the family left the avenue Victor Hugo and moved back to London, into their new house in Rutland Gate. Standing in a tree-lined Knightsbridge cul de sac opposite Hyde Park, it is a substantial, cream-painted Victorian building of six storeys. On the first floor were a ballroom and a large drawing room, on the ground floor a dining room and Lord Redesdale's business room; upstairs, Diana shared with Pam a bedroom overlooking the Ennismore Gardens churchyard. Farve even installed a passenger lift, of which he was tremendously proud. In addition to the house itself, the Redesdales had bought the mews behind it, consisting of a former stable and the flat above it – a flat they dubbed the Garage, and where they spent a good deal more time than in the main house, which was often let.

Sydney, who had insisted on a London house when Asthall was sold, poured all her considerable talents for decorating into Rutland Gate. All the best French furniture had been brought from Asthall, and the drawing room glowed with pale blues, pinks and chintzes. The only gloomy room was David's business room on the ground floor, for which he had chosen curtains in 'a frightful sort of sham tapestry covered in dingy leaves and berries'. His daughters' response was typical: '"Oh, Farve, how ugly," we said; but he imagined he saw birds and squirrels peeping out of the foliage, and this made him feel nearer the coverts at home.'

That Christmas holidays included a visit to the Churchills at Chartwell with Tom. For the first time the two Mitfords (Diana and Tom) and the two Churchills (Diana and Randolph) were no longer considered 'brats', as Churchill cheerfully called his children, but made the leap into the world of the grown-ups, included in the conversation at dinner. Diana's fondness and admiration for 'Cousin Winston' grew still further. For her, though, the holidays were short: it had been decided that she would go back in January to the Cours Fénélon, and stay with two old sisters who took English girls *en pension* in their apartment on the corner of the avenue Victor Hugo and the rue de la Pompe. She could not make the journey by herself ('I never travelled alone on a train until I was twenty-two') and to save the expense and trouble of another chaperone it was decided that she would cross the Channel with Winston Churchill and Randolph, who were on their way to Rome to visit Mussolini (whom at this time Winston 'greatly admired', according to Diana).

At the Gare du Nord Diana was met by one of the two old sisters and escorted to the flat at 135 avenue Victor Hugo, very close to the Cours Fénélon, and to the Helleus'. The ground-floor apartment was hardly luxurious – baths were taken, twice a week, in a shallow round tin filled by a maid with a small kettle of scalding water – and the old ladies were tiresome. It was, she wrote in one letter, 'ugly to the point of wickedness. The French have got a wonderful natural taste, but these old ladies have missed it. One of them is *horrid* and wears a wig, the other is down-trodden and nice.'

Discipline was still strict, but there were many possibilities and Diana speedily learnt to take advantage of them. She was allowed to go on her own to a few chosen places – to school, down the hill to the rue Emil Ménier where the Helleus lived, and to violin lessons near the Lycée Janson, a whole hundred yards away. She had taken up the violin (despite being 'utterly devoid of talent') partly because the music lessons proved so useful. Whenever Diana was meeting a boyfriend – strictly forbidden, of course – she would invent a violin practice, and off she would go, usually to the Bois de Boulogne in a taxi or to a *thé dansant*, making sure to be back in the avenue Victor Hugo in time for dinner. She knew how to have fun, and the sudden, heady discovery of her sexuality and her power over men shows in her reports to friends – naïve but proud, full of an adolescent's affected sophistication, despite the fact that her clothes were still home-made and every night in the gloomy, shuttered ground-floor bedroom she also poured out her sensations to her diary.

One breathless teenage letter written in February 1927 to Tom's friend James Lees-Milne, who was staying in Grenoble, tells of boyfriends ('Charlie is a count, of course. He is fairly rich and extraordinarily handsome but very vain') and of the forbidden exploits ('Round the Bois de Boulogne in a taxi alone with Charlie – you can guess. Don't feel angry with me – I know that it isn't lovely to be so sensual, but it is exciting and wonderful'). Above all, she trills, she feels 'very happy, because wherever I go I am looked on as the eighth wonder of the world, *at last*'.

The source of some of this admiration was Helleu. 'I . . . pose for eternal pictures to M. Helleu whose compliments never become boring because they are always unexpected,' she told Lees-Milne, and her walks with Helleu in Paris parks, or to look at pictures in the Louvre, were an important part of her intellectual as well as her sentimental development. To the naïve Diana he became teacher, mentor, father-figure and sweet friend. She was astonished by her first experience of frank and adult male admiration; above all, he initiated her with enthusiasm and wit into a world of art and aesthetic judgement which she craved. He introduced her to friends and fellow artists; they took long wintry walks in the park at Versailles, and a trip to Rouen to see the rose window he had painted, all the time talking incessantly (and at first mysteriously) about paintings and people. It was an education in taste.

Madame Helleu, too, was warm and welcoming, providing the hungry Diana with 'heavenly food, roast veal, boeuf en gelée, îles flottantes' when she lunched with them, or rich black chocolate cake at teatime after school. Their daughter Paulette, who was a few years older than Diana, was a brusque and critical friend, however, ridiculing her clumsy clothes and lack of make-up (this was still strictly forbidden). Perhaps Paulette was also jealous that so much of her father's attention and affection was directed towards this beautiful but dowdy newcomer.

In the white drawing-room of their apartment, which was also Helleu's studio, hung ornate eighteenth-century gilt picture frames, all of them empty. Helleu maintained that if you couldn't afford the pictures you wanted, you should hang only the frames and use your imagination. It was here that he made his many drawings of Diana, and a dry-point etching of her head, drawn straight on to the sheet of copper as he usually did. The pointe sèche was reproduced in a magazine called *L'Illustration*, which considerably raised Diana's status at the Cours Fénélon. It shows Diana in profile, her head turned hard to the left, in a severe, sleek pose, with the fashionably cropped hair that Helleu hated (and which had predictably caused a huge rumpus at home with Farve). It is as short as a boy's at the back, pushed off her forehead but curling gently down to hide her ears. In photographs of the late 1920s, Diana's eyebrows usually look dark and thick, in the fashion of the time; her deep jawline, accentuated by the shingled hair and the softness of youth, looks heavier than we might now consider beautiful: it was a face to fascinate a classicist, the face of 'La Grèce', one that combined perfect proportion with fashion. Yet Helleu's picture* fails to capture much charm or life, and is too statuesque to convey the luminous beauty Peter Quennell described in *The Marble Foot*, when he likened Diana's skin to an alabaster vase lit from within.

Helleu was the first of a number of much older, clever and talented men who were important to Diana: there would soon be others. They adored her looks, her chatter, her eagerness to learn and her hungry, half-formed mind;

---

* Diana's copy of the engraving, proudly borne home to England under her arm for the Easter holidays, was burnt, with so many other treasures, in a fire in 1956 at Clonfert Palace, the Mosleys' house in Ireland. There are copies in the Bibliotèque Nationale, and in the possession of Paulette Helleu (now Mrs Howard Johnson), and Diana's granddaughter Daphne Niarchos.

she basked in their attention, soaked up knowledge of the world from them and modelled her life on their principles – for a while.

The Parisian episode was short-lived, for two reasons. The first was that towards the end of March, Helleu fell seriously ill. The resentful Paulette turned Diana away from the door when she tried to visit him, and when he died, on 23 March, Diana was deeply upset. It was her first experience of the death of someone she loved and looked up to, and from letters it is also clear that she missed the warm glow of her own reflected image: 'Nobody will ever admire me again as he did,' she wrote.

She returned sadly to Rutland Gate for the Easter holidays, expecting to go back again to the Cours Fénélon for the summer term, but there was trouble in store. One day, when she and Pam had been walking in the park, she heard her mother's voice calling: 'Diana! Come here at once!' To be called by one's proper name in a household so devoted to nicknames could only mean the blackest of rows was brewing. She had made the mistake of leaving her diary, with all its girlish confessions, lying open in the drawing room, where her mother had found it and read it. Even by the standards of Mitford family storms, the ensuing argument was a big one. She was in the darkest disgrace, and for days neither of her parents would speak to her, except to inform her that she would never be welcome in any respectable house if anyone knew that she had been to the cinema alone with a young man in the afternoon.

It did not occur to anyone that Sydney might not, or should not, have read her daughter's diary – parental power was absolute – and the sisters' view was simply that Diana was an idiot to have left it lying around. There was no court of appeal: disobedience like this could not be overlooked, and Diana was not to be allowed to go back to Paris.

She felt her punishment was severe. Not only were the delightful opportunities of Paris at an end, but her entry into the grown-up world was abruptly reversed. She found herself in a kind of social limbo: not yet seventeen, she was too young to go out into society like Nancy and Pam, but too old to go back to the schoolroom and the care of the governess. The house at Swinbrook was still unfinished, and Sydney wanted to get her away from Rutland Gate, busy as it was with the summer's social arrangements for the two older girls, any and chance for further dissipation. It was decided that she should go with Unity, Decca and Debo, the governess Miss Bedell, and of course Nanny, to spend the early part of the summer in a cottage belonging to a great-aunt, Lady Maude Whyte, at Bucks Mills in Devon.

It was a pretty cottage by the sea, but Diana was in no mood for pretty cottages. Her enforced country retreat was 'the terrible, deathly essence of boredom'. She had very few books and no money to send for more; there was no one to talk to, nothing to do – and as the days crawled by the agony was intensified by letters from Nancy, describing her whirling life in London: 'I danced five nights running & a play the 6th night & again Monday Tuesday Wednesday of the next week.' Diana's picture of her own desperation is rather pathetic: the highlight of her day was a walk every afternoon up the hill to the village shop to collect the *Daily Mail*, which was running a serial of *The Story of Ivy* by Mrs Belloc Lowndes, in 'cruelly short' extracts. On Sundays, the *Daily Mail* did not appear. There is nothing quite like the intensity of adolescent boredom and longing, and Diana 'ached' (Mitfordese for aching with boredom) from morning till night. There was a lesson here, and Diana did not fail to learn it: she promised herself that never again would she risk the aimlessness of this existence, the intellectual starvation, the ignominy of being sidelined with the children. She would live at the centre of things. With cool determination, Diana resolved to get away from home as soon as she could.

6 Swinbrook House

Diana, her three younger sisters, Blor and the governess left their tedious country exile in Devon to go straight to the new house at Swinbrook, a house they unanimously disliked. Lord Redesdale was proud of his building efforts, the culmination of a long-cherished dream, but he could not escape the fact that most of his family loathed the place. It was raw and bleak and cold, in comparison with the warm familiarity of Asthall – from which there had been no good reason to move, apart from their father's ambitions to build. It is a big house, with three storeys and eighteen bedrooms, because Farve's plan had been to provide a room for each of the children, for several guests and for each of the staff.

Swinbrook House (as David insisted it should be called – only Nancy continued to enrage him by referring to it as 'The Buildings, South Lawn') is something of a puzzle. Sydney had never had anything to do with the plans or their execution; she never went to see the work in progress. While she was creating her ideal in the Frenchified elegance of Rutland Gate, David was casting his – disastrously, as it turned out – in bricks and mortar at Swinbrook. Sydney was renowned for her excellent taste; David was known to have such an uncertain eye that he could not reliably choose his wife a Christmas present. It is strange that she nevertheless gave him free rein over every detail.

The house was as ugly inside as out. Jessica described the 'large rect-angular grey structure' as having the 'utilitarian look of frankly institutional architecture. It could be a small barracks, a girls' boarding school, a private lunatic asylum, or, in America, a country club.' Nancy, writing to Tom soon after they moved in, gave a typically acerbic account of its effect on the family atmosphere: 'Deep depression has the Mitford family in its clutches. The birds [i.e. parents] never speak save to curse or groan & the rest of us are overcome with gloom. Really this house is too hideous for words & its rather pathetic attempt at aesthetic purity makes it in my opinion worse. I mean I would rather it were frankly hideous Victorian because then at least it would have atmosphere whereas at present it is like a barn . . . filled with extremely beautiful and quite inappropriate furniture . . .' Now twenty-two, Nancy was leading an enthusiastic social life that included regular weekend guests, but with her usual hyperbole she declared that 'one simply couldn't have anybody artistic to stay lest they sicked in the front hall . . .' Diana just thought the house 'monstrous'.

Lord Redesdale was wounded by his family's reception of the home he had planned for them. They had no time for its virtues: its position on top of a hill overlooking the beautiful Oxfordshire river valley, a squash court and a tennis court, gardens and stables. Their reaction was partly dictated by the shock of the new – there has always been a snobbish resistance to modern houses in Britain – but exchanging Asthall for Swinbrook was a sharp contrast, and Swinbrook lost every round in the comparison between the two. In place of the soft charm of the old gabled manor, the new house was brash and grim outside, and inside decorated in a sort of mock-rustic look (not far from what John Betjeman immortalized as 'Ghastly Good Taste'), with ugly fireplaces of rough-hewn stone and heavy oak beams. From Diana's point of view, David's design could hardly have been worse: gone was the secluded Asthall library with its 'peace and delicious smell of books and polished wood', her refuge and her education. Instead, at Swinbrook the books were housed in David's study, to which the children were welcome only occasionally. The piano was in the drawing room now, and Tom seldom played any more because of the inevitable interruptions. The squash court was of no interest to anyone.

The one exception was Debo, who was deeply fond of Swinbrook and greatly enjoyed her childhood there. But she was so much younger at the time of the move, and did not regret Asthall in the same way. For the older ones, though, it was a sad reflection of how little David must have known of his children's talents and preferences. Swinbrook House may even represent some deeper schism in the family – between the parents (how could Sydney have taken so little interest in such an important family project?), and between the two halves of the family (the elder four, who wanted freedom and a social life, and the three little girls still in their childhood world). Many years later Sydney was to say, rather bitterly, that it was with the move to Swinbrook that the family's troubles began.

The one possible consolation, their individual bedrooms, did not compensate for the loss of privacy in the rest of the house. Although Swinbrook had central heating (installed, like everything else, at enormous expense), it was always very cold – there was damp new plaster and draughts from elm doors that had warped – and the children were not allowed fires in their rooms. So the linen cupboard, which was always warm because the hot water pipes ran through it, came to be a favourite place for the girls, and especially for Diana. It was immortalized as the Hons' Cupboard in *The Pursuit of Love*, the place Linda Radlett languishes away her wartime pregnancy. There, in Nancy's novel, the Radlett children gathered to share news of the adult world, to discuss the mysteries of sex (gleaned from a book called *Ducks and Duck Breeding*), and to hold meetings of the Hons Society.

The real linen cupboard at Swinbrook was more like a small room, with a window. Diana valued it as a place to read, and her preferred authors were contemporary, witty and iconoclastic: Aldous Huxley, Bertrand Russell, Lytton Strachey and J. B. S. Haldane. Nancy's heroine Linda borrows characteristics from several of the sisters, but the part that is most closely modelled on Diana, during the brief time in which she lived at Swinbrook, is the 'aching'. Linda mopes, goes for gloomy rides by herself, longs for love and an early marriage, dreams of the glamorous world of 'Lord Merlin' (who was closely modelled on Lord Berners), and wills the hours to pass.

> . . . but oh the days went dragging by. Linda would flop about in the drawing-room, playing (or beginning and then not finishing) endless games of patience, sometimes by herself, sometimes with Jassy, whom she had infected with her own restlessness.
> 'What's the time, darling?'
> 'Guess.'
> 'A quarter to six?'
> 'Better than that.'
> 'Six!'
> 'Not quite so good.'
> 'Five to?'
> Yes.'
> 'If this comes out I shall marry the man I love. If this comes out I shall marry at eighteen.'

Diana also had to endure her exclusion from her older sisters' social activities; she was still treated as a child. But she certainly did not feel like one. She was in love so often, she said, that she couldn't remember the identity of the young man about whom she wrote to Jim Lees-Milne, not long after her return from France. '[Bill] dines here for a dance, and of course I wasn't allowed to be there; but after dinner at about 10 he came up to my room in secret and I rushed out in my pyjamas and kissed him on the mouth. The whole interview lasted about 30 seconds, because after that I pushed Bill away and slammed my door in his face. I was afraid of Muv.' She adds, perhaps disingenuously, 'I have quite chucked the Frenchmen, they are nasty sensual brutes really.'

Jim Lees-Milne was a lifeline to the outside world, and their letters give an insight into the teenage Diana. He had a serious crush on her, although she wrote coyly to dispel it: 'Now listen. I really don't want everyone to fall in love with me you know. I am certainly not a vamp and I don't think I am much of a flirt now. Of course I used to be when I was younger because inordinate flattery and adoration turned my head . . .' He was a faithful correspondent, and often sent books; her replies show a serious-minded and slightly depressed teenager, self-conscious and a little priggish. She is feeling 'broken-hearted and morally ill', and thanks him for his 'wonderfully comforting letter' about her 'grounding' after the Paris disgrace. She takes a worldly-wise tone: 'sex is after all so unimportant in life. Beauty and art are what matter. Older people do not see my point of view.' She decides to hunt once a week to combat the *cafard*: 'The boredom of this place, and my restlessness, and the fact of my staying indoors nearly all day thinking or reading were *very* bad for me. I get such terrible fits of melancholy . . .'

He sent her Francis Thompson's poems, which impressed her, and they talked about André Maurois' *Ariel* ('There will *never* be another Shelley. I wish I had been alive then to marry him. He was more beautiful physically and mentally than any *angel*.') Next she read Harold Nicolson's life of Swinburne, then his *Glorious Apollo*: 'Byron was a selfish beautiful genius, and not really more selfish than many men and most artists. As to Augusta, she was of the same temperament as I am, and just about as silly.'

Diana gave him advice on his own poems, which he had sent: 'Read Alice Meynell's short essay on false impressionism called The Point of Honour. This is *not* meant to be rude . . .' She bats away his continuing compliments – 'you are very kind to admire me, but have you seen the beauties, Georgie Curzon, her mother, Lettice Lygon, Mary Thynne and all the rest? I compare *very badly* with them. I have got dark skin and light hair and eyes which is an unattractive paradox . . .' The same letter continues with a little burst of priggish disapproval: 'In "Eve" this week is a picture of an acquaintance of Nancy, a Mr Byron, in his fancy dress . . . wearing a long white beard à la Walt Whitman. In his hands he holds a bottle & wine glass. Across his shirt front is written GOD. Is this funny? To a very tolerant libre penseur it appears absurd & in the worst taste. It will hurt the feelings of hundreds of the nicest people . . . What a stupid man he must be . . . Warped.'

Within a year, this 'Mr Byron' would be one of Diana's closest cronies, and his outfit that night very like one he would wear just two years later to a fancy-dress party at Diana's house. She was on the point of encountering the first of the Bright Young Things, and she turned with agility from a solemn and melancholy teenager into a dedicated social butterfly.

Quite soon, Swinbrook came alive as the scene of many house parties, filled with the 'sewers' – Farve's disdainful collective term for his children's friends – and none of the artistic guests 'sicked in the hall', as Nancy had predicted. None the less the move to Swinbrook, in the end, suited nobody. David was further from the river he loved, and gradually gave up his fishing parties. Diana thought that his hurt at the family's rejection of his creation was deeper than he acknowledged (especially because Sydney too disliked the house), and he withdrew into himself. In the summer holidays he went to Scotland to shoot; he spent more time in his London club. Worst of all, his finances never recovered from the enormous expense of the new house. From now on, there were more frequent fierce economy drives, when David thought himself penniless: Rutland Gate was often let, as occasionally was Swinbrook itself, and the family retreated to Old Mill Cottage in High Wycombe. Money remained a constant worry to David, straining his already precarious temper. When Gladys, the sewing-maid, departed, the room designed for her dressmaking was colonized by Jessica and Unity; Turner, the chauffeur, eventually had to go too, in keeping with the 'inexorable [financial] decline', which Lord Redesdale's eccentric get-rich-quick schemes did nothing to help.

Diana was increasingly impatient to leave home. Her childhood was over, and she hated the 'schoolroom atmosphere': 'Swinbrook had no charm for me. I wanted to go away and never come back.' Not for her the girlish fantasies of the Hons' Cupboard, or the life of the English countryside: what she wanted was the big world – 'people, an eternity of talk, books, pictures, music and travel'. In fact, she only had to suffer life at Swinbrook for a little more than a year, and some of that time she spent in London or staying at other houses. Tom was away in Vienna, learning German and trying to decide whether to make music his career or to study for the Bar, so Diana's best companion and ally was not available. But in August 1927 her craving for interesting people and interesting talk was satisfied by another visit to Chartwell – more welcome than ever as a contrast to Bucks Mills and a respite from the linen cupboard.

Visitors to Chartwell today will see scores of Winston Churchill's own pictures, mostly landscapes, still lifes and garden scenes. One of the very few group portraits is a small sketch showing the circular tea-table in the wide bay of the dining room that was built as part of the new wing added to the Elizabethan house by the Churchills in 1923. The people it shows around the table on 29 August 1927 were Winston and Clementine Churchill, Diana Mitford and Diana and Randolph Churchill, the artist Walter Sickert and his wife Thérèse, Churchill's political confidant Edward Marsh, and his friend and advisor Professor Frederick Lindemann, 'the Prof'.

This was heady company for Diana. According to her son Jonathan, it was at Chartwell that she first became interested in politics, and in particular an admirer of Lloyd George. Winston Churchill had by this time re-joined the Conservative Party, and was chancellor of the exchequer in Stanley Baldwin's government, but he still expressed great regard for Lloyd George – a view shared by Diana right up until the time she met Oswald Mosley.

Walter Sickert was now in his late sixties, and although the excesses of his youth in France with his Impressionist friends were over, he was still a flamboyant personality. He retained his life-long habit of appearing one day in wildly unconventional garb, the next in dandified formal rig complete with gloves and cane. Diana described his huge beard and cropped grey hair in a letter to a friend, and mentioned him wearing 'red socks with his evening clothes and in the daytime an opera hat to go in the garden'. Hugh Walpole (who sat to him for a portrait in 1928) described a 'courteous, ironical, gentle, interested' man, 'wandering about his studio (which is dirty, tumble-down Camden Town, Charlie Peace, pubs and cabbage) with his little grey peaked beard, his most beautiful eyes . . . blue and affectionate, his forehead of a fine, noble, unstained whiteness . . .' Although Sickert is now seen as among the great English artists of the century, his professional standing was a vexed issue throughout his life. At thirty, he was a leading light in English Impressionism; by the time he was sixty, as his friend and biographer Marjorie Lilly puts it, he was 'a legend in Bloomsbury and Chelsea, with a continental reputation as well, the painter's painter . . . [yet] he was not enjoyed by the multitude he so longed to reach . . .'

Churchill took to heart Sickert's preference for painting by artificial light, even on sunny days: Randolph used to recount a family joke that when Churchill was painting his daughter Sarah the shuttered and darkened room was so airless that she fainted. On this visit in 1927 Churchill himself was the sitter, as Sickert was beginning work on the portrait which was first shown the following year, and which now hangs in the National Portrait Gallery in London.

When Churchill was not discussing the fine arts with Sickert, he was debating the art of politics with Edward Marsh, who became his private secretary, and 'Prof' Lindemann, both regular visitors to Chartwell. Lindemann was a remarkable but spiky character, professor of experimental philosophy at Oxford, who excelled at everything from physics to tennis, although he had some cranky ideas; in the 1920s he was famous chiefly for having solved the First World War aviation problem of 'spin', which until 1916 had caused many casualties. Lindemann worked out, mathematically, how pilots might be able to get their planes out of a spin, then learnt to fly so that he could put his theory into practice. During the Second World War the Prof became a close advisor to Churchill, and head of his statistics section; his contributions ranged from the 'bending' of wireless beams used by German night bombers to research into microwave radar. His Alsatian/English/American background was wealthy, his contacts aristocratic, his personality ruthless and his views extremely right-wing: he had the anarchic arrogance of his type, and he would *épater les bourgeois* with glee. When the dean of Christ Church reproached him for not taking Communion, so the story goes, Lindemann replied, 'I can't; I'm a vegetarian.' He was also straightforwardly anti-Semitic: Diana remembered that of all her undergraduate friends he most disapproved of Brian Howard, because he thought Howard was Jewish.

The Prof took a great liking to Diana, and his interest in her continued after the summer was over, with visits to Christ Church and phone calls after her first balls. When she confessed to the boredom she suffered at home, he insisted she should learn German so that she could read Schopenhauer, and Diana was fired with enthusiasm for the idea – not least because Tom was learning German in Vienna, and in the autumn was to return to Austria, to stay with his friend Janos von Almasy at Schloss Bernstein. When she got home, though, Farve vetoed the idea of German lessons for Diana: 'It's different for Tom, he's a boy.' Nevertheless, the Mitford Germanophilia was beginning on two sides, almost by coincidence, and the family's infatuation with the country, its people, language, arts, music – and, in time, its politics – was to extend from Tom and Diana to Unity, then to Sydney and even (although briefly) to David.

Diana's friendship with the Churchills continued to be a passport to the adult world. Later that year, she went with Diana Churchill to her first ball – the Radcliffe Infirmary Ball in Oxford – and when Tom came home from Austria for Christmas, together they visited friends for hunt balls. Often held in cheerless town halls, and usually full of people who were neither smart nor interesting, these dances often had the added disadvantages of a freezing drive to and fro, and then being trapped there under the watchful eye of one's hostess, with no chance of leaving early. 'Hunt balls,' Diana put it crisply, 'were not my idea of what glamorous grown-up life should be.'

She did not have long to wait, though. The life that began only a few months later was certainly glamorous (if not necessarily very grown-up): she was about to embark on a social scene that has become renowned for its frivolity, its extravagance, the talent of its dramatis personae and the empty-headedness of their behaviour.

Diana often stayed at No. 11 Downing Street, Churchill's official residence as chancellor of the exchequer, when Rutland Gate was let: from this base, or from the Garage, she moved into the conventional débutante orbit of large, chaperoned balls given by the parents of other debs, with young men from suitable families as dancing partners. These parties were, on the whole, too staid, and the young men too respectable, for her taste. 'Sometimes Muv came too,' Diana remembered, 'and sometimes Farve. I waited until they were at supper or engaged in close conversation on the chaperone's bench to escape to a night-club. The charm of the night-clubs was the fact that they were forbidden. After a short time we would return to the ball; there was poor Muv, very sleepy, dying to go home, and only hoping we had enjoyed ourselves . . .'

Diana's circle of acquaintance was much wider than that of many debs, thanks to the energetic social life of Nancy, Pam and Tom. Tom's Eton and Oxford friends (dubbed by Nancy the Fat Fairs, because so many of them were stout and blond) were among the few outsiders welcomed by Farve, while Nancy, gregarious and witty as she was, attracted more exotic company to Swinbrook, giving Diana the chance to meet some of the rich, smart and cynical set which gossip columnists called the 'Bright Young Things'. (Evelyn Waugh always lampooned the phrase by using it of his most sober-sided acquaintances, such as 'Bright Young Henry Yorke', the novelist who wrote as Henry Green, and who was known for his gloomy city suits and melancholy manner.)

Although the four older siblings claimed they disliked Swinbrook, and were perpetually at the mercy of their father's unpredictable temper, for them the house was never the remote fortress that the younger ones felt it to be. 'We had guests every Saturday to Monday chosen by us,' Diana told Harold Acton. 'Farve didn't care for them but put up with it.' Jessica remembered, perhaps rather enviously, that 'at weekends they would swoop down from Oxford or London in merry hordes, to be greeted with solid disapproval by my mother and furious glares from my father'.

Certainly the 'merry hordes' sometimes had to run the gamut of eccentric behaviour on the part of Lord Redesdale. He took violent dislikes to his children's friends, the 'sewers', threatening banishment or horse-whipping for such offences as putting one's feet on the sofa or carrying a comb in one's breast pocket. Selina Hastings, in her biography of Nancy, sums up the confrontation of the two worlds: 'Nancy's young men might have been expressly designed to annoy him. Frivolous and effeminate, they lolled about the drawing-room shrieking with laughter and repeating outrageous stories about each other, in the exaggerated idiom of the period – "utterly divine!", "too too sick-making!" The sight of them in their Charvet ties, polo-necked sweaters and Oxford bags drove Farve, of the canvas gaiters and sensible mole-skin waistcoat, into a frenzy.' And Nancy, without the least sympathy for her father's sense of outrage and invasion, declared, 'The truth is that the poor old man having no building left to do is in a very bad temper.'

From time to time, though, Lord Redesdale replaced his usual loathing for some young man with a distinct partiality. In the family, it was considered a moot point which was worse; the tales of Farve's treatment of the hapless visitors have passed into family mythology, and show that the children themselves were not above using their father's eccentricities as a tease against their friends. Mark Ogilvie-Grant was one frequent visitor who became a favourite of Farve's, but this meant that he would demand Mark's company punctually at an early breakfast. On one occasion, when he pressed the badly hung-over younger man to eat a dish of pigs' brains, Ogilvie-Grant was forced to dash for the door, retching audibly. Jessica and Debo, who on the whole were kept away from Nancy and Diana's 'fast' friends by Muv, celebrated the incident by making up 'a Honnish song, a sort of signature tune for Mark, to be sung whenever he came to Swinbrook, with the lugubrious chorus: "Brains for breakfast, Mark! Brains for breakfast, Mark! Oh, the damn sewer! Oh, the damn sewer!"' We can judge for ourselves how funny Ogilvie-Grant might have found this, after a while.

The Mitfords' myths are all part of the half-ironical portrait of their father as an old monster who made life impossible. But as the legends are retailed through book after book by and about the family, no one remarks on the iciness of the humour, or the callousness that resulted from the self-obsession of this tightly knit family. If feeding the family myth-bank counted for more than a friend's humiliation, then Farve's behaviour was tacitly encouraged by his children, who were enjoying the tease.

Other guests managed to escape this sort of treatment, despite being potentially more dangerous. Nancy quailed at the thought of introducing to her capricious household her Oxford undergraduate friend Robert Byron (the person whose GOD costume had shocked Diana, and who later became a celebrated travel writer), for he made social stock-in-trade of espousing unconventional opinions, denouncing traditional artistic values as trash, whipping up a cult for Victoriana (then at the nadir of its reputation), and performing long, drunken imitations of Queen Victoria with a napkin on his head. Yet, as Nancy wrote to Tom, it was a success: 'Would you believe it, the family really liked Robert! We had a perfectly wild weekend . . . Honestly I've never laughed so much. We got up a terrible hate for Princess Elizabeth . . . we are spreading the rumour that she has webbed feet . . .' Byron's own account of staying at Swinbrook in 1928 (admittedly in a letter to his mother, which might have suppressed some of the sillier details) gives no hint of finding the experience bizarre: 'The Mitford family are very amusing – especially Nancy, and I enjoy being here – the house is modern, built in fact the other day, square, of Cotswold stone, commanding, as they say, a lovely view. Yesterday we went for a nice mild ride on nice well-behaved horses, and I enjoyed it very much . . .'

More perilous still, as a guest, was Brian Howard, a willowy, dark aesthete with flashing eyes, 'a butterfly of sombre brilliance with the self-directed sting of a scorpion'. Although he was a bold rider to hounds, Howard's effeminacy seemed certain to enrage Lord Redesdale, and Harold Acton was among those who wondered what the confrontation between the two would be like. But in *The House of Mitford* Jonathan Guinness takes a cool line, deflating some of the monster-myths about David: 'They . . . coped with each other perfectly well . . . Howard did not spend all his waking hours provoking people, any more than David spent all his in a rage.'

Diana first met Brian Howard in 1925 when she was fifteen, when he came to Asthall for a fancy-dress ball. By 1928 he was a leader of the Bright Young Things, and to be seen at all the most fashionable parties – which, that year, were usually costume parties. These became ever more lavish and esoteric, and those that hit the press included a Circus party given by the dress designer Norman Hartnell; a Cowboy party held by William and Harold Acton; a Second Childhood party at which guests dressed up in baby clothes and arrived in outsize prams (one drawn by a donkey) or with old nannies dragged out of retirement for the occasion. A Noël Coward song of the moment called 'I Went to a Marvellous Party' describes a get-up of Cecil Beaton's: 'Dear Cecil arrived wearing armour/Some shells and a black feather boa . . .', and a letter of Nancy's gives a picture of how seriously the Bright Young People took the business of being silly: 'Nina [Seafield] & I & Patrick Balfour went to the Pageant of Hyde Park through the ages on

Tuesday . . . Mark [Ogilvie-Grant] looked lovely in a white wig & Knee Breeches & Oliver Messel was too wonderful as Byron, I nearly fainted away when he came limping on to the stage, this proves that I must have been Caroline Lamb in a former incarnation He built up his face with putty & looked the living image of Byron. Stephen Tennant as Shelley was very beautiful Lord Furneaux was a modern "young-man-about-town" & Frank Packenham [sic] in a sailor suit rode on one of those enormous bicycles . . .'

Nancy's enthusiasm for this sort of thing seems never to have flagged, but Diana's attitude was cooler. Although they must have commanded more column inches than any similar phenomenon until the 'Swinging Sixties', in later years she described the press reports of these parties as a 'tainted' source. Most of the BYPs, she said, 'played no part in London society', but a number of them were gossip writers whose social life was also their living, and therefore had a vested interest in maintaining an air of fashionability and transforming any event into saleable copy. The guest-lists published in society columns were often inaccurate, and sometimes completely invented: from now on – and more so later, after her first marriage – Diana appeared in print much more often than she did in person. Her social world was more discreet and discriminating. A Swimming-Pool party given by Brian Howard at St George's Baths in Pimlico in July 1928, complete with negro jazz orchestra and guests in 'dazzling' bathing suits drinking a special Bathwater cocktail, was described the next day by Tom Driberg in the Daily Express 'Talk of the Town' gossip column. 'We went to lovely balls,' was Diana's response to her supposed appearance there, 'but not in St George's swimming baths.'

The BYP phenomenon was a powerful one, none the less, and much has been written about the significance of the Roaring Twenties, a moment of iconoclastic pleasure-seeking sandwiched between the grim memories of the First World War and the growing economic Depression of the 1930s. Like the free spirits of the Sixties, these young hedonists had been born luckily too late to have experienced the war that marked their parents, and believed themselves to be rebelling against its shadow; like their later counterparts, too, the BYPs sometimes came to grief. The brittle gaiety glossed over an emotional and sexual immaturity that spelt disaster for many. With sad irony, Evelyn Waugh's own brief and catastrophic first marriage to Evelyn Gardner ('She-Evelyn') came to grief while he was in the middle of writing his novel Vile Bodies, a fierce satire on the emptiness of this social set, which is dedicated to Diana and her first husband Bryan Guinness. His personal pain is reflected in the savage flippancy of his main characters, Adam and

Nina. Getting re-engaged for the umpteenth time (over the telephone), they cut short each other's sweet nothings with a flip, 'Don't let's get intense about it,' and when they finally do go to bed together, Nina's immediate verdict is: 'I don't think this is at all divine . . . It's given me a pain.' The morning after, 'Adam was inclined to be egotistical and despondent; Nina was rather grown-up and disillusioned and distinctly cross . . . Nina said, "Do be amusing, Adam. I can't bear you when you're not amusing." . . . Then Nina said: "All this fuss about sleeping together. For physical pleasure I'd sooner go to my dentist any day."'

We can assume that Waugh intended Nina to be speaking for her peer group. These young women – 'girls' – were not expected to enjoy sex, and so, very often, they didn't. For the first time in Western history women were flaunting cropped hair, skinny hips, flat bosoms and trousers; they played games and smoked and drove and talked as much as possible like boys – but the obvious androgyny of this image betokened very little in the way of sexual liberation. It was not that young women were moulding themselves into young men; rather, they were trying to freeze themselves in a pre-pubertal mode, child-women whose sexuality and emotional range were underdeveloped, while their coltish high spirits held sway. 'Amusing' was the ultimate accolade, and the ultimate defence. 'Do be amusing, Adam . . . I can't bear you when you're not amusing' might be the motto of the era.

Nancy herself was precisely in the mould of Waugh's Nina. She excelled at being amusing, and valued it above most other things, and in 1928 she found herself (as she thought) the perfect playmate. She fell in love with Hamish St Clair Erskine, a small and slender Old Etonian then at New College, Oxford, the second son of the famous gambler the Earl of Rosslyn. Hamish Erskine was notoriously vain, rather silly and extremely amusing. He had early on found his niche in a hard-drinking, camp, theatrical milieu (the actress Tallulah Bankhead regarded him as a protégé), and his lightly worn immorality fascinated Nancy even while she had no idea what it involved. A breathless letter to Tom that ran 'Mark says Hamish is an absolute sink of iniquity and even knows about things Mark had never heard of!' alarmed her brother, who disapproved of the relationship, but it did not surprise him – Tom himself had had a homosexual affair with Hamish Erskine at Eton. It shows the extent of Nancy's naïvety that, throughout the four years of their painful, on-off engagement, she never realized that Hamish was, as Selina Hastings puts it, 'the most shimmering and narcissistic of all the beautiful butterflies of that homosexual coterie'.

To begin with, however, they were like children, revelling in silliness. During a stay with Nina Seafield in Scotland Nancy wrote to Tom: 'My dear this visit is being a perfect orgy . . . Last night we had a dress up dinner. Hamish & I draped our middles in calf-skin chiffon & wore vine leaves I had a wreath of red roses & I curled Hamishes hair with tongs, he looked more than lovely . . . You should have seen the Troll [Hamish] & me standing in a bath together staining our bods with coffee!!!' And so that the world should hold up a mirror to their elaborately created selves: 'Hamish Nina & I wrote the gossip for the next Vogue & put in lovely things about ourselves of course . . . I was "that vivid creature Miss Nancy M. She is a strikingly beautiful & witty girl" & Hamish was a brilliant conversationalist & exceptionally good shot. Oh the fun of it!'

Diana was adept at being 'amusing', too, in the spirit of the day, but these puppyish pranks were not her idiom. Despite Evelyn Waugh's dedication of *Vile Bodies* to her, Diana was no Nina. Her steelier spirit was already emerging, and she was attracted to people who put in a little thought in the intervals between parties. Friends who converged on Diana – Robert Byron, for instance – may have held opinions that were deliberately elaborate and provocative, but at least they had some opinions. Evelyn Waugh had entered the Mitfords' orbit when he married Evelyn Gardner, a friend of Nancy, and other acquaintances included John Betjeman, who became a close friend of Diana and an admirer of Pam.

Although the 'Roaring Twenties' now seem to have been giving off nothing but a shrill squeak, this was the social milieu which surrounded Diana, for at least a short time. The clash between its iridescent shimmer and the earthy, if eccentric, values of the girls' father could hardly have been more dramatic: as Harold Acton put it, 'The contrast . . . evoked extreme burlesque.' For Nancy, it proved a rich source of fictional creativity; for Diana, it was an early training in how two contrasting ways of thinking could co-exist. The seeds were sown, from the time she was emerging into adulthood, of the double-layered personality that would later be so characteristic of her, and so hard to fathom.

Not for Diana, either, was Nancy's prolonged girlhood. Her desire to get away from home was in earnest, and her sights were set on more than the next party and 'Oh the fun of it!' Besides, the débutante season, this round of hectic and competitive social activity, was unashamedly a marriage market in which well-born young women, with the eyes of their peer group upon them, were paraded like prize cattle. They were out to get husbands, the more respectable and the richer the better, and the sooner the better too. To be brilliantly, or at least respectably, engaged by the end of your first season was the pinnacle of success for débutantes, and in this matrimonial competition Diana, aged just eighteen and less than a year after her first grown-up party, carried off a prize.

7 Bryan

In November 1928 Robert Byron wrote to his mother from Swinbrook: 'motored down here with Bryan, who is grotesquely in love with Diana Mitford (who is very beautiful) and goes red whenever she comes into the room'.

The Bryan in question was the eldest son of Colonel Walter Guinness (later Lord Moyne), who was then minister of agriculture in the Conservative government as well as a director of the Guinness Brewery, and Lady Evelyn Guinness. At twenty-two, Bryan Guinness was part of the set Diana knew well, a friend of Harold Acton, Brian Howard and Evelyn Waugh, and an eligible bachelor in the débutante world. He was slim, handsome, an excellent dancer, of good family and very rich.

These were the credentials that mattered to society. But he also had the credentials that mattered to Diana, and which set him apart from the general run of debs' delights: he was highly intelligent and devoted to books, wrote poetry and read hungrily, and although he rode well he was as little interested in most country sports as Diana herself. She wrote that same month to Jim Lees-Milne: 'I *know* you will like him because he is too angelic and quiet and not rough and loathes shooting, and loves travelling and all the things I love.' She was eager to be part of his circle of friends (in 1926 Bryan had travelled to Mount Athos with Robert Byron, and took some of the photographs for Byron's famous travel book *The Station*) and was delighted to find him lodged at the heart of the clever, artistic set she liked best. When introducing Bryan to her family for the first time, she remembers: 'Every time he said or did something uncountrified I glowed with pride and pleasure. Uncle George [Sydney's brother] used to say the countryside was "all mud and blood": I was beginning to agree, and I saw in Bryan the antithesis of a squire.'

Whenever Bryan was described, the word 'nice' was used – and not disparagingly. His manner was gentle and dreamy, he idealized large families of small children, he was a quasi-Tolstoyan idealist, his personality had none of the toughness of Diana's. At eighteen, though, her character seemed more docile and more malleable: she was still very naïve and, while she appreciated Bryan for being so 'uncountrified', he loved in her the fresh country girl he took her to be. Nancy was one of the few who foresaw difficulties, writing to Tom in October, 'The more I see of Bryan the more it surprises me that Diana should be in love with him, but I think he's amazingly nice.' Diana's own early inklings that their rapport might not be perfect – she remembered his dithering at the Swinbrook breakfast table, agonizingly on the point of spilling porridge in his vagueness – were quashed by her desire to be married, her excitement about this lightning romance, and her conviction that she was in love.

They had met at her first débutante parties and balls, when she was still seventeen. Within three months – in July, a few weeks after her eighteenth birthday – Bryan proposed and Diana accepted without hesitation: at that age an acquaintance of three months feels long, and she felt she knew him well.

It was not until November that their engagement was announced, however. Diana told Sydney immediately after Bryan's proposal, but her mother was worried that Diana was too young and Bryan, though four years older, too immature, and she told them they must wait a year before they even thought of getting married. It was hardly a welcome response to a young man 'grotesquely in love' and a young woman impatient for adult life to begin, and they set out to change Sydney's mind.

Their campaign to wear down parental resistance began with a visit by Diana (chaperoned by Blor) to the Guinnesses in the country. Bryan's mother, the indulgent and mildly eccentric Lady Evelyn (a builder like David Redesdale), was in the middle of constructing a faux-Gothic mansion at Bailiffscourt, near Climping, on the Sussex coast. Lacking neither visionary zeal nor the money to accommodate it, Lady Evelyn was having her neo-medieval house built entirely of genuinely old materials which had either been gathered from the site – the house stands beside a thirteenth-century chapel – or imported from other ancient ruins. While this astonishing project was under way, the family and their guests stayed in the Huts – a series of pitch-pine huts, hurriedly put up on brick foundations in the middle of a cornfield at the edge of the sea. Colonel Guinness had escaped on his yacht for a long voyage over the summer recess from Parliament, as he usually did.

Diana was thrust into the middle of a family as large, and, in their different way, as eccentric as her own. Huge picnics on the sun-baked Sussex fields were her memories of that first summer. The wispy, ethereal Lady Evelyn, who rarely spoke above a whisper, allowed her children every indulgence: for

Bryan's brother Murtogh, she had converted one of the two staircases of her imposing London house into a huge polished wooden slide; she spent most of her time in the nursery with eight-year-old Grania; she worried about Bryan underspending his very large allowance while at Oxford. Her passion for rusticity was extreme: at her Hampstead house she watered the paths with milk to encourage moss; she would lean out of the window of the train, while travelling down to Sussex, and hurl fistfuls of wild flower seeds into the surrounding countryside. (The farmers, with their carefully weeded crops, might have thought this a strange action from the wife of the Minister of Agriculture.) Her London houses featured blackened wood panels on the walls, worm-eaten refectory tables on which stood pots of wild grasses, fires that were encouraged to smoke and smoulder. Diana, devoted to other ideas of sophistication, was equally fascinated and horrified.

Lady Evelyn declared herself completely on the side of the young couple, and thought they should be married as soon as they wanted. But she was reluctant to confront Farve, and for any effective intervention they had to wait until Colonel Guinness arrived home in September. Bryan's return visits to Swinbrook were a great success with the family in the meantime (Diana was almost distressed by how much he enjoyed the 'schoolroom atmosphere' of Swinbrook, the thing she particularly disliked). And although she spent part of the summer visiting other people – at her mother's insistence – her parents' disapproval was quickly dispelled: in November their engagement was announced, and their wedding day fixed for the end of January.

Immediately, life improved for Diana, because a few freedoms were permitted: 'Bryan and I have been engaged 4 months secretly and now it is being such fun because we can go about alone and all that,' she wrote. Excitement was high among all the Mitfords. Diana was the first of the six girls to marry, and it was to be a large society wedding. As the hullabaloo of preparation began, the choice moments were quickly recycled into family lore or printed fiction: Lady Evelyn being the best source of anecdotes. When the wedding presents began to pour in – mountains of trays and jugs and vases, as well as more valuable silver, china and glass – she gazed at the display and whispered, 'The glass is easiest: it only needs a good kick.' Nancy relished the good kick and promptly used it in her novel *Highland Fling*. (Nancy's fancy takes over, and the young couple in her book fantasize about a 'wedding present shoot' organized by General Murgatroyd. But in real life Farve thought that kind of joke less than amusing. 'People are very kind to give you presents,' he said reproachfully to Diana.)

They were married on Wednesday 30 January 1929 at the fashionable church of St Margaret's Westminster, with the Earl of Rosse, Bryan's Oxford friend, as best man. Diana could not resist being waspish about this strait-laced youth, whose avuncular letters she thought 'irresistibly comic in their artless pomposity'. Lord and Lady Dulverton (to whom Batsford Park had been sold, and who had remained firm friends of Farve) lent their London house in Wilton Crescent – finances being low and Rutland Gate being let, as usual – to Diana and her family for the preparations. All the society columns ran announcements and photographs of Diana that day, with her short blonde hair swept back and her apparently heavy dark brows, her face plumper than it later became: her exceptional beauty inadequately captured.

The following day, large reports and photographs appeared everywhere, as was usual for society weddings then. The *Daily Mirror* gushed that Diana's wedding was 'the prettiest of the season'. The *Daily Mail* and *Daily Express* both ran half a page of photographs, of Bryan and Diana leaving the church together, and of a group of bridesmaids, while their society columnists listed the titled guests, and all mentioned Winston Churchill. One ran a huge banner headline: 'Picturesque Wedding of a Peer's Daughter'. In its announcements columns, *The Times* listed a mass of family and friends among the guests, and described Diana's dress, 'a modern picture-gown of parchment-tinted satin embroidered with pearls and having long wing draperies and wing sleeves' ('I was dressed in a white satin gown made by Hartnell,' was Diana's own description). 'An old veil of point d'Alençon lace, the gift of Lady Evelyn Guinness, was fastened beneath a tiara in crystal with diamante leaves,' continued *The Times* ('I found it impossibly difficult to arrange,' Diana commented). Her retinue of eleven bridesmaids included four little Guinness girls (in 'long frocks of cream tulle with double frills touching the ground and falling from bodices of gold tissue') and a few grown-up friends together with Nancy, Pam, Unity and Diana Churchill (in 'dresses of parchment coloured silk with gold lamé bodices, the full skirts and long Medici sleeves reaching the ground'). *The Times* report did not include the blow that had struck just before the wedding: wild with excitement about their new dresses and the great day ahead, both Decca and Debo had caught whooping-cough and could not be bridesmaids ('It spoilt the wedding for me,' said Diana).

'Bryan's wedding was quite fun,' Robert Byron wrote to his mother, 'the bridesmaids very pretty for once . . . Michael [the Earl of Rosse] made a rather butlerish best man.' Lady Evelyn, whose taste in clothes did not match her passion for homespun interior decoration, was 'a vision in cream velvet trimmed with sables'. She seemed, Byron noted, 'frankly bored'.

'All I remember of the marriage service,' Diana said, 'is that Tom had got hold of a wonderful trumpeter who filled the church with triumphant sound when the choir sang Handel's "Let the bright seraphim in burning row" and the clergyman pressed his hand on my head so hard that the rickety wreath and veil arrangement fell over my eyes.'

Their reception was held at the Guinnesses' house at 10 Grosvenor Place, among the high Gothic decorations, and at the end of the afternoon the couple left for their honeymoon, 'the Hon. Mrs Guinness wearing a dress of blue printed velvet and a blue cloth coat trimmed with mink fur'.

It was Diana's first taste of adult freedom. Their first stop was Paris, where they stayed in the Guinnesses' flat in the rue de Poitiers. Diana's maid travelled with them, lugging along several suitcases of clothes made at home by Gladys – but these were the last of the home-made things for Diana. From now on she could afford clothes from the great couture houses. Two years earlier, at the Cours Fénelon, when one of the girls had boasted that her mother bought her clothes at the 'grandes maisons', Diana thought she meant department stores like Galeries Lafayette or Printemps, shops which were then beyond her dreams. Now, she wasted no time in buying a dress at one of the couturiers, her first foray into expensive chic.

The apartment was 'pre-Gothic'. Lady Evelyn spent very little time in Paris, and had therefore not troubled to introduce worm-eaten tables or tallow lamps. There was a butler and an excellent cook with nothing to do but look after the young pair: Diana was quickly getting used to the *vie de luxe*. After Paris, they moved on to Sicily, giving Diana her first glimpse of the Mediterranean. She was in something of a daze, judging by one letter to a friend from the San Domenico Palace Hotel in Taormina, thanking him for books he had sent as a wedding present. Gone is the intense schoolgirl; now her tone is already that of a young society matron: 'Oh, it is so lovely being married. This is a heavenly island, we have been here nearly a week and are going on to Syracuse fairly soon, then Palermo and then perhaps Rome or Athens or London I am not sure.'

Their return to England meant a new house – 10 Buckingham Street in Westminster, a pretty town house designed by Lutyens which they had bought before their wedding and which had been decorated for them during the several weeks they were away on honeymoon; a new dog – Rubbish, a nervous and gun-shy black Labrador passed on by Farve; and a new life. It was less than two years since Diana had been considered too young even to come downstairs for a dinner party; now she had a wealthy husband and a substantial establishment. Buckingham Street (now called Buckingham

Place) is a quiet Westminster cul de sac, and the young Guinnesses' house is the most imposing: it has four storeys and a basement, with six long windows across its frontage and an arched front door topped by a crest. Diana's new parents-in-law had made only one stipulation: Colonel Guinness insisted that they have a bathroom each. 'Nothing so barbarous as for a husband and wife to share a bathroom,' he declared.

Although Bryan was always diffident about his money, and always wanted, according to Diana, to be 'just like everyone else' (the very last thing she wanted), his wealth seemed enormous not just to the financially chaotic Mitfords but to most of his friends. Robert Byron, who may have been exaggerating, reported to his mother, 'They have got the most charming house in Buckingham Street – very large – and are setting up housekeeping with innumerable servants, chauffeur, etc. – Nancy says he has £20,000* a year settled on him already, but I don't know if it is true.'

With such means at her disposal, and such a taste for fun, Diana immediately began to be an avid party-giver, as well as party-goer. Buckingham Street was nothing if not spacious, and quickly became open house to all the friends of Tom and her sisters, the Fat Fairs and the Swinbrook Sewers, her new acquaintances as well as her old, who were entertained to dinners, cocktail parties and costume balls, as well as the long, chatty lunches Diana held while Bryan was out studying for the Bar.

The extravaganzas of the Bright Young Things continued: on 4 April Brian Howard celebrated his twenty-fourth birthday with a 'Dionysia', at which Diana was photographed in a toga with a gold wreath in her hair; there were the Heroines of History party at Claridge's, the Catalan party in Lowndes Square, the Baby party in Rutland Gate, and a Literary party where guests had to come as the title of a book. On 25 June Bryan and Diana threw an 1860s party at Buckingham Street, at which Nancy was photographed for the papers wearing a huge crinolined skirt and She-Evelyn as a street urchin in cami-knickers bowling a hoop. The same night there was a Watteau party aboard the *Friend Ship*, a boat moored at Charing Cross pier which was a regular society venue, and where both Evelyns were photographed at a Tropical party a few weeks later. 'We hardly ever saw the light of day, except at dawn,' Nancy remembered. 'There was a costume ball every night . . . soon the door of my tiny room would no longer shut because of the huge pile of costumes I had not the courage to pick up.'

Bryan never liked all Diana's entertaining. He kept saying, 'Let's go to the north of Scotland,' she recalled in later years. His passion was the theatre,

* Equivalent to about £500,000 in current value (1999).

and they went almost every night: to any new play while in London, to the Abbey Theatre in Dublin while staying in Ireland. Bryan even joined a special club so that he could see plays on Sundays when the theatres were normally closed. (In those days, the theatre started late, at about 9.30 p.m., so that it was possible to go after dinner and before a night-club. This was the normal routine of an evening out.) Diana's own enthusiasm for the theatre was considerably less than Bryan's.

Diana's new friends included the well-known hostess Emerald Cunard, and it was in her box at the opera that Diana first met Lytton Strachey. Strachey was one of the older men – in the mould of Helleu or Prof. Lindemann, and later Lord Berners – who held an important place in Diana's life, and when she recovered from her initial awe of the formidably intelligent author of *Eminent Victorians*, he quickly became one of her most valued friends. He was as thin as a streak and oddly dressed, with a long straggly beard and owlish glasses that made him appear older than his fifty years, and he had a high squeaky voice. His mind, according to the writer William Plomer, 'was on the move as swiftly as a bat, with something of the radar-like sensitivity of a bat, and when he spoke it was sometimes in the voice of a bat'. 'He was everything I loved best,' Diana said, 'brilliantly clever and willing to talk for hour upon hour.' They became teasingly close, she nicknaming him Mr Oh Indeed, from his habit of making that supercilious reply to much of what was said to him.

Although he was a mainstay of the Bloomsbury Group, Lytton Strachey managed to straddle the gulf between it and a less intellectual but much richer and more glamorous milieu. 'I've been plunging in the oddest manner among the Upper Classes,' he told a friend that year, although after one curious 'Conversation Piece' tea-party given by the Duchess of Marlborough at Carlton House Terrace he complained that 'the exhaustion was terrific, the idiocy intense'.

He was not the only one to be, or at least to pretend to be, jaded by the swirling round of society. On 20 July, when Evelyn Waugh was in the country writing *Vile Bodies*, and just a few days before he discovered that She-Evelyn had left him for John Heygate, he wrote to Henry Yorke: 'Are you going to Bryan and Diana's party? I might go up for it if I thought there would be anyone who wouldn't be too much like the characters in my new book.'

The summer of 1929 saw the high point of the Bright Young People's shrill antics. They were beginning to pall, but Diana's more adult and intelligent social circle went from strength to strength. Nevertheless she indulged in some pranks, too, and on 23 July she and Bryan held an art exhibition at Buckingham Street which was widely reported in the society pages. The pictures were by Bruno Hat, a German naïf they had 'discovered' in Sussex, and were Picasso/Miro-esque quasi-cubist works painted on cork bath mats and framed with whitened rope (both items from the general goods shop in Sussex run by Mr Hat and his step-mother, according to the biographical notes available at the show). The catalogue, *Approach to Hat*, was a sensitive appreciation by Evelyn Waugh. The artist himself sat in a corner, hunched in a bath chair and peering over a bushy moustache, a thin cheroot in one hand and a glass of iced coffee in the other: as he apparently spoke no English he could not communicate with the crowds of society people, friends and – according to the newspapers – 'eminent art critics and connoisseurs' who filled the Buckingham Street drawing room.

The whole thing was a spoof, however. The hunched figure in the corner was Tom Mitford in a wig and false moustache; the pictures had been painted by Brian Howard in John Banting's studio. The artist's supposed lack of English was purely to avoid journalists' questions, and although Lytton Strachey had bought a picture, he was well aware of the joke as Diana proudly stuck the red spot on the canvas. Next day, the papers were full of the 'art hoax', and in the *Daily Express* a picture of the moustached Tom in his bath chair led a column headed 'Amazing Art Hoax on Experts' in type as prominent as the neighbouring items: 'Chief Whip Snubs Mr Davidson', 'Lady Astor Scene in Parliament', while 'Dragoman', the society columnist, took up the story and named some of the guests (who included 'Mrs Sitwell, who was there with Lady Cynthia Mosley'). It was all carried out in a spirit of hilarity, but Diana thought that in fact Brian Howard was hoping for real recognition for his work. He would have been amused to learn that, even now, a 'Bruno Hat' occasionally turns up in the salerooms.

A few days later, Diana and Bryan left for Sussex, to stay in Pool Place, a house near the Huts lent to them by the Guinnesses. Rubbish, Nanny, Decca and Debo came too. Lady Evelyn's vision was beginning to take shape, and on to that barren, sandy stretch of coast she had imported full-size mature trees, brought by lorry with their vast root-balls and then lowered by crane into position, planted and pegged for stability with a net of enormous guy-ropes. It was a curious sight. Diana thought Pool Place as ugly as all the other Guinness houses, but they used it as a country base for the next two years, until they bought somewhere of their own.

On 2 August 1929 they were joined in Sussex by a distraught Evelyn Waugh, stricken by his wife's abandonment of him. Despite this hard blow to his pride and his heart, Diana found his high spirits undimmed and his company as electric as ever, but this may have been a front – her presence always cheered him up, and he was already adept at taking refuge in comedy. After his marriage ended, and until he married again eight years later, Waugh had no home of his own. He lived at the Savile Club or with his parents in Hampstead, with friends or in country pubs, or on his increasingly adventurous travels and journalistic assignments. His first novel, *Decline and Fall*, had been a great success on its publication the year before, selling 2,000 copies a week throughout the autumn, and all doors were open to him. But he could not settle or decide what to do with himself, and for much of the first year after the break-up, he was seldom away from Bryan and Diana. In September he was writing to his agent, A. D. Peters, from Knockmaroon, the Guinness family's comfortable house at Castleknock outside Dublin; after that he went off with Bryan, Diana and Nancy to Paris, to stay at the rue de Poitiers. He was still writing *Vile Bodies*, which in July he had playfully described to Harold Acton as 'a welter of sex and snobbery', but in September a letter to Henry Yorke bitterly commented that his book had seemed to 'shrivel up and rot internally'. In the same letter he betrays his growing feelings for his young hostess: 'Do you and Dig [Yorke's wife] share my admiration for Diana? She seems to me the one encouraging figure in this generation – particularly now she is pregnant – a great germinating vat of potentiality like the vats I saw at their brewery.'

Diana was indeed pregnant, and although her baby was not due until the spring, she had been told to rest. The Guinnesses' Paris apartment was an extremely comfortable environment in which to do that, as well as to work and play. Of the foursome, three were busily writing novels. Besides Waugh, Nancy was finishing *Highland Fling*, and Bryan was at work on *Singing out of Tune*, which was published in 1933, and was partly based on the break-up of the Waughs' marriage. All morning the three scribbled away, while Diana stayed in bed and read; the afternoons and evenings were pure play time. Their outings to dress shows, restaurants, museums and galleries were spiced with the funny and lightly malicious chat at which Diana and Waugh excelled.

Back in London, Diana and Bryan gave Waugh a birthday lunch at the Ritz. There were other friends with whom he also stayed, but as the autumn wore on into winter, and Diana's pregnancy advanced, he and Diana became closer. She spent many days in bed, or venturing out only for a little 'carriage exercise' in her large chauffeured Daimler, and he would sit with her for hours at a time, often lunching and dining at a small table in her room while

Bryan was attempting to establish a practice as a barrister. The Guinnesses had lent Waugh the house at Pool Place to escape to and write (he was greatly entertained by Lady Evelyn's tree-planting) but whenever he wanted company he took the train back to London and resumed the intense chats in Diana's bedroom. Diana needed a friend to help her while away her pregnancy; her condition made it acceptable to spend so much time alone with an unattached man. They talked, they read, they went to tea with Waugh's parents in Hampstead, they took little trips to the zoo, where they had an elaborate and fantastical relationship with a grumpy Humboldt's gibbon. Waugh was now deeply in love with her.

Many years later, in 1943, his story *Work Suspended* describes the narrator falling in love with Lucy, the pregnant wife of his friend. On his habitual morning call at her house, Lucy greets him 'lying in bed in a chaos of newspapers, letters and manicure tools':

> Couched as she was, amid quilted bed-jacket and tumbled sheets – one arm bare to the elbow where the wide sleeve fell back and showed the tender places of wrist and forearm, the other lost in the warm depths of the bed, with her pale skin taking colour against the dead white linen, and her smile of confident, morning welcome; as I had greeted her countless times and always with a keener joy . . . her beauty rang through the room like a peal of bells . . . So another stage was reached in my falling in love with Lucy, while each week she grew heavier and slower and less apt for love, so that I accepted the joy of her companionship without reasoning.

Many more years later, after thirty-five years of estrangement between them, Diana wrote to ask him about that time. Waugh replied that although he had not meant Lucy to be a portrait of her, *Work Suspended* was 'to some extent a portrait of me in love with you'. (This letter, dated 30 March 1966, appears to have been the last Waugh ever wrote: he died on 10 April.) In the event, however, their intense friendship foundered quickly. In March 1930 Jonathan Guinness was born, and christened a little after that with Waugh and Randolph Churchill as godfathers. These two met at the font that day, beginning a lifelong relationship that alternated between powerful friendship and strong enmity. Jonathan's name was suggested to them because Waugh was at the time planning a book about Jonathan Swift. Nanny Higgs, who had been Diana and Randolph Churchill's nanny, arrived to take care of the baby, and after only a few weeks Diana resumed the social round she had been missing: parties, cocktails, luncheons and balls were available to her again, and she launched herself back into them, both as guest and as hostess, with enthusiasm.

On 19 May Evelyn Waugh began writing his diaries again, after a significant break. His diaries always broke off at telling emotional points: there was a six-month gap immediately after his engagement to She-Evelyn, then again at the break-up of the marriage and throughout his friendship with Diana. The previous month he had published *Labels*, a travel book dedicated again to Diana and Bryan. His diary's daily record gives a picture of an indefatigable social life – although he accused Diana of too much vapid and aimless partying, his own social appetite was prodigious. *Vile Bodies* had appeared in January to huge success; he was lionized everywhere, although according to many friends he was never entirely comfortable in society. He accepted the attentions of the hostesses, but at the same time mocked them in print: 'No-one has a keener appreciation than myself of the high spiritual and moral qualities of the very rich,' he wrote in the *Daily Mail*. 'I delight in their society whenever I get the chance.'

None the less, Waugh's diary reads like a society column, not only in its list of dates but in its bright and brittle tone. On 19 May, he had cocktails at the Savoy, had dinner with Henry and Dig Yorke, then went to a play, then to drink champagne at Quaglino's, then to supper with Diana and Bryan at Buckingham Street ('Good *foie gras mousse*.') The next day it was lunch at the Ivy with his publisher Jonathan Cape, tea at the Ritz with Nancy Mitford, cocktails at Cyril Connolly's; the day after that a cocktail party at Cecil Beaton's and dinner at Quaglino's ('I talked of lesbians and constipation'), and so it went on. (It is interesting to note that most of his many newspaper articles were written at night, after an alcoholic lunch, cocktails, dinner and often a late supper or another party.) Diana gave him tea on 23 May and lunch on the 27th; he saw her on 29 May at a cocktail party given by William and Harold Acton in their massive house in Lancaster Gate, filled with rococo furniture; the following day he saw her again at lunch at Eddie Marsh's, after which they went together to look at the mask Diana had had cast of herself by 'a German who Harold Nicolson has invented. It is very lovely and accurate.' On 5 June Waugh lunched with Diana at Buckingham Street; the next day she lunched with him in a large party he gave at the Ritz, which included Georgia and Sacheverell Sitwell, Nancy Mitford, Cecil Beaton, Frank Pakenham and William Acton, after which they drove down to Pool Place together. On 10 June (Diana's birthday) they drove back to London, and had both lunch and dinner together at Buckingham Street.

The tone of the diary gets increasingly sour. On 12 June: 'Felt very ill indeed. Lunched with Billy Clonmore at Isola Bella. Harold and Peter Ruffer. Peter looking desperately thin and vicious. Cocktails at Lancaster gate after one hour's sleep. Nancy Cunard and her negress and an astonishing fat Mrs Henderson. Michael Rosse. Later the party of Olivia Wyndham and Ruth Baldwin on a Thames steamer. It was not enough of an orgy. Masses of little lesbian tarts and joyboys. Only one fight when a Miss Firminger got a black eye. Poor old Hat [Brian Howard] looking like a tragedy queen. After the party to Vyvyan Holland's [Oscar Wilde's son] where everyone fell asleep.'

Waugh was a perpetual guest, Diana a tireless hostess. On 19 June she gave a large cocktail party; on the 27th she gave another supper. (Waugh 'enjoyed the party, became very drunk and fought Randolph in the servants' hall. All the usual people were there.') It was an unending round of the 'vile bodies' Waugh had already satirized in his novel, and it was apt that at this most hectically social moment in Diana's life he should dedicate the book to the Guinnesses and brand them, as nothing else could, as leaders of the Bright Young Things. Yet it was also ironic, since at heart – though for different reasons – neither Bryan nor Diana was suited to the role, as would very soon become apparent.

From this account it seems that the friendship between Diana and Waugh was still a close one, even though both were socializing frenetically, and Waugh had one or two half-hearted love affairs under way. But their relationship was deteriorating. On 5 July, at Pool Place, Waugh told his diary: 'Diana and I quarrelled at luncheon. We bathed. Diana and I quarrelled at dinner and after dinner. Next day I decided to leave. Quarrelled again with Diana and left.' He had become carping and critical towards her, she felt. On 9 July he saw her at cocktails at the Beatons, but barely spoke, on 15 July he 'went to cocktails at Diana's but she had left'. Two days later, he saw her at a party at John Sutro's, and afterwards wrote her a short letter to say that his unfriendliness towards her was only because he was 'puzzled and ill at ease with himself'. But when she and Bryan invited Waugh to stay with them during the summer holiday at Knockmaroon, he refused. It was the end of an intense year-long *amitié amoureuse*; they were never lovers, and she was never in love with him. From then on, she wrote, 'he bestowed his incomparable companionship on others'.

Diana had to wait more than thirty-five years to have the reasons for this rift confirmed. 'You ask why our friendship petered out,' Waugh wrote to her in 1966. 'The explanation is very discreditable to me. Pure jealousy. You (and Bryan) were immensely kind to me at a time when I greatly needed kindness . . . I was infatuated with you. Not of course that I aspired to your bed but I wanted you as especial friend and confidante. After Jonathan's birth you began to enlarge your circle. I felt lower in your affections than Harold Acton and Robert Byron and I couldn't compete or take a humbler place. That is the sad and sordid truth.'

How much did this love for Diana matter to Evelyn Waugh? He took refuge in her warmth and gaiety at a moment when he had been badly wounded and humiliated by She-Evelyn, but perhaps he had deliberately fallen in love with someone who was not only sexually unavailable, because of her pregnancy, but also very unlikely to reciprocate emotionally. Diana's translucent beauty and high-spirited charm had already accustomed her to male admiration, even adoration, but she was never particularly interested in sexual affairs: what she liked best were clever, chatty friends who would widen her horizons without romantic complications.

It is also true that Waugh, as Mark Amory points out in his edition of his letters, was extremely susceptible to falling in love at this point. He had a large emotional appetite. During 1930 he was beginning to be drawn to the Catholic church, and meanwhile had fallen in love with Theresa ('Baby') Jungman, a rich and beautiful flapper – at the same time as resuscitating an old affair with Audrey Lucas. At this time, too, he met at Lady Cunard's another Diana – Lady Diana Cooper – with whom he formed a deep, lifelong friendship (another non-sexual *amitié amoureuse*). Waugh loved smart, witty women, and his lasting relationships were with those who made no sexual demands on him: Nancy Mitford also remained a friend for life, on the same basis. The next year, 1931, saw the beginning of his passion for an entire family, the Lygons. Lord Elmley and Lord Hugh, the brothers, he had known at Oxford; now he met their four sisters, of whom two became especially close, Lady Mary (Mamie to most people, Blondy to Waugh) and Lady Dorothy (generally known as Coote, although Waugh called her Poll). His letters to these two are written in a web of private jokes so dense they are almost incomprehensible. Their father, the former Liberal cabinet minister Lord Beauchamp, had been threatened with exposure as a homosexual by his playboy brother-in-law, the Duke of Westminster, and forced into exile abroad. Their baffled mother had gone to live with her brother, the Duke of Westminster; the grown-up children, at liberty in their huge house, were a lively brood with money and freedom galore. Madresfield Court not only became the next emotional foster-home for Waugh, but both house and family also became models for *Brideshead Revisited.*

Diana felt hurt by the abrupt falling-out with Waugh, but her social life continued at full stretch. Among a large party of guests that summer at Knockmaroon were the artist Henry Lamb and his wife Lady Pansy (née Pakenham), whom they had met through Waugh because Pansy and She-Evelyn had been friends before their marriages. Henry Lamb was painting a life-size portrait of Bryan, Diana, baby Jonathan and Pilgrim, the Irish wolfhound Bryan had given Diana when Rubbish died ('a dog the size of a grey cow', Dora Carrington called it). They sat separately for this huge picture, partly at Knockmaroon and later in Lamb's London studio.

Henry Yorke came too, with his wife Dig, and another tentative guest was Lytton Strachey. 'In preparation for this holiday,' Strachey's biographer Michael Holroyd tells us, 'he had purchased a very splendid and aggressive suit of orange tweeds.' (Diana also mentions the tweeds, in her pen-portrait of Lytton in *Loved Ones*, adding that they 'set off his beard to perfection'. Strachey's habit of laughing at those who lionized him could easily be turned back on him.) An eventful journey – there was no one to meet him at Kingstown 'owing to the incompetence of the idle rich' – led into a evening of social discomfort: 'Oh dear me!' ran a letter to Roger Fry. 'My new tweeds were far too loud, and . . . quite horrified (I could clearly see) Lady de Vesci – but no matter, she left for England almost at once (whether in consequence of my tweeds or for some other reason).' But this assumed gaucherie in smart weekend company was a pretence, for Strachey was already an habitué of the house parties of Lady Desborough, a list of whose guests – statesmen, diplomats, fashionable beauties, enlivened by one or two men of letters – would appear in *The Times* on Monday mornings. He liked to bridge the gap to his Bloomsbury world by seeming an outsider in society, but he basked in his role of 'literary lion' and, with the Guinnesses, according to Diana, he enjoyed the veneration of a younger audience.

All the same, it was not an easy stay, as Diana remembered it. Bryan's enthusiasm for the theatre was as lively as ever and the Guinnesses used to go twice a week to Dublin's Abbey Theatre, but after one particularly dull play Strachey simply refused to go again. Diana pleaded, in order to keep her house party on track, but Strachey would not compromise. Henry Yorke had sat next to him at the dreary play, and remembered Strachey whispering to him, about one especially uninspiring character: 'I'm feeling rather *low* about *Ignatius*.'

The friendship with Strachey regained momentum later, when he invited them to Ham Spray, the house near Inkpen in Berkshire he shared with the artist Dora Carrington and her husband Ralph Partridge. By this time, however, Partridge was mostly living elsewhere with his lover Frances

Marshall, though both were regular weekend visitors, while Carrington (as she was always known) remained with the homosexual Lytton in a passionate and unofficial *mariage blanc* whose ground rules included sexual freedom for both. It was a typical Bloomsbury arrangement, and although Diana was keenly curious to meet Carrington, Strachey was nervous about the visit.

For the young Guinnesses, the summer first brought a grander trip, to Venice, to Greece and to Constantinople, which was then, Diana said, 'a dying city' full of filth and beggars. Her feelings about the holiday are summed up by her only comment: 'I was quite pleased when we boarded the Orient Express for the endless journey home.' But the Ham Spray visit was an unexpected success. It is not surprising that Lytton Strachey half-dreaded the meeting between the svelte Diana with her super-sophisticated ways and the small, intense and mouse-like Carrington, peering out nervously at the world from under her thick pale fringe.

'I loved her at first sight,' was Diana's reaction. 'She was fascinating. To me, she looked like a little Beatrix Potter character in her unfashionable print cotton dresses, but Lady Ottoline Morrell describes her as a moorland pony . . . Her deep-set eyes were blue, her hands worn with toil – gardening, cooking, working for her beloved Lytton. All summer she had bare legs, sunburnt, sandals and white socks. When she walked she turned her toes in, and her every gesture was that of a shy and self-deprecating person.' Yet Carrington was original, clever and perceptive, and – Diana found this out only years later, by reading biographies of the other members of the set – often juggling a number of lovers, at the centre of a storm of jealous feelings. But she gave no hint of it.

Diana also left a vivid picture of the curious relationship between Carrington and Strachey, and of the Bloomsbury circle itself: '[Carrington] lived for Lytton; nobody else really counted. He accepted her worship in a slightly distant way, I thought. The Bloomsburies – at any rate the ones I knew – although they were a mutual admiration society about their painting, writing and criticism, and despite myriad love affairs within the group, seemed in friendship to be more reserved and chilly than most people. There was something disconcerting, for example, in the way that staying in a country house they would all slip off without wishing one another goodnight. It was supposed to hurt a Bloomsbury if you said goodbye or goodnight.'

Perhaps this style appeared reticent to Diana only in contrast to the exaggerated flappers' idiom of her own set. She also noticed how all the

Bloomsbury group took their verbal style from the witty, sparing locutions of Mr Oh Indeed, and his way of putting heavy emphasis on just one or two words in any sentence. The use of this fastidious, laconic style for non-stop gossip and literary chatter 'served,' Diana put it crushingly, 'to emphasize the contrast between him and his disciples'. She had little time for most Bloomsburys, despite their cleverness. She thought their colours muddy and their style dowdy: they were middle-class.

Also in the house that weekend were Carrington's husband Ralph Partridge with Frances Marshall, the critic and writer Raymond Mortimer, and Roger Senhouse, Lytton's 'beloved': a full display of Bloomsbury's tangled personal relationships. Carrington often did the cooking herself ('typical Bloomsbury fare – that is, a distant cousin of French bistro food') but on the last evening of the weekend her rabbit pie poisoned Diana, who was too ill to go home on Monday morning. So she stayed, sick in bed, at Ham Spray with Carrington while Bryan went back to his legal practice in London. Carrington spent all day in Diana's room chatting, and despite their differences in style and temperament the two women became friends. All Diana's life she remembered Carrington with fondness, and – because Diana was such an improbable Bloomsburyite – her strong feelings for both Carrington and Lytton Strachey epitomize her gift for unlikely friendships.

8 Biddesden

The friendship with Lytton and Carrington became stronger in the autumn of 1930, when Bryan and Diana bought a country house for themselves. Biddesden House, near Andover, is a superb early-eighteenth-century building in brick and stone that stands in rolling chalkland at the edge of Salisbury Plain. It was built by one of Marlborough's generals, and in the two-storey hall Major-General Webb hung a life-size portrait of himself, splendid in red uniform and full-bottomed wig, mounted on his charger, a battle in the background. Hardly Diana's style, but she left it in place – if the picture is removed, the ghost of General Webb is supposed to racket up and down the stairs at night until his portrait is restored to its place. Oddly enough, Lord Redesdale was the only person who ever felt Biddesden to be creepy: he was a reluctant guest. For everyone else it was a warm house, and an immediate favourite with the Mitford family. Tom and Nancy came to stay more often than ever, and the little girls loved the comfort and sophistication of Diana's new house, which was close enough to Swinbrook for Muv to drive them over for the day.

The earthy and country-loving Pam was installed to manage the surrounding 200-acre farm, and she took to the work with gusto: even in those depressed days when many farms were bankrupt, Pam managed to turn a small profit. Her presence gave rise to a large number of visits by John Betjeman, as she was one of the several people with whom he currently fancied himself in love. An old friend of Bryan's, he had met Diana a few months after her marriage, but the growth of their friendship was typically rapid and Betjeman was soon a Biddesden mainstay; for two or three years he spent almost every other weekend there. Quieter and more reticent than the other Mitfords, Pam was not as well tuned as Nancy or Tom to the sharp, witty talk of her sister's circle, and 'Betch' was the only one she felt comfortable with.

'The Huxleys (I hated Aldous) and the Augustus Johns used to come,' Pam recalled, 'and Lytton Strachey and Carrington and Evelyn Waugh (whom I really disliked); Betch made me laugh.' They bicycled over the

Downs together, visiting obscure churches (Betjeman's passion) to attend matins or to collect the evangelical hymns Betjeman used to sing raucously after dinner, to the horror of May Amende, the maid who had come with Bryan from one of the Guinness households, who was older than her employers and a little shocked by their friends. 'I was very, very fond of him,' Pam said of Betjeman, 'but I wasn't in love with him. He said he'd like to marry me but I rather declined.'

At Biddesden for the first time Diana could give free rein to a talent that became important to her, that of doing up houses. Buckingham Street always showed the tell-tale signs of having been decorated while she was away on honeymoon, with some unfortunate consequences. Now she had a beautiful original to work on, and almost unlimited means. Fine furniture was cheap during the Depression of the early thirties; she also commissioned some modern furniture, including a dining table that would seat thirty people. As Diana had been nominated 'a society beauty' by the press, and all her doings already commanded column inches, the house was written up for the woman's page of the *Daily Telegraph* in January 1932: 'There is something more than a little uncanny about the perfection of this Queen Anne house, built in 1711, with its garden and 200 acres . . . Mrs Guinness during the last six months has taken enormous trouble to bring out the exquisite grace of the rooms by the use of clear pastel colours used in a simple youthful way . . . Curtains of Madonna-blue glazed linen are being quilted by the miners' wives in South Wales . . . in the dining room the George III panelling has been painted very pale duck-egg green . . .'

Biddesden was already comfortable, but Diana made it luxurious. A walled swimming pool with a domed gazebo was built in flint and brick by George Kennedy, a well-known architect and old friend of Bryan's, and decorated with mosaics by the Russian artist Boris Anrep, a new Bloomsbury acquaintance who was a frequent and flamboyant presence at Ham Spray. Another Bloomsbury commission was for a large female garden statue, made of lead, from Stephen ('Tommy') Tomlin, the husband of Lytton's niece Julia Strachey (and, incidentally, the person Diana considered the best talker of the group).

Since Ham Spray was only twelve miles away across the Downs, Lytton and Carrington soon became Diana's 'dearest and most welcome guests' among the many. Visits to Ham Spray brought them into contact with the pair's Bloomsbury friends, an artistic and intellectual circle that ran parallel to Diana's, but did not often intersect with it (Lytton's incursions into high society were an exception). Clive and Vanessa Bell, Leonard and Virginia

Woolf, various members of the Strachey family, David Garnett, Stephen and Julia Tomlin, Gerald Brenan, Boris Anrep, Rosamund Lehmann and her husband Wogan Phillips – all these were Ham Spray regulars, in addition to the basic *ménage à trois*, or *à quatre* once Ralph Partridge's lover Frances became a permanent feature. Augustus and Dorelia John were often there, too. The Bloomsburies were, on the whole, rather older (Lytton was now fifty, Carrington in her mid-thirties, while Diana's friends were mostly in their twenties). Diana had still been a girl, devouring the novels of Aldous Huxley in the linen cupboard at Swinbrook, when the 'Garsington set' that revolved around Lady Ottoline Morrell was lampooned by Huxley; in Carrington she had now met the real character who appears in *Crome Yellow*, the novel of the moment, as the sexually reticent, advanced-thinking Mary Bracegirdle.

Diana and Bryan's friends formed a distinct and different group: Harold and William Acton, Evelyn Waugh, John Betjeman, Robert Byron, Roy Harrod, Mark Ogilvie-Grant, Christopher Sykes, James Lees-Milne, John Sutro, the Yorkes, Cecil Beaton, Brian Howard and the artists Mark Gertler and John Banting, as well as Randolph Churchill, who came to Biddesden for his honeymoon and 'practically lived with us', according to May Amende. Most had known each other at Oxford, or through mutual Oxford friends. The other arty élite – the Garnetts, the Stephens, etc. – tended to send their children to Cambridge. These people were reasonably well-off, but seldom rich and never smart; Diana's set, though some were far from wealthy, gravitated towards a more glamorous way of life. Henry and Pansy Lamb spanned the two groups (he an artist, she the daughter of the Earl of Longford). Osbert Sitwell was one older friend who, like Lytton Strachey, appeared in both camps, and Bryan and Diana relished visits they paid with Osbert to his bizarre parents at Renishaw, or to tea with his sister Edith Sitwell, eating stale currant buns in the poet's cheerless flat while she nursed her latest violent literary grudge. The Sitwells, with their brother Sacheverell, were prize guests at Biddesden.

Diana had always lived in very comfortable surroundings. The shivering baths in a tin tub at the elderly sisters in the avenue Victor Hugo were the nearest she had ever come to dingy living – unlike Nancy, who was by now accustomed to a series of flats and bedsits which approached squalor. Since her marriage Diana had got used to real luxury. In spite of the high-spirited conversation and the youth of the hosts, visitors to Biddesden describe the domestic routine there as formal ('rather *comme il faut*', according to the writer Peter Quennell, a guest at the time). This was to Diana's taste, like the formal beauty of the house itself. She never minded the earthy hospitality at Ham Spray because she was fond of Lytton and Carrington, but on the whole the bohemian style, which appealed much more to Bryan, struck her as dreary. Of their one or two visits to Augustus John and his family at Fryern, where Bryan felt at ease, she remarked tartly that 'pubs and shove ha'penny are not among the entertainments I enjoy'. The following year she sat for Augustus John in his studio in Mallord Street, and although she was flattered to be asked – John was an extremely prestigious painter – she found the sittings tedious and the conversation desultory. She did not like the finished work, and felt no obligation to buy it, but many years later it came up for sale and was bought by her second son, Desmond.

Diana was pregnant with Desmond in the summer of 1931, but now there was no Evelyn Waugh to keep her company. Her social life hardly flagged, in London or the country: Lytton was at Ham Spray for the whole of May and June, immersed in editing *The Greville Memoirs*, but weekends brought hordes of guests, and many visits to the 'little Guinnesses'. Towards autumn, when Diana's baby was due, she settled down to wait the last few weeks in Buckingham Street, where Desmond was born at the end of September. They were at the theatre, as they were almost every night, when the baby started, but for once Diana was enjoying the play (*The Front Page*) so much that she stayed to the end, with her labour beginning in the second half.

Friends crowded in to visit as she lay in bed after the birth, and among them – bravely – was Lytton Strachey. He had a famous dislike of babies, and children were never welcome at Ham Spray, so Diana asked her nurse to take the new baby out of the room during his visit. But while he was still there the nurse came back into the room, holding the baby Desmond with his mop of black hair. Lytton was horrified and curious, and the nurse airily explained that lots of babies are born with fluffy black hair and that it would 'all come off'. 'Oh!' replied Strachey with his characteristic shriek. 'Is it a *wig*?'

In those days it was usual to have complete bed-rest for two or three weeks after birth, and while Diana was convalescing in London, Carrington arranged a surprise for her return to Biddesden. She arranged with Bryan that she would paint a *trompe l'oeil* on the west side of Biddesden House, in a large blanked-out arched window. It shows a maid in mob cap and uniform apron, peeling an apple (Phyllis de Janzé, a mutual friend, sat for this portrait), with a striped cat – Lytton's Tiberius – both gazing out at the viewer. It is a quiet, domestic image but one that has a haunting, almost ghostly quality. It is still there, curiously aged by the archaic effect of the maid's uniform.

Carrington, who felt perpetually nervous and dissatisfied about her painting, told Lytton in a letter that she thought 'little Bryan's dummy window' one of the most successful of her works. A domestic commission of this size was a rarity for Carrington, who was perpetually hard up and spent much of her time decorating tiles and crockery for sale in the London stores, so she had been delighted at the opportunity. On 29 October 1931 she wrote to him again, describing the day Diana discovered her present. 'I got up at half past 7 this morning in order to start my picture at Biddesden early [this must have been detailed finishing work – the painting itself had been completed some time before]. Bryan had asked me to breakfast. The car refuses to operate and it is 10 o'ck before I got to Biddesden. Then . . . the moment I started to paint it came on to rain. So all my paints got mixed with water. My hair dripped into my eyes and my feet became icy cold. Diana was delighted. Bryan kept it a complete surprise from her until 3 o'ck. May [the housemaid] joined in the joke and kept my presence dark all this morning and pretended I had walked over from Ham Spray as my car had to be hidden. Diana, of course, thought nothing of my walking over in the rain [a distance of twelve miles] and merely said, "But Carrington you *ought* to have let me send the car for you." I had tea there and then came back. Diana is sweet. She was looking very lovely today, in a curious dark bottle green jersey with a white frill round her neck . . .'

Although Diana and Bryan's London and country lives continued in the same round of friends and family, there were not many more such carefree moments with Carrington or Lytton. Just a few weeks later Strachey fell seriously ill, and all winter wrestled with an agonizing condition that made him progressively weaker. Although it was not diagnosed as such, he had cancer of the stomach, and when he died, on 21 January 1932, Carrington was plunged into despair. He had been her world. Friends rallied around her, fearing to leave her alone; Ralph Partridge, in particular, tried everything he could to 'nail her to life'. When he could not be there, he organized other friends to visit. She had tried to kill herself even during Lytton's last unconscious hours, shutting herself in a sealed garage with the car engine running. Now she began busily disposing of her possessions – she gave Diana an eighteenth-century silk waistcoat, embroidered with flowers, which had been Lytton's.

On 19 February, Carrington wrote: 'Yesterday at Biddesden I came face to face with death.' Out riding in the woods, her horse had bolted and thrown her, but she was unhurt. 'I thought of the irony of fate,' her diary goes on. 'That I, who long for Death, find it so hard to meet him.' On the last

1 TOP: Diana in 1913, aged three, with her brother Tom. ABOVE: Asthall Manor in Oxfordshire, where the Mitford family lived from 1919 to 1926.

2 TOP: Out walking: from left, Lady Redesdale, Tom, Nanny Dicks, Nancy, Miss Bedell, Unity, 'Zella', Pam and Diana. ABOVE LEFT: 'Farve': Lord Redesdale in 1915. RIGHT: 'Blor': Nanny Dicks

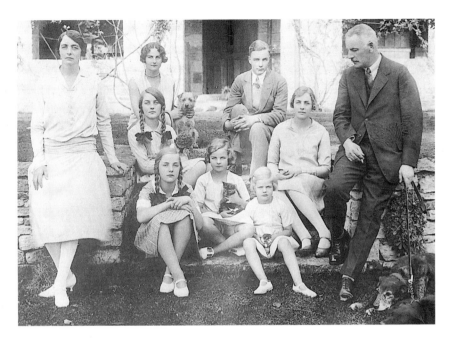

3 TOP: The Redesdales posed for a family group photograph, complete with favourite pets, every year. This one, taken at Asthall in 1926, shows Diana sitting on the left, in the middle row, with long plaits. ABOVE: 1930, the year after Diana's marriage: she is sitting third from left, between Nancy and Tom. Swinbrook House is behind them.

4 TOP LEFT: Swinbrook House: 'Builder' Redesdale's dream. TOP RIGHT: Tom in 1926; Diana aged sixteen: *pointe seche* by Helleu. ABOVE: Winston Churchill's sketch of the tea table at Chartwell: Diana sits second from left; also present are Diana and Randolph Churchill and their mother Clementine, Tom Mitford, 'Prof' and Mrs Lindemann, Mr and Mrs Eddie Marsh.

PICTURESQUE WEDDING OF A PEER'S DAUGHTER.

SEVEN HAPPY BRIDESMAIDS, who attended the Hon. Diana Mitford, in their picturesque old-world gowns.

A SMILING BRIDE.—The Hon. Diana Mitford, daughter of Lord and Lady Redesdale, and Mr. Bryan Guinness leaving St. Margaret's Church after their marriage yesterday.

FATHER AND SON.—Sandland's Pride (left) and his son, White Opal, owned by Mrs. Motion, of Glasgow, winners at the National Terrier Club Show.

5 ABOVE: Diana's wedding in January 1929 was one of the society events of the moment, and appeared in most of the national papers. These pictures appeared in the *Daily Express*. LEFT: John Betjeman, an Oxford friend of Bryan Guinness, soon became a friend of Diana's and a regular guest at Biddesden.

6 TOP: Biddesden House, near Andover in Hampshire: Diana's county home at the age of twenty. ABOVE LEFT: Dora Carrington's *trompe l'oeil* window at Biddesden, a surprise for Diana painted when she was away in London having her second baby, Desmond. ABOVE RIGHT: Diana by Cecil Beaton.

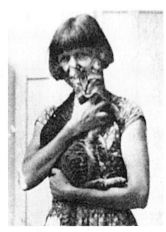

7 The Biddesden set: (clockwise from bottom left) Diana by Augustus John (detail); Robert Byron; Evelyn Waugh in 1930; Lytton Strachey by Henry Lamb (detail); Dora Carrington; Nancy Mitford at her wedding to Peter Rodd.

8 Fancy dress: Diana as Poppaea, with Robert Byron as Nero, at Brian Howard's Roman party at the Savoy, 1932.

day of February, Ralph and Frances took Carrington and David Garnett to Biddesden for another visit. They went riding again, as Carrington loved to do, and a photograph showing the four of them with Pam Mitford and their ponies is the last ever taken of Carrington. That day she asked Bryan (Diana was away) if she could borrow a shotgun, to shoot rabbits in her garden. On 10 March Virginia and Leonard Woolf came to Ham Spray for the day, sent no doubt by Ralph Partridge – a sad and stilted visit at which, Woolf wrote, Carrington seemed 'helpless, deserted, like some small animal left'. The following morning she shot herself with Bryan's gun.

'My life seemed absolutely useless and empty,' Diana wrote. Lytton had been a friend and mentor, but Carrington had been a very close companion, someone with whom Diana had long chats by the fire after supper. All the same, Diana had not then grasped how multifaceted her personality was. 'I thought I knew her intimately,' Diana said, 'but it was an illusion.'

In April 1932 Diana and Bryan moved from Buckingham Street to a large house at 96 Cheyne Walk, overlooking the River Thames at Chelsea, a house that once belonged to the American artist James McNeill Whistler. It is the east part of Lindsey House, a huge mansion originally built in the seventeenth century by the Earl of Lindsey on the site of Sir Thomas More's Chelsea farm, but later divided into three. By coincidence, Bertie Redesdale had lived there before the turn of the century, so Diana found herself only two doors away from where her father had been born. Set back from the road by a front garden, it has four storeys and a basement, with an enormous panelled drawing-room running the length of the first floor with windows looking towards the river at the front and over the garden at the back.

In these surroundings, their social life could become still more expansive. If Diana was feeling bleak and bereft because of the deaths of Lytton and Carrington, and increasingly restless and bored, her social calendar does not show it. There were if anything more parties than ever. Bryan was still trying to establish himself as a barrister, and was out most of the day, but Diana entertained in the daytime too. The dining room of the new house was large and airy, decorated in lily chintz, with tall windows opening on to the garden, an ideal setting for her long lunch parties.

Almost as soon as her redecorating was finished, she and Bryan threw open the house and garden for a ball to which 'we invited everyone we knew, young and old, rich and poor, clever and silly'. It was early July – not long after Diana's twenty-second birthday – and a warm night. The garden was lit up, the trees illuminated from underneath; guests remembered it as 'magical'.

Diana's own recollections show that the party was a lively one; she recalls 'managing to propel Augustus John, rather the worse for wear, out of the house and into a taxi; Winston Churchill inveighing against a large picture by Stanley Spencer of Cookham war memorial which hung on the staircase, and Eddie Marsh defending it against his onslaught.' Her girlish delight is still evident: 'I wore a pale grey dress of chiffon and tulle, and all the diamonds I could lay my hands on. We danced until day broke, a pink and orange sunrise which gilded the river.'

What Diana does not mention, but which no one failed to notice, was that she spent almost the whole evening dancing with Sir Oswald Mosley, maverick politician, socialite and notorious womanizer. It was the first time most of Diana's friends had seen Mosley, as his circle was older and more centred on politics, but it was clear that he was more than a casual guest. May Amende, the maid, remembered him for the first time that night, and she was soon in no doubt about the relationship with her employer: the next morning, before Diana was even awake, May answered the telephone to a breathless man who demanded, 'Darling, when can I see you again?'

In the spring of 1932 the defining relationship of Diana's life had begun. At a dinner party to celebrate Barbara St John Hutchinson's twenty-first birthday in March, she had sat next to Oswald Mosley, and they very soon began a love affair which neither bothered to keep particularly secret. They met continually, walking, lunching and dining together, with private rendez-vous at Mosley's flat in Ebury Street. He was older than she – thirty-five to her twenty-one at the time they met – and well known both in politics and society. He was a dashing figure: handsome in the Rudolph Valentino style then in fashion, elegant, witty, and very charming to women. He had fought bravely in the First World War and entered politics very young; he had had great political acclaim in the Conservative Party and the Labour Party, had left the latter to found the New Party, which had quickly foundered; in 1932 he was working to launch the British Union of Fascists. He was an idealist and a brilliant talker: Diana fell in love with the man, and with his political passion and certainty, at the same time. She said: 'He was completely sure of himself and his ideas. He knew what to do to solve the economic disaster we were living through; he was certain he could cure unemployment. Lucid, logical, forceful and persuasive, he soon convinced me.' Jonathan Guinness put it more succinctly: 'It was the passion of Juliet and . . . the conversion of St Paul; emotion and conviction were inseparable.'

Mosley was fascinating to Diana, and she was just the sort of beautiful young society matron with whom he constantly had affairs. At the start, it probably seemed nothing unusual, and Diana was something of a catch. In the three years since she had married Bryan she had become a small legend as a 'beauty', a personality and a hostess. John Betjeman, always a masterly observer of mores and aspirations, captured the sort of envious awe inspired by her circle in a ditty that began:

> I too could be arty, I too could get on
> With the Guinnesses, Gertler, Sickert and John . . .

Mosley was quite unlike this. 'Up to a point,' Diana said, 'he was not my *genre*. None of my other friends was the least bit like him.'

While relationships in Bloomsbury were famously multifarious, more discretion was required in Diana's world. But it was within the rules of the game for men to take young married women out to lunch and dinner; if they had affairs, no one was surprised. In this affluent class people tended to marry very young and, after they had dutifully provided a few children (preferably at least one boy), there was little to do except pleasure-seeking. Divorce was rare, and usually scandalous; but amorous amusements among the young marrieds were tolerated. Many of Mosley's liaisons were transitory and reasonably discreet, but he could be blatant: only the previous year his more or less public affair with Paula Casa Maury, a beautiful socialite, had caused Lady Cynthia, Mosley's wife, severe pangs of jealousy. That spring Cimmie, as she was known to her friends, was seriously ill with her third pregnancy, and had to spend three months almost continually in bed. She soon knew about the liaison with Diana, but her letters to Mosley show that she struggled to accept her as just another of her husband's 'lovely sillies'. She did not yet realize that Diana, for all her party-going, was made of sterner stuff.

At the Cheyne Walk ball in June Mosley made a proposal to Diana – not of marriage, because he had no intention of leaving his wife and family, but a proposal that their relationship should be of a more committed kind than the usual casual affairs of their set. They were in love; they thought they were made for each other, and indeed they continued to think so for the next fifty years.

Mosley was never called Oswald: his family and friends all called him Tom, and after he launched his movement his political associates called him OM. But as Tom was her brother's name, and she did not want to call him that, Diana re-named him Kit. She said she could no longer remember where the soubriquet had come from. His nickname for her was Percher (pronounced Persia), short for Percheron, a breed of large white carthorse.

It must have been some private joke that made him call the cigarette-slim Diana after a huge and heavy horse, but perhaps he had also been reminded of something he had spotted, or sensed, in her personality. Percherons are almost dazzlingly white, with silky flowing blonde manes and tails – that parallel is obvious enough. And the breed was created by crossing Arab horses with the bull-like drey-horses of Belgium, a mixture that formed the aristocrat of workhorses, immensely strong but with fine lines and slender ankles. As Mosley would write to her many years later, when the going was getting tough: 'Nothing like Perchers for pulling the loads of life.'

9 *John Bull's Grandson*

When Mosley met Diana, they both shone in society, but they also recognized each other at a deeper level. The traditions of the English country squirearchy were in their bones. Mosley was unusual among fascist leaders in that he came from the ruling classes – Mussolini, Hitler and others were of much humbler origin – but the parallels between the old world of England's country estates and the new political world of fascism were many. Both were highly ordered but non-democratic forms of social organization, and both depended on the acceptance of a leader in whom ultimate power was coupled with ultimate responsibility. Diana, like Mosley and most of the English upper classes, had been brought up to accept this idea of responsibility as the counterpart to privilege.

Not too much should be made of this link – otherwise it would be tantamount to arguing that England's traditional social order made it a natural breeding-ground for fascism. This turned out not to be the case, since fascism never gained a secure footing in Britain, and indeed the great majority of English aristocrats who have entered British political life have been devoted parliamentarians, whatever the colour of their politics. But, in their different ways, Mosley and Diana had both had eccentric upbringings within the class to which they belonged, and moreover Diana had an idealistic tendency to hero-worship that welcomed the idea of a single, strong leader who would accomplish wonderful things: a man with natural, if not actual, nobility. When Mosley preached the fascist message to Diana, she was an apt as well as a willing pupil, and an eager convert. 'What else was there?' she said, at the end of her life – she felt both the Tory and Labour parties were dismal failures.

At the time he met Diana, Oswald Mosey had reached a crisis in his political life – and it was a crisis with powerful repercussions in his private life, too. Despite his maverick success in conventional politics, the New Party, which he had recently formed with Labour renegades and other disaffected young MPs, had failed dismally in the autumn election of 1931, and in the spring of 1932 he was ready to turn wholeheartedly to fascism. The British Union of Fascists was founded in that year.

Oswald Mosley's path to fascism may have been hard to predict, but it is not difficult to explain. Historians have often attributed Mosley's political reversals to the fact that he seemed somehow 'foreign', with his hawk-like dark looks, his beautiful clothes, his extravagant oratorical gestures, and his predilection for massed rallies and all the other paraphernalia of fascism. In fact, though, his heritage lies entrenched in traditional England, and in a part of the English landed gentry that was old-fashioned even for its time. Although it is too simple to explain a person entirely in terms of their background – especially with so singular a personality as Mosley – the importance of the feudal traditions of his roots should not be under-estimated.

Sir Oswald Ernald Mosley, sixth baronet, was born in 1896 into a family whose descent can be traced with certainty back to the middle of the fifteenth century, and much further in family lore. Since the Middle Ages the Mosleys had been connected with Manchester and the surrounding areas. Probably yeoman farmers in origin, succeeding generations became merchants in the cloth trade; they laid the basis of a family fortune that soon made them substantial landowners. In 1596 a Nicholas Mosley became lord of the manor of Manchester, and commissioned Inigo Jones to design Hough End Hall for him. Thereafter, different branches of the family added to an estate that included, by the beginning of the eighteenth century, properties in Staffordshire, Derbyshire and Leicestershire – among them Rolleston-on-Dove, in Staffordshire, where young 'Tom' Mosley was to spend a great deal of time as a boy.

Along with the Mosleys' business interests came public position. Nicholas Mosley became Lord Mayor of London in 1599, and his enthusiastic taxing of the London business community, together with his financial success at what was more or less organized piracy against the Spaniards, earned him royal favour: Elizabeth I granted him a knighthood and a family motto, Mos Legem Regit, a play on the family surname which can be taken to mean 'Our Custom is above the Law'. It was a significant motto for his descendant. The royal connections continued: half a century later, when King Charles I needed money, Edward Mosley obliged with a huge loan of £20,000; in return, he was created a baronet. As Robert Skidelsky, Mosley's biographer, puts it: 'The rise of the Mosleys by a combination of business acumen and royal favour is by no means untypical of the social changes taking place in England at the end of the sixteenth and early seventeenth centuries.'

But after these few excursions on to the national stage, the Mosleys settled down on their estates, giving up commercial life in favour of the gentle rhythms of the wealthy landed gentry, while the rents of their rural tenants were swelled by the new leases on their Manchester land as that city grew into one of the first great industrial centres. Unusually for such families (whose seats in Parliament were virtually assured by their position), the Mosleys did not seek election, apart from one Sir Oswald Mosley who became an MP in 1832, and was at first a supporter of Reform. The family's sphere was local rather than national. They remained old-fashioned, anti-cosmopolitan and – perhaps ironically, in view of the source of most of their rents – impervious to the growing affluence of the new middle classes. Nor did they go to university, move into liberal circles, or become affected by the evangelical movement – processes that helped change and modernize sections of the aristocracy in the nineteenth century.

By the early nineteenth century, the industrialists and tradespeople of Manchester had begun to take exception to the medieval manorial rights still exercised by the Mosleys: 'tollage' (a tax on all goods entering the market) and 'stallage' (on the rental of market stalls). The merchants clamoured for the control of their town by means of 'incorporation' and elected local government, and after a fierce fight through the courts, the family had to bow to the forces of the modern world.

The contemporary Sir Oswald – the MP who had begun as a reformer – had a lot to lose. He declared the annual income from his manorial rights at this time to be more than £9,000, which would equal about £1,800,000 in today's value. But even though the feudal taxes could no longer be levied, he retained his property in the city, and many of these freeholds remained in the family's possession until recently. He also retained large tracts of farmland, mostly in Staffordshire. He left Parliament, and retreated to a quiet country life at Rolleston-on-Dove. While the burgeoning centres of industrialization grew up all around them – Derby and Nottingham not far to the east, Stoke-on-Trent to the west, Burton-upon-Trent only a couple of miles to the south, and just beyond that the sprawl of Birmingham and Wolverhampton – the Mosleys made of themselves and their lands an island that defied progress. 'Here,' as Skidelsky puts it, 'a tiny feudal enclave survived into the twentieth century.'

The Rolleston Hall that Mosley's grandfather inherited in 1879 was a rambling Victorian mansion, described by Diana as 'fairly ugly without and hideous within'. The original Jacobean hall, with its elegant Georgian façades added at the height of the family's fortunes, had suffered a serious fire which – as if to reflect the decline of the family's position – destroyed the house and most of the pictures, silver and furniture. This had far-reaching consequences for the young Tom Mosley: in Diana's view, had the fine old house still been standing, he would probably never have left, 'and his life might have taken a different course'.

Sir Oswald Mosley, grandfather to Diana's husband, 'looked like John Bull and was an expert agriculturalist'. He was an earthy but flamboyant character who reigned over his fiefdom in old-fashioned style: when his crested yellow coach raced through the lodge gates, with a postillion blowing a horn and liveried footmen behind, men doffed their caps and women curtsied. He lived apart from his wife. He combined the 'almost complete freedom from inhibitions' which characterized many Mosleys with a great regard for the proprieties and the reputation of the family. By contrast his son, Mosley's father (who was also called Oswald), turned out to be a sort of Jorrocks parody of the hard-riding, bibulous squirearchy. He amused himself with promiscuity and gambling exploits that included, according to his grandson, Nicholas Mosley, shooting out all the lights in Piccadilly with a pistol from a hansom cab. Of these two early models for the young Tom, the grandfather was more significant.

Mosley's father married Maud Heathcote in 1895; Oswald, the eldest of their three sons, was born a year later. Maud – her son described her as 'extremely beautiful' – was tall, strong-featured and purposeful: by the time the young Oswald was five, she had had enough of her husband's dissipations, and she obtained a legal separation and took herself and her three boys away to her own family home, Belton Hall near Market Drayton in Shropshire. From now on, 'Tom' saw his father only rarely. But Maud took her children back to see their grandfather often, and the boys grew up, typically for their class and time, contemptuous of school and enthusiastic about hunting and all other sports, in the enclosed, proud world of old Sir Oswald and Rolleston.

Tom took the place of his errant father in the emotional life of his Mosley grandfather and of his powerful mother: for old Sir Oswald, he was the dashing, sportive but loving and responsible heir his own son was not, while Maud treated him as her 'man-child' and the 'light of her life'. This intense emotional environment gave Mosley the unshakeable self-assurance that marked his adult life. He grew up knowing that he was adored, that he was special, and that anything he did must therefore be justified – the barbs and criticisms of lesser mortals could never touch him.

At Rolleston Sir Oswald was a benign patriarch at the apex of a rigid social pyramid. The majority of the local population were either his tenants or his employees, part of an economic system that his grandson described as 'like medieval life . . . practically self-contained'. Most were involved with the land; there were also craftsmen and artisans ranging from bakers to wheelwrights. The Hall itself employed dozens of maids, cooks, footmen, butlers and other domestic servants inside the house, and thirty gardeners outside. This large number of people provided for and was provided for by the estate in the almost idyllic self-sufficiency Mosley evokes in his auto-biography: 'Farms, the garden, shooting and the large well-stocked cellars satisfied most needs; the same wagon which took our produce a few miles to be sold in Burton-on-Trent would return well loaded with a fine variety of the best beers.'

Sir Oswald built a church, cottages and a school, a recreation hall and almshouses for 'his' people – all aspects of life were catered for in this self-contained universe, one in which everything worked smoothly as long as everyone stayed in their place. Beyond its 'closed and charmed circle' there was no need to go, 'and we children never did', Mosley wrote nostalgically. 'Our time was divided between farms, gardens and carpenter's shop, where the bearded Pritchard presided over a corps of experts who kept all things going as their forebears had done for generations . . . Again in feudal fashion, the warmest and most intimate friendships developed between us and these people, so characteristic of traditional England, not only in their daily occupations, but in the strong bonds of mutual sympathy in life's events, birth, marriage, death, occasions sad and festive . . .' Then, with what appears to be an astonishing lack of awareness, he added: 'this was really a classless society'. That this sentence can begin by describing something as feudal and end by describing it as classless might seem as mysterious as it does preposterous, but what Mosley meant was that modern, urban class distinctions did not exist. It was an order in which middle classes did not exist; certainly, a world in which 'democracy' had no place.

But it was not always the idyll that Mosley described. His son Nicholas tells us that Mosley destroyed almost all the daily diaries kept for fifty years by his mother: the remaining pages, however, are testament to the emotional turmoil that beset this family – the 'quarrels, the separations, the law-suits, the punch-ups'. Diana, however, challenged Nicholas' version. She saw many of Maud's diaries and described them as merely dull and domestic. Whatever the truth about that, it is clear enough that Mosley's father bullied his son, even when very young, and was not above hurting his wife. Surviving sections of Maud's diary also record that, by the time Tom was twelve, his father was telling him tales of London actresses and urging him to kiss the parlourmaid. Maud's disapproving comment on her estranged husband reads: 'No bath, hat on in house, altogether low.'

Old Sir Oswald showed Tom how to live as a gentleman of the time thought proper – responsible to one's land and one's people, but something of a dandy and a playboy, rakish and keen on high-spirited practical jokes. Apart from that, pleasure meant sport. Hunting was more like a religion than a pastime ('the only possible training for a man', Mosley considered it), with other field sports – coursing, shooting and fishing – coming a close second. These were the respectable bloodsports. Through his father, Mosley witnessed some of the more louche – Maud records that during her son's visit to him her husband 'had rats down from London in a box (3 doz) and let the dogs worry them'. Boxing was a family tradition, too. Old Sir Oswald was, like his son and then his grandson, a keen and talented pugilist, and the ballroom at Rolleston was often the scene of bare-knuckle bouts between the Mosley men and local champions. Mosley's passion for fencing, a skill which he would later develop to Olympic standard, also began early.

Boxing, fencing, shooting, hunting: aggressive entertainment, the ancient warrior pastimes. It was a training that engendered in those who were good at it – and Mosley was very good at it – a taste for rough-house and an unquenchable desire to win.

Mosley was taught at home by a Miss Gandy ('an intelligent woman and kindly guide') until he was nine, when he went to West Downs, a preparatory boarding school, and then, a year before time, to Winchester. But even though he continued to excel at sports, was by now strikingly handsome and sophisticated for his age, he was never popular there: he had no interest in what the school offered – a 'trivial existence' based on 'many of the silliest shibboleths of the bourgeois world'. Mosley was already showing his unwillingness to join whole-heartedly any system that was not of his own devising.

His school career ended early, at sixteen, and the question of going to university appears never to have arisen. Throughout his life Mosley had little respect for conventional education, putting his faith in the benefits of self-teaching and focused hard work (his parliamentary career soon showed his extraordinary capacity for this). But it is typical of him that, in his early twenties, he put himself through a series of examinations that pitted his wits and erudition against those of his university-educated friends, just to be sure that they had nothing over him: he emerged quite satisfied with the results. It was only his enforced idleness in prison during the Second World War that allowed him to discover the values of a more contemplative approach to learning; until then, he was a man in a hurry.

After he left Winchester, Mosley went to the Royal Military College at Sandhurst, arriving there in January 1914 to begin 'some of the most vividly happy days of my life', he said. He idealized the army, and his autobiography has lyrical passages about its warm companionship, its 'intimate confidence and complete trust', the 'large family' of the regiment which made every man feel he 'would in all circumstances be looked after'. He quickly formed around himself a group of cadets who 'broke every rule, and off parade had not the least regard for discipline', devoting themselves to all the rowdy high living they could manage. Those with money, like Mosley, could afford illicit jaunts to London night-clubs and music-halls, elaborate dinners that ended in brawls, hard riding at polo matches and in point-to-point races. (The latter were forbidden to cadets, and so involved entering under an assumed name: A. N. Other, or, anticipating disaster, R. S. Upward.) And there were fights. Sandhurst behaviour of the time was notoriously rough, with gang feuds between the cavalry cadets and the infantry cadets over class, or money, or sporting prowess, or almost nothing at all. It seems to have been a combination of all these which caused an incident that proved memorable even by Sandhurst's standards.

In June 1914, Mosley got involved in an altercation over polo ponies (the Sandhurst polo team flourished despite the fact that polo was theoretically banned on the grounds that it got too many cadets into debt). Mosley's team lost a match after their ponies unaccountably went missing, and he considered it a set-up. Later, he and a few friends accosted a suspect in the billiards room; Mosley was carrying a riding crop. 'I thought,' he writes with heavy understatement, 'perhaps mistakenly, he was rude. An argument followed, and ended in a fight, which I won.' But what later transpired was a revenge attack on Mosley by the beaten cadet's comrades; Mosley tried to escape by climbing out of a window, lost his footing, fell thirty-five feet on to gravel and fractured his ankle severely. Although he was confined to the sanatorium by his injury, the full-scale riot that ensued lasted a whole weekend. Mosley was expelled, together with a number of other cadets: it seemed that his army career was over.

However, two months later, on 4 August 1914, the First World War began. Sandhurst was hurriedly recalled, the rustications were forgotten, and the exuberant jokers of the early summer were transformed into dedicated soldiers of the autumn. Mosley – who now passed fit for active service – was commissioned into a prestigious cavalry regiment, the sixteenth Lancers. He was sent first to Ireland, for further training, but felt tormented by enthusiasm for battle. 'Never had men appeared more eager to be killed,' Mosley recorded, and he found a sure way of getting to the front early by volunteering for the Royal Flying Corps.

In 1914 the corps was still in its babyhood: a mere three years old, with only fifty flimsy wood and wire aircraft and some sixty pilots and observers. Already, though, it was known to be extremely dangerous (old Sir Oswald burst into tears when he heard the news of his grandson's transfer). Pilots had to fly their toy-town contraptions low over enemy lines – mostly for observation purposes, as battles in the air were still a rarity – unprotected from heavy ground fire and without parachutes. It was unusual, according to Mosley, for a plane to escape without being hit during a reconnaissance mission. The RFC was obviously not for the faint-hearted, and it involved just the mixture of individual bravery and daredevil recklessness, sense of adventure and technological novelty that suited Mosley. He was a modern knight of the skies, while back in the Mess the danger was masked by the camaraderie and exaggerated gaiety of a *corps d'élite*.

Mosley, then, was a highly mobile observer of the drama of the trenches. He left a vivid account of the second battle of Ypres (and the first poison-gas attack in history). The experiences marked him deeply. In all his subsequent political career, he was conscious of a debt to the friends and comrades left behind dead in the mud. Although later, by embracing fascism, he found himself siding with one of the greatest war-mongers of the century, Mosley had a genuine desire that there should never be another war.

Yet for all this, Mosley's reminiscences of the front betray his enduring romance with war, and the intensity of feeling between soldiers. He formed a strong respect for the fighting spirit of the German troops, their 'order, dignity and dedicated purpose'. Although he never became a Germanophile on Diana's scale, tales of young Prussian officers, forbidden to surrender, pulling on white gloves and goose-stepping ceremonially to meet their certain death, satisfied Mosley's notions of 'natural nobility'. The 'capacity to appreciate a great enemy', he wrote, should not be seen as 'a sinister emanation of the military mind', but as 'a spark of hope for Europe'. It may have been possible sincerely to feel this after the First War – for all its horrors, its legacy was quite unlike that of the Second. When in the 1930s Mosley tried to recreate in his own organization that 'mysterious fraternity of arms', he was still idealistic and sentimental about war, at the same time as he argued for peace. The old soldiers of 1914–18 thought they had seen the worst that war could do; they had no idea what horrors would take place away from the front line in 1939–45.

Mosley's days as a RFC observer did not last long. He was sent back to England for further training at the Flying School at Shoreham, near Brighton. He was no longer as fit as he had been: he had suffered concussion from a piece of shell, and a badly twisted knee from returning in a damaged aircraft that ended up in a pond. Now came another accident. Flying from the aerodrome at Shoreham one day, he was 'in the mood for some mild exhibition' – his admiring mother had come to watch him fly that day – and a misjudged 'pancake landing' injured both his legs, one of them severely. It was the same leg that had sustained an injury during his Sandhurst prank a year earlier.

Nevertheless, he rejoined his regiment, and spent the miserable winter of 1915–16 in deep mud in the trenches. But the leg did not hold up: he was sent home, and the limb was saved from amputation by a complicated operation. It was the end of Mosley's active service. He had survived extreme hazards, in the air and on the ground, only to end up with a disabling injury as the result of his exuberance. His right leg was an inch and a half shorter than the left; from now on he would need a specially made shoe and walk with a pronounced limp.

It was a significant wound. It meant that he had the leisure and opportunity, back in London for the last two years of the war, to launch himself into the social and political circles that determined his future. A variety of jobs ended in a spell at the Foreign Office, but Mosley's time was meaningfully employed in conquering London society. The great hostesses of the time – several, like Nancy Astor and Lady Cunard, were witty and energetic American women – found a clever, self-confident and handsome young officer an asset at their parties. It was in these years, according to Nicholas Mosley, that 'he first got his reputation as a seducer of women'. His many mistresses were always married women; and the smart world into which he moved was more than just a 'university of charm' – it afforded him valuable contacts with people of all political persuasions. While he was working to make himself into a politician, studying history and politics, both Conservative and Liberal whips were already after him to go into Parliament on behalf of their party.

It was the beginning of a golden moment for Mosley, when his 'unlimited capacity for enjoyment' could be indulged at the same time as he looked for 'seriousness of purpose' in a bold, bright future. He was young and talented, and the war was soon over. He had a glow on him; anything seemed possible.

10 *Mosley in Parliament*

A matter of days after the armistice on 11 November 1918, Lloyd George, the Liberal Prime Minister at the head of the coalition government, called a general election, which took place on 14 December. Many of the younger candidates, like Mosley, felt that this election turned on the question of the world to which the men who had fought through the Flanders mud could return, if they returned. The war generation were cynical about the older politicians' promise of 'a land fit for heroes'; they felt the urge for power themselves. And the nation seemed to agree: on a wave of post-war enthusiasm for youth and progress that gave him a majority of almost 11,000, Mosley sailed into Parliament as MP for Harrow – a Unionist, but a supporter of Lloyd George's coalition. It was a month after his twenty-second birthday.

The beginning of Mosley's parliamentary career contained, in embryo, all its later characteristics. From the start, he hardly seemed to care which party he chose (he was courted by both Conservatives and Liberals) – his own views were what mattered, and what he thought he represented was his generation, those who had fought the war. This indifference to the tradition of party loyalty, the basis of modern British parliamentary politics, was later to become acute, as he restlessly shifted his allegiances in search of an ideal platform. His election campaign at Harrow in 1918 also presaged things to come: it was controversial and acerbic, and involved the first of many libel suits. Mosley was no orator yet, and unsure about how to deliver a speech, but he had a speedy wit and a pugilistic instinct, attacking his 65-year-old opponent, who was standing as an Independent, with the first of many quotable quips: 'An Independent is someone on whom no one can depend.'

His first election address, too, was 'one of the key documents of his life', in Skidelsky's words. Mosley never swerved far from the principles it contained, and all the dramatic political volte-faces of the next fifteen years were part of his struggle to find the means of making his vision a reality. When he – as he thought – finally found it in fascism, he embraced a credo that perverted this early idealism.

Mosley's ideals did indeed sound lofty. To the voters of Harrow, he laid out a set of views he described as 'socialistic imperialism', which envisaged 'a high standard of life' for all, under the benign direction of a controlling state. He championed high wages (including a minimum wage), reduced working hours and full employment, to be achieved by greatly increased productivity. Ex-servicemen were to be allotted smallholdings, the land for which should be acquired by the state. Housing was an urgent priority: the slums must be cleared. In education he urged a large number of state scholarships for university and further training; transport and electrification programmes were to be publicly controlled and developed, agriculture secured and protected. His programme put working-class welfare as the chief priority in a Britain for the British, standing firmly at the centre of a carefully protected empire; he argued, too, for improved conditions for workers in the colonies. As a programme devised thirty years before the Welfare State, it was radical and far-reaching. But, naturally, this careful protectionism came at a price. There was to be immediate legislation to prevent the immigration of 'undesirable aliens', and repatriation for those already resident.

The brave new Parliament of 1918, which had no fewer than 260 first-time MPs, turned out to be nothing more than the old guard slightly revamped; Mosley, along with other 'new boys', was soon disappointed at how difficult it seemed to make any mark among the hard-faced coalition financiers grown prosperous on war profits. He became an avid supporter of the League of Nations; he joined a group of young MPs (nicknamed 'The Babes' by the press) on a committee which had half an eye on the formation of a new party of the centre. Then, in November 1919, he went to Plymouth to campaign for Lady Astor, who became the first woman to take a seat in the Commons, and there he came into contact with Cynthia Curzon.

He had once or twice seen Lady Cynthia (she was the daughter of Lord Curzon, the Foreign Secretary) at Cliveden, Lord and Lady Astor's mansion in Berkshire, where the politically heavyweight social circle 'played such a part in our lives in those days', according to Mosley. Cynthia was always known to her friends and family as Cimmie. Now twenty-one, tall and strong-minded, she was canvassing for Nancy Astor's election with her characteristic warmth and enthusiasm. Although she was the daughter of one of the most powerful political figures of the day, she was seen as rather unconventional. The war had allowed her freedoms that would have been unthinkable before – she had done a short course at the London School of Economics that included some social work in the East End of London; she had worked as a clerk in the War Office and even as a landgirl on a farm. She was idealistic and a champion of the underprivileged, at least in theory. Mosley described her as having, when they met, 'advanced Liberal opinions: an instant, automatic sentiment in favour of the underdog'; she considered herself to have 'Bolshevist' sentiments.

Mosley was attracted by her exuberance and energy. Later, gushing social columnists would refer to Cimmie as a 'beauty', but the photographic evidence suggests that, though she was handsome and vivacious, she was hardly beautiful; for the droopy, bland-faced style of the twenties, in particular, her body was too substantial and her square-chinned face too full of character. Even draped in her furs and jewels she radiated sincerity, reliability and niceness rather than glamour. Whatever the appeal, Mosley almost immediately made up his mind to marry her, and his pursuit was characteristically fierce, prompt and tactical. Within a few weeks – before Christmas of 1919 – he had proposed; not surprisingly, since his reputation with women had preceded him, she wanted more time to consider. She may not have been in love with him, at first, but as their son Nicholas wrote: 'Cimmie was a practical, sensuous person and she seems to have adored Tom and never to have ceased from adoring him once her sexuality was aroused.' This did not take long: by March they were engaged; on 11 May they were married.

Mosley himself was in love, it seems, and for the first time. He recognized in Cimmie the qualities of steadfastness and warm-heartedness, combined with intelligence and political acumen, that would make her an excellent counterweight to his colder, flashier temperament. But he was also well aware of how advantageous a marriage it would be, in worldly terms: Cimmie was the daughter (albeit a mildly rebellious daughter) of a powerful, well-connected, aristocratic and rather odd political magnate. She was also extremely rich.

Cimmie's mother, who had died when she was only seven, had been Mary Leiter, the daughter of a Chicago property millionaire who had settled a fortune on each of his grandchildren. Her father was Lord Curzon, at that time Foreign Secretary and Leader of the House of Lords in Lloyd George's government. At the age of thirty-nine he had become Viceroy of India, one of the last and greatest of Victorian proconsuls, and between 1916 and 1918 he had been, with Lloyd George and Viscount Milner, one of the three key members of the War Cabinet. From his years in India he had acquired a taste for elegant and extravagant living, together with a passion for architectural restoration. Much of the Leiter income was spent on the houses where he brought up his three daughters – Hackwood in Hampshire and 1 Carlton

House Terrace in London – and in restoring four great buildings: Bodiam Castle in Sussex, Tattershall Castle in Lincolnshire, Montacute House in Somerset, and his ancestral home, Kedleston in Derbyshire: all now, saved largely by Curzon, belong to the National Trust.

T. P. O'Connor, the Irish Nationalist MP, once observed that Curzon personified those imperial, essentially Victorian feelings that Rudyard Kipling had expressed in poetry and prose. But by 1920 both the poet and the statesman had become anachronistic in style – even if as a political prophet Curzon was often more far-sighted than his more modish contemporaries. For all his industry and intelligence, Curzon's pomp and love of ceremony proved easy targets for legend and caricature, even (at the hands of political opponents) of ridicule. (He gave dinners for the King and Queen at Carlton House Terrace, and the first time that Mosley and Cimmie appeared together at one of these, Lord Curzon had to write to the palace beforehand, asking leave for Mosley, because of his damaged leg, to wear trousers instead of the archaic formal knee breeches still demanded in the presence of royalty.) Behind the stately and self-assured façade, however, was an emotional man, sentimental and easily moved to tears, especially in family contexts. Yet he was a distant father when the three girls were small, and a petulant and censorious parent when they showed independence as young women. Even so the motherless Cimmie, whose step-mother Grace was never close to her, managed to grow up with unusual emotional openness.

Cimmie, however, was in revolt against the magnificence of her background, even if the scope of her rebellion would seem pretty limited to most people. She wanted a quiet wedding, finally compromising on the Chapel Royal, in St James's, which held a mere 100 guests, but Lord Curzon invited several hundred more to a reception at the Foreign Secretary's residence. Among the select few at the church were King George V and Queen Mary, whose progress down Pall Mall was slowed by crowds lining the street ten deep, and the King and Queen of the Belgians, who flew over in two separate two-seater aircraft, as well as a galaxy of society names, the ladies in their twenties regalia of floaty dresses, knee-length strings of pearls and deep-brimmed hats, the men in full morning dress with toppers. Cimmie had the usual brilliant white dress, embroidered with flowers, with a long train; she was attended by seven bridesmaids. The wedding presents of furs, jewels, silver and porcelain were as glittering as the company. Cimmie's quiet wedding had become the society event of the season, and Mosley had moved into the grandest circles.

At first Lord Curzon had been fairly satisfied with Cimmie's choice. He was always (and probably rightly) suspicious that his daughters' suitors were simply after their money, but Cimmie was not to be dissuaded, and his enquiries yielded reasonably good reports of Mosley. Almost immediately, though, the financial squabbles began. The legal arrangement they reached was that, on her marriage, all the capital from her mother's will reverted to her: this produced an annual income of about £10,000. Her father would keep the income from one particular source: about another £3,000 a year. But only a year later, Mosley talked Cimmie into demanding from her father the whole of her inheritance, thereby depriving Lord Curzon of a sizeable chunk of income. When he protested, they exchanged angry letters, and relations were broken off. There were similar financial wrangles with Cimmie's older sister, Irene, and Curzon's relations with his two elder daughters never recovered. Even on his deathbed, four years later, Curzon did not see Irene, who came to make her peace; Cimmie apparently never attempted a reconciliation. It may have been Mosley's part in this nasty quarrel, as well as other reasons, that soon made Curzon refer to him as 'my sinister son-in-law'.

Parental problems aside, the glamorous wedding and the honeymoon in Portofino that followed marked the beginning of a marriage that, at the beginning at least, seemed ideal. The young Mosleys – still in their early twenties – shone among the Beautiful People of the time. The years after the First World War were, in Robert Skidelsky's words, 'Dionysian times' for those who could afford the yearly round that kept the young and rich eternally at play. The press in those years was devoted to recording the goings-on of the smart set, and society people had tabloid fame. Balls and parties were glowingly recounted, entire pages filled with photographs of the guests, and descriptions of clothes and jewels, all couched in deferential and saccharine language. Early in her marriage one such society page cooed over Lady Cynthia as 'the personification of the society girl, tall, willowy, with a slightly bored expression, lovely complexion, and expressive blue eyes. She dresses in the most exquisite taste, and is a fine set-off to her handsome husband in whose company she almost invariably appears.'

The Mosleys continued to be highly visible in smart circles for the duration of their marriage. Their London house – in fact two Queen Anne houses in Smith Square knocked together – was augmented by rented country houses in Surrey and Sussex until, in 1926, they bought Savehay Farm, a Tudor manor house with about 120 acres of land at Denham in Buckinghamshire, not far from London. They had three children: Vivien, born in 1921, Nicholas, born two years later, and Michael, who arrived in 1932. But the life of fashionable pleasure was only half the story. Although Mosley described himself as having an 'almost unlimited' appetite for fun, he and Cimmie were also purposeful and serious, and Mosley, at least, was extremely ambitious. It was also clear from the beginning that, as a politician's wife, Cimmie could hardly be bettered. She proved to be a natural speaker, with charm and sincerity enough to reach straight to the heart of any crowd, and to achieve an instant rapport with people of any social standing. And as a foil to Mosley's more abrasive personality, this easy and genuine charm was a particular advantage. Her loyalty and energy were always devoted to his cause, and over the next dozen years she would doggedly follow and support him through all his various political contortions.

By 1920, the year of their marriage, some significant political storms had already begun to gather around him. At first, these were of a kind that reflected very well on Mosley's character and principles. He fell out with Lloyd George over the latter's policy on Ireland, which involved setting up the infamous 'Black and Tans', a semi-irregular force attached to the depleted Irish police. The new recruits were mostly unemployed English ex-soldiers (and so called because they wore the patchy remnants of khaki uniforms, with black belts). Their purpose, ostensibly, was to maintain order among the Irish population, but behind this thin façade the Black and Tans were employed to carry out reprisals against the guerrilla Irish Republican Army, which too often meant the local population thought to be shielding or sustaining them. In effect, the Crown auxiliary forces were licensed to do whatever they wanted.

The acute situation in Ireland in the spring of 1920 had been building up since the beginning of the First World War. Home Rule (an autonomous parliament for Ireland within the empire) had been passed into law in 1914 but shelved for the duration of the war; in any case, its implementation was obstructed by Protestant resistance in Ulster and a demand there for separate treatment. In 1916 a short-lived rebellion in Dublin had polarized attitudes, radicalizing the whole direction of Irish nationalism. In 1918 seventy-three Sinn Fein MPs were elected to Westminster, and promptly declared themselves to be a separate parliament and Ireland an independent republic. The Irish Republican Army, led by Michael Collins, proceeded to take control of much of the country by force, making short work of the Royal Irish Constabulary. For more than a year Lloyd George and the British government did nothing. Perhaps they believed that any violent suppression of an Irish guerrilla rebellion would be too difficult and too unpopular.

Finally, though, Lloyd George could avoid the problem no longer, partly because of pressure from the Conservatives in his coalition, partly in reaction to an IRA raid that took place on the fourth anniversary of the Easter Rising of 1916. When the Black and Tans came into being, along with another corps of free-booting 'Auxiliaries', they were in effect gangs of mercenaries.

It was a brutal conflict. The activities of the Irish 'murder gangs' provoked severe reprisals from the British-backed groups. There were killings and torture, bribery and trickery, wreckage and destruction of villages and property: the government forces were meeting terrorist tactics with systematic terror of their own.

Mosley was incensed. He may not have cared very much about individuals, but everything in the codes of his gentleman's upbringing and in his soldier's training was repelled. He considered it shameful that a great nation should stoop to such tactics. 'The name of Britain was being disgraced,' he wrote, 'every rule of good soldierly conduct disregarded, and every decent instinct of humanity outraged.' Besides, he opposed the reprisals policy on practical grounds, declaring it 'a very inefficient way of going about things'.

It was over this issue that Mosley's parliamentary character was formed. From now on he would always be a thorn in the side of the established powers; from here, too, he seems to have developed his oratorial brilliance. He played rough, pounding his opponents with blazing sarcasm and piercing personal ridicule. One parliamentarian observed of him that he would 'flay the skin off anyone inefficient in debate'. The row in the House of Commons was such that, on 3 November 1920, Mosley 'crossed the floor', leaving the Conservative benches on the coalition side of the House to face his critics from the opposition benches. He told his constituency association that his action had 'no political significance' – a strange comment to make about publicly leaving a political party – but in fact he never returned to the Conservative fold.

After Mosley's dramatic action, and a rousing attack on the government which one senior parliamentary figure called 'one of the best speeches I have ever heard in the House', a Peace with Ireland Council was formed. Lord Henry Bentinck, a supporter of Mosley in the Conservative ranks, was its chairman, Mosley was secretary and its members included Ramsay Macdonald and Lord Hugh and Lord Robert Cecil; outside the House of Commons, support came from eminent figures as diverse as G. K. Chesterton, Hilaire Belloc, Leonard Woolf, and a handful of generals, bishops and peers. It was an odd mishmash of maverick Tories, Labour figures and Catholic sympathizers; the *New Statesman* was its chief publicity outlet. Significantly, this grouping brought Mosley into contact and sympathy with Labour, on an issue that had nothing to do with economics.

The committee's purpose was to collect information on the individual atrocities committed by the Black and Tans. They called for a truce, a peace conference with Sinn Fein, and the immediate withdrawal of the Black and Tans and the Auxiliaries. They advocated dominion status for an independent Irish state. At an individual level, they could also help to obtain the release of men imprisoned without trial and call for the investigation of particular incidents.

Mosley's campaign went on. Through the winter of 1920 and into the following spring he bullied Lloyd George and the blustering Irish Secretary, Sir Hamar Greenwood, into replying to direct questions about official approval of the reprisals; he accused the government of conducting 'pogroms', of having 'denials on its lips and blood on its hands'. When coalition opponents harassed and heckled him, he replied that he was not concerned with the 'monosyllabic interjections of the otherwise inarticulate'. He attacked the reprisals as being useless as well as disgraceful, saying: 'I am not astonished to find the Government and the Prime Minister committed to a wicked policy, but I am astonished to find them committed to a thoroughly stupid policy.'

The campaign was partly successful. By the summer of 1921 Lloyd George capitulated. A truce was arranged in July, negotiations with Sinn Fein started soon afterwards, and December of the same year saw the signature of a treaty that declared Ireland to be a 'Free State' owing allegiance to the Crown as a dominion, but with wider parliamentary autonomy than Home Rule could have allowed – minus the six counties of Ulster, which remained part of the United Kingdom, though with their own parliament for local affairs.

It was an extraordinary victory for Sinn Fein – not least because its timing was a wonderful irony. The Black and Tans' attempts to beat the Irish into submission had almost worked, and the IRA, by the admission of its leader Michael Collins, was on its knees. 'You had us dead beat,' Collins told Sir Hamar Greenwood. 'We could not have lasted another three weeks.' The delight of the Irish leader was equalled only by his amazement at the British volte-face: 'We thought you must have gone mad.'

Those 'three weeks' linger in the mind as one of the great what-ifs of recent history. There is controversy to this day about the July truce: as R. F. Foster puts it in his *Modern Ireland*, 'those of the IRA who supported [the truce] had a vested interest in privately claiming that they were at the end of their tether; after the Treaty, the irreconcilables had an equally vested interest in claiming that this was not the case'. The debate goes on. But T. P. O'Connor, a Nationalist and MP for part of Liverpool, wrote in 1923 to Cimmie, saying: 'I regard [Mosley] as the man who really began the break-up of the Black and Tan savagery; and I can never recall without admiration and wonder, the courage and self-sacrifice which such an attitude demanded on his part . . . Both your husband and yourself will always be regarded by every good Irishman with appreciation and gratitude.'

'Courage' Mosley had certainly shown; 'self-sacrifice' might be going a bit far. True, he had gambled with his parliamentary career, earned the mistrust of his constituency for crossing the floor, and made a number of powerful enemies because of his insolent and abrasive debating style. But he had also made an almost unprecedented impact on the old guard of the House of Commons, and in this political 'blooding' Mosley had had a taste of the position he most enjoyed, and the kind of fight he was best at. He was at the head of a small, intense group, knitted tightly together by the urgency of their common cause, and doing battle against the full might of government policy. He discovered the heady power of taking on the establishment, with nothing behind him but burning conviction, undaunted energy, sharp wits and sharper tongue. He loved it. And he was still twenty-four years old.

For the next few years Mosley was the darling of the liberal press – the *Manchester Guardian*, in particular – and of progressive thinkers and the growing Labour movement. By the spring of 1921 he was writing to Lord Robert Cecil, his friend and political mentor, to discuss whether the 'psychological moment for an understanding with moderate Labour' had arrived. In the election of 1922 he stood as an Independent, and kept his old seat at Harrow with a healthy majority. His parliamentary reputation, especially as a speaker, continued to grow: the Liberals were talking about him as one of their own; the Labour leadership was wooing him. Cimmie, ever the dutiful wife but perhaps more interventionist than she seemed, was entertaining the Labour leader Ramsay Macdonald to lunch in 1923 – she went so far as to invite him to join them on holiday in Venice. (Ramsay Macdonald, perhaps a little overfaced by the social implications of this invitation, declined politely.)

The Mosleys began to mix with other Labour grandees. Beatrice Webb's first meeting with Mosley, in 1923, produced this entry in her famous diaries: 'We have just made the acquaintance of the most brilliant man in the House of Commons', and, shortly afterwards, in a letter to Harold Laski that showed her eagerness to recruit Mosley to the Labour Party proper: '. . . we had Oswald Mosley to dine here the other night. What a perfect person – almost too perfect for this wicked world.' She described him as being 'a Disraelian gentleman-aristocrat – tall, good-looking, courteous and deferential in manner, open-minded . . . He is the most accomplished speaker in the House, and hated with a quite furious hatred by the Tories whom he has left . . .'

Beatrice Webb had to sound a note of moral caution, though, and the letter to Laski continues: 'But whether he will get through the eye of the needle of great wealth I do not know.' And again: 'So much perfection argues rottenness somewhere . . . Is there some weak spot that will be revealed in a time of stress . . .?' This rather romantic language was replaced, within the next few years, by a more pragmatic approach. Although both the Mosleys quickly became intimates of the Labour intelligentsia, lunching, dining and spending weekends with the Webbs and the Shaws, their fast lifestyle inevitably snagged on the barbs of Beatrice Webb's puritanical disapproval. Others, too, found contradictory the image of this man who looked like Rudolph Valentino, spoke like the fieriest Greek orator, lived like a playboy, acted and dressed like the stereotype of the British ruling class, but professed his deep concern for the working people of the country. When Ramsay Macdonald formed the first Labour government in January 1924, Mosley was his strangest new recruit.

11 *The Road to Fascism*

When Oswald Mosley joined the Labour Party in March 1924, there were fierce attacks from within his own social and political worlds, where he was considered a class traitor: his friends, erstwhile political allies and even his powerful mother wrote to him in distress or anger. By joining the newest of Britain's main parties, his accusers claimed, he was cynically choosing a small pond in which to appear as a bigger fish. Taunts about the couple's wealth and lifestyle came from the trade-union base of the Labour Party: why did he and Cimmie not part with some of their riches to help the poor? The Mosleys made the reply, at first and throughout, that socialism could better be served if they used their money and position to further the cause through organization and propaganda. Journalists amused themselves with the question of titles: although Mosley did not inherit his title until 1928, Cimmie of course had hers. It was half-jokingly decided to dub them both 'Comrade Mosley'; Ramsay Macdonald had gained not one new member but two, since Cimmie herself had joined the Labour Party. The daughter of Lord Curzon was an even more surprising recruit than her husband.

Labour purists were all the more shocked when Mosley's presence – which some considered an affront to the 'political self-determination of the working man' – proved wildly popular. His rousing speeches, and the sight of Lady Cynthia swathed in her furs, drew working-class supporters in their thousands, and he was offered a choice of no fewer than seventy seats to fight at the election in November 1924. John Scanlon, describing the reaction some years after in *The Decline and Fall of the Labour Party* (1932), expressed his horror at the behaviour of party officials: 'It was truly an amazing and saddening spectacle to see these working men, inheritors of a party formed by Keir Hardy in the belief that a dignified Democracy could, and should, run its own party, literally prostrate in their worship of the Golden Calf.'

What Scanlon left out of his account, however, was that the Mosleys' membership did a great deal for the general perception of the party. Labour was tainted by Bolshevism in the public mind, and the association with a few real toffs lent a certain reassurance that this was not a group of wild revolutionaries. Typically proud, or perverse, Mosley turned down all the safe seats he was offered and chose to stand in the election against Neville Chamberlain at Ladywood in Birmingham, a seat which had been held by members of the Chamberlain family for sixty years. He almost succeeded – it was an extraordinary achievement to get such support – and only lost the seat by a very narrow margin.

Perhaps Mosley was relieved to have a little time out of Parliament. Long trips to India and then America with Cimmie provided an opportunity for him to formulate his thoughts on policy, the foundation for his 1925 essay 'Revolution by Reason' and what became known as the Birmingham Proposals. His time away did no harm to his reputation, or the growing legend that surrounded him. The Conservative MP Bob Boothby, a close friend (though political opponent), wrote to Cimmie in 1925: 'I think your husband (damned Socialist though he is by God) will be Prime Minister for a very very long time, because he has the Divine Spark which is almost lost nowadays;' and Mosley's great ally John Strachey, the son of St Loe Strachey, distinguished editor of the *Spectator* and cousin of Lytton Strachey, dedicated his book (also called *Revolution by Reason*) to 'O.M., who may one day do the things of which we dream'. Such disillusioned liberal thinkers were to form the core of his following.

In the years following the 1924 election, John Strachey was one of Mosley's staunchest supporters and colleagues. Both were 'refugees from the upper classes', as historian Hugh Thomas put it in his 1973 biography *John Strachey*; both had incisive and logical minds, and the intellectual interplay between them led to some of the best of the thinking credited to Mosley. Both had a romantic attraction to the Labour Party: Mosley's to 'the rhetorical, picturesque and emotional aspect of Labour politics' (Beatrice Webb), Strachey's to the excitement of smashing middle-class shibboleths. Mosley, of course, did not know the first thing about bourgeois convention, nor could he have cared less. The influence of English puritanism, even English liberalism, had completely passed him by. This was, at first, a great strength.

Mosley was never personally popular with fellow politicians, but in private life his abrasive edges and haughty manner were softened by the soothing influence of Cimmie, who was now learning how to charm audiences as a political speaker; she too began to receive offers of parliamentary seats. In January 1927 Mosley went back to Parliament as Labour MP for Smethwick, in Birmingham; in 1929 he was joined by Cimmie, who had been elected to represent another constituency in the industrial Midlands, Stoke-on-Trent.

Now a powerful pair at the heart of the parliamentary Labour movement, the Mosleys were none the less in an uneasy position, politically and socially. The charge of 'rich socialist' had more powerful bite then than now, in a context of huge disparities of wealth, and the ironies were potent. At Savehay Farm, they would entertain parties of working-class Labour supporters at one moment; at the next it would be their fashionable artistic friends such as Cecil Beaton, Sacheverell Sitwell and balletomane Oliver Messel. In a letter to his wife from Paris, Mosley describes the kind of party they both enjoyed: 'Much dancing in the dark . . . then a lovely romp at supper with little puff balls iced in champagne buckets and thrust down ladies backs . . . Perhaps he [i.e. Mosley himself] had better confess that he invented this game . . .' The Webbs, the Shaws and the other austere Labour intellectuals were hardly the kind to appreciate this sort of 'lovely romp', or Mosley's taste for slightly cruel pranks and practical jokes (he once made an omelette stuffed with tobacco for a pompous guest), let alone his scarcely disguised promiscuity or his delight in making an 'expressionist' home movie featuring Cecil Beaton in drag.

Mosley liked to play hard, and took little account of other people's disapproval, the taunts of the press, or his wife's misery at his multiple infidelities. It would take more than socialist conviction to persuade Mosley to give up his holidays in Venice and the South of France, his shooting parties and winter sports, but he and Cimmie were the targets of the kind of gossip-column attention now reserved for rock stars or actors. Mosley complained that his huge meetings, his speeches to a packed House, his radical policies were all but ignored by journalists, while 'every time my backside hit the azure blue of the Mediterranean, a headline or photograph would ensue'. During the Smethwick by-election campaign Mosley's Tory opponents plied the press with 'rich socialist' stories: Mosley was supposed to have a Rolls-Royce which he would leave on the outskirts of Birmingham before driving into the town in a more modest Vauxhall; Cimmie would change out of her diamond-studded dresses into more suitable garb. The Rolls-Royce was as fictional as the diamond frock.

Although Cimmie tried to keep pace with her husband's exhausting notion of having fun – the round of personal and political entertaining, society parties, travelling – their letters throughout the 1920s show her growing unhappiness at his adulteries, which had begun very soon after their marriage. Mosley hardly bothered to hide his affairs, which were with bored young married women of his own milieu (this was the time when he coined his notorious motto: Vote Labour; sleep Tory). She reproached; he cajoled.

One moment he would icily inform her that jealousy was a pointless, bourgeois emotion, the next he would play the rascally but repentant little boy begging his mummy for forgiveness. He accused her of nagging; she half-hid her pain. As the years go by, the letters tell a miserable tale of arrogance (on his part) and slow corrosive agony (on hers): she could never get the better of him in argument, and never dared to issue an ultimatum. In 1929 he acquired a flat in Ebury Street, only a few hundred yards from the large family house in Smith Square, supposedly so that he had peace and quiet in which to get his ministerial work done, and for political meetings. However, this flat had one enormous and palatial room, with a large bed on a raised dais in a curtained alcove at one end: only the most naïve could have thought it was a place where Mosley might entertain Ramsay Macdonald or other members of the Labour cabinet.

In public, however, they continued to appear as a highly successful couple, and Mosley's behaviour was an open secret only within their own set. It was perhaps partly in order to retain his interest that Cimmie followed her husband into the political arena, where she loyally used her considerable talents to boost his career more than her own – but her socialist beliefs were more heartfelt than his, and her achievements were genuine.

Whatever historians might decide about his policies in these years, Mosley later wrote, 'it would be difficult to deny that they were a serious attempt to meet the problems of the day'. This was quite true. The single greatest problem of the day was unemployment, which in Britain as well as Germany, the USA and other advanced countries was growing inexorably and causing a degree of poverty and social chaos the industrial world had never envisaged. After the Labour Party's electoral victory in May 1929, Ramsay Macdonald gave Mosley a seat in the cabinet and the post of Chancellor of the Duchy of Lancaster, one of four ministers with special responsibility for unemployment. The scale of the task was immense. In the mid-1920s, when Mosley had produced his Birmingham Proposals, the accepted view was that unemployment was a temporary problem, a blip in Britain's economy, to be dealt with in conventionally ameliorative ways. But by 1929, when the unemployment figure in Britain had hardly dipped below one million for seven years, and the effects of the worldwide slump were taking their toll at home, no one could sustain this pretence. The Wall Street Crash of October emphasized the feeling of social disintegration. During the single year of Mosley's ministerial tenure British unemployment doubled to two million.

Mosley was not the senior minister in the group to whom Macdonald had delegated the problem. His superior was J. H. (Jimmy) Thomas, a solid, convivial, but not very bright Labour man who had risen through the ranks of the National Union of Railwaymen. Mosley made his life misery at the time, and trounced him cruelly in his memoirs years afterwards. Thomas couldn't cope. Certainly his indecision, and his rather contrived down-to-earth style ('Beatrice Webb used to say he dropped his aitches as carefully as a beautiful woman puts on her make-up' was one of Mosley's jibes) were no match for his subordinate's flash and fire and speedy brain; in addition, Mosley was the last man on earth suited to committee procedures. He came up with one scheme after another – for the public funding of road-building projects, for early retirement programmes, and so on – which were invariably rejected and often ridiculed by the Labour leadership. After a few months of growing mutual mistrust and contempt for Thomas's ineptitude, Mosley decided to go it alone. He produced a document, soon dubbed the Mosley Memorandum, which summed up his radical proposals not only for long-term strategies to deal with unemployment but also for a series of rapid-fire emergency measures.

In response to the crisis, anti-unemployment proposals were pouring from the pens of theorists. The economist John Maynard Keynes, one of Mosley's heroes and mentors, contributed to a far-thinking Industrial Inquiry organized by Lloyd George and the Liberal Party in 1928; the official Labour Party reply to this was a dull piece of work. Following Keynes's lead, Mosley too advocated large-scale public work programmes directed by the state. He believed the way ahead lay in reviving the home market. In many other plans the British Empire – as the great hope for British economic revival – took centre stage. An imperial tariff system was among the suggestions, and while 200 MPs supported the Empire Industries Association, the symbol of Lord Beaverbrook's *Daily Express*, the knight crusader, emerged as the emblem of his campaign for Empire Free Trade. Mosley was hardly a lone voice, yet his Memorandum has become a minor political legend in Britain. Certainly it is the document which led to his enduring reputation as the 'flawed genius', the great potential leader deflected by an evil creed.

In a diary entry of May 1930, Beatrice Webb summed up Mosley's strengths and weaknesses. 'Hitherto [Macdonald] has had no competitor in personal charm and good looks, delightful voice and the gift of oratory. But Mosley has all these with the élan of youth, wealth and social position added to them. Like Mosley, Macdonald began as a utopian, but today he is a disillusioned utopian, whilst Mosley has still a young man's zeal – and is more able to use other men's brains. Whether Mosley has Mac's toughness of texture, whether he will not break down in health or character, I have doubts.' But this lavish praise is tempered with caution: 'He lacks Macdonald's strongest point – genuine puritanism,' she went on to say. 'He is entangled in the smart set and luxurious habits; he is reputed to be loose with women; he rouses suspicion, he knows little or nothing about trade unionism or Co-operation, he cannot get on terms of intimacy with working men or with the lower middle-class brainworker. He is, in fact, an intruder, a foreign substance in the Labour movement, not easily assimilated.'

Mosley's Memorandum was an all-out attempt to be heard by the cabinet that continued to ignore him. After showing a draft to Keynes in January 1930 (Keynes declared it 'very able . . . and illuminating'), he sent it straight to Ramsay Macdonald, the Prime Minister. Thomas threatened to resign, and a scuffle over procedure and wounded sensibilities went on while the document was batted about from one mildly hostile government sub-committee to another. But the Memorandum managed to reach the country, straight over the government's head, by means of a suspiciously lucky accident: John Strachey, then Mosley's Parliamentary Private Secretary, happened to leave a copy of the document lying around at his home when an inquisitive political journalist happened to be there. The secret was out and all over the press: Mosley could no longer be ignored.

He could be turned down, however, and he was. In May, after much dis-cussion, his Memorandum was rejected by various cabinet sub-committees. It was ostensibly because of the proposals themselves, but there was another difficulty. Part of the Memorandum concerned a mechanism for administer-ing the short-term emergency schemes, which involved a series of working groups with power to act alone, ultimately headed by the Prime Minister but effectively independent of the parliamentary process. That was simply for speed and efficiency, claimed Mosley; his opponents thought it looked dangerously like dictatorship. For all his radical thinking, the current of Mosley's anti-democratic feeling was never far below the surface. The spirit of Rolleston's closed authoritarian world was always strong.

In May of 1930, his proposals finally rejected, Mosley resigned from the cabinet. His resignation speech to the House of Commons brought extravagant praise: it was a brilliant vindication of his ideas and a fine example of his growing talent for oratory ('that strange music by which crowds are swayed like snakes', his son Nicholas called it) – but pointless, except as self-promotion. That was important, though, if he was to realize his dreams of going it alone, and during the summer of 1930 he began to gather around him a loose grouping of like-minded (or at least equally dissatisfied) MPs and thinkers. On Cimmie and the loyal John Strachey he could always count; Bob Boothby and Harold Macmillan were among the Conservatives who flirted with the idea of change; Harold Nicolson, then a journalist, became a loyal supporter. Importantly, the two mighty competing press barons, Lord Rothermere and Lord Beaverbrook, were both regulars in the Mosleys' drawing room, which quickly became a hothouse of debate – especially on the topic of the decay of democracy. To be offered such press support was a great advantage. Like others at this juncture, Beaverbrook believed in Tom Mosley as a politician, but not in his policies.

There was a real sense of urgency, however: the crisis was not just nationwide. Unemployment had reached two and a half million in Britain; five million in Germany; six and a half million in the USA. In the autumn, at the party conference, Mosley made one last, impassioned stand, and was very narrowly defeated. In December his next salvo, the so-called 'Mosley Manifesto' (its real title was *A National Policy for National Emergency*), was signed by seventeen Labour MPs. The following month, the impact of this document, combined with Mosley's discreet approaches to city backers, was rewarded with an enormous donation of £50,000 from the car magnate Sir William Morris, later Lord Nuffield. This powerful vote of confidence gave Mosley a spur to action, and in February 1931 five of the Manifesto's signatories, including of course Cimmie, resigned from the Labour Party and followed Mosley into the political unknown. They included Oliver Baldwin, the son of the Tory leader, and Dr Robert Forgan; the sole defector from the Conservative ranks was W. E. D. (Bill) Allen, who later stayed beside Mosley as he moved towards fascism. Mosley himself never resigned, but in March, when the launch of his 'New Party' was made public, he was expelled for 'gross disloyalty'.

'An amazing act of arrogance' was Beatrice Webb's angry pronouncement on Mosley's actions. All her earlier doubts seemed to be confirmed, and she turned vehemently against him. 'Mosley has bad health, a slight intelligence and an unstable character' was now her verdict. She also commented on a foreign journalist's remark at the Labour conference that Mosley was the 'English Hitler': 'I doubt whether he has the tenacity of a Hitler. He also lacks genuine fanaticism. Deep down in his heart he is a cynic. He will be beaten and retire.'

On this point she was wrong – Mosley never retired. However, Webb was the only commentator, at this time, to recognize a core of cynicism within the man everyone else was hailing as 'visionary', 'idealist', 'radical'. Certainly his New Party did not notice it, in the whirl of activity that the spring of 1931 brought. They embarked straight away on a campaign to fight an April by-election at Ashton-under-Lyne in Lancashire. Allan Young was the New Party candidate; time was extremely short, and Mosley himself was lying ill with pleurisy. Their policies, based on the Mosley Manifesto, could only be put across at a series of public meetings, and the task of spreading the word fell to Cimmie and John Strachey, with one or two hired speakers. Mosley recovered in time to make a few electrifying speeches just before the poll, addressing audiences as large as six thousand.

Was it the brave new political world at last? The New Party must have felt exciting, and enticingly rebellious, when its participants were swapping theories in the comfort of Savehay Farm. Wogan Phillips, the husband of the novelist Rosamond Lehmann, was a typical recruit. In 1980, talking to Selina Hastings, Rosamond Lehmann remembered: 'Wogan, like a number of rebellious left-wing people, joined the New Party, when Tom [Mosley] left the Labour Party, he and John Strachey and Harold Nicolson etc. Tom and Cimmie had these weekends at Savehay Farm at Denham. We went twice, and I was totally out of the group. I don't remember Tom even looking in my direction, but Cimmie and I made friends and had a nice cosy time.'

Despite the 'nice cosy time' at Denham, out in the wider world things were grim. The New Party's public meetings quickly turned out to be very rowdy. The rough-house that became standard at Mosley's fascist meetings began here, as did Mosley's tactics when faced with hecklers. One supporter, Peter Howard, who was captain of the England rugby football team, had recruited a band of young heavyweights to protect New Party speakers, especially Cimmie, on the platform: 'Mosley's Biff Boys', as the press called them, would 'rely on the good old English fist', their leader declared. If this attitude had been formed in private in the ballroom/boxing-ring at Rolleston, it was one that became only too familiar in Mosley's public career.

Some of the violence came from Labour supporters, furious that the defection of a few mavericks had harmed the traditional cause. Allan Young's result – a total of 4,472 votes, against the Labour Party's 11,005 and the Tories' winning 12,420 – had split the Labour vote sufficiently to allow the Conservative Party to scoop victory in a Labour 'safe' seat. When the results were announced, Cimmie had to be ushered to safety out of a back door while Mosley and the rest of his small band faced a mob of Labour militants howling with rage.

At speeches and meetings up and down the country, the New Party was the target of Labour's outrage. 'What is New about the New Party?' thundered Emmanuel Shinwell. 'Did not Brutus stick his knife into Caesar?

The stiletto in the back is as old as the hills.' Mosley's 'treachery' appeared to annoy Labour leaders far more than the defection of so few MPs would normally do – perhaps because they had always been in two minds about accepting Mosley into the heart of the Labour movement. They were aware, too, that John Strachey was having talks with Arthur Cook, the leader of the miners' union, with whom Mosley had been on good terms ever since the General Strike of 1926, and they feared large-scale defections in the New Party's direction.

In fact, they had nothing to worry about. Even within its own tiny ranks, the New Party's doubts and rifts began almost immediately to pull it apart. Harold Nicolson's diaries record the growing anxieties, along with his enduring affection and admiration for Mosley. As early as 10 June 1931, he wrote that 'Allan Young [is] most uneasy lest the Party should swerve too much to the right and be forced into Hitlerism'. Mosley was holding a series of quasi-clandestine meetings with Lloyd George and Winston Churchill, among others, with various apparently pie-in-the-sky associations in mind – including the formation of a 'National Opposition' – yet by the following month Nicolson could write: 'I think that Tom at the bottom of his heart really wants a fascist movement, but Allan Young and John Strachey think only of the British working man. The whole thing is extremely thin ice.'

Left and right diverged sharply. Strachey and Young were agitated not only by Mosley's incipient fascism, but also by his enthusiastic use of organized violence – the Biff Boys, and others like them, had become a regular fixture at meetings, and violent treatment of hecklers was routine. The weekend conferences at Savehay Farm ('a charming little place in which to differ' wrote Nicolson) only highlighted the gulfs. In July, both Strachey and Young decided to leave the New Party. For John Strachey, who had been at Mosley's side for at least seven years, it was a huge wrench. Both wrote bitterly to Mosley, saying how they felt he had changed since his illness in the spring; with hindsight, however, it looks less as if Mosley had changed, more as though he was only now able to flex his ideological muscles in freedom from Tory or Labour Party policies. New Party supporters diverged widely on the political scale, and Wogan Phillips was among several who left to join the communists. Another member, the well-known broadcaster Cyril Joad, resigned because he detected the 'cloven hoof' of fascism, and because the party was out to 'subordinate intelligence to muscular bands of young men'.

Harold Nicolson remained for the moment a leading light in their 'rather sly little movement'. 'I am loyal to Tom,' he explained to his diary, 'since I have an affection for him. But I realize that his ideas are divergent from my own. He has no political judgement. He believes in fascism. I don't. I loathe it.' He felt that 'Tom cannot keep his mind off shock troops and the roll of drums around Westminster. He is a romantic. That is a great failing.' Nicholas Mosley suggests another failing: that Mosley could not keep his mind off non-political pastimes, either. At the end of July 1931 the crisis for which the New Party claimed it had been preparing itself was about to break: the government announced a 20 per cent cut in the already paltry unemployment benefit, and the atmosphere was explosive. Mosley address-ed an enormous crowd of 40,000 at an outdoor meeting in Derbyshire. 'Tom declared: "We invite you to something new, something dangerous,"' Nicholas Mosley reported. Then Mosley and Cimmie went off to the South of France for four weeks. It was a moment when a politician who was not 'a cynic at heart' might have stayed at home and gone to work.

By the time he got back, at the end of August, the widely predicted National Government, a coalition between Stanley Baldwin and Ramsay Macdonald, had been formed. October brought a general election, and the New Party mustered twenty-four candidates. Mosley stood for Cimmie's old constituency at Stoke; Cimmie was not standing as a candidate, partly because she was pregnant. Some of the candidates were bizarre. Though a handful were experienced politicians, and a few others were at least plausible, a Cockney boxer by the name of Kid Lewis had been recruited to stand in Stepney, in the heart of the East End. He was handy in fist-fights at meetings, but less adept at conventional political work. Illiterate, he had been set to learn by heart a single speech which he used time and again. The East End Young Communists learnt it too, and used to chant it in unison at his meetings. A miserable Harold Nicolson, who himself lost his deposit standing for the Combined Universities, recorded in his dairy for 28 October: 'Wake up to read the election results. Tom is out at Stoke [he came bottom of the poll] and we have . . . lost our deposits in all but 2 seats. Even the Communists have done better than we have.'

It was all over. Harold Nicolson bravely kept the New Party newspaper, *Action*, going for another few months. He had managed to persuade some fine writers to contribute articles – Raymond Mortimer, Peter Quennell, Christopher Isherwood, Osbert Sitwell, Alan Pryce-Jones and others – and at its height it had had a circulation of 160,000. By the election it was only a third of that, and in December it fizzled out entirely. During the autumn, too, it emerged how gimcrack the organization was, 'infiltrated by adventurers, incompetents and crooks', as Robert Skidelsky put it. Their few funds were being embezzled by *Action*'s manager; one of their candidates turned out to be wanted by the police under several aliases. The party membership, such as it had ever been, melted away.

Out of Parliament, out of favour and out of funds, Mosley had little to do but take up fencing again in earnest, and go to a lot of parties, not always with the pregnant and increasingly unhappy Cimmie. Politically, there was no place for him in Britain, and he planned trips to Italy and Germany to study 'the modern movement'. In December Harold Nicolson's diary gives an insight into Cimmie's real feelings at this point about the drift to fascism: 'Cimmie,' he wrote, 'who is profoundly working-class at heart . . . wants to put a notice in the *Times* to the effect that she dissociates herself from Tom's fascist tendencies. We pass it off as a joke.'

This difference of opinion between the Mosleys, as well as their personal troubles, had become embarrassingly public; friends and supporters noticed their undisguised bickering. In their letters in January 1932, while he was in Rome being entertained by leading figures in Mussolini's government, the extent of their disagreement over fascism is clear. 'Fascio' was their personal shorthand for his views, 'fatio' for hers. 'Poor Tomby,' Mosley writes to Cimmie from Rome in his teasing mode, 'everywhere he goes hands go up; but as his tiny paw creeps upward in return he hears in his mind's ear [drawing of an ear] an indignant trumpet which pulls it down again – *roar roar*.' The roars, of course, were Cimmie's protests. Not daring to antagonize him much, she nevertheless reiterated her opposition to fascism over and over again.

The New Party was formally disbanded in April 1932. Most of its adherents returned to the Labour ranks eventually, although John Strachey (like Wogan Phillips) joined the Communist Party. In a personal year's-end summing-up on 31 December 1931, Nicolson rather bitterly concludes: 'Of all my years this has been the most unfortunate . . . My connection with Tom Mosley has done me harm.' Confused and wounded by what she felt as political betrayal on Mosley's part, frightened by the fascist tendency, Cimmie Mosley never went back into politics. They had just lost a very large amount of money in a lawsuit over her Leiter grandfather's legacy, and during 1932 both Savehay Farm and the house in Smith Square had to be let, while Cimmie and the children moved into a mews flat behind Tom's Ebury Street flat, which had previously been occupied by their chauffeur.

With nothing else to do, Mosley spent all day working to restore his fitness and skill at fencing – amazingly, at the age of thirty-five, and with his wounded leg, he was runner-up in the British epée championships. Cimmie welcomed a channel for his apparently limitless physical energy, although

Harold Nicolson was more caustic: 'That in fact is what is wrong with Tom: his energy is more physical than mental.' Mosley was also spending more and more time with his 'sillies'. Cimmie still worked as hard as ever to keep her difficult marriage alive, but her ideological rift with her husband had become undeniable.

So ended Mosley's career as a parliamentarian, though not as a politician. As the New Party folded, Nicolson wrote to Robert Forgan: 'If Tom would . . . retire into private and studious life for a bit, and then emerge fortified and purged, he will still be Prime Minister of England. If he gets entangled with the boys' brigade he will be edged gradually into becoming a revolutionary – and into the waste land I cannot follow him.' But the pull of 'the boys' brigade' was strong, and anyway Mosley had never had any real respect for the institution of Parliament. He saw the democratic tradition of one governing party always checked and restrained by a legitimate opposition as the very reason why nothing ever got done. But there is little doubt that Mosley's move into the political wilderness was a talent wasted, as later historians recorded (and as Mosley, typically unencumbered by modesty, quotes in his own memoirs). A. J. P. Taylor said of his ideas that they 'offered a blueprint for most of the constructive advances in economic policy to the present day. [They were] an astonishing achievement . . . evidence of a superlative talent'; R. H. S. Crossman, when Chairman of the Labour Party in 1961, wrote that Mosley, potentially 'the outstanding politician of his generation . . . was spurned by Whitehall, Fleet Street and every party leader at Westminster, simply and solely because he was right. [He] was prepared to discard the orthodoxies of democratic politics and to break with the bankers of high finance in order to conquer unemployment.'

There were many other such accolades. But they all refer to the time when Mosley was still prepared to work within the parliamentary system. After the collapse of the New Party, Mosley turned fully towards fascism, and away from any pretence at democracy. This was no surprise to some of his contemporaries. James Lees-Milne, repelled by the famous oratorial style and by Mosley's 'over-weening egotism', provided a description of a sort of hypnotic monster. 'He did not know the meaning of humility. He brooked no argument, would accept no advice . . . He had in him the stuff of which zealots are made. His eyes flashed fire, dilated and contracted like a mesmerist's . . . The posturing, the grimacing, the switching on and off of those gleaming teeth, and the overall swashbuckling, so purposeful and calculated, were more likely to appeal to Mayfair flappers than to sway indigent workers . . .' Beatrice Webb's increasingly fierce comments about 'that political showman' included the prediction that 'the British elector is too civilized to be taken in by Mosley, with his antics and his cocktails . . .'

But this was still to be put to the test. In politics Mosley had achieved fame by his maverick attitudes; now his radicalism propelled him beyond the accepted limits of the British political arena and into uncharted territory. And it was at just that moment, in the spring of 1932, with his parliamentary career finished, his circle of respectable supporters dispersed and his marriage at its lowest ebb, that Mosley met Diana Guinness.

12 1932: *The Big Gamble*

To all outward appearances, Diana's life had become even more carefree and socially energetic during 1932. At Cheyne Walk and Biddesden, what John Betjeman called 'the endless party' went on. New friends were added to the mix: when staying with Mrs Ronnie Greville at Polesden Lacey she met Lord Berners, a painter and composer, who was to be important to her until his death in 1950; among others were the surrealist Edward James and his new wife, the dancer Tilly Losch, with whom Tom Mitford was in love. More than just a 'society beauty' now, Diana was iconic: this year she was painted repeatedly, by Augustus John, twice by Henry Lamb, by John Banting (an enormous canvas six feet by four, which somehow disappeared), and (with her sons) by Pavel Tchelitchev, a Russian émigré artist and friend of Edward James who was then enjoying a vogue. Tchelitchev shows the little blond boys with hair curling to their shoulders, cuddled against their mother in a soft-focus portrait that remained Diana's own favourite.*

As well as the commissions paid for by Bryan, a durable image of Diana was made by Boris Anrep, who incorporated her portrait into the mosaic floor of the entrance hall of the National Gallery in London. It shows a group of muses, each modelled on a noted beauty of the moment, or a figure from Anrep's circle. In the centre are Apollo and Bacchus, the first a portrait of Osbert Sitwell, the latter of Clive Bell, representing the serious and pleasure-seeking sides of man's nature. Around them are the nine goddesses of Greek inspiration, including Virginia Woolf as Clio, the muse of history; prima ballerina Lydia Lopokova (wife of Maynard Keynes) as Terpsichore, the muse of dance; and Christabel, Lady Aberconway, as Euterpe, muse of music. The only portrait of someone unknown to Anrep is of Greta Garbo (Melpomene, muse of tragedy). Diana is Polyhymnia, the muse of sacred music and of oratory, and thousands of visitors unknowingly tramp across her features every day. Though she admired Anrep, Diana described the work as being made in 'typical dreary Bloomsbury colours', speculating that

---

* It now belongs to Desmond Guinness, but Diana acquired an oil sketch of the triple portrait for her dining room in the 1990s.

if Anrep had fled to France rather than England, he might have been influenced by Matisse's brilliance rather than the 'puritanical muddiness' of Roger Fry.

On 7 July Diana had given her London ball at the house in Cheyne Walk, when she and Mosley had made their commitment to each other. The dance was partly for Unity, now a recalcitrant débutante, and their cousin Joan Farrer, and the *Evening Standard* had previewed the evening excitedly: 'The 300 guests will dance in a white ballroom, and supper will be served at refectory tables in the two sparsely furnished dining rooms with their austere white walls and picturesque arches. The old walls and ceilings – they were built in 1760 – are perfectly plain, in the palest tones of blue, pink and gold.' Osbert Lancaster remembered dining with Jim Lees-Milne before the dance, and then 'as I was going up the stairs two footmen pushed everybody away and two more came carrying Augustus John downstairs. He had already passed out.' Diana insisted this was a complete invention, but one that has passed into legend.

Unity was now getting her chance to meet the friends of her older siblings, but she was not one to appreciate them, nor they her. Almost six feet tall and rather heavy, with enormous hands and feet, she had the same dairy-queen colouring as Diana, and as a girl was often described as beautiful – in fact they could look so alike that in photographs they have sometimes been mistaken for one another. But Unity lacked the essential ingredient that made her sister an adult beauty; one friend described her as like a reflection of Diana in a slightly distorting mirror. Unity was still as determinedly naughty as when she was a child, and she decided to be outrageous as a deb, bringing her pet rat, Ratular, to dances and indulging in any other tease she could think up. 'At deb balls,' her friend Rosemary Peto recalled, 'Bobo amused herself with a yo-yo, she was expert at it, and played it with the hand which was supposed to be at the back of the young man.' She developed a craze for boxing and all-in wrestling, and liked to take a group of cronies in full evening dress to the ring at Blackfriars before a party – a pastime strictly forbidden by Lord Redesdale, although in vain. She enjoyed nothing more than shocking people and spitting in the eye of convention. She had crossed the great divide from the schoolroom to the adult world, and from now on, although they had not been close as children, she was much more important in Diana's life.

After a spring and summer of relentless social activity for Diana, there were the summer holidays – in their different way, no less social. The Mosleys were due to take their usual holiday on the Lido at Venice, and Diana and Mosley arranged to coincide there. She and Bryan were to drive through France with Victor Rothschild and his fiancée Barbara Hutchinson (at whose twenty-first birthday dinner Diana and Mosley had met), and the lovers had arranged a further 'accidental' rendez-vous in Arles or Avignon – Mosley was driving through France on his own while Cimmie, who was still unwell after a difficult pregnancy and the birth of Michael by Caesarian operation, followed by train with the children.

But the plan did not run smoothly. 'My dear Diana,' John Betjeman wrote on 12 August, 'I am so sorry to hear that you are ill in the South of France with pleurisy . . . not so much because of your disease, as because you are in the South of France which has always been in my mind as something worse than Maidenhead although I admit I have never been there . . .' It was not pleurisy which Diana had suddenly contracted. The Guinnesses' sightseeing trip began well enough, with visits to the Saintes Mairies de la Mer and Aigues-Mortes, 'and churches and the Aldous Huxleys'. But one morning at the Jules César Hotel in Arles Diana woke to a severely inflamed throat; at the hospital in Avignon, where she was taken, the doctor diagnosed diphtheria and administered huge injections to the whole party. Diana had a worry apart from her health, however – that a message or a note from Mosley might be delivered to the hotel desk, and be opened by Bryan while she was on her sickbed. Barbara and Victor had to be taken into her confidence, and a message was conveyed to Mosley in Arles.

Diana recovered with surprising speed, but the unfortunate Victor Rothschild had an allergic reaction to the injections that made his skin swollen, itchy and bright red, and confined him to a mosquito-netted bed in a snowstorm of talcum powder. It was not the only blight on this part of the holiday. Despite their help with her clandestine plans, her friends had turned out to be tiresome company: in September Nancy reported to Hamish Erskine that 'Diana is absolutely maddened by Barbara and Victor after 3 weeks alone with them abroad, she says they are much worse and more annoying than any honeymoon couple could be.' This sounds remarkably unsympathetic, from someone who was herself in love. Was this report to Nancy designed to pull the wool over her sister's eyes? Or perhaps the contrast between the two couples – the enthusiastically engaged lovers, and the increasingly estranged Guinnesses – had proved too painful.

In Venice a large band of friends was gathered, almost as if their London set had moved wholesale to the Lido. Tom Mitford was there, staying at Malcontenta, the magnificent Palladian house of Baroness d'Erlanger. Randolph Churchill was his usual difficult self, and during a picnic at Torcello he picked a fight with Brendan Bracken by referring to him as 'my brother' (Bracken was a great favourite of Winston Churchill, and there was a persistent rumour that he was Churchill's natural son). Emerald Cunard was there, as was the conductor Sir Thomas Beecham, her lover. Edward James and Tilly Losch, Bob Boothby, and Doris Castlerosse, who had become close to Diana since she had separated earlier that year from her disreputable husband, the gossip columnist Lord Castlerosse, were among the crowd. And, of course, the Mosleys and their children.

Group sightseeing, meals and parties were the norm, but few people could help noticing that Diana and Mosley were often nowhere to be found between lunch and dinner. Diana once said that 'it was not in [Mosley's] nature to be discreet' about his affairs; that was an understatement. Bob Boothby remembered that at lunch one day, in front of all their friends, Mosley informed him that he would be needing Boothby's hotel bedroom that night between midnight and 4 a.m.: Boothby would have to sleep on the beach. It was the sort of thing Mosley could get away with, by a combination of arrogance and high good humour.

Mosley loved holidays, and enjoyed himself like an exuberant boy, splashing and running, grinning and shouting, indulging his taste for practical jokes, refusing to allow emotional complexities to spoil the 'larks'. In fact, the complicated situation with Diana and Cimmie (not to mention Bryan) was quite normal for Mosley, who was almost always conducting some love affair under his wife's nose, by a combination of deceit and bravado. There is a telling photograph that has survived from this Venetian fortnight: standing in a row are two bare-chested men in holiday mood, Tom Mitford and Mosley, both grinning playfully at the camera, hands on hips, aware of their raffish good looks; and beside them are Doris Castlerosse and Diana, who is dressed for some reason in pearls and white gloves, slender, perfectly coiffed and self-contained as a statue, a tiny smile on her face. She is like a coiled spring. At the front of the picture, slumped despondently on a deck chair is Cynthia Mosley, in her mid-thirties already becoming heavy, eyes averted from the buoyant group behind her. If she had hoped that this holiday was going to restore her marriage, after six months of illness, she was sadly disappointed. The humiliation and pain for Bryan must have been just as intense.

Diana and Mosley were equally ruthless towards their spouses. They were well matched, too, in the way their personalities combined opposing characteristics: an appetite for hilarity and mischief, and an almost priggish high-mindedness. Through the summer, and for most of 1932, Mosley had been at work on his book *The Greater Britain*, his blueprint for British fascism. It is short, idealistic and highly moral in tone, more concerned with political ideas than practical politics. It contains not a single reference to Jews: if Mosley had read *Mein Kampf*, which was published seven years before, it had left no mark. Instead *The Greater Britain* identifies 'decadence' as the enemy – decadence in society and within the individual. To serve the 'high conception of citizenship' it posits, and 'the necessity for the authoritative State', responsible men and women must 'live like athletes' – 'The State has no room for the drone and the decadent, who use their leisure to destroy their capacity for public usefulness . . .' This, from the playboy of the Lido.

Back in England, too, the party went on: 'Tomorrow Barbara H & Victor R, Phyllis de Janzé, Mitty [Tom Mitford], Randolph, George Kennedy & we hope John S are coming,' wrote Nancy from Biddesden in September, 'and on Sunday we're all going to join up with Cecil's party.' (Cecil Beaton had just acquired a country house, Ashcombe, about thirty miles from Biddesden.) But there were two important differences. One was that Mosley was seldom far away from Diana, in London or in the country, and the other was that politics was now an essential part of her life.

It is a tribute to Bryan Guinness's tolerance that Mosley was often to be found staying at Biddesden this autumn, without Cimmie. When Henry Lamb was painting his second portrait of Diana, Mosley was often about. 'Henry became very stuffy about it all,' according to Lady Pansy. Perhaps Henry Lamb was feeling protective of Bryan, who was suffering agonies of jealousy. He had tried forbidding Diana to see Mosley, but realized it was useless. They had begun to quarrel, and the situation was rapidly becoming impossible. Diana 'insisted on the right to choose her own friends', but she obviously couldn't placate him as successfully as Mosley did his wife, or perhaps did not really want to.

The long-suffering Cynthia was still battling with her health. Her pathetic letters to her husband in the second part of this year, after the notorious Venice holiday, show her trying hard to quell her jealousy: she sensed by now that the affair with Diana was something out of the ordinary. But Mosley still managed to quieten his 'squashy-nosed mutton' with baby-talk letters that held an edge of emotional blackmail: they could have a 'lovely' life together, he wrote, if only she would stop being upset about his 'little frolicsome ways'. A surprising term for the kind of commitment he was planning with Diana.

That autumn Diana held a fancy-dress *fête champêtre* at Biddesden House. The Mosleys were prominent among the guests; Cimmie dressed as a shepherdess. 'A number of people,' according to one, 'had costumes designed by Oliver Messel for the C. B. Cochrane production of Offenbach's *La Belle Hélène*. Diana was in white; Mosley in black, suitably. A huge bonfire was lit in front of the house and we danced in the long downstairs drawing room.' Unity made drawings of some of the costumes: John Sutro as a cupid with a bow and tiny wings and gold hair; Oliver Messel himself in a Roman toga, high-heeled buskins and huge feathered helmet; Nancy as a Marie-Antoinette peasant. As at the ball in Cheyne Walk, Diana and Mosley danced together most of the evening, and now her Biddesden circle as well as her London friends noticed that they were 'visibly affichés'. Rosamond Lehmann, who with her husband Wogan Phillips were Biddesden acquaintances through their Bloomsbury connections, remembered the evening vividly. 'I went to a fancy-dress ball at Biddesden where Cimmie was not [recollections differ about this] but Diana was, in a Grecian dress looking greatly beautiful but sinister, which I always thought she was with that huge white face. She danced the whole evening with Tom. They looked as though they were magnetized together, she always laughing with her mouth wide open. Bryan was simply totally silent, he danced with me a good deal but never spoke a word. It was the most awful evening, Tom in triumph with this dazzling beauty, and Bryan, the host, looking like a shattered white rabbit. Dreadful.'

'Diana was telling everyone how thrilling she found him, like having a crush on a film star,' Pansy Lamb recalled. From the start Diana had to reconcile her friends to Mosley's manner. 'Mosley was throwing his weight about,' Pansy Lamb went on. 'Diana must have caught the expression on [Henry Lamb's] face, for she said, You're thinking what a frightful bounder he is . . . Diana's attitude was love-me-love-my-dog.'

By November, it was an open secret among Diana's close friends that she was planning to leave Bryan. Nancy, whose respect for convention was always strong, wrote to her anxiously on 27 November: 'Mitty and I spent the whole of yesterday afternoon discussing your affairs . . . He is horrified & says that your social position will be *nil* if you do this.' And two days later, thanking her for a 'life saving' gift of £5, she says, 'You know, back in the sane or insane atmosphere of Swinbrook I feel convinced that you won't be allowed to take this step. I mean . . . everybody you know will band together and somehow stop you. Oh dear I believe you have a much worse time in store for you than you imagine. I'm sorry to be so gloomy darling.'

What had happened to this marriage, which was only in its fourth year? Diana had believed herself to be in love with Bryan, but she had been very young, anxious to get away from home; tempted by the kind of life he could give her, and they had hardly known each other before they were engaged.

She quickly discovered that her kind, vague, idealistic husband was quite incompatible with her more precise and efficient temperament, hungry for action and determination. There had been no large-scale marital problems involving betrayal or violence or fights. Instead, there was the steady drip of irritation, and the perpetual grating of small differences. He annoyed her incessantly; Mosley, she said, never got on her nerves. He disliked her socializing; she craved people. She wanted the Mediterranean; he wanted the north of Scotland. He loved winter sports and would go every year to St Moritz with the other Mitfords (Lord Redesdale was a very keen skater); Diana would stay behind. Bryan was embarrassed by his wealth, and wanted to be 'just like everyone else'; Diana wanted, above just about anything, to be unlike anybody else. Bryan invited the clerk from his barristers' chambers to dinner: a dull man, Diana reported, whose wife was a do-gooder – 'just the kind of people I hate most'. She was maddened by his Tolstoyan urges: after lunch parties at Biddesden, for instance, he might announce that in place of the relaxed chat Diana enjoyed, they must all go 'roguing' – weeding the rogue oats out of the wheat crop by hand, tramping the fields under a hot sun; he could not have devised anything Diana would hate more. She felt his pretence at 'ordinariness' made him insensitive: once when his architect friend George Kennedy had come to dinner, he told his surprised guests that he had given the servants the evening off, and they were going to make their own supper. 'What that meant, of course,' remarked Diana, 'is that poor Mrs Kennedy, who cooked every night of her life, simply had to set to and peel potatoes yet again – Bryan couldn't do it. They weren't well off. What she would have liked was to have been taken to the Ritz.'

These are small things. In frank moments she admitted that she was bored by Bryan, and she had found someone more to her taste, erotically and intellectually. She had aspired to the life she had with Bryan, but its rich diet had soon turned her stomach and she wanted something bigger, darker, more purposeful and more dangerous. Glutted with the easy hedonism of social life, Diana was attracted by its opposite. Most people rebel away from the workaday aspects of life towards the more light-hearted; in choosing Mosley and fascism, Diana rebelled away from the frivolity of her socializing life into 'seriousness of purpose'. She often told a story about herself and Bryan, early in their marriage, walking the woods at Versailles, getting more and more lost and tired as Bryan insisted he knew the way. Eventually Diana, exhausted and exasperated, sat down under a tree and refused to move until Bryan went to find a taxi. 'I knew that he had no idea of the way,' was her comment.

She wanted to be shown the way, and Mosley was expert at that. In spite of her devotion to parties, she had not been able to shut out the knowledge of the extreme misery, poverty and hunger that existed outside her golden cage. Unemployment was at its height; the slump bred anger. As society events were written up in the press, it was usual for a small crowd to form at the front door, to watch the guests arrive and gaze at the clothes. But these crowds were sometimes in an ugly mood now, their remarks hostile rather than admiring. The pranks of the Bright Young Things were no longer funny. Diana had surrounded herself with clever people, but almost all of them were more interested in aesthetics, ideas and ideals than in practical politics; few had any sense of the urgency of the economic situation or any notion of a solution. Bryan's father, now Lord Moyne, often used to come over to chat when he was in London, and she grew to like and appreciate him. It was a continuation of the thoughtful talk she had enjoyed at Chartwell, the crucible of her political awareness. But since the General Strike of 1926 she had despised the Tories, and even the kindly and clever Moyne felt too slow, too complacent. She had met someone who had a solution and was burning with energy to put it into practice.

At the general election of May 1929, women of twenty-one and over had voted for the first time. Diana, not yet nineteen at the time, had not been eligible to vote, but if she had she would not have supported her father-in-law. At the next election, in the autumn of 1931, Diana had a vote but did not use it. She would have supported a Lloyd George Liberal, but there was no candidate in her area. She felt contemptuous of the National Government created in reaction to the world-wide slump, and led by the 'absurd figure' of Ramsay Macdonald. Though not politically aware in any sophisticated sense, she was becoming sensible of the contrast between her own social stratosphere and the miserable conditions of unemployed millions.

Not that she gave up on a single outing to the opera, dinner party or trip to Venice. But even many decades later, she would talk heatedly about the abysmal conditions of the British poor in the thirties, and was quick to remind younger people, who had only experienced a post-Welfare world, that they could not imagine the conditions in the 'distressed areas'. She became an admirer of Margaret Thatcher – her son Alexander said Thatcher was one of the very few women his mother valued in the public arena – but she was critical of her failure to combat the problem of homelessness. Surely a rich Western country could organize its affairs properly, so that people could eat and be housed? These were all the lessons Mosley taught.

In politics, as in everything else, Diana had a taste for the extreme. Whatever kind of mess the world was in, the slow churning of ameliorative, democratic policies would never have been to her liking. She wanted fire and brimstone, the super-hero with a world vision. Her reading of the Germans had given her that, and such ideas found fertile ground in the Mitford world-view. The family tendency was towards hero worship: other people were *wonderful* or *terrible*, hated or loved. A childhood that made a melodrama from the loss of a mouse turned into an adulthood that demanded highly charged action, and the girls seem to have found significance in their emotional lives by embracing a man and a cause simultaneously. For Jessica it was communism, and her first husband Esmond Romilly; for Nancy it was Gaullism and her beloved Colonel Palewski; for Unity it was Nazism and Hitler. It is a Romantic notion, in the nineteenth-century sense, intertwining love and a burning cause: like the heroes of their girlish pantheon, Byron and the young Wordsworth, they thought it 'very Heaven' to be young and at the cutting edge of politics.

Diana, too, had fallen in love with a man and his ideas simultaneously. In spite of all that Bryan could give her, there was nothing to compare with Mosley. She was properly in love for the first time in her life, and that erotic love was combined with a burning sense of purpose. She was prepared to jettison her husband, her social position, her luxurious life, and the approval of her family and friends for a man who had no intention of giving up his marriage for her. It was an extremely risky step – the position of divorced women in the early thirties was far more difficult than now, and Mosley himself, with his reputation as a womanizer, was hardly a reliable prospect. (In fact, even in 1932 he had not given up all his other amorous affairs.) But Diana wanted to 'nail her colours to the mast' – ruthless behaviour, and reckless too, although Nicholas Mosley described it more generously: 'this was . . . one of the great attractions of Diana: that she would stake her life, as [Mosley] was doing, on something she believed in but which was unlikely to go all her own way.'

Of course, the social censure she faced might have been a perverse part of the attraction, too: she had had enough of being a queen of smart society, and for her milieu this was the ultimate 'tease'. 'I never thought of it as risky, or as a great gamble,' Diana said, 'though all my friends did.' At another time she said that 'The only disapproval I really minded was my brother's. Tom strongly disapproved . . . He was fond of Bryan; he also thought that for a temporary infatuation I was ruining my life and I should bitterly regret it . . . It was a normal reaction which I understood perfectly well. I was only twenty-two; although I was convinced of the permanency of what I had decided to do, other people gave it a year at most.'

Mosley himself was in an idealistic mood, buoyed up by his exceptional self-belief. As he worked furiously to build his new movement, he was striving for what he saw as an ideal in both parts of his life – in the public arena, a hard, clean, relentless new political force; in the private sphere, the happy combining of his home life with a strong commitment to Diana. These two aims now seem equally hopeless, but Mosley apparently thought he could achieve both. He could lead the country in a radical way, and he could lead his private life as he liked, too, with both loyal wife and adoring mistress. He would be the superman of the fascist creed.

By the end of 1932, the family situation had to be faced. Diana had broached the subject of divorce with Bryan, and financial negotiations had begun. In November Nancy wrote to her: 'Mitty says £2,000 a year will seem tiny to you & he will urge Farve, as your trustee, to hold out for more.' Lord Redesdale was forced to act the part of the Victorian father by Lord Moyne, who had returned from one of his long cruises and was horrified by the situation he found. The two paid a visit to Mosley at his Ebury Street flat. It was a not unexpected visit, and Randolph Churchill had asked Mosley what he would do. Mosley had replied, 'Wear a balls' protector, I suppose.'

Nancy, with her usual hyperbole, told the story to Hamish Erskine in a letter dated Christmas Eve: 'Now that lord Moyne is back there seems . . . to be some slight hope of the divorce being off. He & Farve went to see M[osley] (who was dead white and armed with knuckle dusters), they said to him "are you prepared to give Diana up now?" "No." "Then," said Lord M, "we shall put detectives on you." "Very well." Lord Moyne absolutely refuses to have Bryan divorced & Diana is determined not to *be* divorced & isn't going to give a particle of evidence so at present things have reached a deadlock. [This refers to the time when one partner in a divorce had to be the 'guilty' party.] Bryan is going to Switzerland for three weeks,' Nancy added, 'having forbidden Mosley the house. The truth is that Lord M has at last put some guts into Bryan.' Nancy had obviously invented the knuckle-dusters, so her account is hardly reliable: she never let the truth get in the way of a good story. But even a watered-down version of what she said next would show how the Mitfords' habit of wild exaggeration could get them into trouble – and how much the sisters were enjoying the drama of Diana's marital troubles: 'Meanwhile Farve, who is really an extraordinary character, goes to Lord M & says "I suppose you know that my daughter is laying in a store of furs and diamonds against the time when she is divorced." Bobo [Unity] had apparently told Muv this, half out of mischief and half as a joke. So now Lord M is not unnaturally in a fearful rage with Diana whom he was on good terms with before.'

The truth of this incident, Diana told her daughter-in-law Charlotte, was that the 'furs & diamonds' were in fact a pair of country shoes. 'I remember saying to one of my sisters, "I hate country shoes & had better get some while I'm rich."'

By Christmas, although Bryan was in no doubt about what was happening, Cimmie was apparently still in the dark. At any rate, some sort of civilized front was being maintained, for while Bryan was away in Switzerland Diana was a guest of the Mosleys at a New Year fancy-dress party they gave at a rented house in the country. Their big family Christmas had included both Cimmie's sisters. The eldest, Lady Irene, was unmarried, and since the death of her father she had the title Lady Ravensdale – when he realized he might have no sons, Curzon had ensured that one of his titles could pass to his eldest daughter. Cimmie's younger sister, Lady Alexandra, was known to family and friends as Baba, a nickname that originated in India in her infancy. Baba's husband, Major Metcalfe (always known as 'Fruity'), was a royal equerry and friend of the Prince of Wales; they had three children. With the Mosleys' three, this made up the house party for Christmas; and for the New Year celebrations a large number of fashionable guests had been summoned, Diana among them.

The gossip writers had wind of the event, and had asked to come and take photographs; they were refused, but some came anyway, and found plenty of material for their society columns. It is typical of the paradoxes of Mosley's character that just as he was struggling to establish himself as a sober and serious political leader he should allow his own house party to get out of hand: among other antics he threw an éclair that hit Syrie Maugham and caused her to have hysterics. The *Daily Worker* enjoyed this to the full, showing a ludicrous picture of 'fascists at play', describing the pranks of 'the future dictator of Britain' and mocking his 'superman nature'.

The new year dawned, and with it great changes in the public and private arenas. In January 1933 Hitler came to power in Germany, and Diana left her husband to live openly as Mosley's mistress.

13 *British Fascism: The Background*

Mosley's visit to Rome in January of 1932 was the turning-point on his route to fascism. The New Party was not officially disbanded until April, but his mind was already on the next move, and, whether or not it was Mussolini who urged Mosley to adopt the fascist label, Mosley was certainly impressed by what he saw in Italy. His letters to Cimmie – although he admits that because of their differences he was 'piling it on a bit' – glow with enthusiasm for the fascists' achievements: he was shown workers' clubs, model factories, rebuilt roads and reclaimed land, and heard about employment schemes, holidays for poor children, systems of child welfare and youth training, and much more.

Roman society was still there to entertain him, too. He wrote home about parties and dinners, about a 'thirteenth century castle of honey-coloured stone' in the same sentence as a land reclamation scheme; he also managed to fit in sessions with Italy's Olympic fencers. Some of his time, as Cimmie didn't fail to notice, was not accounted for.

Mosley's first meeting with Mussolini took place on 6 January, and over the next few years he saw the Duce several times; Mosley often combined a visit to the Italian leader with his summer holiday. 'I liked him, and found him easy to get on with,' Mosley recorded, adding that he never found Mussolini stilted, cold and unapproachable, as many Italians did. In a letter to Cimmie Mosley wrote, 'He speaks English well', though in his memoirs he says they spoke to each other in French, until one day when Mussolini announced proudly that he had learnt English, and 'after that I understood little he said'. Mosley and Harold Nicolson also met Margherita Sarfatti, the dictator's Jewish mistress and confidante, a clever woman who was a frequent go-between for the Duce, foreign visitors, and the gossip in Roman salons.

When Mosley returned to England, his determination to found a fascist party was set. His experiences in Italy, and his lack of contact with Germany (in 1932 he spoke no German and had never visited the country), ensured that Mosley's fascism was much closer to the Italian model than to Hitler's.

The Italian and British versions were similar in one essential: in 1932, neither considered anti-Semitism an important ideological point. After the Rome–Berlin treaty of 1936, by which time Mosley's own policy had also shifted radically, it was a different matter.

These days, the word fascism is used so loosely that it often simply means anything authoritarian, monolithic or powerful. In political usage it automatically conjures up racism, particularly anti-Semitism, although this was not at first a central tenet of the early Italian fascists. It is also difficult, now, to realize that until the events of 1939–45 a fascist was not necessarily a political pariah. In the 1920s and 1930s – depending on the place and the individual – fascism might have been perceived as terrifying, or unattractive but effective, or merely (as for many people in Britain) rather eccentric, but it was not automatically execrated.

As a political creed born of the dire economic conditions following the First World War, fascism has an unusually precise and brief history: the first fascist party was formed by Mussolini in 1922, and it ceased to be a significant world-wide political force after Hitler's death in 1945, although authoritarian rule lingered anachronistically in Salazar's Portugal until 1970, and in Franco's Spain until 1975. But in various dilute forms (usually extreme far-right nationalist movements centred on anti-Semitism), elements of fascism are enjoying a vigorous after-life in dozens of minority groups across Europe and the Americas, and especially in united Germany, in Russia and parts of the old Eastern bloc.

Mosley, who died in 1980, did not live to see the neo-fascist revivals of the last two decades, and in 1968, when he had declared himself no longer a fascist but 'a European', he wrote: 'Fascism does not exist at present, not because it has been answered, but because it belongs to the epoch before the Second World War.'

Yet even the fascism of the twenties and thirties was hardly a unified ideology. Historians do not agree about whether Italian fascism and German national socialism had enough in common to merit a common label, and where the British version might fit into that. Not surprisingly, given his imperialist patriotism, Mosley's own definition stresses the national differences: 'Fascism was in essence a national creed, and therefore by definition took an entirely different form in different countries. In origin, it was an explosion against intolerable conditions, against remediable wrongs which the old world had failed to remedy.'

There were variations, certainly, but Mosley's claim that it took 'an entirely different form' in different places is hard to justify. A more general description, by Stuart Hood, reads: 'Fascism as a mass political phenomenon was the response . . . to a series of threats: recession, mass unrest, the Russian revolution, the organized working class and its left-wing parties.' It was a powerful triple-headed monster: one part ideological and emotional (playing on the sense of national disgrace and humiliation after the First World War in the defeated countries), another part economic (in response to the consequences of world recession); the third a bewildered reaction to the social tensions brought about by modernization and change. Ex-servicemen and officers, middle-class professionals, and all those on fixed incomes – including some of the aristocracy – felt these factors keenly, right across Europe: there were fascist movements not only in Italy, Germany, Spain and Britain but also in Romania, Hungary, Portugal, Belgium, Austria and elsewhere. The amalgamation of disparate notions and theories made for strange bedfellows. In each country, the compound of radical (left-wing-sounding) ideas and a deeply conservative, quasi-mystical appeal to the glories of a vanished past drew on different traditions: fascism, Hood says, was essentially 'chameleon-like'.

What colouring did the chameleon assume in Britain? The factors that bred fascism elsewhere were less obviously acute there. Although the First World War had taken a terrible toll, there was no national humiliation like that imposed on Germany by the treaties that ended the war. Unemployment in Britain was bad, though not as bad as elsewhere; there was poverty, dissatisfaction and industrial unrest, but the National Strike of 1926, which lasted a matter of days, was a mild affair compared to Italy's 'Biennio rosso', the 'Two Red Years' of 1920–22 that saw the factories occupied and widespread strikes and demonstrations by agricultural as well as industrial workers. Britain's parliamentary tradition was older and stronger, too, than that of Italy or Germany. The British soil, in fact, was not a particularly fertile one for fascism.

Yet Mosley's was not the first fascist group in the country. As early as 1923, Miss Rotha Lintorn Orman founded the British Fascisti, later made into a limited company under the more English title British Fascists Ltd. A 28-year-old from a military family, Miss Lintorn Orman had served in an ambulance unit in Serbia during the First World War, and felt compelled by the Bolshevist threat to follow Mussolini's Italian example. Her organization was to be composed of 'disinterested patriots of all classes and all Christian creeds who would be ready to serve their country during an emergency'. Throne and empire, king and country were its watchwords; its members were not anti-capitalist, anti-democratic or (officially at least) anti-Semitic. Its main function seems to have been the stewarding of Conservative meetings, and Arnold Leese, an early member who successfully stood as a fascist candidate in local elections, scornfully dubbed the British Fascists as merely 'Conservatism with knobs on'. Some members left to form small, more explicitly anti-Semitic groups, all of which petered out after a short time; Leese founded the more extreme Imperial Fascist League in 1929. Violently anti-Semitic from the start, it was principally a vehicle for the bizarre views of its founder; it never attracted more than a handful of supporters, but received a disproportionate amount of publicity.

The membership of the British Fascists, on the other hand, was reckoned to have been substantial in its heyday, from 1924 to about the time of the General Strike in 1926. But, as with all these groups, the truth is hard to establish. The extremist magazine *The Patriot* claimed that the number reached 400,000, while historian Robert Benewick dismisses this as over-extravagant, and puts the figure at a few thousand only. Yet A. K. Chesterton, writing in 1937, declared that the BF's membership had reached half a million – and he was both scornful and hostile towards them. Its appeal was largely to landed gentry and military and naval personnel from 'county' families: its president from 1924 to 1926 was Brigadier-General Robert Blakeney, who later joined Leese's Imperial Fascist League and then Mosley's British Union of Fascists. Other prominent early members included the Earl of Glasgow, Admiral John Armstrong, Lord Ernest Hamilton, the Marquis of Ailesbury and Brigadier-General Sir Ormonde Winter. After 1926 the British Fascists began to decline in numbers, especially in the shires – perhaps because the Bolshevik threat seemed to have receded. As the county membership faded away, the organization also became explicitly pro-Nazi and anti-Semitic.

When Mosley started his fascist party in October 1932, he boldly decided to call it the British Union of Fascists, and quickly moved towards an aggressive takeover of all the other existing organizations that used the name. He described the remnants of the BF, by the early 1930s, as consisting of 'three old ladies and a couple of office boys', which was hardly accurate, and though they were by this time a much smaller movement, they did survive the initial takeover attempt by Mosley. Dr Robert Forgan, who had followed Mosley's political moves from Labour, to the New Party and now into fascism, was deputized to ask all the other groups whether they would place themselves under the umbrella of Mosley's leadership. Some agreed, although Arnold Leese refused on the grounds that Mosley was in the pay of the Jews, and Miss Lintorn Orman on the grounds that he was a communist.

Throughout 1933 and 1934 the BUF waged a strong campaign to eradicate the other fascist groups and absorb their members, and the BF and the IFL fell over each other to appeal to the lowest common denominator by taunting the BUF as 'pro-Semitic' and 'the kosher fascists'. Neither label lasted long, and many of the small fascist groups had disappeared by the end of 1934. Trouble between different fascist parties continued through the thirties, but Mosley's 'Union' of British fascists achieved the predominance he wanted.

14 *The British Union of Fascists*

The British Union of Fascists was launched on 1 October 1932, with a flag-unfurling ceremony in its offices in Great George Street (the former New Party offices). There were just thirty-two members present. Mosley's book, *The Greater Britain*, was published, by a small company of his own, on the same day, so the new group had its manifesto and its policies ready to greet recruits. Also in place from the beginning was the nucleus of Mosley's 'Defence Force', who would soon go into action at public meetings: a handful of young men from the New Party Youth Movement who had been trained to deal with hecklers and 'trouble-makers', and to use their fists with enthusiasm. A few political friends and former MPs had stuck with Mosley – Robert Forgan and Bill Allen among them – but most of the intellectuals who had flirted with the New Party were horrified by Mosley's turn to full-frontal fascism. It is difficult, however, to establish the identity of BUF members at any point, or indeed their accurate numbers. From 1937 onwards Mosley's headquarters kept lists only of 'active' ('Division 1') members, since it was thought that non-active members, who were often clandestine supporters, were wary of their names being included in the files. Even this limited list, which must have been among the records confiscated by the authorities in May 1940 when Mosley was imprisoned, seems to have been inconclusive: a Home Office memorandum on the subject written in 1943 gives only an 'estimate' of membership figures.

The first public meeting was low-key, almost jovial. In Trafalgar Square on 15 October Mosley addressed a small crowd from the plinth at the bottom of Nelson's Column, wearing a white shirt with his suit and tie. He was flanked by eight men in black shirts and grey trousers; there was the occasional scuffle after an interruption, but the meeting passed off without any major incident, or indeed any major impact. Several friends came along, and Cimmie was there with her two elder children: despite her opposition to fascism the year before, and although she had taken little part in preparations, since the launch of the BUF she had decided she had no choice (if she wanted to keep her husband) but to make herself part of it. She never spoke from the platform or stood as a candidate, but she became head of the Women's Section, and she worked on ideas for a fascist flag and a fascist anthem (one notion was to use the tune of Sousa's 'Stars and Stripes' with words by Osbert Sitwell, another was to commission an anthem from William Walton). When the time came for a uniform, she helped to design the black shirt with a high round collar worn without a tie, copied from Mosley's fencing jackets. As usual, Cimmie provided the warmth and humanity Mosley lacked as a public figure, and within weeks she was a great favourite with 'the boys' in the BUF. In her own circle there was no question of being shunned, socially or politically: her Smith Square lunch parties for the rich and well-connected went on as before, and every respectable venue and platform was still open to Mosley at this stage.

This relative quiet was not Mosley's style, however. On the launch of the BUF the *Evening Standard* had described him in a long analysis as 'an astonishing man' but 'an astonishing failure', doomed now to a 'tragic retirement into obscurity', and he was out to prove that analysis wrong. Whatever else he would be, obscurity did not come into it. Recruitment was beginning to pick up briskly, mainly among young, lower-middle-class men resentful that the chaotic state of capitalism – the slump – would rob them of opportunity, and eager for order and progress. On 24 October there was an indoor meeting at the Memorial Hall in Farringdon Street, and this time the atmosphere was quite different. Mosley was at his fieriest: there was nothing he liked more than verbal sparring with questioners, but when some hostile hecklers in the gallery were referred to by Mosley as 'three warriors of class war all from Jerusalem' the fights began, and several people were chucked out with considerable force by Mosley's strong-arm stewards. The march following the meeting saw several more such incidents.

Irene and Baba, Cimmie's sisters, were among many who regretted what turned out to be a typical pattern for BUF meetings. Irene wrote in her diary: 'Baba said his speech had been so fine, why descend to the Jerusalem inanity . . . finally he swaggered in [to Smith Square] like a silly schoolboy only proud of some silly scuffles and rows whilst marching home and glorying over his menials throwing two lads down the stairs at Farringdon Street and possibly injuring them and all this swagger and vanity to Mrs Bryan Guinness and Doris Castlerosse – muck muck muck. When he is such a magnificent orator, and if he had vision, he could have carried the entire hall with him without descending to those Blackshirt rows he seems to revel in, and none of his friends will tell him what a ludicrous figure he makes of himself.'

In more sober language, *The Times* described the procession through the streets, with fascists and opponents chanting at each other: 'Sir Oswald marched in the midst of about sixty or seventy of his supporters along Fleet Street, the Strand and Whitehall, to the headquarters of the British Union of Fascists at 1, Great George St, S.W. Of this party, all young men, many wore either grey or black shirts, without jackets, and nearly all were hatless. They roared patriotic songs and the rallying cries of their organization in turn, and behind them walked a smaller party of men and women roaring revolutionary songs and slogans.'

A slightly rowdy march of sixty-odd people yelling out 'Rule Britannia' and a 'smaller party' raucously chanting 'The Red Flag': it would hardly provoke much comment now. But Mosley was skilled at grabbing headlines, however small his movement at its inception, and those were explosive times. There was real fear about the prospect of crisis and collapse, with capitalism tottering and fascist movements gaining power on the Continent. The language on both sides was inflammatory, and one of the chants that alternated with 'The Red Flag' was:

> Hitler and Mosley, what are they for?
> Thuggery, buggery, hunger and war!

In its muddled but impassioned way, Irene's diary shows the conundrum all Mosley's former friends faced – with such talent, why did he have to behave like this? Could he not see how destructive it was? And why so much posturing and showing off? Over the next seven years, the meetings got bigger, the violence got worse and the stakes got higher, but the reports have a depressing predictability, and the comments of those who respected Mosley's abilities often (though usually in more sophisticated terms) echoed Irene's bewilderment.

Another set-to with protestors took place at Battersea Town Hall in December. Weapons were out: the communists' razors and broken milk-bottles met fascist rubber truncheons, according to some reports. The pattern was set from the start, and Irene was right to worry about it. She was right, too, to worry that his friends would find him 'ludicrous'. Descriptions of Mosley often brought out the comic-opera aspect of his political style; some found it sinister, but many others just found it preposterous. A year earlier, when Harold Nicolson was issuing Mosley with one of his many warnings , he argued that 'fascism is not suitable to England. In Italy there was a long history of secret societies. In Germany there was a long tradition of militarism. Neither had a sense of humour. In England anything on these lines is doomed to failure and ridicule.' Perhaps invoking 'ridicule' was a last-ditch attempt to dissuade Mosley: anyway, it is an appealing idea that Britain might have been saved from fascism by a sense of the ridiculous. But Mosley took himself utterly seriously, and mockery only increased his theatrical style. His model was Mussolini, whose strutting and posturing could not be ridiculed in Italy. In the autumn of 1932 he paid his second visit to the Italian dictator and, on the occasion of a fascist anniversary, he was accorded the compliment of standing on a podium to receive a march-past of troops, and all the ceremony due to a fellow fascist leader.

If Mosley really thought that British fascism should be essentially different from the German or Italian varieties, he was unwise in his choice of party anthems. Gone were the arty ideas about Sitwell or Walton: the rallying-cries of Mosley's faithful were a 'Marching Song' sung to the tune of the 'Horst Wessel Lied', that memorial hymn to the first Nazi 'martyr', and 'Onward Blackshirts', to the tune of Mussolini's anthem 'Giovinezza'. The words of the 'Marching Song' were:

> Comrades: the voices of the dead battalions
> Of those who fell that Britain might be great
> Join in our song, for they still march in spirit with us
> And urge us on to win the People's State!
>
> We're of their blood, and spirit of their spirit,
> Sprung from the soil for whose dear sake they bled;
> 'Gainst vested powers, Red front, and massed ranks of Reaction
> We lead the fight for freedom and for bread!
>
> The streets are still: the final struggle's ended;
> Flushed with the fight we proudly hail the dawn!
> See, over all the streets the Mosley banners waving –
> Triumphant standards of a race reborn!

These songs convey a shorthand version of Mosley's rhetoric, and the key-words that recur in it – soil, blood, patriot, hero, tradition, fight. 'Onward Blackshirts' ran:

> Hark! The sound of many voices
> Echoes through the vale of ages.
> Britain listens and rejoices
> Gazing on tradition's pages.
> Patriots: your cry is heeded!

Heroes: your death was not in vain!
We to your place have succeeded!
Britain shall be great again!

[*Chorus*] Onward Blackshirts! form your legions,
Keep the flag forever high.
For a free and greater Britain
Stand we fast to fight or die!

It is hard to believe that Diana, with her aesthetic sensibility and her friendships with some of the great ironic spirits of the time, could stomach this sort of thing. But where Mosley was concerned, there were to be no jokes.

Early in January 1933 she set up house on her own. Bryan had been away in Switzerland with the Redesdales over Christmas and the New Year, which eased the actual moment of separation, and their arrangements about children, money and staff had all been made. Diana was well organized. She moved into a house at 2 Eaton Square, a fashionable address and only a few minutes' walk from Mosley's Ebury Street flat. It was 'small' by her standards, but it had several storeys and a basement – space for servants and nurseries, if no room for entertaining on the scale she was used to. There was a shortage of tenants for such places during the slump years, and the landlords gave it to her for a token rent, and added a grant to do necessary repairs. She installed herself there with Jonathan and Desmond (aged two and one) and Nanny Higgs, as well as a nursery maid, her ladies' maid, a cook, a housemaid and a manservant – a very much reduced household, by comparison. Bryan gave her the furniture from Cheyne Walk, while he kept everything at Biddesden. Mosley gave her a car, which she garaged in the mews behind Eaton Square for nine shillings a week. So she established herself publicly as Mosley's mistress. She always claimed she did not expect to marry him; he was devoted to his wife and children, and to his political work: she would be there for him whenever he had time to spare.

Her friends told her she was mad, and predicted disaster. Her family was scandalized, and the three younger sisters were strictly forbidden by Muv and Farve to set foot in 'the Eatonry', as Diana's new house was dubbed. 'The whole of London' was savouring the scandal, and in her diary Cimmie's sister, Irene Ravensdale, nearly boils over with fury: 'My heart was in my boots over the hell incarnate beloved Cim is going through over Diana Guinness bitching her life wanting to bolt with Tom and marry him and the whole of London getting at me and Baba with the story he had gone with her and needless to say every Redesdale up in arms and Walter Guinness only wanting to "crash" him and this blithering cow-faced fool insanely ditheringly recklessly trying to ruin Cim's life for her 19-year-old crush on that vain insensate ass Tom.'

Diana always stuck to the same line about Cimmie. She and Mosley 'both seemed so much older than me, and so much more experienced. Kit had had so many affairs, and everyone knew – ten or twelve at least that everyone knew about – so I really didn't think she'd mind. What difference would it make?' She knew perfectly well that it made a good deal of difference: her actions had set her well beyond the usual run of Mosley's conquests. She claimed she never wanted to break up his family. But she had been ruthless with her own life; she was ruthless about Cimmie too.

Early in 1933 Cimmie became extremely upset about the situation with Diana, and from this time dates one of the best-known but least flattering stories about Mosley. He was at a dinner party where one of the fellow guests was Bob Boothby, always an admirer of Cimmie as well as close friend to Mosley, and Mosley asked Boothby if he would go round to Smith Square later that evening to comfort Cimmie, who was in great distress. Why? Because, explained Mosley, he had decided that she might mind less about Diana if she knew about the other women he had been to bed with since they had been married, so he had decided to tell her about all of them. '*All* of them?' Boothby asked in horror. 'Well,' replied Mosley, 'all except her step-mother and her sister.'

This story was told by Boothby, and it is true that Cimmie's sister, Baba Metcalfe, did have an affair with Mosley for several years after Cimmie died, though almost certainly it was only a flirtation before. This affair continued after Diana had made her commitment and left her husband, as she was well aware. Mosley, who had an unusual capacity for juggling the emotional elements of his life, now managed to divide himself between three women. His engagement diary for 6 January 1933 reads: 'Lunch Cim; Baba 4.15; Dine D.' He seemed to have worked out how to have his cake, eat it, and patent the recipe.

Despite Nancy's disapproving words of a few weeks earlier, she liked the Eatonry, where she had a room of her own and could escape finally from home. Diana claimed that Nanny also approved, because it was much nearer Hyde Park (the stamping ground of all self-respecting London nannies), though this was probably said tongue-in-cheek. 'Everyone else was cross,' Diana commented drily. 'However, having delivered a few lectures, they soon settled down . . .' Sure enough, the small dining room in Eaton Square (seating six at a pinch) was soon full of Diana's old friends.

Bryan sold the house in Cheyne Walk and moved into a flat in Swan

Court, where Tom Mitford also had a bachelor flat. He kept Biddesden until the end of his life. He behaved with generosity and kindness: he and Diana had an amicable arrangement about the little boys, who spent alternate fortnights with each parent; he provided handsomely for them all; and if he had hard words to say about Diana, he never said them in public. They remained in touch, and when the little boys were staying with Bryan, Diana would sometimes visit for lunch or tea. In later years they seldom met, but they corresponded until the end of Bryan's life. In 1936 Bryan married again, very happily, and with his second wife Elisabeth he had the large, close family he wanted – 'a much better wife for him than I was', Diana would say. Diana dealt with her lingering guilt about her treatment of Bryan by pointing out that, from her ruthless behaviour about one unsatisfactory marriage, two happy marriages had resulted – hers and Bryan's. But his close friends knew that losing Diana was for Bryan 'like having a limb amputated'. It was a private grief and a public humiliation that never completely healed.

Through the spring of 1933, the BUF expanded rapidly. Recruits came from all political quarters, and Mosley tried to appeal to left-wingers by stressing his radicalism, and to right-wingers by playing on the themes of ordered government and authority. But four of Mosley's most important henchmen who now joined the party were from outside the political sphere altogether: Ian Hope Dundas, who became his chief of staff; Alexander Raven Thomson, a rare and much-needed intellectual voice; A. K. Chesterton, a clever polemicist; and the soon to be notorious William Joyce (later 'Lord Haw-Haw'), whose oratorical brilliance equalled Mosley's own, although the content of his speeches, according to one historian of fascism, 'was often rabid nonsense'. Joyce was to prove an albatross for the BUF, because Mosley – who was no judge of character – could not see that over the next few years Joyce's lunatic anti-Semitic ravings would attract to the party every crazy misfit and bigot, those more interested in hatred and violence than any real political aim. Mosley went so far as to put Joyce in charge of the BUF's official organ, the *Blackshirt*, which began weekly publication in February 1933, thereby giving editorial voice to one of the maddest elements in his organization.

The question of anti-Semitism was not a central one at the start. That is, Mosley did not consider it to be so (in *The Greater Britain* he had made no mention at all of the Jewish question). At this point, neither he nor Diana had had any contact with the Nazis, and Mussolini, his model, had not yet become explicitly anti-Semitic. Even so, it was at least naïve of Mosley not to think more deeply about the issue, just as it was extremely unwise of him to entrust

William Joyce with editing *Blackshirt*. But Mosley assumed he could control the thinking of the BUF absolutely, and his initial line was that because of the empire, Britain was in any case multi-racial, and racial distinctions were inappropriate: 'racial and religious persecution are alien to the British character'. The editorial in *Blackshirt* of 1 April 1933 declared that anti-Semitism was forbidden within the BUF, and membership was open to all British subjects of whatever race or colour. But double standards were already operating: anyone who attacked the BUF was a fair target, and most of the attacks were from Jews or left-wingers. 'We do not attack Jews because they are Jews,' he said, 'we only attack them if we find them pursuing an anti-British policy.'

Extraordinary as it may be, Mosley was genuinely puzzled by growing Jewish hostility towards his movement – to the extent that he asked A. K. Chesterton to prepare a report for him on 'Jews in British Society', so that he could understand the problem. Such a degree of incomprehension is almost laughable, especially given Chesterton's 'later justified reputation of being one of the most rabid anti-Semites connected with British fascism', as historian Richard Thurlow described it. Diana was more vividly aware – if only with hindsight – that after Hitler's accession to power every anti-Semite in England flocked to the BUF, and the movement was bound to become anti-Semitic at its core. Yet for the moment, she claimed, anti-Semitism 'wasn't in our consciousness'. This did not mean there was none – far from it, she described a certain level of anti-Jewish feeling as 'normal' in Britain – but it meant that they had so far failed to grasp how central an issue it was. The leadership stance on anti-Semitism was to change before long.

The BUF's official creed was printed on the back of every membership card. Its aims were:

> To win power for Fascism and thereby establish in Great Britain the
>   Corporate State which shall ensure that –
> All shall serve the State and none the Faction;
> All shall work and thus enrich their country and themselves;
> Opportunity shall be open to all but privilege to none;
> Great position shall be conceded only to those of great talent;
> Reward shall be accorded only to service;
> Poverty shall be abolished by the power of modern science released
>   within the organized state;
> The barriers of class shall be destroyed and the energies of every citizen
>   devoted to the service of the British Nation which, by the efforts and

sacrifices of our forefathers, has existed gloriously for centuries
before this transient generation, and which by our exertions shall be
raised to its higher destiny – the Greater Britain of Fascism.

The references to abolition of class, poverty and privilege sound almost like a
left-wing revolutionary manifesto; what is missing, though, is any reference
to the power structure of this ideal state – i.e. the dictatorship.

Mosley organized his Blackshirts, or 'Defence Force', on paramilitary
lines. They now had a uniform, an insignia (a red flash within a circle on a
black background), a flag and two anthems, and they were encouraged to
think of themselves as an élite squad under the command of Eric Hamilton
Piercy, an inspector in the Special Constabulary of the police, and his
adjutant, Neil Francis-Hawkins, a former salesman of surgical instruments.
They drove about in armour-plated vans, and at early meetings they were
seen to be using knuckledusters and leaded hosepipes to deal with protestors
– although Mosley soon banned these. His instructions to the Defence Force
were that they were not to hit anyone unless they were hit first, and never to
harm a woman, but 'when the hecklers start . . . and the potatoes studded
with razor blades come sailing over, it is the steward's duty to stop the
disturbance'. The instructions end with a clever Mosley ploy, which resulted
more than once in fascists standing by with folded arms while police and
anti-fascists slugged it out: 'If the police come upon the scene, any disorder is
at once left to them. Fascists immediately drop their hands, even if they are in
the act of being struck, and leave retaliation to the police.' So, however the
scuffles began, it was rarely Mosley's men who were arrested.

In theory, Mosley always maintained a belief in public order, and spoke
up for orderly behaviour – his Blackshirts were never supposed to disrupt
anyone else's political meetings, for instance – although as well as the ousting
of hecklers at his own meetings, and an air of general intimidation, there was
some more serious, if unofficial, violence between rival fascist groups during
1933. Mosley had to work to quell the violent tendency in his ranks, trying
to give his movement a reputation for responsibility; in 1933 there were still
a number of middle- and upper-middle-class people and intellectuals who
dabbled with its ideas and went to occasional meetings, as if waiting to see
what the movement would become. On 24 February 1933 a debate between
Mosley and James Maxton of the Independent Labour Party, at the Friends'
House in the Euston Road, was a highlight of the new movement's
honeymoon period. Chaired by a beaming Lloyd George, who later
congratulated Mosley on 'a brilliant debate . . . an unflagging treat', it

attracted an audience that included many of the Mosleys' society friends: 'All Mayfair turned out to watch,' Irene Ravensdale recalled. 'Fascism,' Nicholas Mosley claimed, 'was still on the edge of being respectable.'

Respectable, too, was the dress code. Only stewards had worn the black shirt, up to now, but Mosley started to appear in one more often, prompting the *Evening Standard*, on 17 April, to call him 'one of the best dressed men and the worst dressed fascist in the world'. In Rome, it claimed, Italians averted their eyes from the black shirt swaddled inside his double-breasted Savile Row waistcoat, and his trousers, which were 'in elegant but startling contrast to their own breeches and leggings . . . The beautiful cut of his coat is ill-atuned to the violence of the fascist salute,' it concluded. That dichotomy again.

One eager recruit was Unity Mitford. She had to join the BUF in deadly secrecy from Lord and Lady Redesdale, to whom any mention of 'that man' Mosley was taboo. But Bobo could hardly wait. She was already in thrall to fascism, and at home at Swinbrook, in the upstairs sitting room she and Decca had commandeered for themselves, one side of the room was draped with pictures of Mussolini, swastikas and other Nazi regalia, and stacked with records of Nazi youth songs. Down the middle of the 'DFD' (the drawing-from-drawing room) was a barricade neither sister was allowed to cross: on the other side Decca's devotion to communism was equally strident, with a home-made hammer and sickle and a bust of Lenin, bought for a shilling, adorning her walls. Occasionally they would have pitched battles across the barricade of chairs, or sit mournfully discussing, as Decca said, 'what it would be like if one day one of us had to give the order for the other's execution'. Bobo gave the Nazi salute to family, friends, and the astonished postmistress in Swinbrook village, and drew swastikas in the visitors' books of houses in which she stayed for parties. It annoyed and shocked everyone greatly: a prime tease.

With Diana's defection and Mosley's new party, Bobo suddenly had a real-life outlet for her childish fantasies. She began to refer to Mosley as the Leader (so did Nancy, but that was with heavy irony). She begged to join the BUF, but Diana and Mosley were wary – Bobo's tactlessness was famous, and her enthusiasm could be embarrassing. Mosley had to be as discreet as possible about Diana, as far as his followers were concerned: not only did they love and respect Cimmie, but their leader must be thought a moral man beyond reproach. The Mitfords' sense of humour and idiosyncratic style were not appreciated by everyone. Now and for some time to come, he did his best to play down his Mitford connection.

Cimmie accompanied Mosley on his next visit to Italy, to Mussolini's International Fascist Exhibition at the end of April 1933. There was a good deal of ceremony. The Secretary of the Italian Fascist Party presented the BUF delegates with a black banner that had a Union Jack in one corner and a fasces symbol (a bundle of sticks and an axe) in the centre, and Mosley and his men stood to attention, holding this banner, during a march-past of fascist contingents. For the first time Cimmie seemed reconciled to fascism – because of the speed of its achievements – and she took a liking to Mussolini himself. Diana wrote, many years later, to Nicholas Mosley that his mother had become 'enthusiastic about fascism' in the winter of 1932, and came back from Italy that spring 'enormously impressed' – although Nicholas disputed this.

However, Cimmie had no time to consolidate her new-found enthusiasm. A few days after their return home, on 8 May, she was rushed to hospital with acute appendicitis and operated on that night. Weakened from two years of ill-health, she came through the operation badly and developed peritonitis, which in those pre-penicillin days was a severe danger. Seriously ill, she lay half unconscious for several days, with Mosley almost continuously at her bedside. After a week in which she failed to respond to any treatment, or even encouragement, she died.

Mosley was devastated. For all his philandering and lying, and despite his passion for Diana, he loved Cimmie deeply and was shattered by her death. He was also stricken with guilt: the evening before she was taken ill they had had a bad argument and he had stormed out of the house. He was not there when her attack occurred; it is not hard to guess where he had been. And the sense that he had hastened her death with his treatment of her – the doctors noticed that she seemed to have no will to fight her infection and live – was underlined by the harsh tongues of the gossips. Cimmie had been loved by everyone who knew her for her charm and sweetness of temperament, and considered far too tender a personality to deal with Mosley's cruelties and the public humiliation he inflicted on her. But now his grief was extreme. He planned a lavish tomb for her at Savehay Farm, and until it was ready her body lay in the chapel at the Astors' house at Cliveden, not far away. The tomb – practically a mausoleum – was designed by Sir Edwin Lutyens and built of pink marble. It stood in a clearing in a wooded part of the garden by the river; engraved on it was the inscription 'Cynthia Mosley, my beloved'.

For Diana, Cimmie's death was traumatic. Although it is tempting to think that the sad but natural death of her lover's wife might have been, to put it at its most callous, quite convenient, Diana was probably the person who knew better than anyone how Mosley felt about her. She realized straight away that Cimmie's death, with all its ramifications of guilt and grief and family concerns, might spell trouble for her relationship with Mosley, and she remembered the day as one of the worst of her life. Instead of making them freer to spend time with each other, that night Mosley paid a brief call to say that he wouldn't be able to see her again for some time. The family – that is, Cimmie's sisters Irene and Baba – closed ranks against the trouble-maker, repeating to Mosley that to continue to see Diana would be the worst insult to Cimmie's memory. While Irene devoted herself to keeping up a home for Cimmie's three children at Savehay Farm (the youngest, Mickey, was just a year old), Mosley's mother (usually known as 'Ma') announced to the women's section of the BUF that she would take Cimmie's place as their leader, and Baba concerned herself with filling Cimmie's role in more intimate ways. It was agreed that Baba and Mosley should spend the summer motoring through France together, while Irene took the children away on a cruise: Fruity Metcalfe, Baba's husband, was given a talking-to by Irene and told he must quell his jealousy and allow Baba to comfort Mosley, 'for Cimmie's sake'.

Diana had arranged terms for her divorce just a few days before Cimmie's sudden illness. Bryan, ever kind, did the gentlemanly thing, and set up fake evidence of an overnight rendez-vous in Brighton so that he, not she, would in law be the 'guilty party' in the proceedings, as was the convention in those days. (Evelyn Waugh, who had just been through a bitter divorce himself, describes this process with stinging irony in *A Handful of Dust*.) It looked as though both the lovers would soon be free, and it was surely a moment, once his mourning was over, for Mosley to make some sort of commitment to Diana. Instead, Mosley started playing some of the same games with his two women, Diana and Baba, as he had with Diana and Cimmie. He told Baba he was occasionally having dinner with Diana, 'platonically', because it would be unkind just to let her down flat; simultaneously, he got Diana to agree that it would be a good idea if he was known to be seeing a lot of Baba and going on holiday with her. That would quash some of the gossip about Diana; it would also be wise for them not to do anything that would impede her divorce, which would not be final until the end of the year. As before, Mosley was trying to have his cake and eat it, and he was succeeding pretty well.

In June there was something of a family truce among the Mitfords, and Diana paid her first weekend visit home to Swinbrook for many months. On 15 June she had to make a brief appearance in the witness box at her divorce proceedings, and the evening before there was a full display of sisterly solidarity, with Nancy, Pam and Unity all assembled at the Eatonry. Mosley arrived during the evening, as he still regularly did, despite the chorus of disapproval from Savehay Farm. He greeted Unity, to her delight, with a salute and 'Hello Fascist!' and gave her an insignia pin from his own coat. But Diana found him unsympathetic about the gravity of her divorce, and they quarrelled. There were more dramas before the evening was out: Hamish Erskine, to whom Nancy had been rather listlessly engaged for four years, telephoned to ask Diana to break to Nancy the news that he had finally decided he could not marry her. But Nancy took the call herself, and the letter she wrote Hamish that night shows there was an agonizing scene: only a month later, though, Nancy was engaged to Peter Rodd.

Prodd, as Peter Rodd was called, was extremely handsome, very clever and quite charming. He was also wild, unreliable, unfaithful and an excruciating bore. The Mitfords quickly nicknamed him the Tollgater, after his habit of holding forth on the ancient tollgate systems of England and Wales. He was the most inappropriate person for Nancy, with her mercurial mind, to be happy with, but Nancy longed to be married, and after their wedding in December 1933 she was loyal and supportive. One of the myriad anecdotes about Prodd sums him up. His father, Sir Rennell Rodd, a distinguished ambassador who had taken the title Lord Rennell of Rodd in the spring of 1933, had known Oscar Wilde when he was an undergraduate at Oxford. When Sir Rennell had produced the usual slim volume of poems, as a very young man, Wilde had written a preface to it that included calling Prodd's father 'my heart's brother'. By the 1930s this was not the sort of thing an eminent diplomat wanted to have tucked away in his past. So Prodd, whenever he was short of money, as he perpetually was, used to scour second-hand bookshops and obscure dealers to find copies of the embarrassing volume and sell them back to his father at a premium price.

After Cimmie's death, the work of the BUF went on. Grief-stricken and guilty, Mosley gave up almost all his London social life and applied himself to his political crusade with even more energy. In July he led a thousand Blackshirts on a lengthy route around London, with his mother at the head of the Women's Section, having massed at the start almost under Diana's windows in Eaton Square. This time Irene and Baba – whose enthusiasm for the BUF had already earnt her the nickname Baba Blackshirt from her society friends – were uncritical: since their new places in Mosley's life had become defined, they were fully fledged supporters. The event was more or less ignored by the anti-fascists and there was little trouble. Mosley gave a short speech from the top of a car on their return to headquarters, and the first sizeable BUF march concluded peacefully.

The women continued to fight over Mosley. Just before Cimmie's death Irene and Baba had been on bad terms (there are hints that they had quarrelled over Mosley even then) but they were now united, with Ma, in a concerted effort to keep him away from Diana. They even found Unity's presence in the party suspicious, and claimed she was trying to 'check up' on Mosley. Ma had always been possessive of him; with Cimmie dead, she had got him back. Baba was in love with him, and perhaps thought she might exchange her dull Fruity for the exotic Tom. Irene's feelings about him were vehement, and zigzagged between condemnation and praise, but in making herself a surrogate mother to Cimmie's children she had found a mission in life and a way of staying close to Mosley. Mosley himself played everyone off against each other. 'He had asked Ma,' Irene wrote, 'to tell Baba and me he never contemplated meeting Diana after his trip with Baba.' This was very far from what he had told Diana, but the trip with Baba went ahead none the less.

In the summer of 1933, therefore, Diana found herself alone, half-divorced, half-estranged from her family, execrated by much of London society, while the man for whom she had torn up her life went on a romantic holiday with another woman. She didn't know whether she had a future with Mosley or not. Her children were with their father. Unity was also at a loose end, and they decided to plan a holiday together, well away from the South of France or Venice or the other stamping-grounds of Diana's old circle. Unity was keen to go to Germany. A few weeks earlier, at the house of Mrs Richard Guinness (a distant cousin of Bryan's) Diana had been introduced to 'a very interesting German' named Putzi Hanfstaengl, a close comrade and passionate admirer of Hitler, and now his Foreign Press Secretary. Hanfstaengl held forth, that evening, about the wonders of the new Nazi state and its leader, and issued lavish invitations to one and all to come to Germany to see for themselves what lies were being told about Germany by the British press. Diana had often met drawing-room communists, but 'he was my first drawing-room Nazi'. She quizzed him about the Jews: his reply was one that Diana herself used ever afterwards – the Jews were 1 per cent of the population, but the press only ever talked about them; Hitler would build a wonderful new nation for the 99 per cent. Did they not deserve equal concern? If she came to Germany, Hanfstaengl promised, he would introduce her to this great man.

Diana decided, almost on the spur of the moment, that she and Unity should go to Germany. They arrived in Munich with very few words of German and without the address of Putzi Hanfstaengl, who had given them the impression that everyone in the whole of Germany would know where to find him; they managed to track him down, however, through the Brown House, the grand new Nazi Party headquarters on the Briennerstrasse. Hanfstaengl was delighted to hear from them and fulsomely welcoming: particularly pleased, he said, because the Parteitag in Nuremberg was to start the next day. Like a conjuror pulling rabbits out of a hat, he produced tickets, invitations and a hotel room for the whole four-day extravaganza. This was how Diana came to be a spectator at the first Nuremberg rally of the Nazi era.

15 Germany

The first time Diana remembers hearing the word Nazi was in 1931, two years after her marriage, when she and Bryan went to Berlin to see her brother Tom, who was studying law at the university. His excited talk brought home the realities of German politics, especially among the students, whose rowdy pranks and pitched battles – 'Sozis' against 'Nazis' – often tipped over into serious violence and even death. Tom believed that either the communists or the Nazis would come to power – and added: 'If I were a German I suppose I should be a Nazi.'

When Diana arrived in Germany in 1933 it seemed quite unlike the place she knew. Berlin – the Berlin of Sally Bowles later immortalized by Isherwood and Auden – was then on the European circuit. The rich English would come to sightsee, and hope to be scandalized, in Europe's most louche and flamboyant night-clubs. Diana and Bryan had been to Berlin for the first time soon after their marriage, in the spring of 1929, but Diana had found the notoriously naughty places 'not the least amusing; grim would have been a more appropriate word . . . At one of them there was a telephone on each table, but we could not see a soul worth ringing up.' The Mosleys had also been to Berlin, a few months earlier, with Ramsay Macdonald, when they were taken round the night-clubs by Harold Nicolson, who was stationed at the British Embassy. 'Cimmie and I had never seen anything like it . . .' wrote Mosley, an experienced hedonist. 'The sexes had simply changed clothes, make-up and habits of nature . . . scenes of decadence and depravity suggested a nation sunk so deep that it could never rise again. Yet within two or three years men in brown shirts were goose-stepping down these same streets round the Kurfurstendamm.' Nicholas Mosley, quoting these lines, comments that his father 'does not seem in this description to have been being ironic'. Nor does Mosley make it clear, Nicholas might have added, whether he saw the connection between the two phenomena – his son Alexander, however, believed his father saw the political changes as a healthy reaction.

In the two years since her last visit, Diana had become a different person, or at least a person in very different circumstances, and this was a new Germany. She had cast off a husband and given her life to a doubtful new lover, lost her Olympian social position and found fascism, given up the endless round of parties and chosen a more austere intellectual road. Germany had chosen Hitler and the Nazis, having elected him to power in January. This time, there were no night-clubs on the itinerary, but a sightseeing trip around Bavaria, the heartland of the Nazi movement, with Nigel Birch and Lord Hinchingbrooke.

Diana's interest in Germany had first been fired by Tom, an impassioned advocate of German music and German literature, and stoked by Prof. Lindemann. Her conversion to fascism fuelled her interest, and she was ready to be impressed. The sisters' host and guide, Ernst ('Putzi') Hanfstaengl, was a giant of a man with a bear-like head, a protruding jaw and a sardonic sense of humour. His father was a well-known Munich art dealer, but he spoke good English because his mother was American and he had been educated at Harvard; he was also a fine pianist – a level of cosmopolitan experience and education that was unusual among Nazis. He had been a friend of Hitler from the first days of the Nazi Party, and in the early 1920s he had tried to smarten Hitler up and make him presentable to Munich society: it was a losing battle. The Hanfstaengl family business brought in American dollars, and during the massive inflation of the early 1920s he was able to support the fledgling Nazi Party with quite modest amounts of foreign currency. He helped Hitler to take advantage of the situation and buy a newspaper, the *Volkische Beobachter*. After the disastrous *putsch* of 1923 when sixteen Nazis were shot dead near the Feldherrnhalle in Munich, Hitler was taken in by Putzi's wife and his sister Erna and hidden in the attic of the Hanfstaengls' house at Uffing, on the Staffelsee, thirty-five miles outside the town. Putzi himself, and several other Nazis, including Goering, escaped over the border to Austria, but the wounded Hitler was found by the police in the Uffing attic and led away to imprisonment in the Landsberg Fortress.

Such early comradeship conferred great status in the Nazi Party, to begin with, and Hanfstaengl had been rewarded for his loyalty with the job of Foreign Press Secretary. (He was one of very few senior Nazis who spoke English.) Even so, the position did not last long, for although Hanfstaengl worshipped Hitler, he detested almost all the other high-ranking Nazis, partly for snobbish reasons and partly because he knew they thought him rather absurd. 'Putzi was not ugly,' according to Jonathan Guinness, 'just supremely awkward-looking – an enormous puppet on slack strings.' He and Goebbels particularly disliked each other (Goebbels resented Hanf-staengl's influence over the foreign press), and Goebbels was a dangerous enemy to have. Putzi soon fell from favour and only saved his skin by fleeing the Fatherland in 1937. In 1933, however, he still wielded some influence, although not quite as much as he had claimed – the promised introduction to Hitler did not take place. But he was delighted to be able to usher two beautiful and well-born young Englishwomen into the first Parteitag after the Nazis' rise to power, the 'Party Day of Victory', and he showed them everything, took them to all the parades, kept up a stream of chatty hospitality and charmed them both.

The 1933 Parteitag was characterized not so much by the dazzling, drilled perfection of militaristic theatre – that came afterwards – but by jubilation and triumph. There were few foreigners, and no large groups of diplomats or the crowds of prestigious guests who attended later rallies at Nuremberg. But although Diana made it sound as if they were there almost by chance, and their trip had no connection with the BUF, in fact an official brochure published a few weeks after the rally has photographs of Unity, her black shirt under a tweed suit, together with William Joyce and Alexander Raven Thomson and two visiting French fascists. Diana was not part of a delegation, but she and Unity were not alone in taking the news home to Mosley. Like the others, Diana was deeply impressed: 'The Old Town [of Nuremberg] was a fantastic sight. Hundreds of thousands of men in party uniforms thronged the streets and there were flags in all the windows . . . I often went to the Nuremberg Parteitag in after years, but never again was the atmosphere comparable with this first one after Hitler came to power. It was a feat of improvised organization to bring such numbers of men from all over Germany and feed them and house them . . . Most of them lived in tents near the town. The gigantic parades went without a hitch. A feeling of excited triumph was in the air, and when Hitler appeared an almost electric shock passed through the multitude. In other years the whole thing had become an established political circus marvellously synchronized and with permanent installations to contain the million or so performers; in 1933 it was a thanksgiving by revolutionaries for the success of their revolution. They felt the black years since their defeat in the war were now over and they looked forward to a better life . . . By a strange chance . . . I witnessed this demonstration of hope in a nation that had known collective despair.'

She adds, with her characteristic understatement: 'We heard the speeches Hitler made, most of them very short, and we understood not a single word.'

Had she been able to understand, what she would have heard was the formal launch of Hitler's campaign for racial purity. It was hardly necessary, given the events of the year so far: the boycott of Jewish shops announced on 1 April, the book-burnings in May, and the *Arierparagraph* (the 'Aryan Clause') which banned Jews from employment in a wide range of professions, in June. But Hitler's two major speeches at Nuremberg, *Kultur und Rasse* and *Volk und Rasse*, were a doctrinal declaration which could have left no one in any doubt about Hitler's views, or his ultimate ambitions, on the subject of race.

Although Diana describes the power of the occasion, she hardly conveys its scale, or its self-conscious magnificence. True, the Parteitage, or Party Days, fairly small events which had been held sporadically through the 1920s, got progressively larger and grander until the last and mightiest in 1938, but even by 1933 certain rituals were established. The most hallowed was the quasi-religious 'Blood Banner' ceremony, in which Hitler passed through ranks of standard bearers consecrating each new flag by touching it with a piece of the tattered remains of a bullet-holed, bloodstained party banner that had been loyally held by a dying Nazi during the failed *putsch* of 1923. This rite was the Holy Communion of National Socialism, carried out with great drama and ceremony. As Diana watched in 1933, Hitler performed the Blood Banner blessing of more than 300 vast flags, and between 31 August and 3 September he took the salute of a million men and addressed 60,000 Hitler Youth.

The stage management of the 1933 rally was ambitious. Albert Speer, still a young architect, was given the task of set-dressing the event, and he constructed a 100-foot golden spread eagle on a timber framework to tower above the podium on the Zeppelin Field at Dutzendteich, a huge park southeast of the old city. The Nazis had held rallies there before, but now the site was designated as permanent base of the Parteitage; by 1935 Speer had built a stadium with a capacity of 200,000 on the field (even that was deemed too small after a couple of years), but in 1933 the event was held in the open air. As a propaganda centre Nuremberg was both a symbolic choice and a pragmatic one: it is Bavarian, and ancient (both deeply important to Hitler); it also stood at the junction of seven railway lines, and was therefore accessible to the hundreds of thousands who congregated for the rally.

The event was nothing if not theatrical. Speer worked on the visual effects with Leni Riefenstahl, a film-maker who was never a member of the Nazi Party, but who, like almost everyone else, did what she was told to do by Hitler. She was already well known in Germany as a film star, and had had equal success with the movies she had directed, often dramatic epics set in the Alps. Hitler ordered her to make a film of the event, to be called *Victory of Faith*. The hour-long documentary was believed lost for many years, but a copy has recently been rediscovered. It is not up to the standard of her extraordinary footage of the 1934 rally, *Triumph of the Will*, but served as a rehearsal for the later film. *Victory of Faith* was shown to Hitler and party dignitaries early in December 1933, and although it was never on general release, the London *Observer* managed to report on it: 'The film is one long apotheosis of the Caesar spirit, in which Herr Hitler plays the role of Caesar while the troops play the role of the slaves. It is certainly to be hoped that this film will be shown in all cinemas outside Germany, if one wishes to understand the intoxicating spirit which is moving Germany these days.'

We should be glad the film did not spread more of the 'intoxicating spirit', if the events it portrays affected other people as they did Diana and, more especially, Unity. Unity was smitten by her German initiation, swept away by what she understood of Nazism. It dominated her life from then onwards. And although neither sister understood Hitler's speeches at that first rally, both soon made up for lost time. Unity immediately started to nag her parents to let her go back to Munich to study German. Diana's feelings were also fervent, but much more intelligent. Her concern with German politics was all directed towards one aim and one interest, that of her Führer at home. She realized that to forge close links with the German high command could be very useful to him.

At first the Redesdales were furious with Diana (who was still in disgrace with her family over her divorce) for taking Unity to the Parteitag. 'I suppose you know without being told how absolutely horrified Muv and I were to think of you and Bobo accepting any form of hospitality from people we regard as a murderous gang of pests,' Farve wrote to her. 'That you should associate yourself with such people is a source of utter misery to both of us – but of course, beyond telling you this . . . we can do nothing. What we can do, and what we intend to do, is to try and keep Bobo out of it all.'

But the poor 'Birds' found it impossible to stand up to Unity's single-minded determination. They were even a little relieved by her enthusiasm for Germany. She had finished her second London season without any sense of direction; she was still a handful at home; at least she was now interested in something. Munich in those days was regarded as a sort of finishing-school, like Paris or Florence, only much more economical because of the inflation of the mark. Many of Bavaria's impoverished aristocrats took smart English girls as paying guests, and chaperoned them loosely; several girls of the Redesdales' acquaintance, such as Penelope Dudley Ward, were already staying there. Muv and Farve gave in, and agreed that Unity should go back to Munich the following year to lodge with a Baroness Laroche, who was used to a steady stream of English girls. They were all supposed to learn a little German, but Unity applied herself fanatically to learning the language so that she could speak to Hitler properly when she finally met him. From the spring of 1934, Unity spent most of her time in Germany, where she was often joined by Diana and Tom. It meant that Diana always had a reason to visit, and a companion while she was there: for the next few years it became a regular retreat for her, and later a place where she had a more pressing purpose as a go-between in negotiations for a plan that would secure funding for Mosley's political venture.

For the rest of 1933, Diana did a great deal of travelling. She had decided that it was more tactful to let things in England settle down, rather than go home and face whatever the situation was with Mosley.

On the political front, Mosley was busy: his organization had grown so fast that he had to move his Blackshirt headquarters twice – first to 12 Grosvenor Place, then to enormous premises on the King's Road in Chelsea, a barrack-like building that had been a teacher training college and which, the BUF claimed, could eventually accommodate 5,000 members. It was renamed the Black House, and as well as the officials' offices, 200 Blackshirts were soon installed there, living under military discipline. Like everything else about the BUF, it has been described in diametrically opposed terms. One inmate remembered it, in 1933, as 'filled with students eager to learn about this new, exciting crusade; its club rooms rang with the laughter and song of men who felt that the advent of Fascism had made life worth living again'; yet opponents dubbed it the 'Fascist Fort' and circulated dark rumours that its cellars were used for punishment purposes, while one Special Branch report mentions an incident at the Black House in which a man was badly wounded by a knife in the stomach during horseplay between inmates.

Recruitment soared, boosted by the support of Lord Rothermere's *Daily Mail*, which in January 1934 ran a headline 'Hurrah for the Blackshirts!' over an editorial which declared that the BUF was 'the organized effort of the younger generation to break this stranglehold which senile politicians have so long maintained on our public affairs'. Further articles – 'Give the Blackshirts a Helping Hand' and 'Blackshirts Will Stop War' – had a dramatic effect on enrolment, and centres and offices sprang up around the country. The BUF membership subscriptions were small (a shilling a month if employed, fourpence a month if unemployed), although recruits were required to buy their uniform black shirt for seven shillings and sixpence (an unemployed man on the dole had eighteen shillings a week). High unemployment helped recruitment, because even a menial job at the Black House might mean free accommodation and one or two pounds a week in pay. The other London staff were salaried, too, although regional organizers were still for the most part unpaid. After only ten months of life, the BUF had become a substantial operation. To give an accurate assessment of the numbers of people involved is difficult; as Robert Skidelsky says, 'much ink has been spilt over [this] vexed question . . . The conventional view is that fascism "peaked" in 1934 and thereafter went into a slow but steady decline.' Skidelsky's 'inspired guesses' point to an active membership in 1934 of about 10,000, with perhaps three times as many non-active members and supporters. A total membership of 40,000 would have made the BUF as large as the Communist Party at the time, but this was 'a peak scaled only very briefly with the help of a highly transitory push from Lord Rothermere', Skidelsky adds.

A large lease in central London, paid staff – where was all the money coming from? Mosley had put a good deal of his own money into his movement, but he had suffered financial losses himself and was in any case not rich enough to underwrite such a large operation. Left-wingers were convinced that fascism was funded by Big Business, and tried hard to uncover Mosley's supposed secret backers. Speculation focused on Lord Inchcape, the shipping magnate, Lord Nuffield (who had contributed handsomely to the New Party), Courtaulds, Alex Scrimgeour, a rich stockbroker and friend of William Joyce, among others, but their contributions, if any, are unknown. There are records of a gift from Lady Houston of £200,000, but such largesse was not typical: more common were lesser donations from small businesses and wealthy individuals – Bill Allen, Gordon-Canning, Sir Alliot Verdon Roe, for instance.

Until his death in 1980, Mosley insisted that he had never taken funds from abroad: his movement, he always claimed, was financed by British supporters only. This was not true. From 1933 Mussolini was passing funds to Mosley at the rate of about £60,000 a year (around £1.5 million in today's value). The money came by a circuitous route, so well camouflaged that even after the Second World War, when partial evidence of Mussolini's contributions was announced to the House of Commons by the Home Secretary of the time, Chuter Ede, Mosley could still deny it and challenge the authorities for proof. The money arrived intermittently, usually in monthly bundles of about £5,000, made up of various foreign currencies and remittances, and although Mosley often had the bulky envelopes in his hands, the funds never passed through any bank account of his. They were paid by supporters into a Swiss bank, then transferred into the account of 'an individual in this country', as the Home Office paper put it, and then into a secret account of the BUF. This 'individual' was almost certainly Bill Allen, whose advertising firm based in Northern Ireland had financial contacts and transactions in several European countries: it was a perfect shelter for Mosley's funds from Mussolini.

There is a further twist to this tale. The Italian Ambassador of the time, Count Dino Grandi, was the lynchpin of the Italian connection. He was the main conduit for funds, and in frequent touch with Mussolini about Mosley's progress; the correspondence between Grandi and the Duce, when it came to light after the war, finally established the source of the BUF money. Mosley visited Mussolini on 6 January 1934 to ask for increased funds, and Grandi's letter to the Italian leader confirms that Mosley left Italy on that occasion with £20,000 in used notes of different currencies. But Mosley and Count Grandi had something in common other than politics – for a time during the 1930s Grandi was in love with Baba Metcalfe, and whether or not they were lovers, their relationship was close. Mosley perhaps had an unromantic reason to stay close to Baba himself.

Other extraordinary intrigues surrounded Mosley at this time. One of the oddest is the story of a 'Baroness Marovna', a film actress named Mary Russell Taviner or Tavener, who used a number of other names. Mosley met her a month or so after Cimmie's death, at a film studio he was visiting with a view to making a film about fascism. Mosley was obviously interested in starting an affair with Mary Tavener; more than that, a very long letter she wrote to him in December 1933 refers to a discussion of marriage between them. However, it also tells us that his secretary rang to cancel their next dinner date, and that she had not heard from him since; but that she had received a number of abusive anonymous telephone calls and letters. Mary Tavener's letter is a bizarre document – rambling and ill-written, claiming bogus royal descent (but also mentioning that Mosley had told her he was descended from Cromwell), offering love to his motherless children and repeatedly urging him to stay away from 'that blonde lady of easy virtue who you mentioned was pursuing you' and who 'tried to break up your happy and ideal marriage with your lovely Cynthia'. 'This type of woman will stop at nothing to satisfy their urge to possess,' she tells him, and implores him not to marry her and 'bring endless scandal to your name by confirming the hysterical and fantastic stories that this pitiful creature has caused to be circulated about your alleged love for her prior to Cynthia's death'.

Mosley's ploy with this woman is obvious from the letter. He had talked to her about destiny and his capacity to hypnotize, spoken of marriage and another son, and told her that she must come to him, and soon, otherwise he might be compelled to marry Diana and forfeit 'a deep mutual love of Spirit and mind as well as body [that] can help to set the final seal of greatness on [his] destiny'. And so on. But after that he never returned her telephone calls, and (William Joyce claims) gave orders to his staff that she must not be allowed into the Black House, though she turned up at the door more than once. He never even received this particular letter, for reasons that became clear much later.

We know of this strange document because four years later, in 1937, Mary Tavener launched a lawsuit for slander against Mosley, on the grounds (as far as one can ascertain from a discreet press) of breach of promise and of displaying a 'lightly veiled' photograph of her which his associates dubbed his 'Mermaid' portrait. But the story becomes even more peculiar. By 1937 William Joyce and Mosley had had a serious falling-out, and Mosley had expelled the increasingly manic Joyce from the BUF. Joyce then wrote a lengthy and vitriolic letter to Mary Tavener, which gives a picture of some peculiar goings-on at the Black House in 1933. Mary's letter, it seems, was intercepted (as, Joyce claimed, much of Mosley's mail was – 'such sordid trifles were an everyday procedure in the Black House'). Not only was the small gold love-token Mary had sent Mosley removed from the envelope, but the letter itself was copied and gleefully distributed among 'the Kamaraden'. Joyce claimed it was even translated into French and Italian, so useful was it considered as 'a poisoned dagger for Tom's back'; Joyce had kept his own copy of it, presumably for the same reason. Joyce goes on to spell out to the unfortunate Mary Tavener that the letter never reached Mosley – partly because if it had, the theft of the golden trinket would have been discovered and caused trouble for the culprit, and partly because (this is Joyce's most outlandish claim) it was destroyed at the instigation of 'the Huntress' (Diana). Joyce wrote to Mary Tavener: 'Whilst recognizing the danger to Tom [Mosley], did you never anticipate that said Nymph's [Diana's] possession fixation, as you so aptly described it, might include espionage of the movements to her unsuspecting "target" and that she would *yet again inevitably* pay handsomely for "aid" in the removal of any possible rival. I, and others of my acquaintance, can and will be prepared to testify that the existence of your letter was not only made known to "The Huntress" but a reward was received as a token of gratitude for its interception.'

Joyce's letter rants on for pages, and if there were ever any doubts about the fact that he was insane, this document would dispel them. He is mad for revenge on Mosley, and on Diana, so his remarks about her should be completely disregarded. His hopes of destroying Mosley by helping Mary Tavener in her slander suit are obvious, and he admits them openly in one of his most unbalanced paragraphs: 'Since his craven betrayal of me and my associates, I hold said Tom as beneath contempt and harbour no desire to shield him from the results of his treachery and the gargantuan ego which has reduced him to the purblind, willing puppet of Political pimps, petty sneak thieves, Society strumpets, slimy tongued traitors and the vortex of sub-humanity which has formed his self-forging thrallring since the sad demise of his good angel the loved and respected Cynthia . . .'

This was the prose of a man who had been, until very recently, one of Mosley's closest lieutenants. Joyce did not get far with his destructive impulses, however; although there was a brief flurry of interest among the newspapers in 1937, the case was dismissed. What Joyce's letter does reveal, though, is the atmosphere at the Black House. Even allowing for his crazy exaggerations and inventions, some facts remain: this letter was intercepted, copied and circulated; its valuable contents were pocketed. The extent of the jealousies and intrigues that swirled around Mosley is probably fairly accurate, too: Joyce lists the names of 'Tom's Judas Chorus' – those who joined in this particular scam. (The deceptions began with the 'trusted friend' Mary had paid to deliver her letter to Mosley by hand, and ran almost throughout the organization. One member, apparently, was venting an undying grudge against Mosley because he had been the victim of one of the Leader's practical jokes: a castor-oil cocktail.) More than anything, it shows just how poor was Mosley's ability to select his deputies.

For the time being, Diana was a world away from unemployed men standing to attention at the Black House, or crumpled bundles of money stuffed into envelopes, or filched love-letters. If she knew of Mosley's repeated infidelities during this year, she decided to ignore them, but she may well have realized that Baba was not her only competition; she was probably wise to stay abroad so long. After her visit to Munich she went to Rome to spend a month with Gerald Berners, a recently acquired friend who had a beautiful house at 3 Foro Romano, looking on to the Forum, which became another of Diana's bolt-holes.

Lord Berners was a clever and eccentric painter and composer (he composed ballet music for Diaghilev and for Frederick Ashton), an aesthete and homosexual whose Palladian house at Faringdon, in Berkshire, was renowned for its extravagant visual style – complete with doves dyed pink, turquoise, saffron yellow and cerise fluttering around the lawns. Berners was older than Diana – he was fifty that year, she only twenty-three – and he appreciated her beauty and intelligence and love of fun. He was small, round and bald, with a little moustache, a long nose and a dapper manner. In one of his novels, *Far From the Madding War*, he describes himself as Lord Fitzcricket, the versatile arty peer: 'He was a stocky little man . . . now completely bald, and when he was annoyed he looked like a diabolical egg . . . he did a great many things with a certain facile talent. He was astute enough to realize that, in Anglo-Saxon countries, art is more highly appreciated if accompanied by a certain measure of eccentric publicity.'

He spent his substantial inherited wealth on art – he hung paintings by Corot, Matisse, Dalí and Tchelichev among the eighteenth-century portraits at Faringdon – and on making life into an art. Superb food and beautiful houses, gardens, music, pictures and elegant, clever people were his preoccupations. He enjoyed toys and tricks and surreal objects as much as more valuable *objets d'art*, and he loved visual jokes. On the splendid Palladian double staircase at Faringdon he hung a sign he had found saying 'Mangling Done Here'; on the wall opposite the local church another chance find, a sign that read 'Fire the Canon', showed his disapproval of the clergyman. He kept a selection of bizarre masks to put on when driving around the countryside: whether this caused other drivers to crash their cars in astonishment, he did not say. But he was unusual among the English in being genuinely interested in surrealism. He became a friend of Salvador Dalí, who once had Berners play to him on the Faringdon piano placed in a shallow pool in the garden with chocolate éclairs over the black notes, and in later years he would ask Penelope Betjeman to bring her white Arab stallion, Moti, into the Faringdon drawing room, purely in pursuit of the strange.

In Rome Berners worked all morning, then he and Diana would spend the rest of the day together. He was well connected in Italy, and could take her to the great houses and villas which she loved; he was hospitable and immensely knowledgeable, and his appetite for sightseeing and expeditions was limitless. As before, it suited Diana perfectly to be with an older man, a connoisseur and amusing guide who could show her the city he knew well. Like many beautiful women, she felt relaxed in the company of gay men. He was camp but never outlandish; they giggled together like schoolgirls.

Lord Berners is one of the seven subjects of Diana's book *Loved Ones*, pen portraits of friends published in 1985. The piece is as high-spirited and anecdotal as Berners' own style might have dictated, full of the semi-malicious, semi-fictional stories they loved to tell about their acquaintances.

One of the best concerns Lady Rodd, Prodd's mother, Nancy Mitford's mother-in-law. Berners had been a young attaché at the British Embassy in Rome before the First World War when Sir Rennell Rodd was Ambassador. Lady Rodd, a woman of peculiar tastes who never noticed when other people were making fun of her, was the butt of many jokes. The attachés, a selection of highly educated young men whose working life was hardly onerous, whiled away some of their abundant leisure by holding a competition to see which of them could design the most hideous house imaginable, one that betrayed the least taste and combined the greatest number of different architectural styles. When plans for the winning monstrosity were pinned up on a wall, Lady Rodd happened to catch sight of them and exclaimed: 'My dream house!' More astonishingly, she actually had the thing built, on a superb site at Posillipo overlooking the Bay of Naples. It was a house that, a year or so later, became the scene of a dramatic moment in Diana's battle over Mosley with Baba Metcalfe. It no longer exists, because it was blasted to rubble by the British Fleet during the Second World War – as Diana reports, 'rather a mercy'.

One of Berners' campest and most intricate fantasies was a book he published in 1935 entitled *The Girls of Radcliff Hall* (referring, of course, to the infamous lesbian author Radclyffe Hall). In Berners' book, a thinly disguised *roman à clef* which he had privately printed, Radcliff Hall is a school, he himself the headmistress, and the girls the flamboyant and beautiful gay men who fluttered around him: Cecil Beaton, Oliver Messel (the theatre designer for Diaghilev), his friends Robert Heber Percy, Robin Thomas and Peter Watson. These were the languid, highly cultured young creatures who surrounded Diana in Rome as well as at Faringdon House. Every morning of Diana's Roman visit the following year, Berners would read her the latest instalment of *Radcliff Hall*. Since she knew all the characters, she was greatly entertained – no one else would get much out of it. Berners in his turn appears as the worldly and fantastical Lord Merlin in Nancy Mitford's *The Pursuit of Love*: he and Nancy became friends later, during the war, when she stayed at Faringdon as she was writing the book.

This homosexual world suited Diana, as a refuge and a source of companionship and entertainment. Her beauty was admired, but she was not sought after sexually; she could form close emotional friendships without romantic complications. Loyalty, laughter, the pursuit of aesthetic pleasure, coupled with a slight wickedness – all these she could give and receive with gay men, away from the intensity of the relationship with Mosley and free of any rival entanglements.

From Rome, after that first visit of 1933, Diana and Berners and Desmond Parsons motored back to England at a leisurely pace through France, chauffeured in Gerald's 'lumbering Rolls Royce', stopping to visit places of interest and Max Beerbohm in Rapallo, as well as every three-star restaurant. Beerbohm and Berners had a curious enthusiasm in common: they both spent hours intricately doctoring photographs to transform them into something surreal or monstrous (a picture of George V, for instance, whose uniform would open to reveal a naked female body). Apart from everything else, Berners was an ideal companion for Diana because he was completely indifferent to politics. He accompanied Diana to Munich at least once, and he was embroiled in rowdy fighting at Mosley's fascist meeting at Olympia the next year – like many of their friends, he had gone along once in the spirit of curiosity. But it was true courage, as well as the wealthy individualist's disdain for popular opinion, that took him to visit Diana and Mosley in prison in later years.

It was typical of Diana that she should have switched in a few weeks from a simple inn in Nuremberg to the *grand luxe* of an old Roman house; and that because of her someone like Berners, the most private and fastidious of men, should get caught in a punch-up with a lot of louts at Olympia. She thrived on contrasts.

From 1933 onwards, Diana went to Germany regularly. Perhaps she considered it to be her power-base with Mosley, if the Italian connection was Baba's. Diana saw that the future in fascist terms might lie with Germany rather than Italy. Perhaps she had more sensitive political antennae than Mosley, who was introspective where Britain was concerned. She now set herself to learning German perfectly, to expanding her friendships among the Nazi élite, and to launching a plan on which Mosley's political future might depend.

16 A New Life

Whatever else had happened to Mosley during Diana's long absence, their reunion was sweet; his promise to Baba and Irene, that he would not see Diana again after the summer of 1933, was clearly meaningless. That winter they went on holiday alone together to Provence, staying in a small house near Grasse. Mosley's recurrent phlebitis was giving him trouble, perhaps because of overwork, and they lived simply. Diana went for long walks while Mosley read and worked on his speeches, they sat in the pale winter sun together by day and had supper in front of a log fire at night: it was a time of happiness. Irene and Baba's watch-dog activities had abated a little, and Diana managed to take this holiday without much interference; it did not mean, however, that Mosley's relationship with Baba was over, or that, although they were both legally free, there was any mention of marriage.

Back in London, their social worlds had changed. Many of Diana's friends had reappeared in the little dining room at the Eatonry, after a time of being angry with her for her ruthlessness to Bryan, and she knew the freedom of being beyond the tight confines of social respectability. For some time she had been friendly with Lady Castlerosse, a demi-mondaine who had managed to marry the racketty Viscount Castlerosse and who relied on rich protectors for her keep; Phyllis de Janzé (the model for the maid in the Biddesden window) was another friend for whom the contents of the latest package from Cartier were of pressing interest. It was not that Diana had started to keep louche company, but she was free to choose her friends as she liked, and she relied on them more than ever. The writer and critic Peter Quennell was a regular visitor, and one of several men who was at least a little in love with Diana; at this juncture another faithful friend – he came to lunch almost every Sunday, Diana said – was John Sutro, an amusing, pug-faced, exuberant and wealthy member of Evelyn Waugh's circle from Oxford days. Since Sutro was Jewish, he must have been unusually indifferent to politics, and to the growing anti-Semitism of Mosley's position. But Sutro always occupied a particular place in this circle which contained few Jewish people. In letters to Nancy Mitford Evelyn Waugh, for instance, used to discuss the 'extent' of the Jewishness of Jewish friends or famous figures, worrying at a question he never resolved in himself. 'How Jewish was Proust?' he once asked Nancy. 'I mean like [John] Sutro & [Edward] Jessel or like Brian Howard? Did he go to synagogue? If he was a real Jew it would surely be quite impossible for him to know the haute-bourgeoisie, though he might meet the looser aristocracy?'

Whether Waugh's tone was ironic is hard to tell. John Sutro was the 'real Jew' among his old and lasting friends, as among Diana's, but such was the abiding sense of difference that still, after a visit to Israel in 1951, Waugh could write admitting to 'a shade of anti-jew feeling' because in Israel he had 'realized that all Jews were not like John Sutro and Lord Roseberry'. Although Diana shared the same sense of deep differences between races and nationalities, and would unashamedly admit to racialism, she would put a personal friendship before all that. But her liking for an individual would not change her views about the mass.

New acquaintances joined the old. John Betjeman brought Lord Alfred Douglas to meet her, but although Betjeman treasured him as a 'minor Victorian monument', the notoriously beautiful boy who had proved the downfall of Oscar Wilde had become dull and fat, 'a self-centred bore' living off well-worn tales of 'O.W.' The German songwriter Kurt Weill was introduced by Edward James: he was not yet famous for his links with Brecht, but in Berlin Diana had heard Lotte Lenya sing the *Threepenny Opera* in her inimitable, gravelly voice, and was already interested in him, although their politics were diametrically opposed (Weill and Lenya, both Jewish, had already fled Germany). The previous year Nancy had written a story called 'The Old Ladies' (which was never published) based on herself and Diana, about two relics living in Eaton Square visited regularly by an old gentleman who wears 'a rather terrible curly, butter-coloured wig'. This was Mark Ogilvie-Grant, from nearby in Cliveden Place: the butter-coloured wig reappeared in countless family letters and diaries (often to the confusion of editors). In this story Nancy also took a pop at Mosley, when a character called the Little Leader pays a visit, and 'it was proof of the trust he had for the ladies that he came armed only with two revolvers, a bowie-knife and a bar of Ex-Lax the delicious chocolate laxative' [a reference to the methods of Mussolini's fascists, who were reputed to dose their prisoners with laxatives]. Diana could still tolerate Nancy's jokes about the Leader; later on, it would get more tricky.

Diana and Gerald Berners had a running joke about Violet Trefusis, the lesbian writer and daughter of Alice Keppel, mistress of King Edward VII. At

Faringdon Berners had a wind-up Walt Disney toy of a small fat pig which he would set whirring on the table and shout: 'Look! It's Violet!' Dining with her in Paris on their way back from Rome, they had somehow started a spoof that Berners and Violet (both, of course, homosexual) were engaged to each other; although it was a private joke, it leaked out to the London gossip columns and Berners decided to issue a denial by announcing in *The Times*: 'Lord Berners has left Lesbos for the Isle of Man.'

Since Cimmie's death, Mosley had given up most of the social round he had shared with her. His life was now divided between his work, travelling the country incessantly, speaking at meetings, as well as doing organizational work at headquarters; Savehay Farm at Denham, where his children were looked after by their Aunt Irene, their nanny and a staff of servants (and where Baba was often conveniently to be found); and Diana, who had to accept that she took third place. He was a prodigious worker: from 1933 to 1937 he made about 200 public speeches a year, travelling across Britain by car. Diana occasionally stayed with him at Denham, for a weekend or a few nights, and Nicholas Mosley recalls the furious disapproval of his nanny, who refused flatly to speak to 'that Mrs Guinness', and who told the eleven-year-old boy that if it had not been for Diana, his mother might not have died. They sometimes managed a few days away together in Paris or elsewhere, and Mosley would lunch and dine at the Eatonry if he was in London; otherwise their meetings were often short and impromptu.

On 22 April 1934 Mosley held his biggest rally to date, with an audience of 10,000 at the Albert Hall in London. There was an orchestra to play the 'Horst Wessel Lied' and 'Giovinezza', as well as a new song composed for the occasion ('Mosley: Leader of thousands! / Hope of our manhood, we proudly hail thee! / Raise we this song of allegiance / For we are sworn and shall not fail thee!'). A spotlit procession of standard bearers, carrying Union Jacks and fascist banners alternately, processed up the gangway towards the platform. Then, according to the *Manchester Guardian*, 'the spotlights swung back to the main entrance, and there stood the Man of Destiny . . . Slowly he paced across the hall, chest out, handsome head flung back, while his followers, every man on his feet, cheered and cried "Hail Mosley! Mosley! Mosley!"' He spoke for an hour and a half without notes, 'without a moment's hesitation and without a single flaw in the structure of the speech', one otherwise unsympathetic journalist reported. There were no interruptions, no violent incidents. He claimed his movement was neither racialist nor anti-Semitic. As usual, he started calmly, rationally, some said too technically. 'But the flow of fact and argument', as Nicholas Mosley describes it, 'gave an impression of great control and authority. And then there would be a change; he would stand back from the microphone as if he were a boxer sizing up an opponent before a knock-out attack . . . [Then] my father's voice comes lashing out like some great sea: it is pulverizing: it is also, from a human being, like something carried far away beyond sense. It sends shivers up and down the spine – of both wonder and alarm – what is it all for, this yell for immolation? People at the end of such a speech of my father's were on their feet and cheering; it was as if they had been lifted high on a wave; what did it matter if they were hurled against, or over the top of, a cliff?'

Diana was as impressed by his oratory as everyone else. She kept rather quiet about her attendance at these meetings, for although she often went, it was with discretion, and reports rarely mention her. She began increasingly to see herself as his refuge from the political arena, since she could not be at his side, and this entirely suited her natural inclinations. She hated platforms ('I'd rather die than give a speech,' she used to say) and never had any desire to follow Cimmie's example and move into active politics.

In May 1934 there was a large Blackshirt dinner held at the Savoy: the *Tatler* ran photographs of Mosley, Ma, Irene and Fruity Metcalfe in full evening dress, looking relaxed but carefully well-behaved; Diana was nowhere to be seen. It was part of Mosley's attempt, in that year when fascism 'was on the edge of respectability', to move his recruiting drive upmarket. Groups were set up within the Civil Service, in universities at London and Birmingham, in a few public schools – Stowe and Winchester among them – and there were strong links with the Royal Air Force, partly due to Mosley's background as an airman. There was even a fascist flying club in Gloucestershire in 1934.

In this buoyant phase of the BUF's fortunes, support began to come from surprising quarters, but it is also noticeable that even in its 'respectable' moment fascism never attracted intellectuals in the same way that communism did. Wyndham Lewis used to rush in and out of the Black House, his hat pulled down and his coat collar up around his ears; Ezra Pound wrote an impenetrable pamphlet for the BUF entitled *What is Money For?* The writer Henry Williamson, countryside romantic and author of *Tarka the Otter*, followed Mosley's ideals of peace, convinced that 'usurial moneyed interests' not only caused war but were destroying the British countryside. He tried to get his friend T. E. Lawrence, also a political romantic (or political innocent), to join Mosley, but Lawrence died before he had a chance to commit himself.

George Bernard Shaw had been interested in Mosley since the latter's Labour days, and in a lecture to the Fabian Society, the heartland of correct-thinking Labour, he seemed to taunt them with Mosley's dynamism. He was, Shaw said, 'one of the few people who is thinking and writing about real things and not about figments and phrases. I know you dislike him, because he looks like a man who has some physical courage and is going to do something and that is a terrible thing . . . you instinctively hate him because you do not know where he will land you, and he evidently means to uproot some of you.' Mosley was delighted by Shaw's interest, because he saw himself precisely as a Shavian hero, living out the dilemma of some of the plays: the man of action and ideas confronting the inertia of habit and accepted ideology – especially the dithering National Government headed by the decrepit Ramsay Macdonald.

Although a vigorous leader might have appealed to some radical spirits under such a government, Home Office papers show that there was very little sign of support for Mosley within Parliament, even at the peak of the BUF's growth in 1934. Although Lloyd George described him as 'a very interesting man', Baldwin stuck to his view that Mosley was 'a cad and a wrong 'un'. The Special Branch, who had been making regular reports on the BUF's activities for more than a year, were particularly interested in contacts with the armed services, and therefore in the January Club, a dining club Mosley formed aimed at influencing businessmen and ex-officers. Here, in a convivial after-dinner atmosphere, the fascist word would be spread by Mosley and Robert Forgan, helped by the club's leading spirits – Major Yeats Brown of the Bengal Lancers, Sir Donald Makgill and Captain Luttman Johnson, for example, all BUF supporters if not actually members. As many as 350 people attended some of these functions, people of a very different stamp from the unemployed men who became the foot soldiers at the Black House.

With the growth of the movement, popular opposition grew in strength and energy. Gone were the days when a few dozen anti-fascists trailed behind marches shouting slogans. In May 1934 John Beckett, a Mosley recruit who had formerly been Labour MP for Gateshead, returned there on a speaking tour, and was met by cries of 'traitor' from 3,000 anti-fascists; 5,000 greeted him in Newcastle-upon-Tyne. A. K. Chesterton, then the Midlands organizer, had to abandon a meeting in the same month because of a hostile crowd of several thousands. But the turning point came in June. On 7 June Mosley planned a huge rally at Olympia – the only London venue larger than the Albert Hall – complete with displays of marching men, banners, spotlights, and full militaristic paraphernalia. But because the April event had been a public relations success – the message had been heard, and the rally had passed off without any violent incidents – there was a concerted plan by the Left to make sure that did not happen again at Olympia. The *Daily Worker* published in advance directions for anti-fascist marches and for a full counter-demonstration; on the day itself a map showed the route to Olympia with the rallying-cry: 'the challenge of Mosley will be met by the determined workers . . . All roads lead to Olympia tonight!'

There were 2,000 Blackshirts, of whom half were stewards, lined up to guard the platform and positioned throughout the auditorium and the crowd of 12,000. There was no difficulty about getting into the hall – 2,000 tickets were even given away free on the day – but outside were another 2,000 or so anti-fascist protestors, kept just about under control by 500 policemen, on foot and on horseback. It was the culmination of Mosley's campaign to date, and thanks to the enormous publicity the crowd was mixed. Not only supporters and BUF members, communists and anti-fascists waiting for their moment, but also, for the first time, quite a number of the professionals and intelligentsia Mosley was so eager to reach. When the comments and descriptions began to flood in afterwards, the audience turned out to have contained liberals such as Storm Jameson, Aldous Huxley, Naomi Mitchison, Julian Symonds, Ritchie Calder, A. J. Cummins, Vera Brittain and Claud Cockburn; a number of MPs of different parties; journalists and editors; as well as uncommitted individuals who were curious about the rapidly growing new party.

At last Mosley had managed to attract some of the establishment audience he wanted, but they did not like what they saw. The Olympia rally of 1934 was an epic punch-up, the kind of blood-letting that lives in the legends of both sides. For years afterwards, fascists gloried in the beating they gave the Reds, while the communists wore their wounds with pride and basked in the claim that they had shown up the fascist menace in its true colours. The press had made them ready for each other. The Communist Party had organized four marches to Olympia, the biggest from Stepney, which had a large Jewish population. The *Daily Worker* had been openly advocating the use of force and of weapons. The writer Philip Toynbee, out from his public school for the day, went with his friend Esmond Romilly (the Mitfords' cousin and later Decca's first husband) to buy knuckledusters in an ironmonger's in Drury Lane.

'The largest indoor meeting ever held under one roof in Britain' started almost an hour late, because of the crush of protestors outside and the difficulty of getting the audience seated. As usual, a warm-up band played popular music, until finally the Leader marched into the spotlights in a column of fifty-six Blackshirts carrying banners, to the strains of the National Anthem. Philip Toynbee described the scene in his book *Friends Apart*: 'The procession moved very slowly down the aisle, amid shouts, screams and bellows of admiration; amid two forests of phallic, upraised arms.' Mosley reached the podium, he began to speak, and the heckling broke out. Their plan was to shout him down, whatever the cost. Mosley took his usual stance: he warned that if they did not stop, the stewards would eject them. They had no intention of stopping, and they were strategically spaced out in the hall so that as the Blackshirts moved to deal with one group, another would start. Two protestors climbed into the girders in the roof, pursued by stewards. When Mosley could no longer be heard, he simply stood still and waited, arms folded, while the searchlights played across the milling violence in the audience below him.

The anti-fascists did not merely want to stop the meeting; they wanted to make the fascists appear as brutal and thuggish as possible. They succeeded, at some physical cost to themselves, and those in the audience who preferred to fight with words took up the battle after that. As the clamour rose over the next few days, in the press, on the radio and in Parliament, there were lurid descriptions of what took place. Police reports described people ejected from the building 'in a state of semi-collapse', with tattered clothes and blood streaming down their bruised faces. Several were minus their trousers (a Blackshirt tactic was to cut the belt or braces of the opponent, so that his hands would be diverted into holding up his clothes). There were in fact few reports of weapons; many of group beatings. Geoffrey Lloyd MP reported, 'again and again as five or six fascists carried out an interrupter by arms and legs several other fascists were engaged in hitting and kicking his helpless body'; Gerald Barry, editor of the *News Chronicle*, had seen single hecklers 'being struck on the head, in the stomach, and all over the body with a complete absence of restraint'. In the corridors, he saw 'a man lying on the floor . . . being mercilessly kicked and horribly handled by a group of . . . Blackshirts'; the Reverend Dick Sheppard witnessed one 'being chased by a horde of Blackshirts: some collared him by the legs, some by the arms, and held in this way he was beaten on the head by any fascist who could get near him'.

The Times of the next morning carried a letter protesting at 'a deplorable outrage on public order'. It began: 'We were involuntary witnesses of wholly unnecessary violence inflicted by uniformed Blackshirts on interrupters. Men and women were knocked down and were still assaulted and kicked on the floor.' It was signed by three Conservative MPs – J. Scrymgeour-Wedderburn, T. J. O'Connor and W. J. Anstruther-Gray – who had left before the meeting ended and raced to Printing House Square to catch the presses for the early morning edition. It was the opening round in a rumpus that reached as far as the cabinet, where the Home Secretary, Sir John Gilmour, was put under pressure on the subject of police inside the meeting hall (Mosley had declined to have them there, and it was within his right to do so).

The fascists may have broken more heads than their opponents (though many fascists were wounded too), but they had lost the public relations battle for good. The reverberations of Olympia were catastrophic for Mosley. Because so many of the anti-fascists at Olympia were Jewish, Mosley's attitude towards the Jews hardened considerably, on the grounds that they were organising attacks on him. This only made things worse. True, there was a short burst of increased recruitment, but it was of the worst possible sort – virulent anti-Semites and those attracted by the smell of violence – while Mosley had for ever lost his chance with the more moderate public. Lord Rothermere withdrew his support – Mosley claimed that it was under pressure from Jewish advertisers. The rest of the press boycotted Mosley and his ideas from now onwards, and Mosley's appearance on the BBC on the day after the Olympia rally was his last for more than thirty years, until the ban on him was lifted in 1968. Public opinion against Mosley hardened still further when, only three weeks later, the sinister news came from Germany of the 'Night of the Long Knives', the cold-blooded murder by Hitler's SS of dozens of his oldest comrades. Whatever slight chance Mosley had ever had of becoming a major force in British politics seemed already to be gone.

Diana's memoirs are defensive about the whole Olympia episode. She always reiterated the same simple claim: that Mosley had never set out to attack Jews; Jews had attacked Mosley repeatedly and fiercely, until he was forced to respond. She missed the meeting, although she had intended to go with several friends, because she had a temperature and felt ill. 'I have always regretted this,' she said; such was the controversy about Olympia, 'I wish I had seen it for myself.' But she argued that the tales of violence were exaggerated: 'If half their stories had been true, the hall would have been strewn with dead and dying and the hospitals full of casualties.' [It is true that though many were treated for cuts and bruises only one person, a fascist, spent the night in hospital.] 'As it was they gave themselves a bad fright, and subsequent meetings were quieter.'

As always with reactions to Mosley, the views were as unpredictable as they were extreme. Readers of the Labour paper the *Daily Herald* must have been surprised to find its former editor, Hamilton Fyfe, proclaiming 'how unwise – and even unfair – it was to organize interruption at the Olympia meeting', while Lloyd George, perhaps nostalgic for his own rough-and-tumble days on the hustings, wrote in the *Sunday Pictorial*: 'It is difficult to explain why the fury of the champions of free speech should be concentrated so exclusively, not on those who . . . attempted to prevent the public expression of feelings of which they disapproved, but against those who fought, however roughly, for freedom of speech.' And in a private letter to Mosley he sounds almost wistful: 'You are having a very exciting time and I envy you your experience. At your age I went through a period of riot and tumult in my endeavour to convey my ideas to a resentful public.' Lloyd George was perhaps looking back to a time when rowdiness on this scale was commonplace at political meetings – throughout the eighteenth and nineteenth centuries, and into the early twentieth – but by the 1930s it had become shocking to more educated witnesses.

Diana was never repelled by violence. She believed that at Mosley's meetings the trouble was all that was ever reported, and always out of proportion. In the interests of balance, she wrote her own account of a meeting at the Carfax Rooms in Oxford two years later, another event that became notorious – possibly because of the personalities who were there.

'The hall was full,' she wrote, 'in the front sat some youngish dons. I recognized Frank Pakenham [later Lord Longford] and Richard Crossman [later a Labour minister in Harold Wilson's administration], and some undergraduates. At the back were rougher looking men. When M[osley] began to speak the undergraduates opened large newspapers and pretended to read them. At first M. paid no attention to this absurdity . . . [then] he said, "I am glad to see the young gentlemen are studying, I believe they are very backward in their lessons this year", a mild sarcasm which was the signal for all the undergraduates and their rougher allies in the rows behind to jump up and start shouting. After the customary three warnings from M., to 'give order or leave the hall', our stewards began putting the noisy men out. Crossman leapt at the platform and was immediately seized and chucked out. The iron chairs were freely used as weapons against the stewards and there was a great noise and pandemonium. I flattened myself against the wall in order to keep as far as possible from the assailants. Within twenty minutes calm was restored, all the trouble-makers had been put out into the street, and M. resumed his speech. A large and peaceful audience listened to his economic policy for an hour, and then put questions to him for almost another hour. This was a typical "violent" meeting. It was always a surprise to see how few in numbers the noisy interrupters had been – a couple of dozen in an audience of several hundred on this occasion. Needless to say the fight . . . was all that was reported in the newspapers. The peaceful meeting which followed was not mentioned, nor, obviously, the points made by M. in his speech.'

Unity had missed the events at Olympia because she was already back in Munich, *en pension* with the Baroness Laroche. ('Do write and tell whether you think Olympia was a success?' ran her letter to Diana. 'The accounts in the German papers are marvellous.') Diana was making plans to join her in Munich in the autumn. Diana's enthusiasm for Germany was not dimmed by reports of the Night of the Long Knives, and Hitler's premeditated killing of his old friend Roehm and many dozens of his men in the SA. Unity was at her most childlike in her letter of 1 July to Diana: 'I am so terribly sorry for the Führer – you know Roehm was his oldest friend and comrade, the only one that called him "*du*" in public . . . It must have been so terrible for Hitler when he arrested Roehm himself and tore off his decorations. Then he went to arrest Heines and found him in bed with a boy. Did that get into the English papers? *Poor* Hitler.' Diana would never have taken such a sentimental line: her own memoir of Hitler makes no comment on the incident.

Before her next German trip, however, she had to negotiate the tricky hurdle of the summer holidays. Cimmie's sisters were urging Mosley to continue the family custom of spending a month in the South of France with the children. Irene, Baba and Ma found him a house to rent near Toulon, perhaps thinking they would all be included in the holiday plans. Instead, Mosley solved the problem of his complicated romantic life by asking Diana to join him and the two older children for the first fortnight of the holiday, while Baba was to come for the second. He was nothing if not forthright, and both women agreed. Nicholas remembers a white house with a huge terrace above a rocky sea, his father striding up and down 'contemplating the eternal verities (*joke*)' or teaching Nicky to shoot with an automatic pistol by chucking empty wine bottles into the sea. Diana was practised at living for the moment, and when she could be with Mosley she was happy – they seldom quarrelled, and she knew better than to nag him about the situation with Baba. Nicholas remembers them 'always laughing'.

She was not one to mope on her own, and as Baba took her place in France Diana flew to Rome, en route to staying with Edward James in the

Villa Cimbrone at Ravello, which he rented each summer. She travelled, as ever, with her maid, and on this occasion she was glad to have someone with her, for Edward James was late for his own party at Cimbrone and did not turn up for several days. Finally, though, the guests assembled in the famous villa, whose terrace stretches along the cliffs high above the Gulf of Salerno: among them Oliver Messel, Syrie Maugham (a well-known interior decorator) and – to Diana's delight – Henri Sauguet, composer of the Diaghilev ballet *Les Forains*. She found Sauguet exactly to her liking: witty, well-informed and a brilliant mimic. Edward James was recovering from a messy and much publicized divorce from Tilly Losch, after a humiliatingly brief marriage, but he was in good spirits and took his guests sightseeing in his large open car, spinning them round the terrifying hairpin bends of the Amalfi Drive and entertaining them with a stream of chatter.

There was more travel that autumn. Diana's next stop was Munich, to see Unity and to go to the Nuremberg Parteitag with her. Unity had been installed since the spring at Baroness Laroche's at 121 Königinstrasse, a long road that runs along the edge of the Englische Garten, where she and half a dozen other English girls led an undemanding life: German lessons with Fräulein Baum, a few classes in piano, singing and painting, walks in the Englische Garten, trips to the opera, bicycling out to nearby lakes for picnics, coffee and cakes with friends in cafés, parties and dances partnered by suitable young men. Unity added an extra dimension to her days, however. Apart from studying German with determination, she had discovered from Fräulein Baum, herself a passionate Nazi supporter, where Hitler had lunch whenever he was in Munich.

It was a local restaurant called the Osteria Bavaria. On the corner of two residential streets in Schelling, not far from the Brown House, the place was small and cosy, the haunt of artists of an old-fashioned sort, with dark panelled walls and high-backed wooden settles around the tables. It still exists, now called the Osteria Italia, and a comparison with Albert Speer's account of the place in 1933 shows that it is largely unchanged. To the right of the entrance there is a partition, behind which stands a secluded table for eight or ten; around the sides of the alcove are benches against the wall where Hitler's SS guard could sit. This was Hitler's winter lunching-place, while in summer he would move his party into the small, high-walled courtyard at the back of the restaurant, where there was room for a single table beside a solitary tree. Once Unity discovered the Osteria Bavaria, she would sit there day after day, waiting for Hitler to come in, waiting to be noticed. She was adept at discovering when he was in Munich – by reading the papers, chatting to the sentries outside the Brown House, checking to see whether there were policemen outside his flat in the Prinzregentenplatz, or by asking the one or two young SS adjutants who were her occasional boyfriends. Hitler's usual lunching companions formed a relaxed but influential group that included his political allies and friends – his architect Albert Speer, Heinrich Hoffmann (the photographer), Adolf Wagner (the Gauleiter of Munich), Martin Bormann, Hitler's adjutant Julius Schaub, Dr Theodor Morell and Otto Dietrich – and a few guests like Jakob Werlin of Mercedes Benz or Frau Troost, the wife of another architect. Unity's dream was to be invited to join his table. He was often there on Fridays, on his way to the Obersalzburg for the weekend, and, since he was in the habit of lunching late, Unity's vigil (usually with one of her English friends from Baroness Laroche's) would begin at half-past one or two o'clock and last for several hours. She was never daunted.

This year, even though she and Diana had a letter of recommendation from Otto von Bismarck at the German Embassy in London, Putzi Hanfstaengl was much less helpful about the Parteitag. Perhaps his influence was already on the wane, but he claimed he had no tickets for the event, and he flatly declined to introduce them to Hitler. He told Unity he was embarrassed by their make-up. The highly painted look in fashion in England was a vexed issue, since Hitler was reputed to hate lipstick, and the women of his new era in Germany were supposed to look shiny and well-scrubbed. Hanfstaengl wrote in his book *The Missing Years*: 'They were very attractive, but made up to the eyebrows in a manner which conflicted directly with the newly proclaimed Nazi ideal of German womanhood . . . Goering and Goebbels expressed mock horror at the idea of my trying to present such painted hussies to Hitler.'

Hitler's aversion to lipstick – he liked to claim it was made of animal fats extracted from sewage – was part of a personal fastidiousness that extended to food (he was a firm vegetarian), to a dislike of coffee, tea and alcohol, and a distaste for the smell of cigarettes. Traudl Junge, one of his personal secretaries, remembered lunch-parties at the Berghof when Hitler would regale meat-eating guests with detailed accounts of slaughter-house practices. (When Frau Junge came to marry one of Himmler's staff, she discovered that the Nazi ideal of womanhood extended to a special questionnaire for SS wives that included items like 'Does the wife-to-be enjoy housework?' She protested to Hitler, who laughed. But she completed the form all the same.) Eva Braun stuck to her make-up, however, and so did many of the wives of the senior staff, just as Hitler's guests ate meat around him. Diana and Unity stood firm on the make-up whenever they were in Germany, too, although they were sometimes booed and shouted at in the street.

Undaunted by Hanfstaengl's lack of help, they went off to Nuremberg in 1934 without tickets or anywhere to stay. It was unwise. Hundreds of thousands had congregated in the small town; every street was jammed, every café and hotel packed. There appeared to be no hope of accommodation, and after a weary search Diana urged Bobo to give up and take the train back to Munich. Unity would not budge: she would sit and wait all night, what did it matter? Somehow her fanatical desire to see the parades and hear the Führer speak forced their luck, and just as Diana was on the point of desperation they were rescued by an old party member who found them tickets and a room in a small inn.

Since the previous year, the Parteitag had grown in size (about 700,000 people congregated for this one), in scope (it was extended to a week) and in splendour. Hitler, with his intuitive grasp of mass persuasion and his love of cinema, had begun discussions with Leni Riefenstahl about a bigger and better film of the 1934 rally immediately after the previous one had ended. Her distaste for another propaganda film was considerable, and she had already had angry fights with the jealous Goebbels, but Hitler overrode all the objections of his senior staff. Wriggle as she might, he was not going to let her off the hook. It was not only the film Hitler wanted, but the full catalogue of cinematic tricks applied to the real event. He was not disappointed.

Once again, she worked with Albert Speer, who surpassed his efforts of year before. As well as torchlit processions, he produced for this rally his 'cathedral of light', a technique he had pioneered a few months earlier for a meeting in May. He had seen the Luftwaffe's anti-aircraft searchlights blazing miles into the sky, and to Goering's great annoyance he asked Hitler to let him borrow 130 of these. (It was almost the whole strategic reserve, but the idea pleased Hitler; using so many would make everyone think they had hundreds more, he said.) Speer shone the searchlight beams high into the sky, perpetually moving, crisscrossing and reforming 25,000 feet over the heads of the marching ranks, forming an immense shining 'ceiling' that gave a breathtaking stage-set for even the most tedious parades. (In fact, Speer had come up with the idea as camouflage for the least cinematically impressive part of the rally: the procession of the *Amtswalter*, the minor party officials, whose tubby paunches and bald pates had looked so ridiculous in the 1933 film that he decided to have them march in darkness, with spotlights on their banners.)

Speer thought his 'luminescent architecture' his most beautiful creation. 'The feeling was of a vast room,' he said, 'with the beams serving as mighty pillars of infinitely high outer walls. Now and then a cloud moved through this wreath of lights, bringing an element of surrealistic surprise.' It gave a dramatic setting to Riefenstahl's huge undertaking, and *Triumph of the Will* has provoked as much praise and as much controversy as any film in the history of cinema. 'It is almost impossible to approach it unemotionally,' wrote her biographer Audrey Salkeld; 'we cannot divorce it from the horrors we know happened afterwards. And the fact that it is intrinsically an emotional production, engineered to work on the feelings and senses, makes it almost as hard to argue for a rational assessment as to obtain one.'

The film is a visual extravaganza, mixing beauty and menace into a single theme: the conquest of hundreds of thousands by the will of one man, the subjugation of the mass into a single, mesmerized unit. It opens with shots of Hitler descending from the skies above Nuremberg like some Messiah, his plane nosing through banks of cloud. As the 'Horst Wessel Lied' begins, the aeroplane's shadow passes over the marching columns below. There are abstract patterns of massed humanity, banners jostling like a field of poppies, the Führer meeting the ecstatic Volk, torchlit parades pouring down the narrow streets of the old town like molten lava, jolly scenes like a village fête, all dirndls, lederhosen and concertina music, cut into sinister details of SS men interlocking their hands on each others' belts to form a human chain; because of the power of these images Leni Riefenstahl has been accused of 'inventing' the Nuremberg rallies. That is clearly not true – they began before she was involved, and continued after – but she packaged them in celluloid for new-minted fanatics, and for all time. No wonder a young American foreign correspondent, William L. Shirer, though exhausted and baffled by these seven days of 'almost ceaseless goose-stepping, speech-making and pageantry', realized that 'half a million men would now go back to their towns and villages and preach the new gospel with fanaticism'.

William Shirer's *Berlin Diary* gives one of the best outsider's views of events. He describes the arrival of Hitler, clad in a 'rather worn Gaberdine trench coat', giving feeble flapping salutes with his right hand, 'and for the life of me I could not comprehend what hidden springs he undoubtedly unloosed in the hysterical mob greeting him so wildly'. But as the days went by he began to understand a little how Hitler was bringing pageantry, pride and mysticism to the drabbest of lives. The expressions of ecstasy, especially on the women's faces, reminded him of the crazed expressions of Holy Rollers. Unity had been swept up into the craze, incapable by now of anything but blind adoration; even Diana had been deserted by her usual sharp eye and fluent descriptive ability. And if either of them realized the menace in the air, behind all the careful stage-management, they did not record it. But Shirer, like other foreign observers, was well aware that for the first time since the Night of the Long Knives, only two months earlier, Hitler was facing the SA stormtroopers en masse. The tension in the stadium was palpable – with Hitler's SS guard linked into a human chain in front of him – but not one of the 50,000 SA Brownshirts moved a muscle. He had won.

By now, the Parteitag had become a curiosity, and Nazi Germany was a favourite destination that year for interested travellers. The concentration camp at Dachau, just outside Munich, had opened the previous year, its inmates communists or left-wing dissidents, homosexuals, outspoken writers and trade unionists, only a small proportion of them Jewish; it even featured on the itinerary of some who were taken on official visits – ex-servicemen's associations, for instance, journalists or politicians. The young Donald Maclean, who would later become a notorious spy, was in Munich at the time, with Tony Rumbold and Michael Burn, two other young Foreign Office hopefuls, and Burn remembers that they all considered Unity a bit disreputable for budding diplomats to be seen with. Nevertheless Unity dogged Burn's footsteps, even following his researches into Munich's Ettstrasse prison, where she talked to several young women imprisoned for *Rassenschändung*, personal or sexual contravention of the race laws.

Among the many English people who went to take a look at the Parteitag that year was Baba Metcalfe. She and Diana were obviously unaware of each other's presence in Germany, because Baba sent Mosley a postcard of Hitler's house, enquiring: 'Is Mrs G. still at Denham?'

When Diana did arrive home in London, she and Mosley began to form a plan. The first step was for Diana to perfect her German. After only a few weeks she was back in Munich, installed with her maid in an apartment on the Ludwigstrasse ('with Biedermeyer furniture and a good cook') and enrolled in a German language course for foreigners at the university.

17 *Meeting Hitler*

Unity joined Diana in her flat in the Ludwigstrasse, and their days took on an easy rhythm of German lessons, sightseeing in castles and Gothic churches, entertaining friends to dinner, or sitting for hours in the Osteria Bavaria waiting for two or three black Mercedes to draw up outside and a glimpse of Hitler. Muv and Decca visited, English friends passed through. Brian Howard was especially fond of Munich, and came every year for Fasching, the Lent carnival. Derek Hill, who later became a well-known painter, was studying stage design at the Munich Lehrwerkstätte, and remembers outings every week or so with Unity and any of her family who were visiting; Tim Marten, studying German for the Foreign Office, was another who remembered going to lunch with the 'two great blondes', Unity in a lather of excitement over her latest 'storm' (stormtrooper). Everyone teased Unity about her obsession with Hitler. Tom, who had been to the Bayreuth festival that year, wrote her a card to say he had had dinner there with Hitler and Goering: she was 'miserable for days and frightfully *eifersüchtig* [jealous] and then I discovered it wasn't true so I'm furious with him . . .'

Derek Hill had managed to give her an even closer glimpse of the man than she had at the Osteria. One day in the Carlton Teeraum (Hitler's other regular haunt) Hill was sitting with his mother when Hitler came in and settled down opposite them. Hill could not resist going to ring up Unity, who arrived breathless with hurry and excitement; Mrs Hill saw she was trembling so much she could not drink her hot chocolate. On 9 November 1934 she and Diana had managed to get press passes to stand close to the podium outside the Theatinerkirche to watch the ceremony to commemorate the sixteen Nazis who died in the 1923 *putsch* in the streets around the Feldherrnhalle; to Unity's annoyance, Diana's English maid was the one who got the best view of the Führer.

Diana loved the crisp Bavarian winter, and on this visit she stayed five weeks. It was the prelude, though, to a year or more of travelling repeatedly backwards and forwards to Munich and later Berlin. Before Christmas

1934, Diana went home and Unity moved into the Studentinnenheim, where several of the older English girls had established themselves, free from the watchful eyes of whatever Countess or Baroness they had been entrusted to. Unity was well past such chaperonage. She had carved out her own peculiar way of life in Germany, which was hardly susceptible to any domestic or educational discipline.

Diana's Christmas was spent at Faringdon with Gerald Berners; her little boys were with their father; Mosley was with his children. Two of the other guests – Gladys, Duchess of Marlborough, and Edward James – were recently divorced, and the non-familial atmosphere at Faringdon well suited Diana's semi-rootless state. She continued to make the most of her freedom: she was always happy to be back in the Eatonry with the little boys, and Jonathan loyally claims that they saw more of their mother than most people of their type, but she was away a great deal. Her life now had several parallel strands: at the Eatonry with her boys, family and friends, in Germany with Unity, wherever she could with Mosley. While Mosley kept on travelling, speaking and building his party, she saw him as often as possible but kept her eyes turned firmly towards Germany.

David was the next to visit Unity in Munich, in January 1935. In just over a year, the Redesdales' attitude to Germany had altered completely. They had been angry with Diana for taking Unity to the Parteitag in the autumn of 1933, but within months Sydney had softened, finding 'great beauty and charm' in Germany and its baroque buildings, and was soon making regular visits with Decca and Debo; now even David joined the watchers in the Osteria Bavaria and the Carlton Teeraum. Unity wrote to Diana that Farve not only liked Putzi and 'got on wonderfully well with the Sturmführers' but 'has been completely won over to [Hitler] and admits himself to have been in the wrong until now'. This was probably a great exaggeration of Lord Redesdale's sentiments, but there had been a remarkable shift. The Mitfords' family mythology always shows the children in the grip of their parents' whims and prejudices; in fact, the combined influence of Tom (whom David loved and respected unconditionally), Diana and Unity had taken only a few months to overturn in their parents a lifetime of impassioned anti-German feeling.

The Redesdales were painfully anxious to keep ties with their wayward children, and at this stage both parents were trying to temper Unity's overwhelming enthusiasm. But there was one battle Unity did not win with her friends and family – what Sydney described as 'the daily struggle . . . over giving the Nazi salute at the Feldherrnhalle'. The monument to the dead of the 1923 *putsch* was a shrine, guarded day and night by two SS men, and every passer-by (even motorists) was obliged to give a Nazi salute. Bobo would go out of her way to pass the monument; Muv resolutely refused to salute; in revenge Bobo would deliberately lose her and let her find her own way back to her *pension*. Tim Marten was another refusenik, and recalled Unity's white-knuckled fury when he roared with laughter at a fat man who fell off his bicycle in his effort to stick up his right arm as he wobbled past the monument.

Early in February 1935, Diana received an ecstatic letter from Unity: at long last she had her reward. Diana must come back to Munich immediately, so that she too could meet the Führer, because for Unity 'the most wonderful and beautiful day of my life' had happened. It was a Saturday, 9 February, and Unity had gone to the Osteria alone for a late lunch, rather jaded after a fancy-dress ball the night before. The first account of the day she sent home was to her father ('in those days she was more sure of his sympathy than of mine', Sydney commented). 'At about three when I had finished my lunch, the Führer came and sat down at his usual table with two other men . . . About ten minutes after he arrived, the manager came over to me and said "The Führer would like to speak to you". I got up and went over to him and he stood up and saluted and shook hands and introduced me to the others and asked me to sit down next to him.' Rosa, the friendly fat waitress, brought her a postcard, and she embarrassedly asked for his signature. He wrote: *Frl. Unity Mitford, zur freundlichen Erinnerung an Deutschland und Adolf Hitler* [Miss Unity Mitford, as a friendly memento of Germany and of Adolf Hitler]. She was beside herself with delight. They talked for about half an hour, and she listed the topics for Farve: about England (she said he should visit; he said there would be a revolution if he did); about Noël Coward's *Cavalcade* (his favourite film); about his road-building pro-gramme; about Bayreuth (had she been to the festival? well she must come to the next one); about his determination that international Jews must never again be allowed to make two Nordic races fight against each other (no, she said, next time we must fight together).

This last item is surprising. In all the accounts of social chat with Hitler, especially from the young English people Unity now began to introduce to him, the subjects of conversation are described as unusually bland: the weather and the opera predominate, varied occasionally with dogs and cars. Albert Speer has said that talk of politics was taboo around Hitler, but this directly contradicts Diana's later account. Perhaps Hitler was testing Unity, to see what her reactions were; perhaps she exaggerated. She wrote to her mother about Hitler's 'simplicity' – 'He talked so ordinarily that one couldn't be nervous. And for the most powerful man in the world to have remained so simple and utterly unconceited is surely a miracle and a sign of his super-humanity.'

The next conversation was a few days later at the Carlton tearooms, where Hitler again called Unity over to his table: she was such an assiduous stalker that she was always at hand. On 2 March she again lunched at the Osteria, this time with a quiet English student friend, Mary Widesse; at Hitler's table they were introduced to Goebbels. On 11 March, again at the Osteria, she was able to introduce Diana to the Führer for the first time, since Diana had responded to Unity's excited call and made her way back to Munich via Paris, where she had picked up a new Voisin car, a present from Mosley, and pushed through deep snow in the Black Forest with the help of a driver from the Voisin factory. When Hitler was in a relaxed mood, he liked long chats after meals, and on this occasion with Diana and Unity they talked for an hour and a half, and parted very affably after he had invited them to the next Bayreuth festival, the following year. Such chats, especially with women, were quite unlike the 'Tabletalk' which was later published: that was hectoring, lecturing and often almost ranting. Diana claimed she never heard Hitler rant, in the many times they met over the next four years, nor did she hear the famous monologues, when Hitler would hold forth for up to an hour at a time without brooking any interruption. 'In my experience he liked conversation,' Diana wrote. 'In certain moods he could be very funny; he did imitations of marvellous drollery which showed how acutely observant he was.' They talked about architecture – an abiding interest of Hitler's, who knew by heart the capitals of Europe, though he had never visited them, and their great buildings. He liked talking politics, and commenting on the news; she dreaded the conversation turning to cars, on which Hitler was expert, 'very boring to us'.

Diana took trouble to record her impressions of Hitler because they were so much at odds with the received image of him. His rudeness and bad manners? She found him extremely courteous and formal, his habit was to bow and kiss hands according to the German custom. He always hogged the conversation? Far from it, he could be a good listener. He guzzled cream cakes? Never: he was a most fastidious vegetarian with a delicate stomach, and ate an unvaryingly 'dismal' diet of eggs, mashed potatoes, mayonnaise, vegetables and pasta, with stewed fruit and mineral water. He was exceptionally neat, clean and well manicured. One physical trait she noted that does not appear in most descriptions was his 'high forehead, which almost jutted forward above the eyes. I have seen this on one or two other people; generally they have been musicians.' And she is emphatic that she 'never saw him with a lock of hair over his forehead'.

Perhaps her most surprising claim was that Hitler had a sense of humour and was an excellent mimic. He used to make an elaborate pantomime of himself when he smoked cigarettes in his days of poverty, rolling small shreds of tobacco into the cigarette paper, licking the paper, and all the messy paraphernalia of roll-ups; then he would stop and say, 'You can't do that sort of thing if you're supposed to be a dictator.' (Mosley quotes this as evidence of Hitler's basic sanity: 'It is a small point,' Mosley claims, 'but paranoiacs do not make fun of themselves.') Another of Hitler's party pieces was to imitate Mussolini, strutting and swaggering, being presented with a ceremonial sword by a foreign guest and immediately drawing it from its scabbard and brandishing it theatrically round his head. 'I'm no good at that sort of thing,' Hitler would say. 'I'd just mutter "Here, Schaub, you hang on to this."'

Unity left no useful descriptive reminiscences of Hitler beyond breathless adoration of his 'super-humanity' couched in the language of the schoolgirl crush: he was 'sweet', 'wonderful', and so on. Albert Speer remembered the impression she gave: 'She was highly in love with Hitler, we could see it easily, her face brightened up, her eyes gleaming, staring at Hitler. Hero-worship. Absolutely phenomenal. And possibly Hitler liked to be admired by a young woman, she was quite attractive – even if nothing happened he was excited by the possibility of a love affair with her. Towards an attractive woman he behaved as a seventeen-year-old would.' There was no love affair between Unity and the object of her passion, but an obsession that proved more destructive.

Before long, other Mitfords were presented to Hitler. Sydney was the next to visit, in April, but Unity found translating the stilted conversation a great strain, and wrote complainingly to Diana: 'I fear the whole thing was wasted on Muv, she is just the same as before. Having so little feeling, she doesn't feel his goodness and wonderfulness radiating out like we do . . .' On 14 June Pam arrived, after a tour of the Rhineland with Roger, Joan and Cuthbert Hesketh and Billa Cresswell (who later married the economist Roy Harrod). But Pam had to wait until her next visit, in the autumn for the Oktoberfest, for her turn to meet Hitler: her startlingly inapposite comment was that he was 'very ordinary, like a farmer in his old khaki suit'.

In early June Tom had appeared in Munich, and Unity and Diana were nervous about an encounter between Hitler and their brother, for all his

Germanophilia. For several years Tom had been staying from time to time with his friend Janos von Almasy, whose family castle was in the Austrian province of Burgenland. It had three prominent ghosts, and Almasy was deeply embroiled in the occult. He was enthusiastically pro-Nazi, although his grasp of politics depended largely on casting Hitler's horoscope at every turn of events; perhaps, if communism was the alternative, his interest was just the self-preservation of a precarious middle-European aristocrat. Whether Almasy had influenced Tom or not, the latter had to concede the practical performance of Nazism – he had seen the transformation of Germany in just two years – but he was repelled by its race theories. In his legal work he had Jewish friends, colleagues and clients (Tom probably knew more Jewish people than all the other Mitfords put together; they knew very few), and he felt that the Nazis' persecution of Jews was wrong. This did not prevent him being deeply impressed by Hitler. Unity took him to lunch at the Osteria Bavaria at his insistence, but she deliberately arrived early – that is, before two o'clock – half-hoping that they would miss Hitler, but by chance he was there earlier than usual. In the event, Tom 'adored the Führer', Unity wrote to Diana – 'he almost got into a frenzy like us'. But she added: 'I expect he will have cooled down by the time he gets home.' In the midst of their *folie à deux*, both sisters cared very much about their brother's opinion.

Back in London, Tom did not entirely cool down. He engaged in fierce debates about Hitler's policies with Randolph Churchill and other friends, and when Herr Werlin of Mercedes-Benz paid a visit to England, the Redesdales and Tom gave him tea at the House of Lords. Tom found his interest rekindled. His enthusiasm for fascism grew through the thirties, and he actually joined Mosley's movement – against the prevailing trend of its declining membership – in 1939. He was an officer in the Territorial Army before the outbreak of war, and a press photograph of Tom giving the fascist salute while dressed in British army uniform caused quite a stir, not least within his regiment, the Queen's Westminsters, some of whom complained to their colonel about being officered by a fascist.

Unity's diary, meticulously kept for the years 1935–9, records every conversation with the Führer in red ink. On days when she merely saw him pass in a motorcade or on the street, or he just nodded at her, the entry is in blue or black. The red-letter days, however, number 140 in that five-year period – about two or three times a month. She and Diana were invited to his flat for lunch and tea, as well as to his table at the Osteria Bavaria, and from now until the outbreak of war they were his guests at every Parteitag and at every Bayreuth festival. Unity often travelled with him on long train journeys (some of his entourage altered Mitford to *Mitfahrt*, the travelling companion), and she occasionally went for lunch or tea to Berchtesgaden, Hitler's mountain retreat and headquarters near Obersalzberg in Bavaria, but she never stayed there overnight. Diana was less obviously adoring, never the perpetually available 'groupie', but she began to see Hitler in Berlin as well as Munich, and, unlike Unity, she made contacts with other prominent Nazis.

On 25 April 1935, just before Sydney's visit, Mosley came to Munich and met Hitler. Diana had gone to Paris, to join Bryan and their two sons for Jonathan's fifth birthday, so she was not there. It is generally believed that Hitler and Mosley must have been in regular contact, or at least that Mosley was close to some of the Nazi high command. Not so. On the scores of visits to Germany Diana made between 1933 and 1939, he never accompanied her. She came to know Hitler well, but Mosley only met Hitler twice, and the second time was at his wedding to Diana. He knew no German before the war, and his only contact with the Nazi leadership was through the German Embassy in London.

Hitler was by no means keen to have much to do with Mosley. His investigation of Mosley's movement had revealed it to be small beer in political terms, and Hitler was anxious to forge links with the real powers in British politics. But Mosley's movement was still gaining ground in the spring of 1935 – if it had continued to grow at the same rate as the previous year, it would have started to be a significant player in British politics – and Hitler must have thought it worth taking a look at the British fascist leader. It was nothing like the comradely, uniformed, marching and saluting visits to Mussolini – just an hour's conversation before a lunch party in Hitler's flat at 16 Prinzregentenplatz. Diana described it as 'a private visit', and it was arranged to seem so, but as Hitler was apparently unaware of any relationship between Diana and Mosley, it had nothing to do with her. They talked for an hour through an interpreter, then had drinks before lunch with the other guests. Besides Ribbentrop and Josef and Magda Goebbels, Hitler had asked three women with English connections: Winifred Wagner, the English-born widow of the composer's son Siegfried; the Duchess of Brunswick, the only daughter of the Kaiser and great-granddaughter of Queen Victoria; and Unity Mitford. It was the first time she had had a private invitation to his apartment, and Hitler had apparently invited her without knowing her connection to Mosley. He had thought it would be a treat for her to meet the British fascist, and was apparently surprised that they already knew each other.

Mosley reported that meeting Hitler was 'exactly the opposite of a first meeting with Mussolini: there was no element of posture'. Hitler seemed pale and tired, but 'suddenly came to life when I said that war between Britain and Germany would be a disaster, and used the simile of two splendid young men fighting each other until they both fall exhausted and bleeding to the ground, when the jackals of the world would mount triumphant on their bodies. His face flushed and he launched with much vigour into some of his main themes, but . . . the hypnotic manner was entirely absent . . . He was simple, and treated me throughout the occasion with a gentle, almost feminine charm.'

Goebbels noted in his diary for 27 April: '[Mosley] makes a good impression. A bit brash, which he tries to conceal behind a forced pushiness. Otherwise acceptable however. Of course he's on his best behaviour. The Führer has set to work on him. Wonder if he'll ever come to power?'

'The Führer has set to work on him': what did that mean? Mosley's account of the meeting was written at a much later date, long after the war, and it makes the encounter sound mutually interesting but reserved. It also emphasizes a distance between the two forms of fascism (a distinction that perhaps only Mosley would have recognized): 'In the international issues under discussion we had nothing to quarrel about,' he wrote. 'Hitler and I pursued different paths.' They were looking, he meant, in different directions: 'My ideas for maintaining and developing the British Empire in no way conflicted with what he wanted for the Germans. He did not desire war with Russia, because his aims were limited to the union of the peoples in Europe, but he wanted assurances from England and Western Europe that they would not jump on his back in the event of a clash between Germany and Russia, would not intervene against him during a life and death struggle with communism. If I had been responsible for British Government I would certainly have granted this wish because, while I detest all war, I certainly thought war between national socialism and communism a lesser evil than war between Britain and Germany. In return, he would have been ready to offer all possible guarantees for the support of the British Empire . . .'

In plain language, then, the deal between them was as follows: Britain would have her own islands and her empire, intact; Germany would have the rest of Europe. Britain would not interfere with the process; in return, Germany would dispose of communism. Luckily for this neat plan, 'there was no point on the entire globe at which British and German interests clashed' – so all they had to do was divide the globe between them. If Mosley's account is complete, then there was no mention of the Jewish question. That is hard to believe, but Diana was certain it was true. Presumably it counted as part of the 'process' in which a Mosleyite Britain would not interfere. Certainly, Mosley always deplored the Second World War on the grounds that it lost Britain her empire through interference in someone else's quarrel.

It seems unlikely that Hitler would have adhered to such a deal if Mosley had ever come to power in Britain: it was all in the realm of fantasy. We can assume that Hitler was sizing Mosley up as a potential puppet leader if he, Hitler, ever invaded Britain; but he would have decided straight away that, whatever else Mosley was, he was not puppet material. They had an outline agreement, and Hitler left it at that. They never met again in any meaningful way, although Mosley said that Diana used to pass him messages and information from Hitler, but after 1935 Mosley's movement started to decline and Hitler preferred to concentrate on more central figures. Much more significant to him, for instance, was Lloyd George's visit in 1936.

There are two mysteries about this meeting between Mosley and Hitler. The first is whether Mosley asked Hitler for financial backing. It would not have been surprising, since the spring of 1935 found the BUF in increasing straits: the previous year Lord Rothermere had withdrawn his support and his contributions because of pressure from advertisers, recruitment brought inadequate income, and the costs were spiralling. Mosley makes no mention of it – but he also denied he had had financial backing from Mussolini. There is some doubt about whether any money ever did pass between Hitler and Mosley. Diana was emphatic that she did not know of any, although she had often asked senior Nazis to arrange financial help – never Hitler himself, as that might have jeopardized her special access to him. But, she claimed, her requests were always denied, because Germany had a severe shortage of hard currency.

However, her account is directly contradicted by Goebbels. His diary records that in the summer of 1936 Diana came to him with a plea for funds for Mosley – the huge sum of £100,000. But when (according to the diary) Goebbels took Diana and Unity to see Hitler on 19 June, the best they could get was £10,000, still a substantial contribution (these amounts should be multiplied by about twenty-five in order to assess their current value). Goebbels deputized Franz Wrede, from the party press office, to smuggle the cash to London. Goebbels also records that Diana was back again for the Olympic Games in August, and took the opportunity to make another request; with Hitler's approval, Goebbels turned her down. Goebbels was always doubtful about Mosley and jealous of Diana's access to Hitler, so he was obviously pleased: 'Mosley must work harder and be less mercenary' was his priggish comment to his diary. However, there is a detail in Goebbels' story that does not ring true. It seems improbable that Unity would have been involved: she was too unreliable in her childlike tendency to brag and exaggerate. But if Goebbels is telling the truth (as Diana said, 'It is hard to argue with a diary'), this may have been the only time Diana succeeded in her appeal for funds; certainly she asked and was turned down more often. In 1937, after another unsuccessful request by Diana, Goebbels' diary dismisses Mosley as 'a busted flush' who was 'spending a fortune and getting nowhere'.

There is another mystery about Mosley's lunch at the Prinzregentenplatz apartment: how could Hitler not have known that Unity, Diana and Mosley knew each other? All the sources repeat that he had no knowledge of Diana's relationship with Mosley, but this beggars belief. Hitler was head of state, and – in spite of what Mosley said – a paranoid: would no one have checked the identity and background of these foreign women with whom he was suddenly so friendly? Or put together a dossier on Mosley? Many of his staff were suspicious of 'Mitfahrt', resentful of the Führer's attention to her and astonished that he was so open in front of her; they would have liked to discredit her. It would have been very easy to find out about all of them: the German Ambassador went about in London society, where the gossip about Diana and Mosley was more a roar than a whisper; Unity had been a paid-up member of the BUF for two years, and drove around in England with swastika pennants flying from her car: she was hardly discreet.

Of course he knew. It is more likely that Hitler was playing another game with the Mitfords. The Nazis were aware of the usefulness of the well-heeled young English people who used Munich as a finishing school cum social springboard – the young men who visited as much as the girls who lodged there – and wanted to tap into that network so that the young people would go home to their influential families with glowing reports of the regime. Why else would Hitler put up with Unity bringing girls from Baroness Laroche's establishment to tea at his flat? It must have been extremely boring. Was there another political reason, or were these friendships just what they seemed? Hitler's security services could not believe that British Intelligence was not using Unity and Diana, but there is no evidence for this. Rather the opposite: they were considered trouble. Albert Speer seemed to think Hitler, who sensed Unity's childlike nature, was using her for 'disinformation', or well-placed leaks, on a casual basis. 'It was amazing that someone not German was around Hitler and could listen to details of party politics and far-reaching policy. Hitler made no secret of his thoughts . . . [but] his outspokenness was calculated, talking secrets knowing that rumours would be spread.'

It is hard to say why Hitler was so taken with both Unity and Diana. He was flattered by them, of course, but he was surrounded by flattery and had no need of more. He had the poor boy's enthralment to high-born women; he loved their perfect Aryan looks and their Wagnerian connections; he liked their chatter. Their special access to him enraged his colleagues, and he probably enjoyed that. Although Unity worshipped him to a degree that might have been embarrassing, she was completely unsexual in her adoration, and she made him laugh with her unabashed way of talking. Witnesses remembered how she could say things to him that nobody in Germany would have dared say: for instance, they recalled, to their amazement, Diana and Unity sitting either side of Hitler telling him roundly that von Ribbentrop would be a hopeless ambassador to England. Such bluntness would normally have invoked his intense displeasure. 'The others round Hitler were cautious . . . but she was straight and said things Hitler didn't like. She had cheek,' Speer recalled. Through lack of imagination as much as fanaticism, she was the only person who had absolutely no fear of Hitler. She fulfilled his need for ordinary communication. But Speer also commented on the power this gave her: '[Hitler] was easily influenced by small episodes, so if Mitford brought something to his attention, he could get furious about it and a huge effort would be required to settle things.' One can imagine how unpopular this would have made 'Mitford' with Hitler's entourage. In Diana's case, the relationship was less close, but more intellectual. She was less of a fanatic, more informed about politics, and she did establish a relationship with Hitler that was independent of Unity's. She wanted to charm him, and she set about it with her usual success. If she was as breathlessly smitten as Unity, she hid it better and her attitude had less of the schoolgirl crush about it; after all, she had a Führer of her own at home.

As for Mosley, he and Hitler did not really take to each other. Nicholas Mosley remembers how his father's admiration for Mussolini was lasting, despite all that happened, but that in old age Mosley would refer to Hitler as a 'terrible little man' and tease Diana about him.

However, the spring and early summer of 1935 was the moment when the gloves came off, at home and abroad. The previous October, at the Albert Hall, the next large rally after the Olympia débâcle, Mosley had made his first specifically anti-Semitic speech; in April 1935 he addressed a huge meeting with the words: 'I openly and publicly challenge the Jewish interest in this country commanding commerce, commanding the press, commanding the cinema, commanding the City of London, commanding sweatshops.' He received a telegram of congratulation from Julius Streicher, the most virulent of all anti-Semites among the Nazis, and editor of the ranting periodical *Der Stürmer*. Already Streicher's vicious persecution of Jews was well known, with reports of officially sanctioned torture and murder in Franconia, where he was Gauleiter, as well as an array of personal acts of sadism of which he liked to boast. He was a nympholeptic, his harem consisting of young women accused of sexual 'offences' with Jews but pardoned on condition that they contributed to Streicher's own enjoyment. Unity had become a close friend of Streicher and his family; she was heard to boast in London that at dinner with Streicher a group of Jews were brought up from the cellar and made to eat grass. The story did the rounds, as Harold Nicolson records in his diary; apocryphal or not, it shows the way Unity was behaving, and the way she was now regarded, at home. Diana, at least, was repelled by Streicher's boorishness, if not by his views.

Mosley's reply was quoted by Streicher at a speech on 9 May 1935 in Nuremberg, and published everywhere in the Nazi press: 'Please accept my very best thanks for your kind telegram which greeted my speech in Leicester. I value your advice greatly in the midst of our hard struggle. The power of Jewish corruption must be destroyed in all countries before peace and justice can be successfully achieved in Europe. Our struggle to the end is hard, but our victory is certain.' Diana believed this telegram had been sent in Mosley's absence by one of his staff – presumably William Joyce. Whatever the circumstances, this kind of rhetoric, which had not been Mosley's style even a year before, intensified. By the autumn he was concerned by the situation in Abyssinia, where war threatened: Abyssinia was a member country of the League of Nations which some people in Britain felt bound to protect against Italy's imperialist actions. Over the whole dispute, Mosley declared, 'rises the stink of oil, and stronger than even the stink of oil is the stink of the Jew'. Small wonder that he was losing any chance of attracting half-way sensible supporters – for which he still hoped – and was about to begin a year of street warfare in the East End.

A combination of circumstances account for why Mosley's anti-Semitic remarks became increasingly overt at this point. Throughout his career, Mosley was a political weathercock: he knew which way the wind was blowing, even if he did not always choose to point in that direction. He was influenced by his recent visit to Germany, and Diana's growing enthusiasm for Hitler's regime must have had its effect on him – it was, after all, the one that was getting results. In 1935 his movement was at a crossroads – would he go with the tide of European (that is, Nazi-led) fascism and turn towards a full racist platform, or would he continue to try to appeal to a more moderate membership? The moderates were not responding well, and there was a pull towards anti-Semitism within the senior ranks of the BUF. It is significant that the next year, 1936, Mosley changed the name of his movement from the 'British Union of Fascists' to the 'British Union of Fascists and National Socialists', always shortened simply to 'British Union'. At the same time he changed the symbol displayed on its uniform badges and armbands from the 'fasces', or bundle of sticks, to a Nazi-like jagged flash within a circle. His opponents dubbed it the 'flash in the pan'.

The question of a name was always a significant one. Several years earlier, it was Harold Nicolson who had warned Mosley that 'fascism [was] not suitable to England'. In 1935, after Unity got to know Hitler, she wrote in a letter home to Diana that Hitler had said that Mosley was unwise to attempt to import the term 'fascism' and to adopt the black shirt – both, Hitler thought, were 'foreign', out of keeping with British traditions, and likely to impede Mosley's success. A successful political movement had to grow from deep national roots, Hitler believed, and, according to Diana, he always said that 'National Socialism is not for export'. He had a brilliant grasp of the mechanics of mass appeal, and knew how to conjure up the power of the past. When Unity asked him what he would have recommended for a British-based fascist movement, Hitler replied that Mosley should have referred back to an important national moment – namely, the revolution of Oliver Cromwell – and called his men 'Ironsides'.

In June 1935 Unity's craziness reached its peak. Apparently on a whim, she wrote a letter to *Der Stürmer*, expressing her admiration for the paper 'as a British woman fascist'. 'If only we had such a paper in England! The English have no notion of the Jewish danger . . .' and so on. She ended by saying, 'We think with joy of the day when we shall be able to say with might and authority: England for the English! Out with the Jews!' and added a postscript to the effect that if the letter were published, she wanted her full name printed, because 'I want everyone to know that I am a Jew hater.'

What was the purpose of this extraordinary document? A love-letter to Hitler, perhaps. Streicher knew how to make the most of it. He printed it on a full page, with an enormous photograph of Unity, and he invited her to a midsummer festival at Hesselberg, near Nuremberg, where she was not only treated as a honoured guest but suddenly asked to make an impromptu speech before a crowd of 200,000. She was being paraded as a sort of trophy, and it was not the only time Streicher did this. Once he asked the 'two great blondes', Diana and Unity, to stand up before a huge crowd at a meeting, like prize cattle at a show: 'They are taller and more beautiful than we are,' proclaimed the short, dark and corpulent Streicher, 'but they are of the same blood.'

The British press were on the trail in a moment. There had already been articles about Unity ('She adores Hitler' over a large photograph), but from now on she became a sort of public monster. This kind of publicity never attached itself to Diana. She was far too smart to use openly anti-Semitic language beyond the confines of a sympathetic audience, but her letters to Unity show that she was capable of racist talk of the same type. Writing in 1936 about a dinner with Hitler in Berlin, she refers to Tom's Jewish sympathies: '[Hitler] was so wonderful . . . He asked after Tom and I said, *"Der Judenknecht ist fast Nationalsozialist geworden"* [The lackey of the Jews has almost become a National Socialist] and he roared with laughter and said, *"Ihr Bruder ist ein fabelhafter Junge"* [your brother is a splendid young man] twice over. Isn't Tom *lucky?*' And Unity replied by inventing an extra verse to the hymn 'There were Ninety and Nine by the River', with Tom (whose family nickname was Tuddemy or Tud) as the lost sheep recalled to the fold: 'And up from the mountains Communist-ridden / Up from the Jewish mud, / There arose a cry to the Reichskanzlei / Seig Heil! I have found my Tud! / And the Nazis echoed round the throne, / Seig Heil! For the Führer brings back his own!'

With Diana, this sort of talk would never have leaked into the other parts of her life, and she would never impose her views in non-political company. After all, Diana retained her many friendships with civilized and liberal people, and she had a whole other social world; the pathetic Unity had no one but Nazis to impress. If Diana was questioned, then or ever, she was skilful and charming enough to sidestep or laugh away the challenge. The social codes of Britain have always dictated that fierce political debate in polite company is very bad form. Diana's ability to step between the two worlds – an ability she kept to a remarkable degree to the end of her life – meant that she was never socially ostracized in the thirties, or connected with the lunatic fringes of racism. She even kept in contact with several Jewish friends, although their comments were sometimes pointed: one, a singer who was half-Jewish, used to say when they greeted each other, 'You can only kiss half of me.'

The Redesdales were upset about the publicity surrounding Unity's letter in *Der Stürmer* and her Hesselberg speech, and even more about an interview about the BUF she gave to the *Münchener Zeitung*. They cancelled their next visit and wrote angrily to her. Decca wrote affectionately though disapprovingly; she still loved her favourite sister, through thick and thin, while Nancy showed her distress in her usual way, that is, in farcical mode:

> Darling Stony-heart. We were all very interested to see that you were Queen of the May this year at Hesselberg.
>
> > Call me early, Goering dear
> > For I'm to be Queen of the May
>
> Good gracious that interview you sent us. Fantasia, fantasia.

Nancy and her husband Prodd had been among the family visitors to Munich, but, unlike the others, Nancy remained unimpressed by the Hitlerite dream. At the beginning they had attended a few meetings of 'Sir Ogre', as she called Mosley behind Diana's back, but it was mostly out of curiosity. Prodd had been enthusiastic at first, and Nancy went along with him: as she wrote in 1955 to Evelyn Waugh, 'Prodd looked very pretty in a black shirt, but we were younger & high spirited then and didn't know about Buchenwald.' After Olympia, their short-lived interest in fascism came to an abrupt end. Now, although her political thinking was unsophisticated, Nancy considered herself a middle-of-the-road socialist, a shade of pink Diana dismissively described as 'synthetic cochineal'. She only ever had one potent weapon: satire and laughter. They both used it (Prodd, who liked a tease as much as Nancy, replied in Yiddish to an invitation from von Ribbentrop – the invitation had been written in German). And Nancy herself thought that fascism was ripe for a spoofing.

'Darlingest Bodley,' she wrote to Diana in Munich in November 1934. 'Peter says I can't put a movement like Fascism into a work of fiction *by name* so I am calling it the Union Jack movement, the members wear Union Jackshirts & their Lead is called Colonel Jack.' Nancy's latest novel, entitled *Wigs on the Green*, was about to cause a full-scale Mitford family row, this time with Diana and Unity on one side, Nancy on the other. The moment fascism had burst on the family, Nancy started fictionalizing it, but this spoof of 'Eugenia Malmain' and her country village fanaticism was too much for Diana. She knew that Mosley would be furious at having his movement lampooned, especially by his almost-sister-in-law.

Nancy's novel used her family mercilessly, as usual, magnifying and distorting them with the lens of comedy but still planting painful darts of truth. Eugenia (Unity), a huge girl with glittering eyes, is a crackpot who shouts Nazi slogans and racial insults from a tub on the village green, with her dog Reichshund beside her, 'dressed in an ill-fitting grey woollen shirt, no stockings, a pair of threadbare plimsolls and a jumper made apparently out of a Union Jack. Round her waist was a leather belt to which was attached a large bright dagger.' Eugenia quarrels incessantly about the movement with Nanny (as Bobo did with Blor), and with her grandparents Lord and Lady Chalford (who are referred to as TPOM and TPOF, another bit of family slang served up for the reader), in the most hyperventilated dialogue: 'Get out you filthy Pacifist, get out I say, and take your yellow razor gang with you . . . the time is not ripe for a bloodbath in Chalford.'

It was all ridiculous, hardly to be taken seriously as satire. Nancy's letter promised that Diana could edit the text – 'although it is very pro-Fascist there are one or two jokes' – justifying herself because 'they are set off by the fact that (a) the only nice character is a Feedjist [Fascist], & (b) the Conservative is a lunatic peer. But I don't want to Leadertease . . .'

Leadertease is just what Nancy did, however, and by the following summer when the book was ready for press the tone of the sisters' letters was becoming anxious. To Unity Nancy kept up a stream of lightly barbed Mitford-speak: 'Darling Stone-Heart Bone-Head,' she wrote in May, 'I am very glad to hear that you are returning anon. Do leave all your rubber truncheons behind & pump some warm palpitating blood into that stony heart for the occasion. I have taken out all reference to the F. [Führer] (not the P.O.F. [Poor Old Führer = Mosley], the other F.) in my book, & as it cost me about 4/6 a time to do so, you ought to feel quite kindly towards me now.' But by the end of June she had taken refuge in gushing mock-remorse: 'Oh dear oh dear the book comes out on Tuesday . . . Oh dear I wish I had never been born into such a family of fanatics . . . *Please* don't read the book if it's going to stone you up against me . . . Oh dear *do* write me a kind & non-stony-heart letter to say you don't mind it *nearly* as much as you expected, in fact you *like* it, in fact after *I Face the Stars* it is your favourite book even more favourite than mine comf [*Mein Kampf*]. I wonder what Mr Wessel [Hitler] will think of it? . . . Oh dear I am going to Oxford with Nardie [Diana] tomorrow, our last day together I suppose before the clouds of her displeasure burst over me. She doesn't know yet that it's coming out on Tuesday. I have spent days trying to write her diplomatic letters about it. Oh dear I wish I had called it mine uncomf now because uncomf is what I feel whenever I think about it . . .'

Nancy knew that Diana would not be fobbed off with this sort of patter. In their different ways they were as tough as each other. Diana and Mosley had together given Nancy a list of things they objected to in the typescript, ending with the fact that her style was an 'unsuitable medium' for dealing with a serious political movement, but she had ignored most of their points. The 'diplomatic letter' Nancy finally sent to Diana is crisp, almost business-like. 'My book comes out on the 25th inst. & in view of our conversation at the Ritz ages ago I feel I must make a few observations to you,' she wrote. 'When I got home that day I read it all through & found that it would be impossible to eliminate the bits that you & the Leader objected to. As you know our finances are such that I really couldn't scrap the book.' But Nancy was probably wary of Mosley, who was highly litigious and would not have hesitated to sue her over an unfavourable portrait of himself. He often won large amounts from newspapers, and it amused him to do so. So she went on: 'I did however hold it up for about a month . . . in order to take out everything which related directly to Captain Jack, amounting to nearly 3 chapters & a lot of paragraphs.' She tried to persuade Diana that the book could do no possible harm, and that it was 'more in favour of Fascism than otherwise'. Besides (though this she did not say) the satire fell mainly on poor crazy Bobo, a soft target, not on the adult sister who might bite back.

The other famous lampoon of Mosley and his movement came from P. G. Wodehouse in *The Code of the Woosters*, where a character called Roderick Spode is the founder and leader of the Saviours of Britain, a fascist organization also known as the Black Shorts (by the time Spode formed his association, there were no black shirts left, so they had to use black football shorts instead). Gussie Fink-Nottle explains to Bertie Wooster that '[Spode's] general idea, if he doesn't get knocked on the head with a bottle in one of the frequent brawls in which he and his followers indulge, is to make himself a Dictator.' Spode is mixed up in the tangled love story of the novel, and at one point there is a showdown in which a terrified Wooster musters his courage to rail at Spode: 'just because you have succeeded in inducing a handful of half-wits to disfigure the London scene by going about in black shorts, you think you're someone. You hear them shouting "Heil Spode!" and you imagine it is the Voice of the People. That is where you make your bloomer. What the Voice of the People is saying is: "Look at that frightful ass Spode swanking about in footer bags! Did you ever in your puff see such a perfect perisher?"'

Wodehouse's book did not come out until 1938, however, and it was written by a stranger. It had little power to sting. Nancy's spoof came at a more sensitive moment in the BUF's development, and was from the inside – a hurtful piece of family disloyalty, as Diana saw it, and all Nancy's blandishments were in vain. Diana's famous sense of humour deserted her completely over *Wigs on the Green* – the charge of ludicrousness was obviously too painfully apt – and she stuck to her view that fascism was too serious a matter to be dealt with in a funny book. Mosley's annoyance and sense of insult were implacable, and the publication caused a coolness between the sisters that lasted until well after the war. The book had brought their political differences to light; Mosley disliked the sharp edge of Nancy's tongue, and Diana's loyalties lay with him. The rift hurt Nancy, who relied heavily on her sisters' friendship, but in another few weeks she was laughing about it. To Mark Ogilvie-Grant she wrote: 'I hear that Bobo and Diana are going to stand outside the Polls next polling day & twist people's arms to prevent their voting, so I have invented (& patented at Gamages) a sham arm which can be screwed on & which makes a noise like Hitler making a speech when twisted so that, mesmerized, they will drop it & automatically spring to salute . . . I saw Diana at a lunch of Syrie's [Maugham] 2 days ago, she was cold but contained & I escaped with my full complement of teeth, eyes, etc.'

Nancy could mock Diana in letters to friends, and behind her back, but not directly, as she did in letters to Unity. She never took on Diana as a satirical target: perhaps they had been too close in the past, perhaps she knew that Diana, with her iron beliefs and her devotion to Mosley, had a seriousness of purpose that was out of Nancy's league.

18 Wootton Lodge

If last year's summer holiday, dividing the time with Baba, had been tricky but negotiable, the summer holiday of 1935 proved a double disaster. Once again Mosley made a similar plan: he rented the Rennells' outlandish villa at Posillipo, on the Bay of Naples (the winner of the ugliest house competition among the young attachés at the British Embassy in Rome), and planned a month there with Nicholas and Vivien. This time, Baba was to come for the first fortnight, Diana for the second.

Before the holidays began, however, Diana had a car accident. Late at night on her way to Mosley's house at Denham for the weekend, she collided with a large Rolls-Royce and her small car was badly mangled. Badly mangled, too, was her face, which was deeply cut by the broken glass of her windscreen. Her nose and jaw were broken, although the rest of her was only bruised. At the hospital she was stitched up roughly by a harassed young doctor who could not find any fine thread, and used a coarser one; Diana was too dazed and shocked to protest, or to think about anything except her spaniel, who had been in the car with her, and the panic Mosley and her children would feel when she did not turn up as expected. She managed to put through a telephone call to Mosley before she spent the rest of the night, her face heavily bandaged, in one of the hospital wards.

Tom came the next day to take her home to Eaton Square in a hired ambulance. Mosley visited, her sisters came, Bryan arrived with armfuls of flowers, and Lord Moyne, Bryan's father, also came to see her. Still rather dizzy from the crash, she could not understand why everybody looked so grave and worried, but the gossip columns were quick to pounce: would this great beauty be scarred for ever? The *Daily Express* ran a leader on the mutability of human fortune. But Lord Moyne had more practical ideas, and insisted on a specialist plastic surgeon for Diana. When Sir Harold Gillies investigated the mess under her bandages, he was horrified. He had to wait a week, until some of the swelling had gone down, to operate on her nose and jaw, and to graft skin; in the event, two very painful operations were needed. And what was he to use for a model? It was Bryan who remembered the mask of Diana's face which had been cast in plaster a few years earlier by the 'German whom Harold Nicolson has invented', the mask she went to inspect with Evelyn Waugh on one of the last days of their friendship. Were it not for this, Diana might not have got her face back; as it was, Gillies did a perfect job and Diana not only looked just the same but was also quite unscarred.

During her weeks in the London Clinic, Mosley departed for Posillipo to begin his holiday. Passing through Rome on his way south, Mosley was again given star treatment by Mussolini, saluted on a podium with the Duce at a march-past of 'innumerable fascists', as Nicholas, who was then twelve, remembers it. When they reached Posillipo, they were all impressed. The Rennells' villa may have been built in an absurd jumble of styles, but its clifftop position was superb, looking out across the bay to Vesuvius, with the island of Capri lying in the sea to the right. Mosley had bought a 30-foot yacht called the *Vivien*, which was anchored in an inlet at the foot of hundreds of steps down the cliff below the house. It had a crew of two, and several cabins at the front, but they rarely slept there; Mosley preferred to sail across the bay to Capri or Sorrento, drop anchor and swim in deserted coves, or to eat at a small restaurant on the island before returning. Nicholas remembers this as a happy holiday, with his father at his most affable, inventing excursions and urging adventures, playing games with 'a vast histrionic exuberance', laughing and teasing – 'he had a way of making ordinary things seem hilarious'. Baba was an excellent 'mother-companion', swimming, exploring and playing with the children; she and his father seemed happy together, he thought.

Stuck in the clinic in London, Diana was miserable and restless, longing for some Italian sunshine and to recuperate with Mosley by the sea. Her doctors insisted that she was not ready to leave, but she pleaded with Farve to smuggle her out very early one morning, drive her to Croydon and put her on a plane to Marseilles. There she changed to a seaplane, and arrived that evening in Naples. As it was several days before she was expected, she sent a cable to announce her coming: unfortunately, it arrived just as she did, in the middle of dinner.

Whether she had forgotten that Baba was there, whether she had mistaken the dates, or whether perhaps she had thought that, given her state of health, Baba would quietly make way for her, is not clear. Mosley had written to her in the clinic, telling her to hurry up and get better and join them quickly, but this sudden arrival was obviously not what he had in mind. Nicholas remembers the day vividly, not least because in the morning they had had a visit from the Crown Princess of Italy, a childhood friend of

Baba's, and had taken the yacht for a long trip to Ischia. Then, after the children had gone to bed, 'there seemed to be strange comings-and-goings in the grown-up world; doors banged here and there; what might one expect with Crown Princesses?' Vivien told him the next day that she had heard a row in the middle of the night, and when he found out that it was Mrs Guinness who had arrived it was, he thought, 'a social and a personal challenge worthy of the mettle of someone like my father – on his tightrope, as it were, juggling with his plates above Niagara'. Perhaps for once the juggler dropped the plates. That same day Mosley, Baba and the children left on the *Vivien* for a three-day cruise to Amalfi, until the time when Baba was due to continue her holiday in Tunisia; Diana was left alone in the villa in the care of the servants.

At the end of his life Mosley confided to a friend that 'through the thirties I really had two wives – was that so bad?' The two wives, early on, were Cimmie and Diana; now they were Diana and Baba, and this situation went on for many years. In the telling of the Posillipo incident, as well as through the whole litany of Mosley's infidelities (which continued throughout his life with Diana, even after the war), one wonders at Diana's real feelings. In later years she would say that his peccadilloes 'never threatened' her position, but to closer friends she admitted agonies of jealousy. She was occasionally humorous about it all: she told Nancy's biographer, Selina Hastings, that there was a difference between Mosley and Gaston Palewski, an incorrigible womanizer and the man Nancy was in love with. They differed in only one thing. In the vicinity of any pretty woman 'Gaston would just lunge', according to Diana, 'whereas Kit would at least wait for an answering gleam'.

In Diana's published account of the summer holiday in 1935, however, there is not a word of any contretemps. Nicholas remembered that as she sat recovering under a sunshade, 'Viv and I would approach her cautiously like animals looking for food', until she began to feel better and taught them to play poker; she recalled her contentment with Mosley and the healing effects of the sea. Whatever Diana really thought about the situation with Baba, she decided to play poker herself, and to keep a completely straight face until someone showed their hand. Questioned, she would put on her most sphinx-like manner, and merely say that of course Baba's presence was perfectly natural, because of Cimmie's children; as for Mosley, 'I always knew he liked me best.' After such a show-down, the situation could not continue, surely. Yet it did, for at least another year. Mosley's ability to keep his options open was extraordinary; the two women's tolerance was perhaps even more unusual.

Then it was the Parteitag again, and this year there was no problem about hotel rooms, tickets, or too much lipstick: Diana and Unity were Hitler's guests, they had rooms at the Grand Hotel and in the stadium excellent seats from which they heard Hitler's official announcement of the Nuremberg Laws, depriving German Jews of their nationality. There could be no doubt, now, that German anti-Semitism was not a passing phase.

Mosley never went to a rally at Nuremberg, and Diana was accompanied in 1935 by Unity and Tom, together with a number of their English acquaintances. By now there were many witnesses: Henry Williamson, the Mosleyite nature writer who venerated Hitler, left an account of the rally in *Goodbye West Country* (1937), and his friend John Heygate, also a BUF sympathizer (and the man for whom Evelyn Gardiner had left Evelyn Waugh), wrote about it in *These Germans* (1940). Before the festivities began at Nuremberg, however, Diana and Unity had been guests of honour at a warm-up act for visitors, the Congress of Nazi Groups Abroad, a jamboree characteristic of Streicher in its mixture of folk-dancing and racial hatred. Streicher interrupted one of the many speeches to introduce the ladies at the top table: Leni Riefenstahl, Frau Troost, Unity and Diana. Prize specimens at the show again. The *Fränkische Tageszeitung* reported that the two English-women had 'heard the Nazi message in their blood'.

In Nuremberg on 10 September, the sisters met up with Tom and their friend Mary Widesse shortly before Hitler's ceremonial arrival at the airport. That first night they attended a performance of *Die Meistersinger* conducted by Furtwängler at the opera, where Hitler went with Streicher and local dignitaries. When they got to their specially reserved seats the next day, they found Hitler had arranged for them to be placed next to Eva Braun: it was his way of introducing them, although they had hardly any further contact. Eva Braun was *maîtresse de la maison* at Obersalzburg, where Unity was seldom invited, and Diana had not been, but she never appeared with him anywhere else; Hitler kept his life in careful compartments.

The heated atmosphere of the summer's political events must have made its mark on Diana, because in October there was an incident which was quite untypical of her restrained political style. On 28 October in Hyde Park she came across a large demonstration against German cruelties organized by the British Non-Sectarian Anti-Nazi Council, with Clement Attlee, leader of the Labour Party, as chief speaker. When a boycott of German goods was proposed, a sea of hands went up in support of the motion, and then a single hand to vote against it. The *News Chronicle* had the story. 'Mrs Guinness, daughter of Lord Redesdale, stood in the crowd on her own and recorded a lone vote . . . Some of the crowd jeered, others laughed. "I simply wanted to give my opinion like everyone else," said Mrs Guinness. During the singing of "God Save the King", while the crowd stood bare-headed, Mrs Guinness raised her hand in the fascist salute.' The crowd began to turn nasty, but two BUF members who happened to be there whisked Diana away before any trouble started. This would have been quite normal for Unity; it was very unusual behaviour for Diana.

By the end of 1935, things did not look rosy for the BUF. Membership was falling, and Mosley had been obliged to take notice of the criticisms that the movement was out of control, especially in the regions. He sent A. K. Chesterton on a fact-finding tour of provincial branches, which proved revealing; in one district, Chesterton reported, the organization's office was 'part thieves kitchen and part bawdy house'.

Mosley was a brilliant orator with superb debating skills, but essentially an individualist. He was so busy travelling and speaking that he had no time to keep a tight rein on his organization, nor was he good at it; neither was he judicious in his choice of lieutenants. Of the many thousands (according to some figures, hundreds of thousands) who joined the BUF on a wave of enthusiasm immediately after one of Mosley's meetings, 90 per cent never went any further in the movement. There was no efficient follow-up organization for whatever ordinary members it might have attracted, and they simply melted away as quickly as they had come; for the most part, only fanatics and misfits stayed to staff the various centres and offices.

The experience of Margaret White, who married William Joyce in 1937, was typically haphazard. Her comments should be seen in the light of the bitter rift that later occurred between Mosley and Joyce, but even so it is clear that it took some persistence to remain in the organization or establish a local branch. She joined the BUF in 1934, when she was twenty-three, after hearing Mosley speak in Carlisle. She had toyed with the communists, but found them 'unnecessarily unwashed and envious', yet she had a deep dislike of 'Conservatism and High Finance'; when she heard Mosley she felt he was putting into words everything she thought. However, 'Mosley loved the bright lights and cheering but hated organization,' she discovered. 'I heard nothing after my application had been accepted and I'd bought a badge. Then I met a girl wearing a black shirt and a badge on the street, and she told me of others, who met. At long last we got the applications back from London and were able to gather up all the odd people who'd joined after the Mosley meeting . . . We still weren't many but enthusiastic – there was the usual high percentage of cranks and crooks – but it was fun. I was about the only one who could speak semi-educated English and we got a propaganda man sent to look us over and I got pushed on to platforms . . .'

In response to his critics, Mosley reorganized more tightly, and on increasingly militaristic lines. This suited his core members; as Robert Skidelsky points out, a very large proportion of them were ex-servicemen – not just enlisted men, but career soldiers. The ex-officers, in particular, felt at home with the military style ranks, titles and orders. Mosley's Chief of Staff, Ian Hope Dundas (ex-Naval Office and son of an admiral), said of the BUF that it provided 'the same spirit as the navy – but without the sea-sickness'. In the summer of 1935 Mosley gave up the Black House and moved back to offices in Great Smith Street; he no longer wanted 'a clubhouse or playground' for his men. The only growth of the movement at this time was in the East End of London, where there were about 150,000 Jews in a population of 500,000, and its main impetus came not from Mosley but from one of his district officers, the 24-year-old 'Mick' Clarke.

Clarke had a powerful and vicious tongue, and was a tireless speaker at rough and ready street-corner meetings; he had a certain brutal charisma, and he built up a following that was almost independent of Mosley. By the end of 1935 Clarke's men were everywhere on the streets of Bethnal Green and Stepney, Hackney, Shoreditch and Bow – the heart of the East End. They would swoop in with loudspeaker vans and drums, set up a stall with lightning speed and bellow out the rhetoric for as long as it took for a fight to start, or for the police to arrive. The racial abuse was open and extreme; there were many fights and many arrests on both sides. Not surprisingly, Clarke's men fell foul of the real rulers of the East End streets, the underworld gang leaders, and there were often violent clashes. They included the infamous Jack Spot, who got a six-month sentence in 1937 for causing grievous bodily harm to a fascist.

Although so far he had concentrated on the industrial towns of the north, Mosley now turned his efforts to help this swing towards London's East End. In June 1936 he led a 'half-mile column' (*Blackshirt* claimed) to address thousands of people in Victoria Park in Hackney; he announced that the BUF's effort would now concentrate on the East End, and that they would put up candidates in the municipal elections. The most noticeable thing about this march was Mosley's new uniform: gone were the plain, subdued black shirts; instead he and all his senior staff turned out in a military-style get-up of officers' peaked hats, fitted black military jackets with Sam Browne belts, breeches and high, gleaming jackboots. It was strongly reminiscent of the Nazi SS, as the press were quick to notice; or, as one caustic observer put it, more like King Zog's Own Imperial Dismounted Hussars. It certainly did not improve relations in the East End, where the violence was getting worse. William Joyce and Alexander Raven Thomson were often to be found there, egging on the most vitriolic elements, and although Mosley tried to lay down the law ('Mere abuse we forbid . . . it is bad propaganda and alienates public sympathy'), he failed to stop the chanting and taunting and racist slogans chalked on walls, let alone the broken noses and smashed windows.

The 'King Zog', SS-style uniform – with its connotations of links with foreign fascist movements – was misleading in one way. In these years, just when European fascism was at its most apparently successful, Mosley seemed to turn more and more inwards towards Britain and have less interest than ever in what went on abroad. Although he had information about Germany from Diana, he made no attempt to repeat his visit to Hitler of 1935, and by 1936 his Italian connection – the relationship with Mussolini – was effectively over. But it is more surprising that he took little interest in the other important international event of this year, the Spanish Civil War, which began on 18 July. As he later wrote, he saw himself and his British Union as being 'engaged in a military operation against the highly trained guerrillas of communism' in Britain, yet he seemed to feel no link to that same struggle taking place in Spain. 'On this major issue for the British left,' wrote Robert Skidelsky, 'the BUF had little to say.' Mosley approved the British government's policy of non-intervention, and although 'the fascist press supported Franco, Mosley confined himself to attacking the Labour Party for putting Spain above England.' In this curious lack of interest, he showed himself to be out of touch with the pulse of the times, since the Spanish conflict fired the imagination of young British people as few political events have done before or since. Diana's sister Decca was only one of many who ran away to assist the cause in Spain, mainly in support of the Republicans. There is no record of similar initiatives from Mosley's ranks, volunteering to fight for Franco.

Rather than widening to encompass events on the continent of Europe, Mosley's focus narrowed into a few areas – chiefly the industrial Midlands and the East End of London. Yet while his movement went downhill, into some of the poorest parts of the capital and into some of the most degraded forms of behaviour, Mosley and Diana were transforming their private lives into a haven. The contrast could not have been more extreme. More than three years since Diana had made her commitment to Mosley, they were still spreading their lives between various establishments. Mosley had his Ebury Street flat and Savehay Farm, where his children lived and where he stayed for some weekends; he spent an enormous amount of time on the road around Britain. Diana had Eaton Square, but she, too, spent a great deal of time travelling – to Lord Berners in Rome, to Munich, increasingly to Berlin as well. When Diana was in London, she would drop anything at a moment's notice to see Mosley, but all the same it was often difficult to meet.

During 1935 their relationship had changed significantly, perhaps because it had been a traumatic year. Diana had suffered her car accident, and they had weathered the emotional intricacies of the summer holidays. When Diana was due to set off for Rome to stay with Gerald Berners, however, she was delayed by another short stay in a clinic, to terminate a pregnancy. 'Hurry up with your illegalers,' Berners wrote to her cheerfully, and although she was characteristically discreet and buoyant about the abortion, many years later she recalled the pain of the experience to a friend. She wanted more children, with Mosley, and it proved a catalyst. Early in 1936, three years after Diana had left Bryan and a full two and a half years after Cimmie's death, Diana and Mosley decided to get married and to set up a home together outside London.

The obvious and easy thing would have been for Diana to move into Savehay Farm, but even now Mosley had no wish to unify his households; very likely, Diana had no desire to take on the full step-motherly role towards his children either. Anyway, the household there had its own routine: there were Nanny and Andrée, Cimmie's former lady's maid and now the housekeeper, to take care of the children, and usually Irene Ravensdale in residence when Mosley was not there, Baba Metcalfe when he was.

So Cimmie's old home remained, almost as if she were still alive, while Mosley and Diana found a spectacular, huge, beautiful and extremely impractical seventeenth-century stone house called Wootton Lodge, in Staffordshire, close to the big industrial centres of the Midlands where Mosley's work often took him. Wootton Lodge stands at the end of a mile of drive lined with beeches; at the approach, there are two plain stone lodges with pitched roofs either side of a gate that opens on to a circular lawn, round which the formal double driveway loops up to the sweeping stone steps in front of the large, pilastered door. The house is a symmetrical box, almost a cube, with rooftop pennants on the high Jacobean chimneys, and each of its four storeys has the same enormous mullioned bay windows. Like Hardwick Hall, its more famous contemporary, Wootton is 'more glass than wall', and the architectural historian Mark Girouard described it as one of the most beautiful English houses of its period. The house sits on a sort of promontory with wooded hills around it, and the terraced garden slopes down sharply behind the house to a series of lakes. In the depression years houses like this were of little value: they were hard to keep up, and the land around Wootton was nothing but bluebell woods; there was no profitable farmland, no hunting, few pheasants, and only a few old trout in the lakes. The house agent called it a white elephant, and Diana rented it on the spot – 'for almost nothing' – hoping that they could buy it later.

Wootton was 'like a castle in storybooks', Nicholas Mosley wrote, and he remembers Diana in that setting as a storybook princess: 'You went up a wide flight of steps into a panelled hall; the drawing room was to the left where there were Chippendale chairs and a settee shaped curiously like sea-shells; here Diana would sit like someone in a painting by Botticelli.' This move meant a distinct change for Diana. She turned her back on London and much of her social life; Wootton was remote and they had few visitors. Nancy, in the dog-house because of *Wigs on the Green*, was never invited; the rest of the family came occasionally. Diana would have filled the house with people, as usual, but Mosley liked to find her alone there when he came back weary from work. He fished and rode, they walked in the woods and potted at rabbits; it was a world away from the hurly-burly of fascist meetings. They even gave up their routine of going to the Mediterranean every summer, preferring to stay at Wootton for what turned out to be the last three summers before the war. When Diana remembered Wootton in those years, the word she always used was 'happy', and Nicholas described the atmosphere that surrounded the two of them, in their private cocoon at Wootton Lodge, as the invisible force-field of those in love.

19 Marriage

Soon after she had moved into Wootton on 1 July 1936, Diana left for Berlin and the Olympic Games. On 7 March of that year Hitler had ordered his troops into the Rhineland, reoccupying it after it had been de-militarized under the terms of the Treaty of Versailles, and thereby moving a step closer to confrontation with Britain and France. At the end of March he called an 'election' to ratify his actions, and Diana and Unity, devoted groupies that they were, had been in Cologne to 'surprise' him when he arrived on the eve of the poll, as the bells rang in Cologne's great Gothic cathedral – part of a huge publicity campaign superintended by Goebbels. (The election results were a triumph for Hitler, and it would have been very remarkable if it had been otherwise, since the ballot paper gave no opportunity for dissent. On Sunday 29 March 98.6 per cent of the voting population turned up at the polling booths, and 98.7 per cent of them voted for Hitler: a total of 44,399,000 people.)

By now, Diana and Unity's activities in Germany were regular fodder for the British press, and half the reports were patent nonsense. Writing about the reoccupation of the Rhineland, various papers claimed that Diana and Unity rode into Cologne on 7 March immediately behind the German army in the car of Field Marshall Blomberg ('the heavenly B', the sisters called him). But Diana's version, backed up by Ward Price, a *Daily Mail* foreign correspondent, is more plausible: on the eve of the election, a few weeks later, they merely booked into the Hotel Dom and waited. Hitler spotted them in the foyer of the hotel, invited them over to join him for tea, and during the course of a jubilant conversation asked them to be his guests that summer, first at the Olympic Games and then at the Bayreuth Festival.

Diana was back in Germany again in June, as we know from Goebbels' diary; and back yet again in late July for the start of the Olympics on 1 August. The Olympic Games of 1936 were a showcase for the new Germany, a chance for the Germans to display themselves to the world and for the Nazi regime to try to win back some respectability. They were also a celebration of the achievements within Germany in the last three years, a great display of national order, progress and pride. But there had been serious international disquiet about the games being hosted by Germany, and about the position of Jewish athletes. The Germans had had to agree that Jewish and non-white athletes from other countries could compete; ultimately they even had to agree that a quota of German Jewish athletes would appear. (The one thing everybody now remembers is that the outstanding performer of these games was the 22-year-old black American from Ohio, Jesse Owens, who won four gold medals and broke eleven Olympic records in the first week. 'O-*vens*, O-*vens*,' the crowd chanted.)

Berlin was packed with foreign visitors to the games, and Goebbels was determined not to miss his propaganda opportunities. He had given Leni Riefenstahl a budget of 1.5 million marks for her film of the games, but as before he quarrelled with her constantly; he said she was impossible to work with; she claimed it was because she had spurned his sexual advances. (In fact, Riefenstahl later denied that her *Olympiad* film was made under the Nazis' auspices at all, claiming that her commission was directly from the International Olympic Committee.) Whatever the truth, her two-part, four-hour epic is now considered one of the greatest documentaries ever made.

To foster better public relations with the foreigners, Goebbels was also determined that the party should keep a low profile. What is now referred to as 'the Olympic pause' – when for propaganda reasons the Nazis tried to play down some of their harsher policies, especially in relation to the Jews – was under way, and indeed lasted most of the year. Sharper observers were not fooled – in her articles Martha Gellhorn described her instant dislike of the young Nazis in 'clean blond khaki-clad formation', lacking 'one parrot brain among the lot' – although other visitors (many of them young, since Germany had provided greatly reduced rail fares for young people) were pleasantly surprised by the country's air of modest prosperity and order. Some things could not be disguised, however. An American writer and journalist from New Orleans, Howard Smith, recorded his shock at the number of men in uniform. He noticed 'long caravans of camouflaged tanks, cannons and war-trucks lashed to railway flat cars' and freight depots 'lined with more of these monsters in hooded brown canvas'. To see anything like this, however, he must have taken himself well away from the determinedly festive streets of Berlin, where red bunting and swastika banners decked the main avenues, and where Albert Speer had designed huge gold and red linking garlands to festoon the trees all along the six-mile route from the Brandenberg Gate to the Olympic stadium.

Historians refer to 1936 as the heyday of fascism, and this summer was undoubtedly the high point of Anglo-German relations in the thirties. Although the *Daily Mail* was the only major daily newspaper still openly enthusiastic about the Nazi regime, Richard Griffiths, in his *Fellow Travellers of the Right*, draws a distinction between the moderate public's distaste for Germany's internal policies and some degree of sympathy – or perhaps merely indifference – towards her external ones. The Italian war in Abyssinia occupied British minds more than the situation with Germany, which it virtually banished from the headlines during the spring of 1936; and the letters columns of *The Times* indicate that the Rhineland coup evoked as much tolerance as censure. For the Rhineland to have been a de-militarized area, one correspondent felt, was as if British troops had not been allowed into Colchester.

The Germans' efforts at greater respectability within the international community were directed towards their re-entry into the League of Nation. With the British, their attempts to foster better relations had to some extent paid off. Joachim von Ribbentrop, newly appointed Ambassador to London, did not take up his post until October, but from the spring onwards he was busy wooing the likely elements within Britain. Lady Astor complained that Ribbentrop kept 'bad company' in London when he paid a long visit in May, but at this moment, Richard Griffiths claims, 'a section of smart London society was . . . not only pro-German but pro-Nazi'. The leading hostesses among this 'empty-headed' group were Lady Cunard, Laura Corrigan and Lady Londonderry, and although Ribbentrop was also concerned with more solidly influential figures – he tried for most of this year to bring about a meeting between Baldwin and Hitler, for instance – he clearly had a taste for the drawing rooms of the rich. 'Chips' Channon, the American-born socialite and politician, was typical of those 'impressed by the glamour and excitement of the new regime', as Griffiths says, 'and shallowly unconcerned by the realities behind it'.

Chips Channon and his wife Lady Honor (a Guinness) were among the many Ribbentrop met in London and invited to attend the Olympic Games as Germany's guests. Literally hundreds had received official invitations, and hospitality was lavished on them. On 14 July the Duke and Duchess of Brunswick were guests of honour at a dinner of the Anglo-German Fellowship in Berlin: Lord Mount Temple was in the chair, Lord Zetland, Secretary of State for India, was an official guest, speakers included Lord Rennell, Lord Lothian and Major-General Sir Frederick Maurice. Once the games began properly on 1 August, the attendance was enormous. 'The English pour in', Chips Channon wrote in his diary, 'and are jealous of one another's activities and privileges', while one commentator after another in the British press praised the Germans' 'friendliness', 'community spirit' and 'national zeal', and British sportsmen were reported as claiming that only such a regime could produce Olympic winners.

Diana and Unity were guests of the Goebbelses at their country house at Schwanenwerder, by the Wannsee lake just outside Berlin. It was a large and pretentious villa which had belonged to a Jewish family who had already left Germany. There Goebbels and his family entertained generously (Unity and Diana had often been guests at lunches and picnics), and Goebbels could keep his fast cars and his speedboat. Every day a car was sent to take them to the games. Luckily, Diana reported, their seats were a long way from those of their hosts, so as soon as they got there they could wander off; Diana thought watching athletics was 'the very essence of boredom', and got out of it whenever she could. In fact, Diana was always dismissive about the Olympic fortnight, describing it as dull, just glad when it was over. Yet other foreign observers describe a mesmerizing show of extravagance throughout, culminating in a closing ceremony on Sunday 16 August which again featured Speer's cathedral of light. The American Ambassador, William E. Dodd, sent dispatches home wondering about the incredible cost of it all: how can they pay for this? he kept asking.

In particular, William Dodd mentioned the parties. The Nazi *prominenten* competed with each other to give the most spectacular and lavish entertainments of the fortnight. Chips Channon's diaries record these occasions with relish. The Channons, friends of Edward VIII and Mrs Simpson, were extremely wealthy and devoted to society; a great social climber, Channon wrote of himself that he was uninterested in 'all the things most men like' (sport, business, war and the weather) but 'rivetted by lust, furniture, glamour and society and jewels'. He was disliked by many (Robert Byron is said to have attacked Channon's pro-German sympathies by saying: 'I suppose I should not be surprised that you are prepared to sacrifice the interest of your adopted country in the supposed interests of your adopted class'), but his acute social antennae made him sharp enough to spot, after only forty-eight hours in the country, the tensions between Goering and Goebbels, and the hints that Ribbentrop's star was on the wane.

The first large function was the state banquet on 6 August, a dinner at the Opera House for 2,000 people 'glistening with flashing jewels and orders', the royalty and aristocracy of middle Europe mixed with the grander foreign visitors and home-grown political arrivistes. 'Berlin has not known anything like this since the [First World] War,' Channon remarked, likening the evening to 'the fêtes given by the Directoire of the French Revolution, with the upstarts, tipsy with power and flattered by the proximity and ovations of the ex-grand, whom once they wished to destroy'.

Next, the 'upstarts' gave a series of parties. Ribbentrop was obviously very attentive to the English guests, and invited many to the dinner for 600 he gave on 11 August at the Dalheim villa 'transformed into a scene of revelry'. Channon described him as looking 'like the captain of someone's yacht, square, breezy, and with a sea-going look . . . He is not quite without charm, but shakes hands in an over-hearty way, and his accent is Long Island without a trace of Teutonic flavour'. Ribbentrop's wife Channon rudely called 'distinguished in the Berlin manner, that is she has intelligent eyes, appalling khaki coloured clothes and an un-powdered, un-painted face'. The guests that evening were 'a fantastic collection of notabilities', according to Channon, who sat next to the Old Etonian Duke of Saxe-Coburg and Gotha, a grandson of Queen Victoria who was so enthusiastic a Nazi that he was usually to be seen in a Brownshirt uniform. Ribbentrop's large but decorous evening event was eclipsed, two days later, by the ostentation of Goering's 'dazzling' gala in the floodlit park of his house on the Leipziger Platz, 'where the Goerings live in theatrical magnificence', Channon noted. There were bands and dance floors, but this was just the beginning. After an elaborate dinner for seven or eight hundred, a corps de ballet danced in the moonlight, and Goering's old air-ace chum Udet put on a display of stunt-flying. Then there was a sudden lighting-up of a dark end of the gardens to reveal a procession of white horses, donkeys and actors in eighteenth-century peasant costumes to lead the guests in a specially built Luna Park – carousels, cafés with beer and champagne, roaring music, peasants drinking and dancing, a complete Petit Trianon fantasy cast in Germanic mood. '"There has never been anything like this since the days of Louis Quatorze," someone remarked. "Not since Nero," [Channon] retorted, but actually it was more like the Fêtes of Claudius, with the cruelty left out . . .'

'There is something un-Christian about Goering,' was Channon's impression, 'a strong pagan streak, a touch of the arena, though perhaps, like many who are libidinous-minded like myself, he actually does very little. People say he can be very hard and ruthless . . . but outwardly he seems all vanity and childish love of display.' Goering's vanity and curiously flamboyant habits of dress were well known, and Diana left a reminiscence of him that makes him sound something of a joke (her remarks about Goebbels, by contrast, were always tinged with wariness). Although Goering was usually to be seen in his air-force uniform, one dark winter's day Diana encountered him wearing 'a pale yellow soft leather jerkin over a white silk blouse with voluminous sleeves caught at the wrist; on his fingers were several rings set with emeralds and sapphires. I believe the jerkin had something to do with his being Reichsforstmeister [Head Forester of the Realm]; in any case he was an amazing apparition. That evening, I could not resist telling a German acquaintance about [Goering's] astonishing get-up; the only reaction was: "Yes, he dresses like that because he gets so hot."'

Two nights later, on 15 August, it was Goebbels' turn to show off: 'the last of the fantastic entertainments, and in a way the most impressive', for Channon. The house at Schwanenwerder where Diana was staying was transformed into a staging-post for 2,000 guests, who congregated there before they made their way over a series of specially laid pontoons, lined with ranks of young female dancers holding blazing torches, to a smaller island in the lake, decked with lanterns, with orchestras, dancing, displays. After dinner 'fireworks began on a scale which would have impressed the Romans . . .'

Diana's brief remarks about this orgy of ostentation were surprisingly colourless. Since she was their guest, the Goebbelses took her about with them, and, she said, they went to 'several of those awfully large rather dull receptions the Germans like'. Memory plays strange tricks, especially when time has passed and shame or distaste has intervened, and the whole issue of the Nazis' entertainments causes embarrassment to many. Chips Channon had no bashfulness in telling his readers about playtime with the Nazis ('the memoirs of the frivolous will always be eagerly read' was his comment on himself), but Diana cultivated a more serious political stance. As for Leni Riefenstahl, the 'walling-up' of her memory has been well investigated by Susan Sontag, and others. Despite photographs showing her with Diana and Unity, and reports of their meetings, Riefenstahl, when asked about them by Unity's biographer David Pryce-Jones, said: 'I don't remember them at all. I am sure I never met them.'

Such extravaganzas would not have been much to Diana's taste, anyway, and she was distracted during this Olympic fortnight – by the boredom of the games themselves, by her fruitless mission to get money from the Nazis for Mosley, and by the strain of staying with the Goebbelses. She became fond of the unhappy Magda Goebbels, and enjoyed the little children Magda was producing at the rate of one every year or so. She was a bright, pretty, dyed blond who had no choice but to stay in her ostentatious but miserable marriage, because Hitler refused to let the couple part. And although Diana is restrained in her description of Goebbels (she called him 'intelligent, witty

9 TOP: Wootton Lodge in Staffordshire, 'fairy tale' house or 'white elephant', which Diana and Mosley rented in 1936. ABOVE LEFT: Gerald Berners, composer, painter and writer, Diana's frequent host during these years. RIGHT: Diana near Lord Berners' house in Rome with his friend Desmond Parsons.

10 The many faces of Sir Oswald Mosley: (left) with his first wife, Cynthia, and Labour Party collegues in th 1920s; (above) in 1934, not long after Diana met him; (below) speaking in Trafalg Square, in the early days of British Union of Fascists.

11 TOP LEFT: Mosley in jovial mood: fencing for Britain. The original blackshirt uniform was derived from this type of fencing jacket. TOP RIGHT: Inspecting his men in the later, SS-style uniform of 1936, worn at the battle of Cable Street and banned by Act of Parliament in December that year. ABOVE: barricades in Cable Street during the disturbances of 4 October, when police fought Communists and East End protestors as the fascists stood by silently.

12 Germany: (clockwise from bottom left) Josef and Magda Goebbels and their children at their house Diana married Mosley in 1936; Diana and Unity pose for a *Daily Express* photographer in front of marching Nazis; Diana with Adolf Hitler in 1936; Diana and Tom at Nuremberg. On the home front, Mosley in domestic mode with baby Alexander and Nanny Higgs, 1939.

13 ABOVE: Lady Redesdale and the three younger girls on a cruise in 1936. ABOVE RIGHT: Lord Redesdale in Canada. RIGHT: Decca and Debo in 1935. BELOW: Holloway Prison in London as it was in 1940 when Diana was arrested.

THE MOSLEYS IN
NEW HOME

IN the yard of the Shaven
Crown, at the old-world
village of Shipton-under-
Wychwood, walk Sir Oswald
Mosley and his wife. This is
their home since their release from internment a
short time ago.

Sir Oswald's chief exercise
seems to be coal-fetching. In
a blue
boiler - suit,
carrying
bucket and
shovel, he
limps to the
coal - cellar.
The white
gloves in
which he
used to take
the salute
from his
Blackshirt
followers
now — just
keep his
hands clean.

ASKS LABOUR, '
MOSLEY AGITA

LOCAL Labour Parties
London area are a
recognise that the
affair is settled.
'They are urged to turn
other vitally important
which face the party.'
Mr. D. H. Daines, actin
tary of London Labour, w
this advice in a circular
stituent bodies, adds:
'Above all, we should be
guard against the effort
being made by bitter
opponents to exploit this
to the detriment of the
Party.
'The Communist Par
be quick to use this an
spontaneous outcry as an
tunity for sowing disunity
Labour Party.'

Dec 15 194

14 ABOVE: Diana and
Mosley snapped by press
photographers in the yard a
the Shaven Crown, 1944.
TOP LEFT: Crowood House
in Wiltshire, where Mosley
took to farming. ABOVE
LEFT: Mosley on the Lido in
Venice, a favourite holiday
destination. LEFT: Diana on
the *Alianora*, the boat Mosl
bought in order to defy the
ban on foreign travel.

15 FAR LEFT: Family life at Crowood: Diana and Mosley with Alexander and Max. LEFT: the Temple de la Gloire at Orsay outside Paris, Diana's home until 1999, with its fine drawing room (below left).

ABOVE: Mosley with supporters in an East End pub in the 1950s. LEFT: Diana and Mosley photographed arriving at London airport in the 1950s; such pictures were often accompanied by hostile editorial comment.

16 Veiled and aloof, Diana at a Union movement meeting in the 1950s.

Ball at Chatsworth: Nancy, Debo, Pam and Diana in evening dress, with Cecil Beaton (left of picture) and the Duke of Devonshire.

The sisters gather for Nancy's funeral in 1973: Diana (left), Pam and Debo are shown. Jessica too was present on this occasion, the first time she and Diana had spoken or seen each other in almost forty years; they never met again.

The literary life: the Mosleys with Christina Foyle in 1977, on the publication of Diana's *Life of Contrasts*.

and sarcastic'), he was also sinister and lecherous, power-mad and capable of adding public humiliation of his wife to his rampant infidelities: the happy family façade could surely not be kept up for long. Diana's mind was on her new house, and the plans for the summer holidays which – despite the change in her relationship with Mosley, and their plans to marry – yet again included Baba Metcalfe on a time-share basis.

However, as soon as the hated Olympics were over, Diana could leave Berlin for Bayreuth and the Festspiele, where she heard Wagner's Ring Cycle with intense pleasure, and *Parsifal* for the first time. When she told Hitler she liked *Parsifal* least of all Wagner's operas, he told her that as she got older she would appreciate it more and more. (It was his own favourite; yet for some reason after 1941 he forbade its performance at Bayreuth.) In the long intervals Diana and Unity had dinner with Hitler at a local restaurant, and Diana met Winifred Wagner, the reigning queen of Bayreuth. They had in common not only Diana's grandfather and his friendship with Siegfried Wagner but also their shared devotion to Hitler. Winifred Wagner was one of the few women for whom Hitler had any intellectual respect, and he was often at Haus Wahnfried, the emotional epicentre of his Germanizing mission.

The summer holidays that year were spent in a hotel in Sorrento. Nicholas remembers that there was 'as usual a good deal of jockeying about who would be where and when and with whom', but events intervened to rule out Baba's presence. Mosley got appendicitis and needed an emergency operation, so at the last moment the older children went to Cornwall with Irene Ravensdale and little Mickey; by the time they joined their father, he was already convalescing in Italy with Ma and Diana. It cannot have been a very comfortable group, given Ma's feelings about Diana, but during this holiday Mosley and Diana began to make firm plans for their wedding.

The arrangements were complicated. They were anxious to avoid the press at all costs: not only the gossip columnists and political opponents, but also the danger of violent demonstrations if the marriage were announced in advance. What is more, Mosley had decided they must keep the marriage secret, even from their families. The reason he gave was that his political life had become extremely rough, and Diana was now going to be alone a good deal in the isolated house at Wootton, but there may have been other motives. They planned to get married in Paris, but when they discovered that banns had to be posted at the British Consulate, they realized there would be no secrecy. Diana found out that British subjects could be married by an ordinary registrar in Germany, and appealed to Hitler to instruct the Berlin registrar to marry them in secret. That September, at the now routine visit to the Parteitag, Diana made arrangements.

The Germans' effusive propaganda towards the British was still in full swing, and there was another influx of official invitees, Irene Ravensdale among them. She confessed her reservations in her characteristic style, but decided that she 'had better try and go to the Nazi Congress, and look if only once on this firebrand Hitler'. She had no idea how warmly welcomed she would be. 'Requesting Prince Bismarck at the German Embassy to secure me one ticket for one session, I was startled by being told I would receive an official invitation from the Führer himself for the whole session. This flung me into great agitation . . . But when I discovered that many English people were going, already invited by von Ribbentrop . . . I accepted rather than be over-pernickety.'

Among many others who were not 'over-pernickety', or who were simply curious, were BUF sympathizers such as Sir Harry Brittain, Lord Mount Temple, Admiral Sir Barry Domvile, Sir Frank and Lady Newnes. A long list of MPs accepted invitations as *Ehrengäste* (guests of honour), and attended an informal party in the specially designated guest house adjoining the Grand Hotel in Nuremberg, a couple of days before the Parteitag began, to enable them to meet Hitler, Goering, Goebbels, Ribbentrop, Hess, von Shirach, Blomberg and other party notables.

On the eve of the opening of the Party Congress, Unity and Diana arrived late, with their friend Mary Widesse, and Putzi Hanfstaengl had sent a car to the station to take them straight to the opera to hear *Meistersinger*. They had no chance to change and found themselves in Aertex shirts and crumpled cotton skirts among crowds of formally dressed people: an embarrassment when they were called to the Führer's box in the interval. Tom arrived the next day, with Janos von Almasy; Hitler's adjutant had third-row seats for them all. Among the other foreign visitors were two who remained lifelong friends of Diana's, Prince Jean-Louis de Faucigny-Lucinge and Comte Jean de Castellane, the latter strongly pro-Nazi. But Unity and Diana, Tom and Janos were among the few non-Germans invited to a strange evening event in the middle of the week, a bivouac supper given by the SS. The special role of this unit was already clear, and – perhaps because they thought themselves superior, perhaps because the rest of the German army feared them so much – they camped apart from all other units. Their guests were seated at long tables in a huge tent, presided over by an affable Himmler, while the band played cheerily and the men sang.

The British reactions to all this hospitality have been well documented by

Richard Griffiths. After the war, many of the guests claimed not to have been fooled, to have had lurking suspicions and premonitions, and perhaps many did: Meriel Buchanan, in her book *Ambassador's Daughter*, described shaking hands with Hitler and looking into 'those strange mad eyes, lit up by a fanatical glare' and feeling a cold shudder 'as if I had seen a snake rearing up in front of me'. But this sort of language was common after the war, much less so before it. Contemporary accounts were often more in the vein of Sir Arnold Wilson, who described the ceremony of the *Arbeitsdienst* as 'so simple, so solemn, so moving and so sincere as to merit . . . the title of worship'. It was not only the already converted, like Lord Rennell, who wrote of 'that remarkable man of vision who directs the destinies of Germany'; Lloyd George's visit of the summer had led him to give an interview to the *News Chronicle* on 21 September describing Hitler as 'unquestionably a great leader'. 'The Germans have definitely made up their minds,' Lloyd George added, 'never to quarrel with us again.' And Beverley Nichols, in the *Sunday Chronicle*, praised the 'moral strength' of the nation and declared, 'There is so much in the new Germany that is beautiful, so much that is fine and great. And all the time in this country we are being trained to believe that the Germans are a nation of wild beasts who vary their time between roasting Jews and teaching babies to present arms. It is simply not true.'

With such focus on Germany, and so many of those who were interested in German politics flocking to one or other of the year's large events, it seems even more strange that Mosley should have stayed resolutely at home in Britain during 1936. He had also been out of the political frontline for a couple of months, convalescing from his operation, but he was laying plans to pull the pieces of his fragmenting organization back together with a grand gesture. He decided on the biggest demonstration to date, a huge march on Sunday 4 October that would start outside the Royal Mint, opposite Tower Bridge and the Tower of London, and head eastwards along Cable Street into the East End – Shoreditch, Limehouse, Bow and Bethnal Green. He would make speeches in four or five different locations along the way. It turned into the famous Battle of Cable Street, the best known of Mosley's escapades, and it is generally thought to have been a battle between fascists and anti-fascists. In fact it was not.

There was a flurry of publicity about the march, and both sides mustered their manpower. The Police Commissioner allocated 6,000 policemen to keep order, while local anti-fascists and street leaders, Jack Spot among them, made their preparations. They built a series of enormous barricades across the route of the march, one using an overturned lorry full of bricks, and their chant that day was a gesture of solidarity with the defenders of Madrid in the new Civil War in Spain: 'They shall not pass.'

Mosley's powers of stage-management were at their sharpest. About 3,000 fascists had assembled for the march, and his Blackshirts were standing to attention in military formations, their uniforms immaculate. The much larger press of people around them jostled and jeered, chanting and shouting, so that the police were forced to grapple with the crowd to keep them away from the stiff, silent fascists, thereby creating a cordon around them. Suddenly Mosley appeared, standing to attention in his open Bentley, his regalia and jackboots gleaming, his arm raised in the fascist salute, while the big car crawled through the throng of people. It was 'the rummiest sight I've ever seen in the East End', said Jack Spot. Slowly Mosley stepped out of the car and began to walk intently along the Blackshirt lines, inspecting them: still the crowd surged and tried to attack, causing the police to set about them. There were several arrests before any Blackshirt had moved a muscle. Then the Police Chief, Sir Philip Game, told Mosley he could not start his march until the police had cleared the barricades, and he ordered his constables to open up the street. The anti-fascists fought back, however, and as the police charged the defences there was an onslaught of bricks, bottles and stones, with broken glass scattered under the hooves of the police horses. Each time the police broke through, the anti-fascists retreated to another barricade, and the vicious battle began again. As the fighting raged between police and protestors, the fascists stood silently to attention. They still had not moved.

It was not that the police were pro-fascist, as many people later claimed. Sir Philip Game wanted to impose his authority on both sides, and was not about to surrender rule of the streets to the East Enders any more than to Mosley's men, but he was outmanoeuvred by Mosley's tactics. It was an extension of his rule for stewards at meetings – if the police arrived, they were to stop fighting instantly and just stand still – and it was a brilliantly effective way of getting the police and protestors to fight each other.

After two hours of bitter skirmishing with police that extended to the whole area and left more than 100 people wounded, Sir Philip Game telephoned the Home Secretary, Sir John Simon, to request authority to call the march off. When he relayed the order to Mosley, Mosley turned his troops around and marched back westwards, along Great Tower Street and Queen Victoria Street to Charing Cross pier, where he dismissed his men with a rousing speech. Communist leaders declared it a 'humiliating defeat' of Mosley, but he had behaved exactly in accordance with the law. At the same time, there had been eighty-three arrests of anti-fascists. Mosley's men may have been disappointed that the march did not take place, but they felt it a victory of a sort; Mosley had won the battle of wits.

That night, it was impossible for Mosley to evade the press and get away, so it was not until the evening of 5 October that he managed to catch a plane and leave the country. On the morning of 6 October he married Diana in the drawing room of the Goebbels' house in Berlin.

Goebbels and Magda had had a row about this wedding. In September when Diana came to dinner at Schwanenwerder, Magda had floated the idea tentatively, wanting to help her friend; Goebbels grumbled to his diary that she was getting too involved. According to him, he and Hitler were both wary of association with Mosley, and one of the other guests of the day, Heinrich Hoffmann's daughter, recalled that Hitler kept his distance from the British leader. This contradicts Unity's account in her diary, where she says that Hitler and Mosley disappeared with an interpreter at one point to talk privately; Diana said that their contacts that day were purely social.

None of these undercurrents affected her, if she knew about them. She remembered the day as bright and golden, and as she dressed in a yellow silk tunic she looked out of the upstairs window and saw Hitler walking through the autumn leaves in the park that separated the house in Hermann Goeringstrasse from the Reichskanzlei. An adjutant trotted behind him, carrying a big box and some flowers. The box turned out to contain Hitler's wedding present to them, a large photograph of himself in a heavy silver frame topped by the double-headed German eagle. The small party gathered in 'an ordinary middle-class drawing room, very bright and clean', Diana said. Unity and Magda Goebbels were Diana's witnesses, Bill Allen and an ex-officer of the Fourteenth Hussars, Captain Gordon-Canning, were Mosley's, and the only other people present were Hitler and Goebbels. The registrar conducted the ceremony in a few minutes. Afterwards, they all drove out to Schwanenwerder for a luncheon at Goebbels' house by the lake, with posies of flowers collected by the little girls. The rest of the day was spent at the Sportpalast, where Hitler made a speech to open the Winterhilfswerk (an organization that distributed coal, blankets and basic food to the needy in the cold winter months); this was the only time Mosley saw Hitler in action, in front of a crowd of 20,000. Sefton Delmer in the *Sunday Express*, as well as other journalists, reported that Hitler's speech contained a furious attack on European democracy and on Bolshevism. Mosley understood no German, but it interested one theatrical performer to observe another at work.

Then it was back to the Reichskanzlei for a dinner hosted by Hitler. Diana remembers that the long day was a strain: having to interpret everything meant that conversation was intermittent and banal. 'We were both exhausted by the hopeless language difficulty,' Diana later wrote to Nicholas, 'and I was very sorry that your father and Hitler couldn't have a real talk. It was so boring for both of them.' It must have been very strange for her. Here were the two men who mattered most to her, both extra-ordinary talkers, face to face for the first time in her presence, but they could only exchange trivialities. She was relieved when Hitler left to catch his special train back to Munich, taking Unity with him, and she and Mosley went off to spend the night at the Kaiserhof Hotel.

One conversation that day had far-reaching implications, however. In an effort to entertain her grumpy host, the new Lady Mosley gave Goebbels the inside story of the royal love affair between Edward VIII and Mrs Simpson. Goebbels and Hitler seemed shocked, but they did not forget that, as Prince of Wales, Edward had spoken publicly in support of Hitler's social programme. From October onwards the newspapers of America and the rest of Europe were full of the scandal, while the British press kept silent, and Hitler and Goebbels decided to support the King in the same way – Goebbels put a total ban on any mention of the royal goings-on in the German media. After the abdication two months later, Nazi wiretappers intercepted a comment from one British Embassy official, to the effect that the former King would be sure to remember Hitler's decision with gratitude.

The eagle-decked photograph graced the drawing room at Wootton for several years – to the discomfiture of some visitors – but it disappeared in a domestic fire at the Mosleys' Irish house in the 1950s. However, Magda Goebbels' present was one that Diana treasured until the end of her life: the complete works of Goethe in twenty small volumes, bound in bright red leather with flimsy blue water-paper, inscribed in Magda's formal script:

My dear Diana
in reminiscence of 6 October 1936
and the happiness of being with you both on your wedding day
With very loving wishes
and everything for your success and happiness
Magda Goebbels

20 *Air-waves*

Not a word about the Mosleys' marriage leaked to the press in either country, although journalists strongly suspected it and often pestered Tom and other family members for confirmation. But they could find no proof. The secret was tucked away in a German registrar's files, and Diana continued to be known as Mrs Guinness. She told her parents, who were greatly relieved that their daughter was no longer living in sin, and she also told Tom, who was still her close confidant, but none of the other sisters apart from Unity were aware of it. It seems that on this occasion Unity managed to be discreet. Mosley told no one, not even his children, Irene, Baba or Ma. The reasons he gave later – that he did not want Diana mixed up in the hurly-burly of his politics – were flimsy. (Baba, for one, was bitterly angry when she found out a full two years later about the marriage. After that, her relationship with Mosley abruptly ended.) There was one other more substantial reason, however, which concerned a plan that he and Diana had been hatching for re-financing his movement.

By 1936 support for the BUF was at a low ebb, and the organization's reputation was becoming increasingly unsavoury. Not only had the overt anti-Semitism hardened attitudes, but the authorities could no longer tolerate the civil disturbances caused by the fascists and their opponents. The Battle of Cable Street provided a spur to official action, and in December 1936 a new Public Order Act was passed through Parliament. It banned the wearing of the Blackshirt uniform and regalia, and gave local police chiefs the power to ban fascist marches. Now, Mosley found it almost impossible to get a booking at a large hall in any of the big cities, which meant that both his most powerful weapons – the marches and the huge public rallies – were denied him. Furthermore, the Act contained a clause that obliged movements like his to reveal the source of all their funds. Financial help from Mussolini's government in Italy had come to an end – probably in the summer of 1935, although the records are incomplete – and perhaps because the Duce discovered that Mosley had been in Germany to see Hitler: the two European leaders were possessive and competitive about what they saw as satellite fascist organizations. Grandi, the Italian Ambassador to London, had been urging Mussolini to cut his ties with Mosley – although he had been a keen supporter two years before, he now wrote to the Duce that 'with a tenth of what you give Mosley . . . I could produce a result ten times better'. Diana has suggested that there might have been some personal jealousy over Baba Metcalfe involved in this sudden change of attitude.

At the beginning of 1937, then, Mosley realized that his organization was almost bankrupt, and that the BUF was facing a severe internal crisis as well as its many external problems. In March 1937, after the east London municipal elections had brought very limited success for his candidates, Mosley took drastic action, reducing his headquarters' staff from 140 people to 30 in a single afternoon, and cutting his budget by 70 per cent.

Even this was not enough, and money was urgently needed. During this period Mosley put at least £100,000 of his own into the movement, but he knew he could not personally support it for very long. As early as 1934 Mosley had begun to think about setting up a commercial base to finance his political organization, and he had formed a cigarette manufacturing company, New Epoch Products Ltd, with Lord Rothermere. A factory had been acquired and production was due to start when the break with Rothermere put an end to the scheme. During 1937, Nicholas Mosley remembers, 'one or two business schemes were bandied about', sometimes half-jokingly, over the dinner table at Wootton. One idea centred round making and marketing a pill that would deodorize breath – there was nothing like that then available, and just think how many marriages might be saved, they joked, by removing the smell of drink! Since Nicholas describes his father in earnest conversation about the scheme with a young scientist who paid a visit to Wootton, it was obviously at least half serious. Another ruse involved obtaining the concession for organising football pools in France. These proposals, whether mere pipe-dreams or more realistic, were never modest. Mosley was already, of course, a rich man by most people's standards, so the aim, as Nicholas remembers, was 'an enormous fortune'.

But unknown to Nicholas, and almost everyone else at the time, one get-rich scheme was already under way. Since 1936 Diana had been negotiating with the German government for permission to set up a commercial radio station on German territory to broadcast to the south-east of England, and this was why her visits to Germany had become so frequent. It was also, she claimed, one of the reasons why they had kept their marriage secret.

At that time, the BBC held a monopoly over the domestic air-waves, so any independent radio venture broadcasting to Britain had to site its station on foreign soil. Despite this complication, there were already a few successful mavericks: Radio Luxembourg was supplying a diet of light music and lighter advertising, and in 1930 a company called International Broadcasting Co., the brain-child of one Captain Leonard Plugge, had secured a licence from the French government to operate Radio Normandie, which broadcast to Britain from the French coast. Although, like Radio Luxembourg, Radio Normandie could only reach a small part of the country, Captain Plugge's initiative had netted a handsome profit, and was an encouraging precedent. The British advertising industry was beginning to expand – by 1935 about £400,000 a year was being spent on commercials, and within three years the figure had increased to about £1,700,000 – but it was short of outlets. The BBC monopoly, with its strict policy of no commercial input, meant that advertisers had no access to the air-waves at all in Britain; they welcomed any new commercial radio venture.

The advantages for the franchising countries were equally simple: they benefited from the influx of sterling and a share of the profits; all they had to do was part with a wavelength. But the Mosleys' radio station was not intended as a political vehicle. Their agreement with the Germans emphasized that there was to be no political message, either from the BUF or the host country; all propaganda was specifically forbidden in the contracts for fear of scaring away advertisers. The aim was purely and simply to make money, using a gentle programme of light music to advertise domestic products to housewives (as Americans were doing with the new 'soap' operas). According to Diana, the Mosleys became so enthusiastic about the opportunities that they even planned to start manufacturing cosmetics and other products that could then be sold over their own air-waves. Ambitious as ever, they saw the German scheme as merely the first in a chain of radio stations surrounding the British Isles on several sides – in Ireland to the west, the Channel Islands to the south, as well as Germany and Belgium to the east.

The practical demands of the plans were eased by the fact that Mosley already had an advertising expert in his inner circle. His long-standing friend and political ally Bill Allen was chairman of a large family advertising business, David Allen and Sons, based in Northern Ireland. Allen was central to the plan from the beginning, and acted throughout as the front-man for the organization; he was especially keen, through his family and business connections, on the prospects of an Irish franchise. For technical expertise in broadcasting they recruited Peter Eckersley, also a BUF sympathizer, who had been a chief engineer at the BBC until sacked by Lord Reith in 1936 for the sole offence of getting divorced. The only other individuals who knew about the project were Gerald Keith, Mosley's solicitor, and one or two BUF sympathizers who tried to secure franchises in other places: Sir Oliver Hoare (the brother of the then Home Secretary Sir Samuel Hoare), who negotiated (unsuccessfully) for Mosley in Belgium in 1937, and Colin Beaumont, the son of the Dame of Sark, the quasi-feudal ruler of that Channel Island. All the players in the scheme understood the need for intense secrecy: if the press, or anyone else, had caught a whiff of the connection between the proposed new radio stations and Mosley, the advertisers would immediately boycott them and the dreamt-of fortune would never materialize. Consequently, they all signed a secrecy pact, which the Mosleys stuck to with rigour: even Unity had no idea why Diana came to Germany so often in the two years between the summer of 1936 and the middle of 1938.

Disguising Mosley's involvement meant setting up companies with suitably anodyne names. A firm called Museum Investment Trust was used to conceal Mosley's identity when, in the spring of 1937, a thirty-year broadcasting agreement was reached with the Dame of Sark, through Colin Beaumont (Mosley was to finance the construction of the station, and Beaumont to have 25 per cent of the profits). They hoped – unsuccessfully, as it turned out – to establish that Sark was outside the writ of the BBC monopoly. The German plans entailed even more elaborate provisions. There was a holding company called Air Time Ltd, of which the directors were Peter Eckersley and a partner named Carpenter, set up with an initial capital of £10,000, and another firm called Radio Variety (directors Peter Eckersley and an accountant) to sell the advertising and develop programmes. Most of the capital was Mosley's own.

Mosley, of course, did none of his own negotiations. Diana thought that, through a combination of her access to senior Nazis and the lure of the hard currency Germany needed so badly, she might be able to win the concession from the Germans (if they agreed, the Mosleys believed, other countries would be more likely to follow). But in trying to persuade the Germans to grant them a wavelength – especially on medium wave, which was essential for a strong enough signal to run a popular station – she faced tough opposition. Josef Goebbels was firmly against the plan. He was not only loath to give up one of his wavebands, but he also hated the idea of any broadcasting from German territory which would not be under the control of his propaganda ministry. In the days before television, the radio was the most powerful political instrument for reaching the masses, and Goebbels was aware of its importance as a fighting weapon: as war approached, and later, during the early 1940s, Goebbels thought up all sorts of inventive and bizarre broadcasting schemes. In 1937, though, Diana's plan also came up against objections from the high command of the Wehrmacht and the Luftwaffe: such foreign intervention went against the nationalist grain so deep in Nazism.

It was formidable opposition, but Diana kept trying. Her personal friendship with Magda Goebbels was an important channel to the weaselly propaganda minister, but that would not be enough. She knew that her best hope was to ride in on the whim of Hitler himself – the only person who could overrule Goebbels – but the Führer couldn't really be bothered to discuss the idea – 'he was never interested in the details of things like that', Diana said. Most of the franchise negotiations took place with Dr Wilhelm Ohnesorge, the Postmaster-General, who was sympathetic to Diana's ideas because he was convinced of the advantages to Germany that a steady flow of hard currency would bring. But Ohnesorge, despite his position, was not a Nazi, and had limited influence. Throughout the winter of 1936 and the summer of 1937, Diana repeatedly left Wootton to travel to Berlin, where she would stay at the Kaiserhof Hotel, just opposite the Reichskanzlei, and try to move the discussions along. Sometimes she travelled with a young barrister called Frederick Lawton, who had been instructed to advise on the legalities. These were often boring times for Diana, who spent the days waiting in her hotel room, eating meals in the hotel, too, for she dared not go out during office hours in case she was called to the telephone. When 5.30 came, and there had been no call, she would rush out to a museum, or to shop; otherwise, she was strict about the business in hand.

On occasional evenings, however, often very late, the telephone would ring with a message from Hitler, over the road in the Reichskanzlei. Diana became skilled at finding out when the Führer would be in Berlin, and timed her visits accordingly: restless and insomniac after the day's formalities, he liked to summon some spirited company to chat to him, or watch a film, or eat supper (he lived with little ceremony, and meals were usually impromptu and informal). In a large, rather bare, private room, in front of a huge fireplace, Hitler liked to unwind by talking half the night, and he and Diana were often left alone by his weary staff. There was nothing sexual in these encounters, although Diana is eloquent about the power of his charm, and he was obviously in thrall to her wit and beauty: he liked to talk about politics, as ever, and he liked an intelligent listener. Years later, when Diana once mentioned in Mosley's hearing that she enjoyed the company of politicians, he snorted and said, 'Politicians are bores. You like them because the only ones you've ever met are Hitler, Churchill and me.'

On the radio discussions, though, progress was slow. Diana was too clever to risk her relationship with Hitler by nagging him for a decision in her favour. She just had to bide her time, and continue to charm and reassure the Germans; but in October 1937 came a blow that seemed to be final. A letter from Captain Wiedemann, Hitler's adjutant, written from Obersalzberg on the 9th of the month to Mrs Guinness (as she was still known), ran: 'I have today finally reported to the Führer the whole matter concerning the advertising transmissions. I had also in this connection to report to the Führer that apart from considerations of the technical matters and so on that the Ministry of Propaganda has raised – considerations which under some circumstances could have been disregarded – the greatest objection was raised by the appropriate military authorities. The Führer regrets that under these circumstances he is not able to agree to your proposal. I am very sorry that I cannot give you any other answer . . .'

Undaunted, Diana tried again early in 1938, and this time her efforts met with more success. In February Wiedemann wrote again, saying that the Führer's interest was sufficiently rekindled for him to have taken the documents to read, although 'whether he has got round to reading them in these last few stormy weeks [Hitler was on the point of annexing Austria] I do not know. I would advise you,' Weidemann continued, 'to come to Germany again when things have settled down, and then get your decision from the Führer himself.'

Given the opposition she had to confront (the combined power of Goebbels, the Luftwaffe and the Wehrmacht), as well as the increasing speed of world events and Hitler's indifference to plans that were not a direct part of his military mission, it was almost miraculous that Diana finally got his consent, but get it she did. It shows that Hitler must have had a very high opinion of her; it also shows that she had remarkable skills as a negotiator and diplomat. After the Anschluss in March 1938, when Germany took over the Austrians' wavelengths along with everything else, Goebbels was at last persuaded to authorize the leasing of one of his newly acquired medium wavebands (the former Polish Kattowitz frequency) to Air Time Ltd. Hitler then authorized a meeting to exchange contracts; Diana remembers that she and Mosley celebrated her success at Wootton on her birthday, 10 June.

By the following month, the contracts were ready, and a meeting took place in Paris on 18 July. Bill Allen represented Air Time Ltd; the German signatories (for Gemona AG, a German-registered company set up for the purpose) were Dr Johannes Bernhardt and Kurt von Schroeder, a prominent industrialist and Nazi. Mosley, once again, had no contact with the Germans.

The deal pleased both sides. The Reichspost owned 55 per cent of the equity; Air Time Ltd the remaining 45 per cent. The Germans were to finance the building of the radio station at Osterloog, near Norddeich, in the furthest north-west corner of Germany, from where broadcasts would reach East Anglia and the south-east of England. They were also to cover the operating expenses, while the British company would be responsible for selling advertising, programming and supplying announcers. Profits were to be divided: 45 per cent would go to the British, the rest to the Germans. The Mosleys, it seemed, were in sight of their 'enormous fortune'.

The construction of the station was scheduled to take fourteen months, and as far as Diana knew it was completed. She often wondered, she said, whether it was used for broadcasting during the war, since the completion date for the construction coincided almost exactly with the outbreak of hostilities in September 1939. Other sources suggest that it went on air as Bremen I, broadcasting propaganda to Britain during the war years.

When the war began, Air Time's plans came to nothing. Many years later, Mosley wrote of how nearly he had become 'the first revolutionary in history to conduct a revolution and at the same time to make the fortune which assured its success'. The money, he claimed, 'would have been clean money, made by our own abilities and great exertions'. Then, with his characteristic mixture of self-congratulation and delight in the chance to cock a snook at the establishment, he went on: 'We should neither have double-crossed nor capitulated to capitalism. We should have beaten it on its own territory with good clean weapons of relatively decent commerce, which at least provided the people with an entertaining alternative to the dreary schoolmasters at the BBC. Last but not least we should have had a good crack at the press Lords.'

Considering how far advanced their plans were, and how close they came to success, it is all the more extraordinary that the whole project remained secret for so long. Nothing was known about it until the 1970s. It was typical of Diana that she took the secrecy oath so seriously that even when the war was over, the map of Europe transformed, most of the protagonists dead and the wireless-station plan nothing but a memory, she still never spoke about it. She made no mention of it in her memoirs, and none of her sisters knew of the scheme until details were published by historians. She once said, 'No, I don't think it ever occurred to me to tell my family about it after the war.' If she had, some of the stigma of her flirtation with the Nazis might have been mitigated (in Nancy's eyes, for instance) by the fact that she was doing business, as it were, for the family firm; but Diana really didn't care what anyone thought of her relationship with Hitler.

In fact, the broadcasting scheme may have tipped the balance of the Mosleys' wartime fate more strongly than they knew at the time. For it now seems likely that MI5 knew all about the project, probably through Bill Allen, who, it turns out, was working for MI5 throughout the time he was Mosley's friend and a publicly acknowledged BUF supporter. Even more oddly, Mosley apparently knew of Allen's secret-service connections all along. Nicholas Mosley quotes him as saying that Allen was 'very much involved with MI5, and made no bones about it', and that he had probably contributed 'largely fictitious reports' on their conversations; Allen was, according to Mosley, a 'tremendously boastful man'. But perhaps Mosley was happy to have an MI5 informer at the heart of his organization: better to be watched by the authorities than ignored by them, and anyway it showed them his true intentions, which he never wished to hide. He enjoyed the double-dealing game of cat-and-mouse. In Diana's opinion: 'We were always sure MI5 knew all about the wireless project, and it never seemed to Mosley to matter in the least. It was the Press that mattered, in connection with secrecy.'

It is more than likely that British Intelligence also knew of Diana's late-night visits to Hitler, as well as their many more public appearances in each other's company, and this may have been a strong factor in the later decision to arrest and imprison Diana. In any case, the German contract was found among Mosley's papers by MI5 searches after his arrest, and when Diana was questioned, after her own arrest, by Norman Birkett's Advisory Committee, the whole thing was treated as suspicious. 'It was preposterous' in Diana's view. 'They accused me of planning to "help" Germany by playing Beethoven and Wagner over the radio, and so making German culture more respectable!' The authorities found it hard to believe there were no direct propaganda intentions, but although to be engaged in a new business deal with Germany in the summer of 1939 looked at best foolish and at worst thoroughly suspect, it was not actually illegal or treacherous. As usual, Mosley and Diana treated the British authorities' reactions with disdain, and at her interrogation Diana was openly contemptuous of Norman Birkett's 'silly' questions. Air Time Ltd became a victim of what Mosley called the 'accident' of war, and receded into historical obscurity.

21 *Prophesying War*

In 1936 Lord Redesdale decided to sell Swinbrook House, even though he had completed the building of it less than ten years before, and the estate around it. The large family for whom it had been designed was almost dispersed, and Tom had no interest in country pursuits or a country house from which to pursue them – he preferred the law and travel, music and love affairs. But David, having divested himself of one large and expensive property, soon acquired another that was also large and expensive, and this time extremely remote. He bought the island of Inchkenneth, a tiny tadpole-shaped piece of land that lies in the shelter of Loch na Keal to the west of the Isle of Mull in the Inner Hebrides. On the island is one large bleak house, a bare white box with castellations on top of its five storeys. There is an ancient ruined chapel, a cottage, a walled garden, a single field and a small jetty. Getting there was described by Nancy as 'The Worst Journey in the World' (the title of a book about Scott's Antarctic expedition); once there, Jonathan claims, it is the most beautiful place on earth. David put the island in Tom's name.

In 1936 Pam was also married, a few weeks after Diana, to a brilliant and wealthy physicist, Derek Jackson, and the eighteen-year-old Decca eloped to Spain with her cousin Esmond Romilly, who was nineteen. The Spanish Civil War and Decca's communist sympathies, coupled with her boredom at Swinbrook, made her the next to follow what was becoming a family tradition, to make a wild gesture for her man and her cause. (An Austrian friend of Janos von Almasy, who met Lord Redesdale with Unity in 1935, remembers him saying mournfully to her, 'I'm normal, my wife is normal, but my daughters are each more foolish than the other.')

Decca's elopement with Esmond Romilly was a great crisis for the Redesdales: letters flew between them, arrangements were made, Nancy and Prodd were dispatched to get them home again. As they were both under twenty-one, they could not be married without parental consent, but this was eventually arranged between the families and a hurried wedding took place in France. Diana sent Decca an amethyst and pearl necklace and earrings – perhaps not the most useful present under the circumstances, unless it was intended to be usefully saleable. Otherwise she was kept well out of it. Given her politics, her involvement would only have been inflammatory, and she had never been particularly close to Decca in any case. The strange thing is that Decca and Unity were still almost as devoted as they had been since their young childhood: 'my Boud', they called each other, and, despite their ferocious differences of political opinion, Unity was devastated by the fact that Decca had not confided her running-away plans.

Diana's marriage had reassured her parents a little, but its secrecy caused some difficulties. 'Living in sin' was still in those days considered beyond the pale, and Irene Ravensdale – who was not in the know – would not let the teenage Vivien stay with her father and Diana at Wootton (although Nicholas came often). Diana could not even spend Christmas with Mosley in 1936, as he was back at Savehay Farm with his children, Ma and the sisters-in-law; she went to stay with friends. A ridiculous situation arose when Muv would not allow Debo, the only daughter over whom she still had any control, to visit Diana – even though Sydney knew that Diana was respectably married, Debo did not, and no one else did, and the eyes of the world were what mattered. Mosley and Diana's youngest sister did not even meet until 1938, and then it was a visit made on the quiet.

With their worries about Decca, Unity and Diana, the Redesdales were among the very few whose attention was diverted from the national crisis of the moment, the abdication of King Edward VIII in December 1936. Although the British press had kept silent on the subject of the King's love affair with a twice-married American, Mrs Wallis Simpson, by that autumn most people in society, or with parliamentary connections, knew what was happening. Many had been aware of the relationship between Edward and Wallis for much longer. Chips Channon, who never liked the King but saw in Wallis an admirable courage and tact, made a diary entry at the beginning of 1936 that proved to be far-sighted. As the old King, George V, lay dying, Channon wrote of the then Prince of Wales: 'he will mind so terribly being king. His loneliness, his seclusion, his isolation will be almost more than his highly strung and unimaginative nature can bear. Never has a man been so in love . . .' Although the Mosleys were not part of Edward and Wallis's social circle at this point, they had other close informants because Baba's husband, Fruity Metcalfe, was one of the King's friends and confidants.

Edward did in fact mind being king, and most historians agree that he was barely equal to the job. Though popular at first – he was handsome, charming and sympathetic – he found his duties irksome when they clashed with his private interests. During the autumn of 1936 his popularity went rapidly downhill, because of his extraordinary tactlessness – on the day, for instance, when he had claimed to be too busy to open a new hospital in Aberdeen, he was seen not far away at Ballater station meeting Wallis Simpson off a train. He was obsessed by Wallis, and determined to marry her; his grasp of the political realities was feeble. He had been brought up to believe that he could do anything he wanted; it was Wallis who realized what the consequences might be. Yet during his brief reign, 'Nothing seemed to matter to [Edward] but the pursuit of his heart's desire,' wrote even the most partisan of his biographers, Michael Bloch.

The British political establishment was in turmoil at the unprecedented constitutional crisis, and there was serious concern that the institution of monarchy itself might be damaged. 'If he married her,' Chips Channon put it succinctly, 'he would have to abdicate immediately, for if he did not, we would have unrest, Socialist agitation, and a "Yorkist" party [in support of the Duke of York, the next brother in line to the throne and eventually King George VI]'. Nevertheless, Channon typically added: 'What a temptation for a Baltimore girl.'

After Wallis's divorce hearing in October the factions for and against Edward, and the abdication question, became more pronounced. Winston Churchill was among the 'King's Party', ready to support him; but Baldwin, the Prime Minister, and the majority of senior political figures were by now simply anxious that the King should go without causing too much scandal. Throughout November there was intense political and personal intrigue and speculation. Baldwin told the King his government would resign if he persisted in his intention to marry Mrs Simpson, and on 3 December the British newspapers finally abandoned their reticence and blazoned the story to the country: their King was in love with a twice-divorced American, generally thought to be an adventuress, and set on marrying her. The judgements were unsparing, on the whole – only the Beaverbrook and Rothermere papers were sympathetic, since both those press barons were friends of the King.

There was a public furore. 'The plain fact is that nobody could envisage a king married to a lady with two ex-husbands living,' Diana wrote many years later, in 1980, when she published a life of the Duchess of Windsor. There is no doubt that the contemporary prejudice against divorce was the main factor, and the difficult position in which marrying a divorcée would place Edward (who as king was Supreme Governor of the Church of England); but others had different views. Many remember the anti-American feeling of those years, which amounted to a fear of full-scale economic subordination; the King's own growing unpopularity, as he became increasingly offhand about public duties, did not help. Feelings ran high, on the streets as well as in Parliament, where a stand-up row between Churchill and Baldwin took place in early December. When the Prime Minister told the House of Commons that his government was not prepared to introduce legislation that would make a morganatic marriage possible for the King, Churchill shouted: 'You won't be satisfied until you've broken him, will you?' Lloyd George, who was also a supporter of the King, echoed Churchill's belief that Baldwin's animus against Edward was political as much as constitutional. Lloyd George was in the West Indies and unable to return in time for a debate in the House of Commons on 7 December, but he sent his son Gwilym and his daughter Megan, both of whom were Members of Parliament, a telegram which was obviously for public consumption. It began: 'Hope you are not going to join the Mrs Grundy harriers who are hunting the King from the Throne' and continued with the fierce view that 'Had [the] King not as prince and sovereign exposed continued neglect by Government of chronic distress, poverty and bad housing conditions amongst people in his realm, [I am] convinced they would not have shown such alacrity to dethrone him.'

Diana's book *The Duchess of Windsor* paints a sympathetic portrait of both Wallis and Edward, so it inevitably emphasizes this side of the argument. Like Lloyd George, she conjures up a picture of a much-loved, caring, even radical monarch whose only transgression had been to challenge the complacency of a staid and stuffy government. It was not a view shared by many – although it became Edward's own version of events during his long exile. In 1936 when the revelations about Wallis broke in the press, the public was reminded of Edward's playboy years as Prince of Wales, and to this essential charge – a lack of seriousness and proper sense of his office – was added the suspicion of pro-German sentiments. Whatever the Duke of Windsor later claimed, at the time he was so preoccupied with marrying Wallis that he behaved as if he could hardly wait to leave the throne. He was quite unrealistic about the consequences of his action, and the bitter wrangles of the coming years – about Wallis's title, about money, about his own role – were indicative both of his own naïvety and of the royal family's determined lack of forgiveness.

On Friday 11 December, the British people woke up in the reign of Edward VIII and went to bed in that of George VI, after the first abdication of a British monarch for 537 years. The dramatic speech, broadcast from a small room in Windsor Castle where the King sat alone with his lawyer,

Walter Monckton, was heard all over the world. Wallis Simpson listened to it lying on a sofa in the Villa Lou Viei at Cannes, where she had taken refuge with her friends Kitty and Herman Rogers – covering her eyes with her hands to hide her tears, as she later wrote. The hate-mail which arrived daily by the sackful only increased in volume and virulence. Diana remembered listening to the speech on the wireless at Wootton with Jim Lees-Milne. Since she had been living so far outside London society for the past year, she had not been party to the rumour mill of London drawing rooms, and especially that of her old friend Emerald Cunard, Wallis Simpson's champion. But she heard at second hand much of what was going on in the next few months. The new Duke of Windsor was advised by Walter Monckton that he must not even be in the same country as Wallis until her divorce became final in the spring, in case there were even now legal moves to stop their marriage. Edward had chosen Schloss Enzesfeld in Austria, Baron Eugen Rothschild's house, as the place to while away the weeks of waiting, and as his companion he had chosen his old friend Fruity Metcalfe, Baba's husband. It was not an association that gave either much pleasure, apparently, and through the five long months of this vigil Metcalfe's letters to his wife complain of the boredom, the tension, and of the Duke's meanness about money.

On 3 June 1937 Edward and Wallis finally managed to get married. Friends had offered them various locations for the wedding. For reasons of comfort and privacy from the press, they chose the Château de Candé in Touraine, which belonged to a French-American entrepreneur, Charles Bedaux; Wallis had been staying there for some weeks. The Reverend Anderson Jardine married them in defiance of his bishop's instructions; Cecil Beaton came to photograph the couple on the eve of the wedding. Baba Metcalfe and Randolph Churchill were among the dozen guests (none of the bridegroom's family appeared); Fruity Metcalfe was the Duke's best man.

Apart from the hospitality he gave the couple, Charles Bedaux occupies a small but distinct place in their story because it was he who arranged for the Windsors, soon after their marriage, a trip which was probably their greatest piece of mistiming and tactlessness: a visit to Nazi Germany. They were never forgiven for this by the public, and the charge of pro-German feeling – even active support for the Nazis – became a lasting stigma. In her book Diana stoutly defends their decision to visit Germany, pointing out that there was still nothing strange in such a visit – Halifax, the Foreign Secretary, paid an official visit even later, and Diana claims that there was no 'war fever' in Britain until the following year, 1938.

The visit had come about because the Duke of Windsor was so stung by his family's refusal to countenance any royal status for Wallis, wounded by financial quarrels with his brother, the new king, and anxious for some active role for himself after months of enforced idleness, that he was susceptible to Bedaux's flattering suggestion that he might now become a sort of freelance statesman, travelling on his country's behalf and promoting international understanding. Through his business empire Bedaux arranged for the couple to make two 'study tours' of industrial conditions, the first to Hitler's Germany, the second to Roosevelt's America. The Duke was pleased: it was a sort of quasi-royal progress for him and his bride; the Duchess was glad because she looked forward to a visit home to America. They had nothing else to do, and for the moment they had nowhere to live – the Duke still believed that, after an interval for the dust to settle, they would return to Britain.

In the event, the proposed American tour in November and December 1937 was cancelled, because Bedaux had fallen foul of some powerful American labour unions over his ruthless 'time and motion' practices, and the arrangements were abruptly called off. It avoided some tricky diplomatic moments: although the trip was supposed to be unofficial, the President and Mrs Roosevelt had invited the couple to the White House, as well as on a tour of housing projects in which the First Lady was especially interested – yet the British Ambassador in Washington had instructions to ignore them. Wallis was particularly disappointed, and had to make do with the German trip and a forced-march tour of German factories (the photographs show the couple's faces getting progressively grimmer and their smiles increasingly forced throughout the October fortnight). Their guide was the dull and drunken Dr Ley, of the Nazi labour organization Arbeitsfront; however, they were enthusiastically received by Goebbels, Goerring, Hess and Ribbentrop, among others, and their visit ended with tea at Berchtesgarden with Hitler.

They talked through Hitler's interpreter, Paul Schmidt, even though the Duke's German was good – good enough, Diana reported, to correct the interpreter on occasions. Records of the conversation are lost (although Schmidt left an account of it). Diana says there were 'certain areas of agreement' between Hitler and Edward, but blandly lists them as 'admiration for the British Empire, hatred of Communism'. She knew, however, that Hitler was a political realist, and however friendly the Duke's disposition towards Germany might have been, his potential usefulness to Hitler was nullified by his position. And in a footnote she adds, 'The author [i.e. Diana herself], who saw Hitler from time to time, cannot remember hearing him mention the Duke and Duchess of Windsor.'

The debate still continues about the Windsors' degree of sympathy with the Nazis, at this date or later. The visit generated several fantasies, not least in the mind of Ribbentrop. Some time later he apparently tried to persuade Hitler that Edward had lost his crown because of his sympathy for Nazi Germany, and that he might therefore be interested in the idea of getting it back under the auspices of the Germans. Another myth that arose was that Wallis became ardently pro-Nazi, but there is little evidence: Wallis's diaries recorded a common reaction to Nazis – a mixture of fascination and horror – and in any case her political interests and acumen were restricted to dinner-party diplomacy. Diana quotes the 'Dook' (privately, she referred to Edward like this, since that was how Wallis pronounced it) as telling her that 'Every drop of my blood is German', but that unlike his pro-Nazi cousin, the Duke of Saxe Coburg Gotha, Edward was no National Socialist. He was a fervent monarchist who assumed, at this point, that within a few months he would be back in England, living at his country house, Fort Belvedere, and fulfilling some appropriate and highly patriotic role. He had no idea that he was facing permanent exile.

But the facts of the visit, and its aftermath, are of less consequence than the general perception of it, as Diana knew. She quotes a message sent in the autumn of 1937 from the British Ambassador in Washington, Sir Ronald Lindsay, to US Undersecretary of State Sumner Welles on the subject of the Windsors' aborted American trip, describing 'on the part of all the governing class in England a very vehement feeling of indignation' against Edward, for having reneged on his royal responsibilities, adding that 'in Court circles and in the Foreign Office and on the part of the heads of political parties, this feeling bordered on hysteria'. In such a climate, only the most politically unaware could think a visit to Hitler would not have extensive repercussions, and leave an ineradicable taint.

It is perhaps surprising that Hitler never spoke of the Windsors, because it was in the autumn of 1937 that Diana saw him most regularly. For her, much of that year was taken up with Germany and the plans for the radio station. There were tedious and solitary weeks waiting in the Kaiserhof Hotel for day after day until she had a chance to talk to someone in authority and inch the scheme forward. Diana's life at Wootton was solitary too, but she said she was never lonely or bored. She had given up almost all her social London friends, partly by choice, and only a few faithfuls were invited to Wootton. Nancy was in bad odour with Mosley, and the sisters were 'on non-speakers' for these years. Jim Lees-Milne, with whom Diana had almost lost touch during her first marriage, reappeared. Unity sometimes brought her Austrian friends, and Henry and Dig Yorke, rare remnants of the Biddesden set, also visited occasionally. Diana's sons were with her for half the time, and whenever Mosley came home he liked to find her alone. More and more it became a refuge for him, and during this year, when a brick was hurled at his head during an open-air meeting in Liverpool and found its target with painful accuracy, he stayed at home to convalesce for several weeks. In the winter of 1937 he took two months off from the political round and stayed at Wootton to write his next book, *Tomorrow We Live*.

Mosley had given up his flat in Ebury Street and acquired a house on the River Thames in Grosvenor Road, in Pimlico. It is a strange and completely undomestic building which had been a restaurant, with a huge central room held up with pillars and wide windows looking over the water – just the kind of sparse but imposing room Mosley liked best. But when Diana visited London she often stayed with friends, usually Gerald Berners in Halkin Street, and recreated some of the gregariousness of previous years.

For the first time since her marriage to Bryan Guinness, Diana felt short of money, even though – or perhaps because – she was living in such a large and beautiful house. Wootton Lodge was a very substantial place to keep up. Mosley paid the rent, and installed heating; Diana paid the wages. She decided to dispense with her lady's maid, for the first time in her adult life, so that she could have another gardener. But she was determined that, at Wootton, there should be no clouds on the horizon, and Nicholas remembers his holidays there as happy interludes in a difficult childhood. He chose to divide his time between Wootton and Savehay Farm. Often he was alone with Diana, when his father was away, the two of them taking meals together in the big dining room. She was close to being a real step-mother.

In Germany, while Diana concentrated on Berlin, her radio discussions with Ohnesorge and her occasional fireside chats with Hitler, Unity in Munich was at the centre of an incident which seems to illuminate the peculiar reality of her relationship with the Führer. It is clear that Hitler used Unity's blind devotion, her credulity and her lack of discretion to circulate 'rumours', usually aimed at the British Consulate in Munich, where Unity spent quite a bit of time; diplomatic reports confirm that her remarks about conversations with Hitler were often passed back to London. But one of the reasons why Hitler's staff loathed and even feared her was the reciprocal power she had. While his *Umgebung*, his little court, spent their time trying to pacify the Führer, Unity would repeat to him every trivial complaint she heard, careless of whether or not she triggered his anger. Fanatically, she sniffed out the faintest whiff of dissent or disloyalty. Erna Hanfstaengl, Putzi's sister and Unity's close friend, warned her time and again of the extreme dangers of careless talk in the prevailing climate of denunciations, disappearances and arbitrary arrests. Erna once became seriously frightened when she heard Unity laughing about Frau Himmler, a pathetic woman who had suffered shellshock while nursing at the front in the First World War. Even within high Nazi circles Himmler was feared: no one else would have got away with mocking his wife.

Now Putzi Hanfstaengl himself fell victim to Hitler's displeasure, and realized he had to flee the country to save his neck. The story has many versions, but it apparently began in February of 1937 when Diana, Unity and their cousin Clementine Mitford (later Lady Beit) were in Berlin. They had dinner with Hitler at the Reichskanzlei, then watched a film with him; during their chat they were laughing about the awkward and timorous Hanfstaengl. Unity told Hitler that Hanfstaengl, nostalgic for the Nazis' 'days of struggle', had said he half-envied the men fighting in Spain's Civil War, and a scheme was formed. 'He plans wonderfully funny joke on Putzi' was Unity's diary entry. Hitler would issue orders for Hanfstaengl to report to the military airport for a top-secret mission. Once in the air, the pilot would hand him further orders informing him he was to be dropped behind the Republican lines in Spain, but after circling harmlessly a couple of times the plane would land at Munich again.

There was much hilarity at this absurd idea, but in fact Hitler gave the orders, and they were carried out to the letter. Was this a classic Mitford tease, elevated to international proportions via the Reichskanzlei? Can one really believe that Hitler had the time for elaborate and expensive practical jokes on his staff? Hardly. Hitler's game was to let the Mitford sisters think he was just playing a joke on their friend, while issuing to Hanfstaengl the kind of deadly warning that was quite unmistakable to anyone in his circle. Safely back on the ground but badly frightened, Hanfstaengl lost no time in leaving the country. He took refuge first in Switzerland, then in London, where Unity in a flurry of concern invited him to the Garage. She tried to intercede for his rehabilitation, and to secure a pension for him from Hitler, but Hanfstaengl remained bitterly convinced to the end of his life that he had fallen from favour because Unity had repeated to Hitler some critical remarks he had made to her in private about the country's 'crazy militarism and soldier-cult'. At the time she had replied that if he thought like that, he should not be the Führer's press attaché . . . Diana then took up the case with Goering in Berlin in May, but although she obtained verbal assurances that Putzi would be welcomed back in Germany, he was too frightened to be tempted in this way. Once again, Diana and Unity may have been being used by the Nazis – if they could have coaxed Hanfstaengl back to Germany, a vocal critic would have been removed from Britain at a moment when the Nazi regime was still hoping to smooth Anglo-German relations. Probably wisely, Hanfstaengl chose to remain in exile. He thought Unity did not even realize what she had done in repeating his words to Hitler: we can only guess how many similar but unknown repercussions might have rocked other lives. Still, in Putzi's case it enabled him to survive the war, and live out a prolonged old age in the family house in Munich where he had sheltered Hitler in the 1920s.

It is no wonder that Diana, though she was endlessly loyal to Unity, did not tell her about the radio plans.

The autumn routine of Bayreuth and Parteitag continued in 1937, the Nuremberg events even bigger and grander than ever. The sisters were with Tom and Janos again, and this time they stayed in a big modern hotel that had been built to accommodate the thousands of foreigners who poured in: Diana was nostalgic for the atmosphere of the little inns of her early Nazi days. Tom was increasingly under the spell of the fascist ideal. Janos, who had in any case no loyalty to Austria – his properties had been in Hungary until the treaty of 1919 folded them into Austrian territory – hoped for the Anschluss that would bring Austria under the Nazi regime; as it turned out, he had not long to wait. It also turned out that this was Diana's last Parteitag. The following year, Unity took her mother and father to Nuremberg, and, because Tom was ill, his place was taken at the last minute by Robert Byron (although he was anti-Nazi). Diana could not go because she was seven months pregnant.

Alexander Mosley was born in November 1938 in the house by the Thames in Grosvenor Road, and when Diana took the baby home to Wootton and the care of Nanny Higgs, it became a family house for the first time. Her domestic happiness must have seemed a reward for the years of uncertainty with Mosley. Once the baby was born, they had to go public about their marriage – anyway, the wireless station negotiations with the Germans were almost complete, and Mosley's links with it very well covered up. The news of their wedding made a great splash in the press – 'Hitler was Sir Oswald's Best Man' ran one headline. The announcement meant that Diana was relieved of the strain of pretence. In her family, the most important people had been party to the secret, and the others had probably guessed, but Mosley now had to face the feelings of his mother, his children and his sisters-in-law. They were hurt, angry and outraged, according to the nuances of their relationships with him. Not only had the marriage been a secret, but so too had Diana's pregnancy: she had been quietly at Wootton for some months. Nicholas learnt the news that he had both a step-mother and a baby brother from a newspaper a day before the letter from his father arrived; Baba Metcalfe read about it by chance on a train from Paris to London. Although Baba's part in this story had not always been particularly laudable, she felt she hardly deserved such treatment. Many years later she told David Gilmour, her father's biographer, that she believed one of the reasons why Mosley insisted that the marriage be kept secret was so that he could continue his affair with her – a liaison she would have ended if she had known of his marriage to Diana.

The autumn of 1938 had seen Neville Chamberlain's now-infamous Munich agreement. He had become Prime Minister in May 1937, and set himself to decelerate the drift towards war with Germany by reaching an accommodation with Hitler. Although the Anschluss of Austria, in March, had provoked some sympathy (Lord Redesdale, in April 1938, had made a rare utterance in the House of Lords to the effect that 'the gratitude of Europe and of the whole world is due to Herr Hitler for averting a possible catastrophe of such magnitude [i.e. civil war in Austria] without shedding one drop of blood'), many people in Britain had foreseen that the problem of the Sudeten Germans in Czechoslovakia would provide Hitler with his next excuse for aggressive action. To judge by letters to *The Times* that spring and summer, a substantial section of public opinion – which included Mosley – thought that the Sudeten Germans had a strong case for re-unification, and that there lurked a sense of the righting of wrongs imposed by the Treaty of Versailles. The whole issue, however, was set against Czechoslovakia's alliance with the Soviet Union. Fear and loathing of communism underlay everything, and after Chamberlain's initiative, those who welcomed it did so mainly on the grounds that the Sudetenland was not a sufficient cause for war with Germany, and its possible consequences – that is, the strengthening of the mighty Soviet Union. The Duke of Windsor – though not usually a perspicacious man – summed up this view when he wrote to Robert Bruce Lockhart in October 1938 that 'war would have destroyed both the democracies and the dictatorships, and the victory would have gone only to communism'. Yet many prominent voices in the cabinet, the Foreign Office, the press and the country were firmly against any attempt to make terms with the Nazi leader. Not only did Chamberlain's appeasement policy lack popular appeal, it soon became, as Robert Skidelsky put it, 'a byword for surrender'. Skidelsky also thought Mosley had 'put his finger on the fatal flaw in Chamberlain's methods when, following [Anthony] Eden's resignation (February 1938), he remarked, "Eden's policy means war – Chamberlain's policy means humiliation."'

Which would Mosley have preferred – war or humiliation? On the surface, at least, he professed to believe that neither was necessary. He saw 'the Munich achievement' as 'an act of courage and commonsense' on Chamberlain's part, but continued to pretend that none of it had anything to do with Britain. 'I don't care if three and a half million Germans from Czechoslovakia go back to Germany, I don't care if ten million Germans go back to Germany, Britain will still be strong enough, brave enough to hold her own.' Either way, he told his BUF audiences, it was irrelevant: 'Has the British Empire sunk so low that we have to shut up shop if another ten million Germans enter their Fatherland? If not, what is the fuss about?'

Yet he knew quite well that Britain was in no position to negotiate from strength – he himself had persistently criticized the neglect of rearmament. And he was prescient in his predictions that Hitler had outmanoeuvred Chamberlain, when the German leader immediately demanded the occupation by German troops of the Czech territory Chamberlain had conceded, and so challenged Britain 'with an apparent choice between war and abdication as a Great Power', as Mosley put it. So although Chamberlain's version of 'appeasement' was not very different from Mosley's campaign for 'peace' – the two words now have completely different emotional weight, but mean much the same thing – Mosley did not like to acknowledge this. Later historians, Richard Thurlow among them, confirm that until March 1939 'it is not at all clear that BUF policies . . . with regard to Nazi Germany were radically different from that of the British government'.

Meanwhile, Mosley's campaign tried its best to concentrate on another war. 'The War on Want is the War We Want' ran its London slogans in September 1938. 'Give British Union its chance and we'll declare war – war on poverty and suffering,' he roared to an audience in Hackney. He set this fine-sounding declaration in its inherently racist context, invoking the 'alien' power of 'finance': 'Tonight I come to you and ask you to answer finance – answer the alien and say – We'll fight for Britain but we will not fight for you. Break the system – smash the tyranny of money. Endow our people with the wealth of modern science and let us dedicate ourselves to building the Britain of our dreams.'

The irony of these demands to 'smash' the international financial system, coming from a man who lived his whole life on inherited and invested wealth, seems to have escaped the speaker himself, as well as his audience.

Typically of Mosley, too, his words might have sounded impressive and brave, but they were irrelevant to the moment. In only a few weeks, on 9 November 1938, Chamberlain's Munich dream of 'Peace in Our Time' was abruptly shattered by the death in Paris of Ernst von Rath, a secretary of the German Legation who had been shot by a young German Jewish man, Herschel Grynzpan. The news of this shooting unleashed an officially sanctioned orgy of violence against Jews throughout Germany: the *Kristallnacht*, the night of breaking glass, in which Jewish businesses, shops, homes and synagogues were attacked, looted and destroyed. While the Western world reacted with horror, Mosley again stood out alone, thundering on in *Action* in December 1938, attributing the events of *Kristallnacht* to 'the simplicity of the German character' and demanding to know 'How many minorities have been badly treated in how many countries since the [First World] war without any protest from press or politicians? . . . Why was it only when Jews were the people affected that we had any demand for war with the country concerned?' By now Mosley had succumbed completely to the theory of a Jewish world plot. 'There was only one answer . . . that today Jewish finance controlled the press and political system of Britain. If you criticize a Jew at Home – then gaol threatens you. If others touch a Jew abroad – then war threatens them.'

Early in 1939 the threat of war became ever more real. In March Hitler moved into Czechoslovakia, and the official British attitude towards the international situation altered radically. Hopes of appeasement were at an end, except where Mosley was concerned: his campaign for peace went on into 1940. As Hitler's troops entered Prague on 15 March 1939 they were certainly not cheered, as they had been in Vienna. Yet on the personal front Hitler behaved as if peace were still assured: he instructed the housing office in Munich to find Unity a flat of her own (she could no longer stay with Erna Hanfstaengl), and in June she was shown a pleasant modern apartment on Agnesstrasse in Schwabing which was hers for the asking. 'It belongs to a young Jewish couple who are going abroad,' she wrote to Diana, although they must both have realized that the couple had been forcibly dispossessed. It was a strange time for Hitler to arrange permanent accommodation for Unity – months after foreigners had been advised to leave Germany. Was it another of the 'messages' he passed through her, implying that he did not want or expect war? If so, it was of course a bluff, since he was at that moment preparing the Wehrmacht for the invasion of Poland in September. But Unity, who spent half her time in misery about the prospect of war, the other half in cloud-cuckoo-land, busied herself setting up her first home, bringing her things from England and scouring local junk shops for bric-à-brac, settling down in Germany.

Diana was under no illusions. The coming conflict between the two countries would, she knew, mean ruin for Mosley and the end of all he had worked for; for Unity it meant separation from her beloved 'Wolf', as they referred to Hitler in their letters, and an impossible dilemma. Unity had always said she would kill herself if war broke out, and for some years she had carried a small pistol everywhere with her in her handbag.

Hitler had invited both Diana and Unity to be his guests at Bayreuth again. Throughout the Festspiele of 1939, they again dined with Hitler almost every evening during the long intervals, spent hours with the Wagner family, and hobnobbed with other Nazi leaders. Some foreign friends were there: the situation seemed almost normal. (It also seems extraordinary that Hitler, who was within a few weeks of going to war, felt he had time to listen to hour after hour of opera.) On the last day, 2 August, Hitler invited the sisters to lunch in the Wahnfried annexe where he always stayed in Bayreuth. Afterwards, taking them aside so that he could talk to them alone, he told them that war was inevitable. That evening's performance was *Götterdämmerung*. 'Never had the glorious music seemed so doom-laden,' Diana wrote. 'I had a strong feeling . . . that I should never see Hitler again, that a whole world was crumbling, that the future held only tragedy and war.' As for Unity's fate, 'there was nothing to be done. She and I had talked it over and over; I dreaded her iron resolve.'

Indeed, Diana never saw Hitler again, and by the time she next saw Unity her sister's life was changed beyond repair. Stubborn to the last, Unity stayed on in Germany despite Hitler's warnings, but Diana hurried back to England and her family. She was soon caught up in whirl of activity. Mosley travelled and spoke more assiduously than ever, campaigning for peace up until the very minute when it became illegal. There was already widespread fear of bombing, and the Home Counties were thought unsafe: Irene Ravensdale, Nicholas, Vivien, Mickey and his nanny moved to Wootton Lodge, while Savehay Farm was closed up. They made immense black-out curtains for the windows at Wootton. Diana was pregnant again. She divided her time between Wootton and London, and it was in Grosvenor Road, on the blue, cloudless morning of 3 September, that she and Mosley listened to Chamberlain's announcement of the beginning of the war.

Mosley's peace campaign was at an end, although for the next few months he did not stop holding meetings and making speeches, urging negotiations even at this late stage. In July 1939, just before the outbreak of the war he was opposing, he could claim to have held the largest indoor meeting in the world up to that date. He had learned the lessons of Olympia as far as organization went, and he had no trouble with organized thugs. The meeting took place in the main building at Earls Court. 'It was perfectly peaceful,' according to Alexander Mosley; 'the audience was enthusiastic, so it was a non-event, not newsworthy.' Even after war was declared, the BUF was still a legal organization, and *Action* continued publication, with weekly analyses on position and strategy from Mosley. His position on the war was always the same: it was a great mistake, it would be a disaster for Britain and lose her the empire, it was someone else's quarrel. Britain could not win, but she could prevent Germany from winning: in this stalemate, why not try to make terms for peace? But his fascists were patriots, he insisted, and he publicly instructed his members to join up and fight for their country.

There was no news of Unity. After a few days, Diana began to hope she might be all right, given that there were still a few journalists from neutral countries in Berlin and Munich who could have conveyed news of her. But weeks of silence went by and nothing came until 2 October, when Muv and Farve got a letter from Teddy von Almasy, Janos's brother, to say that Unity was ill in hospital. Telegrams and letters to Budapest brought brief replies to the effect that she was 'improving' – but still no mention of what she was recovering from. Then more weeks of silence: only on Christmas Eve did a telephone call from Switzerland convey the news that Unity had tried to shoot herself, but was still alive and lying in a hospital in Berne.

It took some time to discover what had happened. After Bayreuth, Unity saw Hitler twice more, on 4 and 5 August, and later in the month she was writing chirpy letters asking her mother to come and stay in her new flat, which was 'perfect joy and heaven'. Diana wrote that she was planning to come at the end of the month for the Parteitag, but this cannot have been a very serious proposition, especially since she had said she would bring Jonathan, Desmond and Vivien Mosley with her. A few brave foreigners were still travelling in Germany – William Douglas Home, the playwright and close friend of Debo, was in Munich for a couple of days in August – but by the end of the month Unity wrote to Diana: 'I feel awfully cut off, since all the foreigners and even journalists left . . .' On 2 September she wrote to thank Diana for a letter: 'You can't think how thrilling it is every time I hear the letter box click, as I always expect every letter to be the last that will get through . . . I tried to ring you up last night but it was a few hours too late – no more calls to England allowed.' The links between the countries were closing. Unity was adrift now, and her panic showed. The letter went on: 'I fear I shan't see the Führer again. Nardy, if anything should happen to me, and the English press try to make some untrue story out of it against W[olf, i.e. Hitler], you will see to it that the truth is known won't you . . .'

The next day, Unity heard the news of the declaration of war from the British Consulate. She immediately sat down and wrote her parents a letter which was effectively a suicide note:

Darling Muv and Farve,

I came round to the Consulate to get your telegram and hear that war has been declared. So this is to say goodbye. The Consul will kindly take this to England and send it to you. I send my best love to you all and particularly to my Boud [Decca] when you write. Perhaps when this war is over, everyone will be friends again, and there will be the friendship between England and Germany which we have so hoped for.

I hope you will see the Führer often when it is over.

With very best love and blessings,

Bobo

Fondest love to Blor.

And I *do* hope Tom will be all right.

By this last postscript she must have meant she hoped Tom, a single man of fighting age, would not be killed in the conflict. Perhaps it was prescience: Diana considered Unity the first casualty of the war, and Tom was to become one of the very last.

Next Unity went to see Adolf Wagner, the Gauleiter of Munich and a regular of the Osteria Bavaria circle, to ask whether she would be interned as an enemy alien. He said that she would not. She handed him a large envelope which contained her Nazi Party badge, her best signed photograph of Hitler, and a letter to the Führer. She asked Wagner, if anything should happen to her, to see that she was buried in Munich with the photograph and the badge. She appeared quite calm, but he was sufficiently worried about her to have her followed, and her 'tail' did not have long to wait before he had something to report. She walked straight to the middle of the Englische Garten, settled herself on a bench, took the little automatic out of her handbag and shot herself in the temple.

22 *Holloway*

The bullet lodged in Unity's brain, but it did not kill her. She was taken to hospital in Munich, and a network of friends, nurses and officials undertook her care. Janos von Almasy was notified, and several visits from Hitler – it is astonishing that he found time for hospital visiting, when he had just gone to war – were enough to ensure that everything possible was done for her. The doctors decided it was too dangerous to try taking the bullet out of her head, so there it stayed. After about six weeks, when she could speak a little, Hitler asked her whether she wanted to stay in Germany or go back to Britain; she chose the latter. He arranged for her to travel with Janos to Switzerland, and from Berne they were able to telephone the Redesdales. Then, in the eerie calm of the 'phoney war', Sydney and Debo set out to fetch her back.

Diana wanted to go, but was heavily pregnant by now. It was as well that she did not try, because this truly turned out to be The Worst Journey in the World – in mid-winter, from Switzerland across a shambolic Europe, in cold jolting trains packed with troops, in slow, freezing ambulances, every step dogged by a press pack in pursuit of the great scoop. They all wanted the first interview with Unity: every trick was tried, every inducement offered. Sydney turned down the enormous sum of £5,000 from the *Daily Express* for a five-minute interview with Unity while they were waiting at Calais for a boat across the Channel; once on the other side, David met them with an ambulance that broke down as it was crawling at a snail's pace through the blackout of the January night – a breakdown, they were sure, which had been engineered by the press, who were immediately behind in a procession of about twenty cars. Eventually David allowed one reporter to speak to Unity, for nothing. She said, 'I am glad to be in England, even if I am not on your side.' The transfer to another ambulance meant that the press got their photographs too, flashbulbs popping in Unity's face on her stretcher, and a roll of newsreel film that was played at cinemas across the country. She was Public Monster Number One.

When eventually they got back to Old Mill Cottage at High Wycombe, they were unprotected from the reporters, and life became intolerable. They were forbidden to take Unity to Inchkenneth, because it was a Defence Area, so Muv and Unity moved into a small cottage in Swinbrook village (also called Mill Cottage); Farve retreated after a time to Inchkenneth. He could not bear the proximity of his messy, brain-damaged daughter. Unity could speak but she was often incoherent, could remember a little but only erratically, was incontinent and incapable of feeding herself properly. When she learnt to walk again, she lumbered clumsily, half-paralysed down one side. She had become vastly bloated and her features were distorted. Her fanatical turn of mind had converted itself into unpredictable mood swings: a huge young woman raging around a small cottage.

David, a man so fastidious that he could hardly abide even the sight of a child dropping a little food on a tablecloth, found the care of Unity impossible, but that was not the only thing that drove him away to his Scottish island. Politics had cut a deep rift between him and Sydney. While he had turned firmly against Hitler, repudiating any interest he once had, Sydney was concerned to pacify Unity on the subject of Hitler, and David argued with Sydney constantly. After the Mosleys' imprisonment, it only got worse: Sydney could not get over her sense of outrage, whereas David realized that it was probably a necessary wartime measure. The couple parted, as if temporarily, but although they wrote to each other almost daily, they never really lived together again. Their marriage was another casualty of fascism and war.

After the declaration of war in September, nothing seemed to happen for a long time. A few mothers and babies came to Wootton, evacuated from the cities in the first wave of panic, but after a while they drifted away again. The Mosleys quickly realized, though, that it would be impossible to keep Wootton through the war. It was too big to manage when all the staff were called up, too far from a railway station when there was no petrol, too cold to heat with little fuel. Every penny of Mosley's was going into the BUF, and Irene Ravensdale, who held the purse-strings of the children's money that had made it possible to keep up both Wootton and Savehay Farm, rebelled against providing funds for Wootton – or perhaps she found it impossible to live in Diana's house. Certainly the framed photograph of Hitler, which she had always found hard to stomach, now seemed disgraceful. Mosley and Irene had a blistering row, but she was immovable: the threat of bombs in the Home Counties had receded, and they were going back to Denham.

The Mosleys spent a last glittering white Christmas at Wootton in the hard winter of 1939, when the boys could skate on the lakes, and finally left on a sunny morning early in 1940. It was supposed to be a temporary move, but Diana never believed she would go back there. In London, too, they gave up the inconvenient house in Grosvenor Road and moved their London base to a flat on the seventh floor of Dolphin Square, a block just opposite. On 13 April Diana gave birth to her fourth son, Max.

War had achieved what peace never did: the bringing together of the two parts of Mosley's family. Diana and her little babies, her Guinness boys when they were with her, Mosley and Mosley's children, all settled into Savehay Farm at the end of April. The weather was beautiful, the countryside was lush, and Diana's private life had never been happier. The war had not begun in earnest: she thought that there might be a little bit of quiet time ahead. However, in the first week of May the German armies invaded France and the Low Countries, on 10 May Churchill took over the reins of government from Neville Chamberlain, and on 23 May Mosley was put in prison.

The police were waiting at the entrance to their flat in Dolphin Square. As he and Diana got out of the car that afternoon, just arrived from the country, Mosley was presented with a warrant for his arrest. There was no charge: he was being arrested under Defence Regulation 18b, which had been passed on the outbreak of war the previous year, giving the Home Secretary the power to imprison anyone of 'hostile origin or association, or . . . recently concerned in acts prejudicial to the public safety or the defence of the realm'. However, this rubric clearly did not apply to Mosley, and he could probably have established that in court: he had campaigned for peace, but publicly urged his members to fight once war was declared. At the beginning of September he had instructed them 'to do nothing to injure our country, or to help any other power . . . to obey [their] orders and in particular obey the rules of their service'. Only a fortnight before his arrest, in *Action* on 9 May, he had addressed the current rumours of an invasion of Britain with another rousing call to patriotic activity: 'In such an event every member of British Union would be at the disposal of the nation. Every one of us would resist the foreign invader with all that is in us. However rotten the existing government, and however much we detest its policies, we would throw ourselves into the effort of a united nation until the foreigner was driven from our soil.'

In the face of this kind of public statement, the regulation obviously had to be amended to encompass Mosley and his supporters, and on the previous evening, 22 May 1940, an amendment passed by a special Order in Council, as 18b 1A, added the power to arrest anyone belonging to an organisation if 'the persons in control of the organization have or have had associations with persons concerned in the government of, or sympathies with the system of government of, any Power with which His Majesty is at war'. The order was retroactive, and enabled Mosley to be detained, as Diana said, with 'a semblance of legality'. There had been a raid that morning on Mosley's headquarters, and many of his staff were already on their way to gaol. More policemen were waiting on the seventh floor at Dolphin Square, to search the flat and confiscate Mosley's papers, while others escorted him to one of the waiting cars and drove him away. Diana was told he was being taken to Brixton prison; she could visit him the next day. She recorded her feelings of icy fury.

She returned to Savehay Farm, and that evening as she was having dinner with Vivien, another posse of police arrived to search the house, making a lot of mess. They confiscated nine sporting guns from Mosley's gunroom. The safe domestic world of Savehay was shattered before it had formed.

The next few weeks were anxious and confused. On Diana's first visit to Brixton, the next day, she found out that several hundred men had been hurriedly interned there, but she did not yet realize that they had been accommodated in a disused part of the prison which had been due for demolition. It was filthy, and the rotting wooden frames of the beds were infested with what Mosley judged 'the most variegated collection of bedbugs I had encountered since the First World War'. He and most of the other men decided that it was too unhygienic to shave, since even small cuts quickly became infected, so they began to grow beards.

Mosley asked Diana to send a solicitor to see him as soon as possible, and this quest gave her a first taste of what was to come. The BUF solicitor flatly refused to have anything to do with them, as did Mosley's family lawyer; Diana's lawyer made kindly excuses. Suddenly, they had become untouchables, and the newspaper headlines howled in triumph. 'Wherever I went,' she said, 'I was met with glances not so much hostile as terrified.' Finally she found Oswald Hickson, an 'old radical' lawyer who was indifferent to public opinion at a moment when everyone else was succumbing to the atmosphere of panic. After all those months of stagnation, the war had suddenly gone into high gear.

Diana did not know whether she would be arrested or not. She had taken so little active part in Mosley's work, and Max was only five weeks old. But it is now clear from Home Office papers that she was left at liberty when Mosley was arrested simply so that she could be watched: her movements were reported, her telephone was tapped and her letters opened by special order of the Home Secretary, Sir John Anderson. But a widespread campaign for Diana's imprisonment now began to gather speed, and it is interesting how many people use the word 'dangerous' in connection with her. The press campaign was to be expected, but from her personal life even people who were once fond of her weighed in. Nancy wrote to Mark Ogilvy-Grant, 'I am thankful Sir Oswald Quisling has been jugged aren't you, but think it quite useless if Lady Q is still at large.' She did more. She went to the Home Office in person for a meeting with Gladwyn Jebb, Principal Private Secretary to the Under-Secretary, to tell him that her sister was as dangerous as Mosley himself, and that she should be locked up. 'Not very sisterly behaviour, but in such times I think it one's duty?' (Diana did not know about this until after the war: Nancy continued to all appearances to be the supportive sister, writing chatty letters and sending books.) When Gerald Berners came to see Diana at Denham after Mosley's arrest, by means of a tedious bus journey, he reported that all the Oxford dons he knew had tried to persuade him not to come: to spend a day with Diana was 'dangerous'. Lord Moyne, Diana's former father-in-law who was once close to her, added his weight with a letter to Lord Swinton, chairman of the Security Executive, warning of her 'extremely dangerous character' – all those cosy chats in Buckingham Street, then, had obviously left him with a high opinion of her abilities. Nancy and Lord Moyne were people who knew the steel in Diana's character.

Was she 'dangerous'? Because of her many solo trips to Germany, she seemed to have an independent political life, yet in fact she only followed where Mosley led. She was in thrall to the ecstatic, Holy Roller aspects of Nazism – although not to the extent that Unity was – but there is no evidence that she undertook any political tasks (for instance, obtaining information for the Nazis) on her own. Everything she did was for Mosley, and in accord with his plans. To the general public, her visits to Germany seemed suspicious, and her friendship with the madman whose tanks were rumbling through France both shocking and sinister, but to the authorities there cannot have been any mystery. They must have known all along the purpose of her visits and their outcome, if it is true that Bill Allen was working for the Security Services. After all, he had been at the heart of Mosley's movement. He was the conduit for funds from Mussolini; he was a lynchpin of the Air Time plan; he was a witness at their wedding; he was a close associate of Mosley. Yet all the time he was relaying this information back to the authorities, and Mosley knew he was. And if the authorities knew the extent of Mosley's operation and Diana's place in it, they could not have considered her particularly dangerous.

In all, about 800 British Union members and sympathizers – 700 men, 100 women – were interned in the summer of 1940, in prisons at Brixton,

Holloway and Liverpool (where conditions were worst), as well as at the specially created camp on the Isle of Man. Some were dedicated paid-up fascists; others were arrested for association with the movement, or even on the vague tittle-tattle of neighbours. On the whole, it was the older members who were arrested. Mosley claims in his memoirs that 'the mass of our young membership was in the forces by May 1940, as we encouraged those of military age to join, while the peace campaign was mostly conducted by men who had fought in the first war', and there is no evidence to contradict this. At the time Mosley was imprisoned, he reckoned that 'four out of five of our district leaders – usually men in the early thirties – were in the forces, and very few of them were ever detained'. The older BUF members – many of them experienced soldiers of 1914–18 – made silent protest against their imprisonment by wearing their decorations in gaol, and Mosley records that 'every medal given for gallantry in the British army was being worn in the prison yard at Brixton, except the V.C.' One of his members had been awarded the Victoria Cross but, Mosley could not resist adding, 'even that government had not the effrontery to arrest *him*'. The atmosphere and camaraderie was distinctly military, too: there was an ex-Guards officer called Captain Ramsay (then the Conservative MP for Peebles, imprisoned for his membership of the 'Right Club'), with whom Mosley swapped notes on vermin, as one connoisseur to another, agreeing that only one particular dug-out just behind the front line at a place called Vermelles could surpass the bedbugs of Brixton.

Clearly, young men who were useful to the war effort were not put to languish in prison. But in general the imprisonment of fascists was so haphazard that while many minor characters were interned, an able and highly informed figure like Mosley's associate Major-General J. F. C. Fuller was at liberty throughout the war. Not surprisingly, Bill Allen was never imprisoned either. The naturalist Henry Williamson, who was running a farm in Norfolk, was not detained, yet a Welsh farmer who had never before left his home county found himself incarcerated on the Isle of Man. The elderly Viscountess Downe, a keen member, was probably saved from prison by the fact that she was an old friend of Queen Mary; but Admiral Sir Barry Domvile, a former chief of Naval Intelligence, did not escape despite his rank, as he had been the organizer of an Anglo-German friendship society called the Link. (When the time came, the discharges seemed just as illogical: one BUF member was imprisoned for almost three years on the Isle of Man, released without warning, and four days later received his call-up papers for the army.)

In such a climate it was prudent, perhaps, to have Diana under lock and key. More than anything, however, her arrest was a response to public opinion. In June, several weeks after Mosley's arrest, the War Office commandeered Savehay Farm for the Ministry of Supply (it became a Chemical Warfare research centre) and Diana was given a few days to leave. Mosley's family was beginning to fracture: the complicated arrangements whereby Cimmie's substantial fortune was held in trust for her children, and supported the household at Savehay Farm, came under scrutiny again. For some years this money had been in the control of the courts – the sisters-in-law, as well as the legal authorities, were determined to prevent Mosley spending the children's money to finance his movement. Now he insisted on appearing before the Chancery Court in another hearing about provisions for the children of his first marriage. Although Mosley opposed the move, Irene Ravensdale was appointed their guardian, Mosley effectively renouncing all responsibility for them because he refused to have guardianship without the right to decide their education and their future. According to Diana, 'Kit was extraordinarily incensed' by the court's decision, which seemed both insulting and unnecessary. He sent a message to Irene Ravensdale that he was 'through with them [the family]'. 'God in his inimitable way has handed me Cim's children,' Irene wrote triumphantly, while he, in a letter to Diana that sounds more annoyed than distressed, drily commented that 'the children today were duly removed'. He tells her that he successfully resisted the idea that Mickey should be evacuated to Canada with his school ('on the grounds that it was disgraceful for well-to-do children to run away to Canada leaving nearly all the rest of the nation's children to whatever is coming') but he had no other authority over them. 'I am afraid they will keep Nicky at Eton until he is eighteen and try to make him as big an ass as most of that class: however I think he will survive it.'

Nicholas thought he survived the next years because of Eton, not despite it. His father's imprisonment was more painful than the publicity about Mosley's marriage had been two years earlier, but 'still not the sort of occasion at which Etonians showed any venom'. 'It is almost the one place on earth, I suppose, that has such a built-in confidence in itself – in the virtue just of Etonians being Etonians – that this is stronger than any stray occurrence such as that of some Etonian's father being locked up in jail.' As to the others, the faithful aunts rallied round, and all the children went on holiday to Scotland with Irene that summer, Baba and her family taking a nearby house.

When Savehay Farm was requisitioned, therefore, Diana had only herself, the two little boys and Nanny Higgs to worry about. The Dolphin Square flat was out of the question: no one was moving into London for fear of the air raids that were expected any day. So she had decided to make arrangements to go as paying guests to her sister Pam, and to stay at Rignell, the Jacksons' country house near Banbury in Oxfordshire, for the time being. It was a long way from Brixton, but it was something. On 29 June, a Saturday and their deadline for leaving the house, Diana had packed everything, fed the baby and settled him in the garden, and was reading in the bright sunshine that persisted that summer. When a maid came out to inform her that three men and a woman were at the door, she knew they must be police: the journalists only hunted in pairs. They produced a warrant for her arrest.

She had to leave immediately, but she was uncertain about whether to take the baby. She was breastfeeding him, and he was only ten weeks old, but the female officer told her to pack just enough things for the weekend as it was only a temporary detention. She would be back in a few days. She decided to try to keep her breast-milk flowing, so that she could go on feeding Max when she came back – at the moment of leaving her thoughts were distracted by such concerns. She kissed the babies, said goodbye to a weeping Nanny Higgs, and asked the policemen to drive her to prison via a chemist so that she could buy a breast-pump.

On arrival at Holloway, the 'reception' procedure was harsh. Diana was locked into a tiny box-like cell, about the size of a cupboard, with no window but a wire-netting roof that let in light: if she sat on the single wooden ledge her knees touched the door. She was there for four and a half hours. The book she had grabbed at random as she left Savehay Farm was Lytton Strachey's *Elizabeth and Essex*: a voice from another world which did not provide much distraction. Slowly the neighbouring boxes filled up with other new arrivals, and for the first time she heard 'the odd noise made by women prisoners, particularly prostitutes. They shout to one another in a sort of wail that is more like song than speech. It was to become a familiar sound over the years; also the accompanying shouts of the wardresses: "Be quiet, you women."'

In F wing, the BUF women were about to be locked up for the night. They crowded around Diana when she joined them: although few of them had even seen her before, since she took so little part in Mosley's work in Britain, she was a celebrity in their midst. They also knew that she had left behind a little baby, and their sympathy was aroused.

The cell to which she was taken was below ground level, and its one small high window was covered from the outside by rotting sandbags, so that no light and very little air could filter through. The floor was wet – a hasty attempt to remove some of the encrusted dirt – and there was no bed, only a thin mattress on the soaking bare floor. There was a single naked light bulb, of low wattage, and two hours after the cell doors had crashed shut this was turned off, from outside, without warning. Diana sat all that first night in her clothes, hugging her aching breasts, and learning what a locked cell door looks like from the inside.

In the morning, she began to learn the other realities of prison life. The lavatories were filthy; there was always a queue. There was one split-second chance each day to ask for a doctor, the governor, or anything else, when the wardress with a notebook hastily unlocked each door and shouted 'Are you all right?' before rushing on to the next. Food arrived with a wardress and convict (the convicted prisoners did domestic work), and the first meal was enough to make Diana's stomach turn. Some bread, some sugar and a small pat of margarine accompanied a greasy metal container holding some strings of yellowed cabbage and a couple of blackish potatoes, and in a lower compartment a few bits of gristle swam in oily grey gravy. With this food, the all-pervasive filth, and her aching breasts, Diana was terrified of infection: in the days before antibiotics lactating women were warned to be extremely careful about hygiene. She spent her first few prison days avoiding the food in its half-washed dishes and taking every opportunity to scrub her hands, but she quickly discovered that one bath a week was the most she might hope for. In the time that followed, she learnt that this was typical of the prison routine: visits to the dentist, for instance, were allowed once a year.

She did not know whether Mosley knew about her arrest, or whether anyone had told Jonathan at Summerfields, his prep school, or whether he would be informed only by the screaming headlines – 'Lady Mosley Arrested at Last' – amid purple passages about the downfall of 'the Nazis' ideal woman'. Jonathan remembered that he was called into the headmaster's office (he was ten) and curtly informed, 'They've shut your mother up'; he felt a surge of anger.

After the first, punitive night, Diana was moved to a more reasonable cell – though still dirty, like the rest of the prison, at least it was not verminous like Mosley's. The cells were nine feet by six, each with a small barred window with one or two panes that opened to let in air, a narrow hard bed with canvas sheets, a chair, a small heavy table. Perhaps it was the memory of these sheets that prompted Diana, when she appeared on the radio programme *Desert Island Discs* more than fifty years later, to choose as her hypothetical luxuries 'a soft pillow and a soft rug'. On the table stood a battered jug and basin, under the bed a bucket with a lid; nothing else. When the weather got colder and blankets were distributed, Diana said they were encrusted with 'every variety of human filth'. This was probably not just her fastidiousness: at the beginning of the war most convicted women had been evacuated from Holloway, which is in the centre of London, to Aylesbury prison, and most of the supplies had gone with them. The 18b intake, both men and women, had to make do with disused cells and discarded equipment.

Nothing more was heard about the idea that she was only there for the weekend; she knew she was not going home for some time. Nanny Higgs had taken the 'foals', as the Mosleys called their babies, to Pam and Derek Jackson at Rignell; after several days and nights of pain, Diana's breasts had returned to normal and the risk of infection receded. But both she and Mosley were optimistic at first, believing that as soon as their properties had been searched and their papers thoroughly examined, they would be let out. The 18b prisoners had no trial – there was no charge against them – but they went before an advisory committee which examined each case and made a recommendation to the Home Secretary about whether that prisoner should be detained or freed. Through the autumn of 1940, hundreds of women who had been arrested in the early panic were released, especially those with young children. But the committee's premises were in Burlington Gardens, which took a direct hit from a bomb soon after Diana's arrest, so her hearing did not take place until the autumn.

She had no choice but to get used to prison life. At the beginning, the wardresses were out to get 'the Nazis' ideal woman', handing her a filthy rag and telling her to scrub the landing on her knees, and similar tricks; she in turn was haughty and disdainful. But soon the barriers broke down. She made particular friends with three of the wardresses, Miss Davies, Miss Andrews and Miss Baxter, all well-intentioned women who helped the prisoners as much as they could within the limits of the system. She was quickly on good terms with the other inmates, whose ages ranged from eighteen to sixty-five, and came from all walks of life – German and Italian women who may have been prostitutes, or ordinary housewives married to British men, refugees, or even just visitors trapped in Britain by the outbreak of war.

The 18b prisoners had 'remand' status, so at least Diana did not have to wear the coarse prison uniform with its stained underclothes. They could wear their own clothes and have food sent in from outside, as well as receiving parcels with other essential items. (One well-to-do and very religious Italian woman, who carried her numerous jewels everywhere with her in a basket rather than entrust them to the prison authorities, used to pray loudly for food parcels. When they arrived, she would claim that God had provided, although the packages were clearly marked Harrods, where she had an account.) The prison food got no better, though Diana liked the bully beef, and she learnt to live off Stilton cheese, which could be sent in large chunks. She got very thin, but she was not seriously unhealthy. There were other important items in prison life. Instead of the prison's chipped enamel she got a china plate to use, which felt like luxury. Sydney sent fruit cake; Pam sent marmalade. Books were unlimited, and she joined the London Library in order to get a regular supply by post. (In the 1990s, when her eyesight became too weak to read in quantity, she resigned her membership. The Librarian wrote to her, as he did to all long-standing members, tactfully recalling that she had joined the library when she was resident 'at an address in London N7'.)

At first letters were restricted to two a week, both incoming and outgoing, and Diana asked for letters from friends to be held back so that she could get one from Mosley and one from Pam or her mother or Nanny Higgs, giving news of the little boys. The authorities were strict about outgoing post, too: she was not even allowed two separate sheets of paper for Desmond and Jonathan, so she had to write to one on one side of the paper and the other on the back. When the letter arrived, they fought over it so fiercely they pulled it in pieces.

After a few months the incoming letters rule was relaxed, and Diana got a packet of held-up, heavily censored letters from friends and well-wishers. She discovered who had written to her on the day her arrest was known: Gerald Berners, his friend Robert Heber Percy, Lady Mary Dunn (Hamish Erskine's sister) and Henry Yorke, friends who earnt her lasting gratitude. Berners' letter had barely survived the censor – not surprisingly, since part of it read: 'Are you burrowing a passage under your cell with a teaspoon? Shall I send you a tiny file hidden in a peach?'

By 2 October 1940, when Diana was at last called before the Advisory Committee, it had found temporary premises in the Berystede Hotel in Ascot, so another item was added to Diana's jokes about prison vocabulary: 'going to Ascot' meant the Advisory Committee, a 'garden party' meant a group of prisoners digging vegetables, and so on. She looked forward to the outing, but held out no hope for her release. Mosley had been questioned by the committee for a total of sixteen hours, over four days in July, and it had made no difference. Mosley was up against a couple of old adversaries: Norman Birkett KC, the committee's chairman, a celebrated barrister and later a judge at the Nuremberg trials, had been the opposing counsel a few years earlier when Mosley won large damages in a libel action against the *Star*, and Herbert Morrison, the Home Secretary in whose hands their fate ultimately rested, had been a Labour leader with a constituency in east London when Mosley's movement started to make headway there. They had clashed on many occasions. Mosley also had undisguised contempt for Morrison because he had been a conscientious objector during the First World War, that conflict which had so powerfully shaped Mosley's ways of thinking.

The records of the Mosleys' interrogations by Norman Birkett's Advisory Committee are now available to read only because of a campaign waged in the early 1980s by Diana, Nicholas and several left-wing Labour MPs. At the end of the war the documents were placed under a 100-year rule of secrecy, instead of the usual thirty years, and Robert Skidelsky had no access to them when he wrote his biography of Mosley published in 1975. After Mosley's death in 1980, however, pressure on the authorities began gradually to increase. A television playwright, Ian Curteis, who wanted to write a play about Mosley, was surprised to find his access to the documents blocked by officialdom, and to discover that they were under the control of the Lord Chancellor. He began a correspondence with Diana. In 1981 a Labour MP, Stan Newens – then leader of the left-wing Tribune group in the House of Commons – put a question to Sir Michael Havers, the Attorney-General, about the 100-year ban. It was a surprise to Diana, who did not know Newens, but she contacted him to thank him for his question and at the same time wrote the first of several letters on the subject to *The Times*.

Sir Michael Havers was slow to reply, but in the meantime pressure mounted. Newens managed to co-opt several MPs from different parties – his Labour colleagues Peter Shore and Ian Mikardo, as well as a Scottish Nationalist and two Conservatives – to join him in urging the Lord Chancellor to action. Finally, in 1983, a large number of Special Branch and MI5 reports on the BUF, as well as 140 files on Mosley and Diana's arrest and imprisonment, were opened. Others remained closed for varying amounts of time; some are still under wraps in 1999.

Each of the campaigners had his own motives. Diana felt that the continuing secrecy of the documents implied that 'there must be something very fishy which the authorities were anxious to hide'. She was concerned to prove that Mosley had had nothing to conceal, and that he was no traitor.

They had done nothing wrong, in her eyes, and certainly nothing illegal: she wanted the world to be able to see this. The help she received from Stan Newens is more surprising. Diana thought that the men of the Left must have 'imagined that thrilling plots would be disclosed, "names" would be mentioned, damaging to the Conservative Party'. They hoped to find evidence of widespread fascist sympathy at the heart of the establishment. In fact no prominent names were named: 'not even minor dukes' – as Robert Skidelsky noted, rather despondently – let alone the Duke of Windsor or other notable suspects. 'I knew they were going to be disappointed,' Diana remarked, 'but I gratefully accepted their push and drive.'

What the files tell us can be interpreted in several ways. Prisoners were not allowed defence counsel when they appeared before the Advisory Committee, so Mosley himself had to pit his wits against one of the ablest barristers in the country – a series of encounters he relished. But was it ever anything more than a charade? The transcripts show that although the panel accepted most of Mosley's case – that his and Diana's detention was illogical – it had no intention of releasing him on that basis, or possibly on any other. Birkett was sufficiently impressed by Mosley's fluency to write to the Home Secretary, afterwards, that Mosley was obviously 'an exceedingly able man' and 'more important, an exceedingly able politician'. Their exchanges were elaborately polite, if sharply barbed, and Mosley time and again used his habitual method of countering a charge: first, he would deny the accusation point-blank, demanding proof, then he would demand to know what harm there would be even if the charge were true? For instance, he flatly denied all knowledge of the money paid to the BUF by Mussolini because he had decided to distance himself from all fund-raising activities – but immediately went on the offensive to point out that such help would not in any case have been illegal, since Britain and Italy were not at war at the time. At other moments, he waved questions away with a supercilious tone – Why had Hitler attended his wedding? Because Goebbels' house was just opposite Hitler's residence and 'it was no trouble at all to walk across'.

Mosley's interrogation is most revealing about his anti-Semitism. Years later, in his writing, he denied that he had ever held specifically anti-Semitic views, but these transcripts tell another story – 'as no retrospective apologia can, [they show] the malevolent mentality of the time', Skidelsky comments. Throughout, Mosley stresses his identity as an upper-class English patriot of old family: how could someone like him *not* fight for his country, *not* be suspicious of outsiders? On Jewishness, he points out – as if it explained everything 'chronologically' – that his grandfather had led the House of

Commons opposition to Jewish emancipation half a century earlier. Such views were unfortunately traditional, he believed, 'a whimsical British brutality' and 'a very old growth in British soil'. But, Mosley told Birkett, he himself had 'never looked into the problem in any shape or form. I always actually thought [anti-Semitism] was the work of cranks.' Yet as the violence between Jews and the members of his movement grew worse, he said, 'I was compelled to look at the Jewish problem by their opposition to us and having looked at the Jewish problem I developed what is called anti-Semitism.' Did he accept that the British Union had fomented anti-Semitism? 'Yes,' Mosley answered, 'I think it is partly them, and partly us.' And he offered the Advisory Committee his solution: 'constructing a national home for them which would put an end to all this friction . . . which is as harmful to the Jews as it is to us. It changes his [sic] character into a gangster and arouses in us a certain brutality and it is bad for the Jew and bad for us.'

Diana's own interrogation was brief, no more than an hour long. With Norman Birkett sat Sir Arthur Hazlerigg ('a dear old boy who blinked in friendly fashion') and Sir George Clerk, a reminder of another era in her life – she and Bryan had lunched with him in Constantinople ten years earlier, when he was Ambassador there. None the less, the elaborate courtesies of Mosley's questioning were absent this time. 'Birkett was very hostile towards me, and I was very hostile towards him,' Diana recalled, and she was as scornful of the committee's methods as of the content of their enquiries. 'Few of the questions put to me . . . would have been allowed by a judge at a proper trial.' They mostly wanted to know about her acquaintance with the Nazi leaders. Was she a fascist? Yes, Mosley had converted her. Her visits to Rome in 1933 and 1934 came under scrutiny, but the committee accepted that these were private visits to Berners and nothing to do with politics. She was questioned about the incident in Hyde Park. The panel seemed almost baffled by her answers, because she appeared to be completely without guilt or guile – she had no hesitation in confirming her friendship with Hitler or her admiration for his achievements. Why was she married in Germany? Because they wished to keep the marriage secret, and it was not possible to do that in England or France. Why was Hitler there? Because he was a friend of hers. Was he still a friend of hers, now that he was bombing London? It was frightful – that was why she and Mosley had always argued for peace. Would she welcome Hitler if he invaded Britain? She could not continue to live if Britain were invaded, but she would like to see the German system of government in England because of all that it had achieved in Germany.

And so on. When questioned about the radio concession, she denied that her friendship with Hitler had secured it: it was a business proposition. The only point at which Birkett seemed put out, Diana said, was when he asked her about her last conversation with Hitler, at Bayreuth in August 1939. 'Did you tell him that there was no doubt war was coming?' 'No, he told me.' There was a current idea that Hitler had formed the impression, perhaps from Ribbentrop, that Britain would not fight, and Birkett seemed to have assumed that this would have been Diana's message to him too. Far from it, she told them: Hitler knew that the British guarantee to Poland made war practically inevitable, and he also knew from his English contacts that the most powerful influences in Britain were anti-appeasement. Even Sydney, when she and Unity were entertained by some of the German high command at the Parteitag of 1938, had startled them by her rather bellicose response to a query about Britain's willingness to make war.

Then came the subject of the Jews, and prominent Nazis of her acquaintance. Diana was asked about Goering, Hess and Himmler (the latter she had met only once), although not about Goebbels, whom she knew best. Of Streicher she said, 'He is a very simple little fellow, quite uneducated.' He had little influence, and his paper *Der Stürmer* was amusing as pornography, but 'nonsense from beginning to end'. Did she agree with the Nazi policies towards the Jews? Yes, up to a point. 'I am not fond of Jews.' And did she know about the atrocities against Jews? 'I saw the book called the *Brown Book of the Hitler Terror*, but I did not pay much attention to it.'

With answers like these, it is clear that the committee was not troubling to press her very hard – there was obviously no question of freeing her anyway, so it hardly mattered what she said. Their unanimous verdict was that she should be kept in prison. They did not really need information from her either; they knew all they wanted from Intelligence sources, from the Mosleys' confiscated papers and files and from telephone tapping. Mosley recounted that the Advisory Committee did not even bother to hide the bugging of telephones, although its practice was strenuously denied in the House of Commons; Diana was questioned about a joke she had made on the phone to Lady Downe after Mosley's arrest. The committee got its information in haphazard ways, with all the usual idiocy such a system entails – Mosley used to enjoy telling a story about one BUF member who was locked up for two years on the basis of an entry in his diary that read: 'Remove English queen and replace with Italian.' The man was a bee-keeper.

Those who live a long life, like Diana, get a chance to comment on their own history, and the history of their times as it appears to subsequent generations. (Albert Speer, the longest survivor of the senior Nazis, had a similar opportunity to contribute – perhaps very creatively – to the record.) When Diana saw the transcripts of the Birkett Committee, more than forty years after the events they record, she was convinced that deletions had been made in her own files, and believed that Mosley's had been tampered with too. 'Two passages I well remember have disappeared,' she felt sure. 'One was an intervention by Sir Arthur Hazlerigg . . . who, when Birkett was asking me about my last conversation with Hitler, at the Bayreuth Festival in 1939, interjected: "You mean to say you saw Hitler last August? [i.e. August 1940]" This made me laugh, and I imagine somebody removed it because it so clearly showed the sort of people who served on the committee and the unreality of the whole proceedings.'

A second, more substantial deletion was apparently made by the 'weeders' – the Whitehall officials who decide what is left in files in the Public Record Office and what should be suppressed, and have the power to remove material they consider sensitive. Diana reported that when Birkett asked 'whether I disapproved of the bullying of Jews in Germany, I said I always disapproved of bullying: that for example I strongly disapproved of the treatment of black people in the southern states of America, where they had no civil rights and there were frequent lynchings which went unpunished, but that I did not therefore consider Britain should declare war on the United States'.

Not only were passages deleted, according to Diana, but perhaps added as well. There is a comment in Mosley's transcript – he is quoted as saying that the three women Hitler most admired were Winifred Wagner, Magda Goebbels and Diana – which she considered very unlikely and quite out of character for Mosley, who had never had that sort of conversation with Hitler in any case. Whether Diana's memory was accurate, whether her guess about Mosley's questioning was correct, whether these questions were asked and answered, deleted or added, will never be known. The purpose of tampering with the records was obvious to Diana: Anthony Blunt had been one of those who were in a position to alter the documents relating to 18b prisoners, and he had later been revealed to be 'a spy working for Russia' throughout. Other traitors subsequently unmasked were in similar positions of power over the written evidence: 'and that they were our enemies I am proud to acknowledge', was Diana's comment.

One could speculate endlessly about this. If the Mosleys' transcripts were doctored, why were the changes not more significant? Why did the enemies of fascism not insert some really incriminating material? The striking thing about these documents is the fact that they contain no real surprises. In a system that allows the censorship of declassified documents, under the provisions of the Public Record Acts of 1958 and 1967, historical truth is a precarious concept.

Diana got a decent meal out of her Ascot visit, somethig that had interested her more than the committee hearing ('a low diet generates fantasies about feasting'). She had lunch on a tray in the stables of the hotel, with her wardress; they shared a half bottle of claret which was delivered to her 'with the compliments of Sir Arthur Hazlerigg', and then it was over.

Even during that first summer Diana shuddered with cold in the prison, since the ground-floor cells of F block were half underground, and she asked Muv and Pam for woollen clothes and hot-water bottles at their first visits. This request leaked somehow to the press – Diana was never allowed to see visitors alone, not even her lawyer ('unlike murderers and burglars'), and several of her remarks found their way to the outside world via the wardress standing in the corner. The hot-water bottle request made the William Hickey gossip column in the *Daily Express*, which was written by Tom Driberg, and Diana found out some years later that after its appearance dozens of hot-water bottles had arrived at the prison, although they never reached her.

The tabloid press kept up a barrage of taunts, and the Mosleys' captivity was a sort of national joke. 'This one for Lady Mosley's suite,' the bus conductor used to sing out as the bus stopped outside the gates of Holloway. The journalists felt themselves safe to print anything they wanted while the couple were imprisoned and disgraced, but they reckoned without Mosley's litigious instincts. Three times he took legal action while he was in Brixton. He made legal history by being the first prisoner successfully to sue the governor of the prison in which he was incarcerated: Mosley claimed the governor was denying the BUF men some of their rights, and he won. He sued a Norfolk MP, Sir Thomas Cook, for calling him a traitor, and Cook was forced to pay substantial damages. But the newspaper actions were the biggest. Several publications had been gaily making up stories about the life of luxury the Mosleys had organized for themselves in prison; the *Sunday Pictorial* of 4 August 1940, for example, concocted a fantasy about Mosley along these lines: 'Every morning his paid batman delivers three newspapers at the door of his master's cell. Breakfast, dinner, and tea arrive by car . . . Mosley fortifies himself with alternate bottles of red and white wine daily. He calls occasionally for a bottle of champagne. His shirts and silk underwear are laundered in Mayfair.' Locked for twenty-one hours a day in a dimly lit, bug-ridden cell, Mosley decided to make the most of this, and the resulting libel suit at least allowed both him and Diana a day out of their

DIANA MOSLEY

prisons, and they were able to see each other for a few minutes for the first time in several months. The newspapers had to pay up handsomely, and Diana asked Sydney to spend her share on a fur coat, which she wore day and night through the freezing winter. Other than this, there was no way to keep warm except to burn anything flammable in the chamber pot in the cell, helped along if possible by a dollop of cheap eau-de-cologne.

The bombs that fell throughout the autumn and winter were frightening, and many prisoners asked to be transferred lower down the building. Mosley, whose prison letters show unfailing jauntiness, claimed that when the barrage was severe all the 'more simple souls' among the Brixton warders would cluster into the cell immediately below his – they thought Hitler's aim was so good that he would arrange not to harm Mosley even if the prison was bombed. Holloway did receive a direct hit, however, to a central section of the building: one young Frenchwoman walked out of her cell and fell three floors from the blasted-away landing, breaking her legs. It was after this incident that the cell doors were unlocked on the nights of the Blitz. Even more seriously for the rest of the women, the bomb blew up the water mains, and the inmates were restricted to half a pint of water each a day. The sanitary facilities, grim at the best of times, became truly horrible, and on the second night the noise of the bombardment was accompanied by the sound of several dozen women retching repeatedly in their cells. They had eaten a prison stew made in a pot that had not been washed.

The weekly visit by Sydney, Nanny or Pam, bringing one or other of the children with them, was Diana's only highlight at the beginning. It was hard for the visitors, crawling along blacked-out roads from Swinbrook or Rignell, eking out the petrol ration, then waiting in a bleak room before a quarter of an hour's stilted and supervised conversation. Jonathan remembers the waiting room by the gate, 'like a small country station', then walking across the courtyard to a cell with bars. He had to sit across a table from his mother, whom he thought looked 'funny' because she was thin and white-faced and wore no make-up: he had always known her in the bright lipsticked mask fashionable in the thirties. Diana did not see her baby, Max, for ten months after her arrest, as it was thought so dangerous to bring him into the bombing zone; and Alexander, aged two, found the visits to his mother very upsetting. He often had to be forcibly dragged away from Diana, his tears soaking her clothes. All the BUF women with small children had been released before Christmas, apart from Diana. Mosley and Mr Hickson, their lawyer, never stopped complaining and campaigning, however, and in the spring of 1941 interned husbands and wives were allowed to visit each other once a fortnight. Mosley and Admiral Sir Barry Domvile used to be escorted over together from Brixton to Holloway, as chirpy as boys on a spree, for half an hour's conversation with their wives.

Quite abruptly, there was a change in their circumstances. Winston Churchill appears to have had a slight conscience about the detainees, as he had in the past thundered against detention without trial, calling it 'in the highest degree odious'. He had intervened for Diana once or twice, asking the governor if she and the other women could have extra privileges – books, letters and so on – but now he altered their lives at a stroke. Early in December 1941, Tom was on leave from the army and came to visit Diana. He mentioned that he was going to Downing Street for dinner that night. Was there anything she wanted him to ask Churchill? Yes, said Diana – tell him that if he must keep us locked up, at least let us be together. It was a request the Mosleys had been making for more than a year, and representations had been made through every political friend they had. There were very few fascist couples left in internment now; it would not be difficult to house them together, but the answer had always been that it was 'an administrative impossibility'. At this latest request, however, made by the persuasive Tom, Churchill suddenly capitulated and gave orders to cut through the red tape. By Christmas Oswald Mosley had become the first male in the prisoners' records of Holloway – Prisoner No. 2202 at Brixton had become Holloway's Prisoner No. 1, written in red in the ledger to indicate his unusual status – and he and Diana were together. Diana wrote that 'one of the happiest days of my life was spent in Holloway prison'.

With three other couples, they were housed in a disused 'Preventive Detention Block', effectively a small cell block detached from the main buildings, right underneath the huge prison wall, with a patch of waste land around it which they were allowed to dig and plant as a vegetable garden. They were given their rations directly, to be cooked as they wished, so they were free at last of prison slop. And each couple had the privacy of two or three cells for themselves (a 'suite', as the newspapers soon dubbed it, as if it were Claridge's). Two of the couples were very soon released, leaving only the Mosleys and a Major and Mrs de Laessoe, an elderly pair who had been prominent members of the BUF. The men stoked the boilers and gardened; the women cooked but did not need to clean: nice Miss Davies sent them some convicts ('sex offenders, because they are so clean and honest') to do the chores. Diana was not supposed to talk to them but she usually did, and always left some small item of food out in the kitchen for a pretty bigamist she had befriended.

Two more years passed, the seasons measured by the single tree in their yard. They walked round and round the vegetable patch, which had become positively exotic: the soil was almost pure soot, Diana said, but some plants thrive on that, and she 'never grew such fraises des bois again'. The children could come and spend a whole day, even a night occasionally. 'Alexander and Max used to stay,' Jonathan recalled, 'though I never did – but I used to spend days out from Eton there.' At school, the other boys were 'a bit suspicious' of Jonathan and Desmond, but they would also sometimes ask him to get the Mosleys' autographs. At Eton in 1944, he said, the stigma of having such a family was 'about on a par with being Jewish' – a remark that shows he had adopted the family mode of supercilious defiance.

Nicholas, who had left Eton and joined a Rifle Brigade, visited for a day at a time when he was on leave from the army. Nancy came, as did Debo, Pam and Unity. The faithful Gerald Berners trotted across the bleak prison yard; Henry Yorke came too. Diana and Mosley read extraordinary quantities of books, Mosley making up for lost time in a literary education he had never had. He had learnt German in Brixton – there were several Germans interned there with him – and his letters to Diana during that first year and a half are full of Goethe, Schiller and Nietzsche. He took to it with his usual determination, using it as an escape from his surroundings and his enforced idleness, and became very proficient in the language.

Both Diana and Mosley had been seriously ill – Diana had dysentery (Major de Laessoe dosed her with some ancient anonymous pills he had saved from his years in Angola, and she suffered a severe case of opium poisoning) and Mosley was almost crippled by his recurrent phlebitis, a condition caused by inflammation of the circulatory system which is exacerbated by inactivity. He was thin and ill and was forced to spend a good deal of time in bed; Diana worried about how he would survive another winter. In 1943 Diana decided to plead with her mother to go and ask Clementine Churchill to intercede with Winston to get them released. The two women had known each other for more than forty years, when Clementine had been Sydney's bridesmaid, but now they faced each other across a chasm of hostility. Muv thought Winston a war-monger; Clementine was rigid with disapproval of Sydney's fascist sympathies. The encounter went downhill still further when Clementine informed Muv that the Mosleys were much better off in prison, because if they were released they would be at the mercy of the furious population. (Nicholas's version differs: he remembers accompanying his grandmother to the Home Office on the same mission; perhaps Sydney did both.)

Whether this meeting had useful results, or whether the prison doctor's reports were so grave that the authorities feared the consequences, in November 1943 the Home Secretary, Herbert Morrison, decided he had to release Mosley on medical grounds. He told Parliament that there was 'no undue risk to national security' and he had no wish to 'make martyrs of persons undeserving of the honour'. Like most official decisions affecting the Mosleys' lives, it was sudden and rather confused: the public announcement on the wireless on 20 November was made before they had been informed themselves, and they first heard the news when one of the wardresses, Miss Baxter, ran in to Diana, burst into tears and told them they were to be free.

Released, but not really free. They were to be under house arrest for the remainder of the war. They were not to live in London. They were not to have a car. They had to live in a place approved by the Home Office. They were not to move without permission. They were not to associate with any political allies. They were not to talk to the press. Any form of speech-making, publication or political action was banned. There seemed to be a web of restrictions, and there was the overriding problem of where to live: Wootton was gone, Denham was requisitioned, their flat was in London. Once again Pam came to the rescue, and offered to have them at Rignell, a house large enough to accommodate them all, and the authorities accepted this suggestion.

The next difficulty was how to get them away without a riot. The announcement of the Mosleys' release had brought an immediate outcry from the press, from Labour MPs and trades unions. Crowds had formed outside the main gate at Holloway as soon as the news broke. The press erected a tower for the photographers, who waited round the clock; the communists organized protest marches. 'A girl I know was in Trafalgar Square that day, trying to get to the tube,' Nancy wrote to Diana a few weeks later. 'In order to do so she was obliged to join a queue and shout in unison *Put Him Back*. If you didn't shout you were flung out of the queue and no chance of getting to the underground. Then she had to stop and sign things . . . after which she was very late for tea. You must say –.' On 29 November Osbert Lancaster's *Daily Express* cartoon had a party of mackintoshed marchers with 'Put Mosley Back in Jail' on their placards, accompanied by a single, monocled and bowler-hatted figure whose placard read 'Put Christabel Pankhurst Back in Jail'. Some placards went further, and demanded 'Hang Mosley!' The *Daily Herald* called him 'a symbol of the evil against which this country is fighting to the death'. The *Daily Worker* published a picture of a carefree Diana taken several years earlier at Ascot racecourse, to demonstrate that she was in such good health she should go back to gaol. Personalities of all sorts were interviewed and questioned about their views. George Bernard Shaw, always a maverick defender of Mosley's maverick nature (if not of his opinions), went on record to say that 'it was high time to release [Mosley] with apologies for having let him frighten us into scrapping the Habeas Corpus Act . . . The whole affair has become too silly for words.' Decca, now living in America, joined the fray with an open letter to Winston Churchill insisting that 'they should be kept in jail where they belong'.

After three days the governor decided to smuggle them out of the prison by a side entrance, through a little door in the wall and into some waiting police cars, before it was light. They drove through the snowy countryside to Rignell as the dawn broke, a scene of breathtaking beauty for people who had not seen the outside world for three and a half years. Their arrival at Rignell – the fine food, the wine, the chatter, the soft beds and the surrounding, open country, and above all the company of their children – seemed a dream. Mosley was confined to bed, weak and thin, but it hardly spoilt the happiness of their release.

After a day or two the press found them, inevitably, and laid siege: 'every laurel, shrub and hedge or ditch concealed some unfortunate half-frozen reporter', Diana remembered. Since there was no activity and nothing to report, 'they made up thrilling stories about a mansion and baying hounds [the Jacksons had two dachshunds]'. And as the Mosleys were forbidden to go anywhere or do anything, the journalists had nothing to do but wait while the hullabaloo died down. Diana thought they would not be going anywhere again for quite a while.

But another turn of events was in store: euphoria turned not to tragedy but to farce and, as Mosley put it, 'British officialdom staged one of its brightest pantomimes.' One night after less than a fortnight at Rignell, they were awoken in the small hours by dogs barking and megaphones stuttering orders. The Chief Constable of Oxford was outside; the house was surrounded by military police. The reason? By one of those bureaucratic blunders that are worthy of *Catch-22* or Evelyn Waugh's *Men at Arms,* the War Office and the Home Office had managed to billet Mosley, Public Enemy Number One and the most controversial figure in Britain, in the house of a man who was engaged in top-secret work. Derek Jackson, inspired physicist, arch-individualist and himself a Germanophile and fascist sympathizer, had joined the Royal Air Force, but his work was mainly theoretical: he was one of the inventors of 'windows', a system using strips of metallized paper to foil the enemy radar, and involved in several other highly sensitive projects. He was a disdainful, cuttingly sarcastic man, funny, very wealthy, indifferent to public opinion and delighted at any opportunity to goad the establishment. When the Home Secretary, Herbert Morrison, telephoned the house to say that the Mosleys must leave immediately, Derek Jackson took the chance to say that he would take no lessons in patriotism from a man who had spent the First World War dodging about in an apple orchard.

It was hardly logical. Mosley could not have understood Jackson's work even if he had seen it, and, as Jonathan Guinness put it, 'he was so closely supervised that his only means of communicating with Germany would have been telepathy'. But the couple had become symbolic. Morrison had hated having to release Mosley anyway, and had taken a barrage of criticism for his actions; he was not going to risk that again. They had to go. Housing was in extremely short supply, however, and all they could find at such notice was a dirty disused pub called the Shaven Crown at Shipton-under-Wychwood, not far from Swinbrook. The innkeeper still used the bar (which was put out of bounds to the Mosleys); the rest was empty. Diana and Mosley, Nanny Higgs, Alexander and Max moved into the cold, semi-derelict living quarters, which had not been used for four years. Jonathan and Desmond came when the school holidays began, and the Home Office contributed a detective named Jones. It was here that they spent their first free Christmas since 1939.

23 Country Life

Diana was thirty-three when she was released from Holloway. She had the greater part of her life before her, yet what she and Mosley had lived for – their political dreams and ideals, their guiding sense of purpose – was already over. Fascism was a spent force: Mosley was the first to say it. He did return to politics, as a 'European'; he started the Union Movement, he wrote and spoke and stood for Parliament twice, but there was no real future for him in the political arena.

After Holloway, however, there was a domestic life to be remade, and Diana was good at that. It needed all the happiness of release to hide the grimness of the months at the Shaven Crown. Diana found a girl to help clean the place of the accumulated dirt of years, but did not really know what to tell her to do – Diana was used to trained servants, and had no experience of housework. She had no idea how to wash a floor. Mosley was miserable, ill, mostly in bed. The four children all got whooping-cough at Christmas. The press siege continued, along with preposterous stories about the 'country hotel' where they lived in luxury. Diana cooked and kept house; Mosley was photographed carrying a bucket of coal across the yard by a journalist who leapt from a patch of nettles to snap him. In these pictures, he looks old and stooped, often walking with a stick. There was little to do: the crime stories told by Jones the detective were a main source of entertainment. Gerald Berners came to stay in the middle of the whooping-cough episode, although Diana tried to dissuade him, as she knew how uncomfortable he would be.

Forbidden to have any contact with politics, or to go to London, the Mosleys had little choice but to settle down to be rural gentlefolk. Food was in short supply, and since they had to be in the country, they thought of farming and began to look for some land. Diana busied herself with estate agents, searching for a house and farm. The first house she found was near Newbury, and when she appealed to the Chief Constable for permission to go and see it, he sent two policemen with her in a car and allowed her to stop at Faringdon for lunch with Berners: a taste of pre-war luxury. Lord Berners was his usual skittish self, remarking, when he saw Diana's police escorts, that in these austere days nobody else could still manage to maintain two footmen.

The house she saw was a rambling old brick structure called Crux Easton, with eight acres, a garden stocked with fruit and a gardener to look after it, and a wonderful view out over the Hampshire countryside. Diana bought it on the spot, and moved into action. 'I know what Perchers are when they start galloping,' Mosley had written to her from Brixton when they were about to be transferred to the Preventive Detention Block at Holloway. 'The air anyhow will be pink and blue and gold.'

The 'pink and blue and gold' was a reference to Diana's passion for interior decorating, and now even with wartime shortages and all their restrictions, she could start again to make a home. There were carpets; they sent for their furniture from Wootton. They bought a cow and some chickens, and obtained seeds for every vegetable they could think of for the slow and ancient gardener to plant. Jones was recalled by Scotland Yard and replaced by another, grumpier policeman called Buswell, whom the little boys called 'that battleship Buswell'. Or so Mr Buswell thought; what they were actually saying, in their new thick country accents picked up from friends round about, was not 'battleship' but 'bugger-shit'.

Alexander and Max, now five and four, had quickly discovered the electrifying effect of such words on Nanny, and added this to their considerable range of pranks. Diana taught them both to read and write and count, and tried hard to weld them all into a coherent family. But despite the pleasure of being reunited, the stresses on the little boys had been great. In Max's case, his parents were virtual strangers – he knew them only from his few prison visits. Alexander, who was just one and a half when Diana was taken away, had been deeply disturbed by the experience of separation. He was rebellious and angry, prone to tantrums and hard to settle. He knows that Diana did her best, but already, he said, the important bond had been broken, 'the damage was done'. Nanny Higgs was the nearest they had to a mother; Pam and their grandmother were both more familiar figures than Diana. Diana knew this, and it weighed heavily in her resentment about their imprisonment.

The Mosleys' conditions of house arrest still applied. They were not allowed a car, and they could go as far as Newbury but not Oxford or London – no more than seven miles. Buswell left, and instead they had to report weekly to the police. They had bicycles, and used to cycle to nearby pubs from time to time, but mainly the world came to them. Sydney and all the sisters came (except Decca, who had long left the family circle and had settled in America); Tom used to come for weekends from the Staff College at Aldershot, where he was stationed. Perhaps surprisingly, he had become very keen on soldiering. Vivien and Mickey came to stay, and Nicholas visited when he had leave – he had just won a Military Cross in the Italian campaign.

Throughout the war years, Nicholas and Vivien had effectively had no home; now they could make a base with their father and Diana. When the war was over, Nicholas recorded his homecoming: 'I arrived in the middle of the night. I have a memory of everyone – my sister was there too – in the kitchen in their dressing-gowns giving me eggs and coffee. My father and Diana looked absurdly young: they were in their pretty, rather bourgeois house: we were behaving as a family! Everything was so correct: I hardly knew how to deal with this.'

Diana was happy at Crux Easton, but there was not enough land for the serious farming Mosley wanted to embark upon, and they were unable to get more acreage round about. Early in 1945, after less than a year at Crux Easton, they heard of a property not far away at Crowood, near Ramsbury in Wiltshire, with 1,100 acres of mixed farming around an eighteenth-century stone manor house. However, the Home Office ('with its usual senseless spite', Diana wrote) refused to allow the Mosleys to go and look at Crowood, because it lay beyond their seven-mile limit, so they had to buy it sight unseen. The price, Jonathan Guinness recalls, was £40,000, but Mosley was not short of money at this point, even though he had not yet sold his requisitioned pre-war home at Denham. According to Nicholas's figures, Mosley had spent about £100,000 of his own (at least £2.5 million in today's value) on the British Union in the years just before the war, but he claimed to have recouped this on the stock market during the war and immediately afterwards. As soon as the war in Europe was over in May 1945, Regulation 18b restrictions came to an end, and the Mosleys wasted no time in getting hold of a car and going to have a look at the property they had bought.

They continued for a while to live at Crux Easton, but they had to take the Crowood farm in hand immediately, and Nicholas remembers haymaking there in the heat of that summer, when he had just been demobbed. All seven children were gathered: himself, Vivien and Mickey, Alexander and Max, and Diana's Guinness sons Jonathan and Desmond. 'We were like Bacchanals and Cherubs,' he wrote with an unusual flash of sentimentality, 'my father and Diana were like Zeus and Demeter.'

This picture of family togetherness did not quite reflect the reality, however. Still smarting from the insult of having Irene Ravensdale imposed as guardian of his children, Mosley refused to resume responsibility for Mickey after the war. There were visits, but his second son never lived with him, and Mosley and Irene were not on speaking terms. Baba and Irene were not on speaking terms either, Nicholas reports (we are left to infer the reasons for this) – even though they shared the care of Mickey in his school holidays. Jonathan's experience of Mosley as a step-father was reasonably benign: he could be rather frightening, the Guinness boys found, but he was very funny, constantly teasing and telling jokes. It impressed the schoolboy step-sons that Mosley was so interested in the classics, talking to them about the ancient Greeks and extolling Julius Caesar as his hero.

The summer idyll over, the household was fully re-established at Crowood by September. Diana was sad to go, because she had liked Crux Easton, but Mosley preferred Crowood and the land was to be their livelihood. Apart from the farm workers, there was a cook-housekeeper couple and a housemaid for the indoor work, a gardener and a gamekeeper outside. (The gamekeeper was black, according to Diana, and had been there for many years.) The house had an eighteenth-century front and a later high drawing room at the back, which before long Diana had transformed with her signature pale colours and French empire furniture, to create, as Nicholas remembers it, 'an air of extraordinary elegance and benignity about surface life'.

Just before the end of the war, Tom was killed. 'My second personal tragedy,' Diana called it – meaning that Unity's suicide attempt was the first. In the spring of 1945 it seemed likely that Tom's regiment was going to be sent to Germany, and he could not contemplate the idea of fighting against, or crowing over the victory of, a people to whom he had felt so close. So he volunteered instead to go to the Far East, as part of the dangerous Burma campaign, and on 3 April he was shot in the stomach and died the following day. James Lees-Milne wrote an 'appreciation' of his old friend for *The Times* after his death. For Lees-Milne his death was particularly bitter, not only because they had been so close but because the other 'new boy' he and Tom had befriended on their first day at Locker's Park in 1919 – Basil, later the Marquess of Dufferin and Ava – was killed outright on the same day. Lees-Milne heard of both deaths in the same morning. And Tom's regiment was, in the event, sent not to Germany but to Athens.

The effect of Tom's death on Diana cannot be overestimated. Fifty years later, she still missed him, still thought of him several times every day. He had been her companion, mentor and intellectual twin, her ally in that complicated and often cold family, and he had moved in step with her towards fascism. Her relationship to Unity could not compare – Unity was never her intellectual equal. Tom's fate mirrored Unity's, though: to volunteer unnecessarily for service in Burma was quasi-suicidal, and it was done for the same reasons. Like Unity, he loved two countries, and he was torn apart by the prospect of the destruction of either. He was always somehow in two camps at once – for instance, he was the only one of the family who stayed on excellent terms with Decca and Esmond, and Decca did not know until many years later that he had actually joined the fascists. Neither did Jim Lees-Milne. Tom had become a member of Mosley's movement at the time of the Munich crisis. His attitude to the war was the same as Mosley's: if your country goes to war, you fight, even if you think the war wrong or misguided. But it was Tom's view, not Mosley's, that you do not have an obligation to live on into the post-war reality. He hated the thought of a humiliated Germany, but even more he could not stand the idea of a mediocre Britain stripped of its empire.

Tom was committed to fascism, but he was not an anti-Semite. There is no telling what he would have thought if he had known of the Holocaust. Perhaps, like Diana, he would have felt that it was all part of the appalling price innocent people pay for a misguided war, and that it would never have happened if Britain and France had not declared war on Hitler. The breathtaking illogic of this proposition did not perturb her; it might have troubled his lawyer's mind more.

As soon as Diana heard the news of Tom's death, she hurried up to London to be with her parents – it was in defiance of the regulations, but no one stopped her. Nancy, Unity and Debo were with the Redesdales at the Garage (Mosley, still persona non grata with David, stayed outside in the car). They did their best to comfort each other, but it was difficult: in that tangled pack of relationships, Tom was the one to whom each had felt especially close. In their separate ways (for they were no longer together), neither Sydney nor David really recovered from Tom's death.

It was the last of the personal disasters the war had brought to this family, especially to Diana. As Mosley's life had been marked by the First World War, hers was scarred and divided by the Second. Unity was the first Mitford casualty; Tom the last, but there were many more. Decca's husband Esmond was killed; so was Debo's brother-in-law – everyone had their losses. But Diana's family had also been torn apart by ideology: her parents separated, their only son dead, Unity a physical wreck, Diana herself a pariah, Decca at a contemptuous distance from them all. Beyond that, Diana had been imprisoned and estranged from her sons at the most sensitive moment in their lives, Mosley's work was cancelled out and her ideals were void, sucked into the maelstrom of war. Perhaps that was what she meant when she told Nicholas Mosley, decades afterwards, that her meeting with Hitler had ruined her life. 'And,' she had added, 'I think it ruined your father's.'

This had an urgent current meaning for her fractured family: if she had known, she said, that having tea or dinner with Hitler would cost her three and a half years in prison and away from her children, she would obviously not have done it. In the wider sense, she wrote many years later, Hitler's 'fatal intransigence, and above all his obsessive anti-Semitism, endemic throughout Central Europe, antagonized the rest of the world and saddled Mosley with a problem unknown to him in his previous life both private and political.' Thus the Jewish 'problem', she always claimed, was foisted on to Mosley. She went on to reiterate the same defence of Mosley's anti-Jewish policies from which she never deviated: the Jews attacked him first, he was obliged to defend himself.

The Mosleys' state of mind after the war was paradoxical. Robert Swann, a schoolfriend of Jonathan's who as a teenager became close to the Mosleys in the Crowood years, described Mosley as 'completely unembittered', and others corroborate this. He thought the war had proved him right ('with dreary regularity', Diana put it, his predictions had come true). But he was also quite unapologetic. 'Mr Churchill observed to mutual friends that we adopted an attitude of defiance,' Mosley wrote, and at the same time quoted John Bright's advice 'to those in political trouble': 'Say it again, but be ruder the second time.' Despite this, Mosley did not in fact 'say it again', in terms of pre-war versions of fascism; although he was eager to get back into some sort of political activity, he was to change his angle considerably. In Diana, the war left a deep well of bitter sadness, and an anger and a sense of resentment that never quite left her and could bubble up at unlikely moments. But remorse and guilt were never part of this web of emotions, either for her or for Mosley, and there were plenty of justifications they could use. They had espoused the same political system as Hitler, yes, but they had strenuously opposed the war, and had argued for a negotiated peace and the creation of a Jewish homeland in one of the 'many waste places of the world possessing great potential fertility' – though not in Palestine or anywhere in the British Empire. Diana quoted a letter to Mosley from Osbert Sitwell, written in 1945: 'The only comfort for you [in having been imprisoned] must be that it is impossible to blame *you* for anything that happened in those years.' The crispest and clearest self-absolution, in her view, was that they simply 'never considered that Hitler's excesses were anything to do with [them]'.

To square this attitude with remarks both she and Mosley made in front of the Birkett Advisory Committee, for instance, might seem impossible. Diana's relentlessly logical answer in later years was that an admiration for an efficient system of government, such as the Germans had in the 1930s, did not automatically involve condoning genocide, and that anti-Semitic remarks do not automatically lead to mass murder. She would often quote the genocidal record of Stalin – in numerical terms far worse than Hitler's – although this tit-for-tat argument curiously weakened her case, as it made her appear to be justifying the Nazis' behaviour on the grounds that others had done the same, rather than condemning both. During the immediate post-war period, however, the Mosleys found out about Hitler's crimes in the same way and at the same rate as the rest of the general public. 'This was a time,' Nicholas remarked of that first post-war summer, 'when the worst stories of German atrocities had not yet come out: there was not much news of the extermination camps, which were in territory overrun by Russia: the news was of Belsen and Dachau, the horrors of which could just conceivably and to some extent be explained by the disease and starvation resulting from the chaos and bombing of the last stages of the war. There would be just a flash from my father's eyes: a guillotine look from Diana's bright blue ones.'

However they came to terms with such knowledge, the horrors of the Holocaust were far distant from the realities of Diana's world. Whether Hitler had 'ruined' her life or not, she was young, energetic, healthy, beautiful, well-off, at liberty and in love with her husband. Her new house, Crowood, was a place where a traditional and tranquil country life offered itself. There was shooting and a briskly run farm. Mosley was busy: as well as trying to manage a large estate of which he had little experience – the land was quite different from his Staffordshire home – he employed two secretaries and wrote two books, *My Answer* and *The Alternative*, in the next few years. Diana was a devoted home-maker, and Robert Swann remembers how she 'orchestrated everything so that [Mosley] should be happy', while Nicholas saw that Diana 'cherished and protected [Mosley] from both past and future: she created a garden with him in the present'. 'Diana's laughter swooped on to every plan one made, every subject one discussed,' Swann recalled, and described a family life full of the talk and jokes Mosley liked: teasing, games of charades, a cow named after an unpleasant Holloway wardress, tea in the nursery and limericks with the boys.

As a father to his second family, Mosley's attitude seems to have been more challenging than protective. 'He loved to see Ali and Max doing something a little bit wild,' Robert Swann noted: fights with bigger boys from the village were treated with interest but not discouraged. The children retained their 'rich collection of swear-words and strong local accent', and Alexander, already a difficult child, was hardly soothed by a father who 'loved to get him to talk in Wiltshire with as many of the forbidden words as possible'. Although this caused difficulties for Diana, because her younger sons were never easy, she rarely crossed or confronted her husband in anything; her reaction to anything in him that annoyed or displeased her was more often simply to close her eyes, smile calmly, and murmur, 'Silly'.

As far as Mosley's work was concerned, the authorities were still truculent, and made objections about allowing a paper ration for the printing of Mosley's books (during the war, while *Mein Kampf* was available to anyone who cared to read it, every word of Mosley's had been banned). To circumvent this, the Mosleys effectively established a general publishing company, Euphorion Books, so that Mosley's work could form part of a larger list of classics, translations and a few original works. The name Euphorion – he was the son of Faust and Helen – was meant to represent the fusion of the Gothic and the Classical in European culture: Diana's ideal, as well as Mosley's. In the service of her husband's work, Diana now became a publisher.

Their list was varied. Euphorion Books produced Virgil's *Georgics*, plays by Webster, an old translation of *Faust* with a new introduction by Mosley. There was a first novel by Desmond Stewart called *Leopard in the Grass*; Nancy translated *La Princesse de Clèves*; Diana translated some stories by Balzac. And they had one bestseller. It was Hans-Ulrich Rudel's *Stuka Pilot*, in a very poor translation (which seemed to discourage nobody) and with an introduction by the British flying hero and double amputee Douglas Bader. Rudel was the latter-day Red Baron, perpetrator of incredible feats in the air, a legend of the war who had destroyed Russian tanks by the hundred and sunk a battleship. Bader's introduction shows that he was respected by fliers on both sides, and Rudel tells the story of Douglas Bader undertaking an extremely dangerous flight behind enemy lines in order to drop a pair of artificial legs to Rudel when he heard of the German pilot's serious accident. Perhaps it is strange that the story of an enemy flier's exploits should sell in tens of thousands so soon after the hostilities were over, but by chance Rudel had never bombed or shot anyone British or American – only Russians. Every small publisher needs one hit, and *Stuka Pilot* (perhaps appropriately) underwrote the whole of the Mosleys' publishing enterprise.

Crowood was neatly situated for a small but choice group of friends: Gerald Berners at Faringdon, John and Penelope Betjeman at Wantage, and Daisy Fellowes at Donnington. Daisy Fellowes was the daughter of a French duke and an American Singer heiress (Daisy is supposed to have made the sign of the cross every time she passed an advertisement for their sewing machines) and a famous society figure who had been referred to as one of Europe's best-dressed women before the war. Berners and Daisy had a stream of weekend guests of all nationalities and types, and the luxurious standards they each maintained in their houses seemed to defy the realities of rationing and hark back to an earlier era.

The extended family also came to stay at Crowood, bringing friends. For the five years they were there, the Mosleys hardly needed any other society, and if they hardly had any, they did not mind. It is generally said that they were shunned, and Candida Lycett-Green, John Betjeman's daughter, says in her commentary on her father's letters that her parents' loyalty to them never wavered although they were, at that time, 'virtually ostracized by polite society'. Diana always denied that they were the objects of social ostracism. Then, slightly wickedly, she would amend it to saying that 'the local colonels did not come to call'. This suited her perfectly: she dreaded 'neighbour life' in the country and became quite worried when one young man who came as tutor to the boys started to make friendly links with local worthies. As far as social life went, the Mosleys had just what they wanted, and on their own terms. Their grown-up children brought younger people home, there was clever, bookish company, jokes and delicious food to be found at the Betjemans', visits from a few persistent admirers of Mosley, and the frivolous, cosmopolitan non-political set they encountered through Daisy Fellowes and Gerald Berners. It was, wrote Jonathan, 'all the more enjoyable because, in their circumstances, no one who was going to be uncongenial would be likely to come at all'.

This shows Diana's talent for avoiding the whole issue of social censure by creating a sealed and self-sufficient world. None the less, in the wider sphere there were difficulties. Diana could not persuade a school to take her younger sons, and she wrote to John Betjeman in 1946: 'You really are an *angel* to have found a school which might accept Alexander and Max as pupils – or should I say a genius . . . I was beginning to despair, as I had so many furious refusals. Isn't it odd in a way, if I had a school I should welcome reds, in the hope of converting them.' Other people have left evidence of the same sort of feelings towards the Mosleys. Lady Gladwyn, wife of Lord Gladwyn (formerly Gladwyn Jebb, whom Nancy had visited before the war at the Home Office to urge Diana's detention), bumped into Mosley and Diana in Heywood Hill's bookshop in the summer of 1947. She wrote that he 'had that look in his eye (they both had) that people no doubt acquire when they are accustomed to being shunned – a kind of studied indifference'. The next part of the diary entry shows a different side of the general perception of them: 'Both Diana and Oswald Mosley are evil characters, Lucifer fallen from Heaven, and he in particular has a sinister and almost hypnotic power.'

Not everyone felt like this. One old friend who returned after the war was John Sutro – even though he was Jewish. In the letters between Evelyn Waugh and Nancy Mitford in 1963, Waugh, who was by then reclusive but always interested in news of old acquaintances, asked Nancy whether Sutro and Diana 'were chums again', and whether Sutro had been among the guests at a lunch party at Gunter's when she came out of prison. Nancy replied: 'I rang up Diana & said is it true you had a coming-out party at Gunter's? Quite true, YOU gave it. She is on the best of terms with Sutro now – was there ever a coldness? Oh I suppose while they were actually baiting there must have been.' (This party at Gunter's almost certainly took place when the war was over, rather than when Diana was released, since under house arrest she was not allowed into London.)

Shunned or not, the Mosleys did some shunning of their own. They made it a rule never to speak to any member of the government at the time of their imprisonment unless they knew that person to have been vocal in their support. This cut down on the social contacts they might have had, and sometimes led to icy moments in the lift at their own block of flats in London, but they were resolute. A few other political figures remained affectionate friends despite all their differences: Bob Boothby was one.

Some things had improved, but the authorities persisted in imposing restrictions on the Mosleys' movements, even after their house arrest was over. They were refused passports, despite many applications, so they could not travel abroad. They were keen to go back to Venice and other favourite haunts, to see friends, revisit the Mediterranean and eat Parisian food instead of dull British rations – but mostly it was the principle of the thing which made Mosley come up with one of his characteristic establishment-baiting schemes. Mosley knew that by ancient right Britons could leave their country and return to it at will, in peacetime, with or without a piece of paper. He had already made overtures to the authorities in Portugal and Spain, to ask whether he and his family might be allowed to land without passports: but of course, came the reply. No airline or commercial ship would carry them without passports, but there was no obstacle to a trip abroad on their own boat. So in 1949, bored with having his passport requests turned down time after time, he bought a sixty-ton yacht, the *Alianora*, which was registered for convenience in the name of Robert Heber Percy. 'We were determined at all costs to assert our freedom,' Mosley wrote. 'It was a liberty,' he added, 'no more available to all than the freedom to sleep in the Ritz instead of on the Embankment. But a little money worked, as so often in our land of the free.' Mosley made no secret of his intentions, repeating them to sympathetic parliamentary friends such as Brendan Bracken and Hugh Sherwood, and word obviously reached the Foreign Office that they were about to be made fools of. The Mosleys' passports arrived the day before they set sail.

It was not a smart boat, according to Diana, but a broad and sea-worthy power-and-sail ketch, built to withstand the Atlantic gales around the home of its first Irish owner. There was a hired crew of two sailors (Mosley's experience of the sea, he quipped, was restricted to the swimming-pools of ocean liners) and room for about six passengers. They left in June, with Max and Alexander, and 'our equally inexperienced butler', and travelled south to Bordeaux, Corunna and Lisbon, where Diana celebrated her thirty-ninth birthday. It was a long summer and autumn of harbour-hopping around the Mediterranean she had not seen for more than ten years – to Tangier, Formentor, Antibes, Monte Carlo, Portofino – and, creating a virtue from necessity, they made up for all the years of being grounded in England. They left the boat and travelled in Spain, forming some significant political contacts which included Ramón Serrano Suñer, Franco's brother-in-law and former Foreign Minister, who was to prove important in Mosley's post-war political efforts. They renewed old friendships and kindled new ones; they visited the familiar scenes of years before (Mosley had not been out of Britain since 1936) and explored fresh sights. Friends came aboard: Nancy was first, followed by Desmond and Debo. In the south of France Daisy Fellowes shadowed them in her larger and more luxurious yacht (the eighteen-year-old Desmond removed himself to that one), and provided her particular brand of entertainment, which usually involved some sort of quarrel, acrimony or mischief. It was a four-month trip, that year, after which they left the boat in Cannes for the winter and motored home with Debo. Another, less lengthy trip followed the year after, but in 1950 they sold the *Alianora*. Diana was never keen on life aboard, Mosley felt it took up too much of his time, and the boat had served its purpose.

When the war ended, the official prohibition on Unity's movement was lifted, and Inchkenneth, where Lord Redesdale had sat out the war in the company of his housekeeper, Margaret, was no longer a Defence Area. Sydney, who still had the heavy task of caring for Unity (although Unity often stayed with Diana at Crux Easton and Crowood), was tired of being cooped up in Mill Cottage, and she took Unity north to join David. But for the second time it proved too difficult. Now, Sydney and Unity stayed put on the Scottish island, while David retreated to a cottage on the family estate at Redesdale in Northumberland. He spent the rest of his life there. Diana took her boys to spend a long holiday on Inchkenneth in 1947. In the spring of 1948 Sydney and Unity were in London; Diana saw them off on the return train north. After a few weeks, the telephone rang at Crowood to say that Unity was in hospital in Oban. The old wound in her head had started to hurt; the bullet had begun to move. Unity was already unconscious and there was nothing to be done. Muv and the sisters congregated at Crowood on the way to the funeral at Swinbrook, where Unity was buried. It was the end of a life which had become pitiable, and although Diana was sad, it was not the same loss as Tom had been. The Unity who had been an exuberant companion of her youth had disappeared years before, in any case. Diana never really admitted how much of an embarrassment Unity had been, both to her and to Mosley – her family loyalty was too great. But Unity's fanaticism and ill-judged remarks had repeatedly damaged Mosley's efforts – as Diana's sister, and wildly outspoken, she was always good copy for the newspapers, and she lent Mosley's cause the air of craziness and extremism he least wanted. Carved on Unity's tombstone in the graveyard at Swinbrook is 'Say not the struggle nought availeth' – a sentiment almost as impenetrable as her mind and motives when she was alive.

24 *The Aftermath*

When Mosley published *The Alternative*, in 1947, it was to announce his new political identity as a European and put forward his ideas 'as an offering to the thought of a new Europe', 'beyond both fascism and democracy'. His basic notion was that Europe should become a single nation, using Africa as its 'estate' to provide raw materials for a closed Euro-African economic system; to escape the barbaric behaviour of past colonialists, a new and higher type of white man would be required. For Diana, the ideological switch to this new 'United Europe' agenda was welcome. 'It was an idea,' she said, 'that I could embrace unconditionally. I preferred it.' She might have preferred it, too, if the ideas had remained in the realm of thought. But although he called himself 'a man without a party' and declared, 'Deliberately, I refrain from forming again a political movement in Great Britain in order to serve a new European idea,' within a few months of the publication of *The Alternative*, Mosley launched a new political movement.

Diana believed it was the loyalty of some of his followers, who had paid for their beliefs with years in prison, that put pressure on him to start again. That was 'probably the principal reason', she said; 'his own dreams were shattered'. While he was claiming that he was only interested in books and farming, his British Union lieutenant Jeffrey Hamm had started a 'British League of ex-Servicemen' which established a proto-fascist presence on the streets of the East End and soon attracted the same kind of fights and disturbances as those of the pre-war years. Rebecca West, reporting on the phenomenon in the *Evening Standard*, described a communist street meeting broken up by 'boys and girls between sixteen and twenty, adolescents who were children during the war . . . and now miss the excitement . . . singing and shouting about a Mosley whom none of them has ever seen'. And Nicholas describes driving his father and Diana to a reunion of old BUF members, in 1947, in an East End pub. At the street-corner rendez-vous their car was flanked by a motorbike escort; outside the pub two lines of men stood to attention with arms raised in salute. When the Mosleys entered the pub, 'people clapped and cheered; there were hundreds of them; as he walked between them from the door to the bar they touched him, just touched the hem of his garment, as if they wanted to get some magic from him'.

If all this was orchestrated by his supporters as a lure to get Mosley to return to the active political arena, as Rebecca West thought, it was successful. In February 1948 he announced the start of Union Movement, his new identity as a European, and his campaign for 'Europe a Nation'. He launched a weekly paper, *Union*, with the help of his stalwart followers Jeffrey Hamm and Alexander Raven Thomson. He was back to the round of meetings and speeches, when he could get a hall – most were closed to him by Labour councils, but he held large meetings at Porchester Hall and Kensington Town Hall in London, as well as at substantial venues in Manchester and Birmingham – but at a greatly reduced level.

In terms of policy, Union Movement was not just a post-war version of the British Union. 'By adopting the European cause,' Robert Skidelsky pointed out, 'Mosley renounced the old nationalist support which had sustained the pre-war Movement.' Diehard nationalists turned to Arnold Leese's League of Empire Loyalists. Meanwhile Mosley, sniffing the wind of change, turned away from explicit anti-Semitic rhetoric, and tried to discourage it within his ranks by 'refusing to recognize a Jewish question', hoping to send the cranks and extremists off to join Colin Jordan's White Defence league, or another such fringe group.*

Although Union Movement welcomed Jewish members, in theory, and even appointed a half-Jewish youth to lead the Youth Section in the early 1950s, many of its members were still vocally anti-Semitic. Naturally enough, it attracted fierce opposition from anti-fascist groups like the Jewish '43, and Robert Swann remembers that Mosley was still worried about Diana's safety. 'Jonathan and I were doing our National Service and dressed as two conspicuously unmilitary Privates escorted Diana to one of [Mosley's] first meetings which the Jewish '43 tried to break up violently. Kit had some fairly dotty idea that we might discourage aggressors from Diana, who, typically, had insisted on being there.' Between 1947 and 1950, anti-Semitism was still the strongest issue; Mosley's main platform in the 1950s, however, was to campaign against non-white immigration.

Trevor Grundy was a London boy who grew up in the shadow of

* Jordan's White Defence League merged with John Bean's National Labour Party in 1960, calling themselves the British National Party. This group in turn later joined up with the Empire Loyalists to form the National Front. From the mid-1950s onwards, they were all opposed to non-white immigration, and later to Britain's entry into the Common Market.

Mosleyism, with a mother who 'confused the Leader with Jesus' and a father who spent four wartime years in prison under Regulation 18b. His vivid reminiscences of the post-war years, when he was a Youth Section leader, include a Union Movement dinner of the 1950s which shows that Mosley was hard put to control his members' obsessions: 'The debate following the Leader's speech had turned to immigration. Members had said that too many West Indians were coming into Britain and that there'd be trouble. My father [i.e. Grundy senior] rose and said that the problem wasn't the blacks, it was the Jews. Red-faced and with great passion he'd screamed, "And if you're looking for the first man in Britain to turn on the gas taps, I'm here!" He hit his chest with his clenched fist and waited for applause, It did not come. He sat down, looked around several times and then looked at Mosley. I watched the Leader's face. For a few moments he stared at my father and then Jeffrey Hamm . . . announced that we'd have a short break.'

Diana always attended these dinners, which continued even after Mosley's death in tribute to him. By the 1980s they had become an extraordinary mixture of old members, newer sympathizers, and a few tattooed, lurid-haired punk-rock bands with names such as No Remorse.

The Union Movement differed from the pre-war organization, too, in that Mosley did not devote all his time to it, and was only intermittently active. This was partly because he spent more and more time spreading his European ideas abroad, and partly because, in 1951, the Mosleys decided to leave England.

The battle with the authorities over their passports was one of several. Mosley fought a complicated tax case through the courts, and when he lost his lawyer said, 'I could have won that case for anyone but you.' He was restless, ready to be on the move again, and tired of the prejudice against him. Gerald Berners had died in 1950, to Diana's great sadness; there was an empty space in their life at Crowood. Mosley could not easily combine farming, which demanded his settled presence, with his extensive travelling. They decided to move to Ireland – Pam and Derek Jackson had a large house at Tullamaine, where hunting was more like a religion than a sport, and Debo, whose husband had succeeded as Duke of Devonshire in 1947, was châtelaine of Lismore Castle; Diana had connections too from her Guinness days. Mosley had connections from long before, the days of his campaign against the Black and Tans. Moreover, the Irish were nicely flexible about tax, and about politics other than their own.

They found an old bishop's house, Clonfert Palace, in County Galway, standing on the edge of the bog less than a mile from the Shannon, a river which often floods. It needed everything – bathrooms, electricity and heating. The work was immense because the structure was so ancient, and while it was going on Diana, Alexander, Max and Mr Leigh Williams, the boys' tutor, stayed with Pam at Tullamaine. Crowood was emptied and sold, for a handsome profit (Jonathan Guinness remembered that it fetched £80,000 – a 100 per cent increase in five years). The move was a substantial operation because Mosley had been using the house as an office and it contained all his papers. Everything was put into storage in Cork, and survived very haphazardly: it was a huge upheaval.

If that were not enough, the Mosleys had simultaneously found another unusual and old house which they had seen while visiting friends in France: the elaborately named Temple de la Gloire in the Chevreuse valley, some fifteen miles outside Paris. Built in 1800 by the architect Vignon, who had also built the Madeleine, it was a gift from the grateful French nation to General Moreau, to celebrate his victory at Hohenlinden. Perfect, jewel-like, small but with grand Hellenic proportions, it too was in need of restoration. Here Diana could really indulge her passion for pink and blue and gold: it is more like a stage set than a house. A single central drawing room, as high as it is wide, occupies the whole middle section of the raised main floor: on one side windows look out to the gates and the drive, on the other french doors lead out to a narrow balcony behind the massive pillars of the garden façade, and stone steps sweep down each side to a lawn that slopes down to a lake. Symmetrically on each side of the drawing room is a small sitting room or study, a bedroom and a bathroom; downstairs is a dining room and spare bedrooms; it is like a grown-up dolls' house. The Mosleys now had a 'temple' and a 'palace', and a flat in central Paris too, but the French house turned out to be the one that lasted until the end of their lives.

A new yearly routine was established. They went to the Temple from March to July, and always spent August in Venice. In the summer of 1957 they took a flat and stayed for a full seven weeks, but the usual routine was to stay at the Europa, later the Cipriani, and take a hut on the Lido. In the mornings they bathed and walked; Diana used to sightsee in the afternoons while Mosley snoozed; the evenings were devoted to their many friends, some of them former fascists among the Italian aristocracy. They spent the winters in Ireland – Max's principal interest was hunting – but returned to Paris for Christmas, where a round of parties included those given by Mona Bismarck and the Duke and Duchess of Windsor. They had met the Windsors again through Paris society, and renewed the links they had had before the war; and once the Mosleys moved into the Temple, they were not far away from the Windsors' Moulin de la Tuilerie (known as 'the Mill') at Gif-sur-Yvette. The 'Dook' enjoyed talking to Mosley about current affairs, and to Diana about Germany: there was obviously a sympathy between these two couples both so fiercely at odds with the British establishment.

Although the Windsors, unlike the Mosleys, were received at the Paris Embassy, both were objects of undimmed hatred for sections of the British people. As Diana began to know the Duchess, she started to appreciate the grit in her character which impelled her to make the best of her situation. Diana recognized the similarities between them. Like Diana herself, Wallis devoted much of her time and ingenuity to making life seem full enough for a man who had lost his *raison d'être*, as both Mosley and the Duke had done, and who was used to a role in the limelight that was now denied him.

Mosley's response to this enforced idleness was to keep moving, and it is obvious that he had in fact very little time to devote to Union Movement. After the first period of time abroad, they were allowed ninety days a year in the UK (more than this would incur British tax), so Mosley's appearances among his followers were very limited. Theirs was a restless life now, spread between different places of great beauty, although their many house-moves were almost at an end. The seasonal migration between various houses and places was not an unusual pattern for people of their class, although fewer could afford it after the war. On top of their regular migrations, however, Mosley followed 'the familiar neo-fascist trail', as Robert Skidelsky called it, forging and maintaining political links in Spain, South Africa and elsewhere. He went to Argentina to meet Perón. His Spanish contact with Ramón Serrano Suñer flourished enjoyably. In Italy he knew Giorgio Almirante, a leader of the neo-fascist MSI (Movimento Sociale Italiano). He had contacts in Germany – Diana had none left apart from Winifred Wagner – and made some well-attended speeches there after the translation of *The Alternative*, but it was the Italian connections that embarrassed Nancy and other friends, because the fascist tendrils strayed into their social world, especially in Venice. In 1962 Mosley was the British representative at a congress of extreme right-wing groups in Venice, but by this time even he had accepted that his one-nation European ideal was obviously going to make no headway.

Politics apart, Diana and Mosley devoted their energies to finding the finest of everything, and incorporating it into their life. Their food was always superb (at Crowood their cook was so good that he went on to Chatsworth); the furniture and décor perfect; the clothes and manners immaculate. It was a strange life for their sons. Diana's eldest boys were both at Oxford by now. Their upbringing had hardly been smooth, with their mother's divorce, imprisonment and long periods away, but they had a steady influence in their father's family. Bryan had married for the second time not long after Diana, and produced eight more children: the Guinness clan, centred on Knockmaroon, Biddesden and the other houses, was a powerful stabilizer. During the last part of the war, Jonathan and Desmond had had the umbrella of Eton, too – like Nicholas, Jonathan found it comforting for the simple reason that nobody was sufficiently impressed by his wicked mother to bully him about her.

For Alexander and Max, Diana's Mosley sons, it was different. They had had a traumatic beginning, and a difficult time since. There was no school for them, no normal routine, nor the company of other children. Diana taught them to start with, and then they had lessons with an old Scottish hermit, Mr Watson, who lived in a small cottage on a hill near Crowood. It had been impossible to find a school that could accommodate Alexander and Max for any length of time: at the establishment John Betjeman found for them, Alexander lasted just one term. He was made too miserable by yet another separation to settle down; the school said he was unmanageable.

Diana decided they should stay at home and have a tutor. Mosley, in any case, had maverick ideas about education, and little regard for the conventional establishments. He was always on the point of taking Nicholas away from Eton, 'that idiot school'. Mr Leigh Williams arrived to teach both boys; he moved with the family to Ireland when Max was eleven and Alexander twelve. Max was in his element: he loved the life at Clonfert, because he lived for riding, especially hunting. The ponies had come with them from Crowood, and Max settled in straight away. It was much harder for Alexander, who was not horse-mad, and who was upset again by the move. There was nothing to interest him in Ireland; he had no school life, and now his parents were away a great deal in France and elsewhere, leaving him and Max and Mr Leigh Williams on the edge of the Irish bog. He was extremely clever, very bookish, very bored, and ready to become very wild.

During the second Irish winter, Mosley let Max off lessons altogether so that he could hunt every day – Mosley considered hunting the perfect education for a gentleman. Mr Leigh Williams had left, and Alexander had finally gone to school at Pontoise, at St Martin de France, so Max spent much of the winter alone in Ireland. He was thirteen. The next year Max did go to school too, at Stein an der Traun, an establishment recommended by Frau Wagner. Alexander joined him there, his career at Pontoise having come to an abrupt end, and both boys were duly expelled not long afterwards.

Alexander said he got his brother kicked out with him, but the school authorities told Diana that both her sons were 'uncontrollable', and had no discipline at all. (In fact, their offences sound minor: it should have been easy for the school authorities to diagnose homesickness and lack of stability rather than naughtiness.)

They were soon to move house yet again. In the middle of winter in 1954, Mosley and Alexander were at Clonfert, and Diana was due home from London the next morning. When she landed at Dublin airport, she was surprised to see an unshaven Mosley waiting to meet her: she had not expected him. He had come to tell her that there had been a serious fire at Clonfert in the night: all the people and animals were safe, but the fire had destroyed most of the furniture, books, pictures and papers, and indeed most of the house. It had started in a chimney in one of the maids' bedrooms, where peat and wood fires burnt in the little grates, and caught the ancient beams that had been dried out by the new central heating. A nearby farmer's wife had been woken by the whinnying of the horses, had seen the smoke and flames and had sent her son to run down and throw stones at Alexander's windows to wake him up. But since in a fit of rural idealism the Mosleys had decided not to install a telepione at Clonfert, it took a long time to summon the fire engines and get the blaze under control.

A large number of their things were burnt, although some of their favourite objects had already been moved to France, and some were saved. Family furniture and portraits of the Mosleys, some furniture Diana had from her parents, countless things of sentimental value went up in smoke. Less than three years after they had half rebuilt the ancient house, it was a complete ruin. It was never lived in again, and its remains are overgrown, with no trace of life left.

The fire was just before Christmas, and Diana's first grandchildren, Jonathan's family, had been expected. They all went to stay with Debo at Lismore Castle instead, and there heard of another house, not far away, which they took almost immediately. Ileclash, in County Cork, has none of the ancient romance of Clonfert, but it is less isolated and sunnier in mood, standing on a cliff above the Blackwater, with views of the river winding away through hills and between water meadows. There was just as much hunting for Max. But this house, too, was a staging-post, and when in 1963 they realized they were spending more and more time away from Ireland, they decided to sell up and divide their time between the Temple de la Gloire and a large London flat in Lowndes Court.

In 1953 Diana suddenly became an editor. Mosley decided that he needed a publication that would reach a more intelligent audience – it was the old problem of bringing in the intellectuals, or at least some middle-class support. Two competing periodicals were trickling out from Union Movement, *Comrade* and *Action*, both of poor quality. Diana dreaded the commitment of editing a monthly review, but she knew the work would fall to her in the end – Mosley would never have kept it up – and insisted she would not be involved at all unless she was completely responsible. She had already got John Betjeman to lecture Mosley about the scruffiness of his books (he said everything Mosley published looked 'underground'), but Mosley simply couldn't see the problem about misprints, or poor production standards – ideas were what he cared about.

So Diana launched *The European*. She insisted that contributors be paid, even if modestly, and she always did the proofs herself. They printed in England and distributed it through Mosley's office and through W. H. Smith, but her editorial work had to be done wherever she was on her peripatetic yearly round. The magazine had a small bound format like a booklet, and a plain cover with names and type: it looked restrained, intellectual without being frightening, and it bore no outward indication of the political colouring of the contents. The 'European' editorial was a commentary by Mosley on current events and issues, its language strong but never tub-thumping. Other than that, Diana preferred to fill it with book reviews and notices of plays and films, even articles about food and cookery, as well as a few general articles. She wrote a fairly light-hearted diary every month, to the dismay of some of the old guard; it certainly contributed to the magazine's readability. Mosley wrote non-political articles, too: his 'Wagner and Shaw: A Synthesis' argued against Shaw's interpretation of Wagner's *Ring* in *The Perfect Wagnerite*. Desmond Stewart and Alan Neame were mainstays among the contributors, but Diana also published Henry Williamson, Ezra Pound, Roy Campbell, Anna Kavan, Hugo Charteris and (occasionally) Nicholas Mosley. The tone was bantering and ironic, often making sport of the pinkos (Stephen Spender was a favourite target, as were *Encounter* and the *New Statesman*, which they referred to as *Sissies' Weekly*). The overall standard was not bad, and some of Mosley's supporters thought he should have given up the Union Movement and concentrated on *The European*, as it was the most dignified of the movement's activities.

One of Diana's longer pieces has lived on. For the issue of July 1956 she wrote a coruscating attack on 'The Writing of Rebecca West' (a leading light among the pinkos) which was separately reprinted in 1986 in a limited edition. It has some strange contemporary resonances, because Rebecca West wrote much about Serbia, Croatia and Bosnia. West also wrote, for *The New Yorker* in September 1945, an account of the trial for treason of William Joyce. During the course of this 7,000-word article (which West had completed within a day of the end of the trial) she made some inaccurate remarks about Mosley and his wartime policy: hence the reason for Diana to expend many thousands of well-written words on the work of a writer she so dislikes.

Rebecca West had a curious emotional empathy with Joyce. At the end of her book *The Meaning of Treason*, a study of a number of such trials, she concludes that there is a case for the traitor – all 'revolutionaries' (among whom she numbers William Joyce) should have a drop of treason in their blood, otherwise they will never challenge the prevailing order. Yet she thought the questionable decision to hang Joyce, who was accused of treason after his wartime broadcasts from Germany as 'Lord Haw-Haw', was the right one. Diana, whose watchword was patriotism and who always sought to defend Mosley from the least taint of treason, disagreed on both counts: she thought treason unforgivable, but also believed that a hypocritical British court had no right even to try William Joyce, who had never been a British subject, let alone to convict and execute him.

The battle of words between these two haughty, opinionated women is an interesting one, and shows what Diana might have been in a different environment. Rebecca West's writing is emotional, full of fantasies, generalizations and personal additions; Diana's is cool and crisp, with an often devastating turn of understatement. Their intellectual collision makes them seem like two sides of the same coin. If Diana had turned her writing talents to an outlet that achieved more public notice and prominence, her reputation as a writer might be as high as that of her sisters Nancy or Jessica. Those who suspect that Diana might have been a better writer than either could entertain themselves with her review of Rebecca West.

The European was very hard work for Diana, and too expensive a hobby for Mosley, and after six years they decided to close it. It may have had little effect politically, but the effect on Diana was decisive: it had turned her into a writer, editor and reviewer. In the next years she produced three books and countless reviews, as well as keeping a firm editorial eye on Mosley's publications. A memo she wrote to Mosley pointing out some of the more unfortunate stylistic devices in *Action* shows that she was keen to intervene if she could. It gives a glimpse of the interplay of ideas between them, cast in a formalized structure, as would suit both, and always with the careful separation of politics and personal life. In the memo she called a passage 'repugnant to intelligent people who might otherwise heed our economic argument: "Fuzzie Wuzzies", "Hottentots" . . . Do not play into the hands of those who imagine our policy is based on hatred of the blacks.'

Anyone who heard Mosley's campaign speeches in 1959, however, when he decided to stand as a parliamentary candidate for Notting Hill, would certainly have imagined that. He campaigned on a single issue: opposing unrestricted black immigration. Though his economic arguments sounded more elevated when he explained them properly – his view was that the economy of the Caribbean islands should be strengthened sufficiently so that West Indians would not have to leave to find work – his oratorical style got the better of him when he was in full flood from the back of a lorry, and his language became lurid. Max and Alexander campaigned for him, and Diana did too (although she loathed electioneering and thought it 'impertinent'); she remembered that although the middle-class voters were rude and hostile, the working-class voters, as usual, had more time for Mosley. But he only achieved a tiny percentage of the poll, and lost his deposit.

He was downcast. Through the 1950s his Union Movement had rumbled on, helped intermittently by Alexander and Max, and in 1958 one of Mosley's sons (Nicholas) had been pelted with rotten eggs by another (Alexander) during the course of an Aldermarston anti-nuclear march. (Although they were on opposite sides, Alexander left the Union Movement ranks at one point, to the consternation of onlookers, to chat to his brother among the peaceniks.) Skidelsky estimated that Union Movement reached its peak in the early 1960s, with about 1,500 active Mosley supporters and as many as 15,000 sympathizers. But the Leader himself had all but gone. Part-time since the early 1950s, he withdrew increasingly, and after a second resounding defeat at Notting Hill, in 1966, he formally gave up the leadership. He was seventy, but he claimed he was not retiring. He worked on his autobiography, *My Life*, which came out in 1968 to surprisingly favourable reviews. It is by far the most readable of Mosley's publications, thanks in large part to the fact that Diana demanded to see the day's work each evening, and would edit the pages with a stern eye. By now, Mosley had achieved the status of a sort of historical curiosity rather than that of a dangerous political animal, and when in 1968 the BBC at last broke their thirty-four-year ban on Mosley with a *Panorama* programme featuring him, it was watched by eight and a half million people. A visit to New York to promote the book brought, Diana said, some 'very very hostile' questioning; but, she added, 'he didn't mind'.

By the time Diana published her own memoirs, *A Life of Contrasts*, in 1977, she could do little travelling because Mosley was already ill with Parkinson's disease. The reviews of her book were in a different vein. She said that it was 'the truth – but not necessarily the whole truth', and she showed great agility when dancing round what she called 'the tricky bits'. Her liveliness of style was praised, but the word 'unrepentant' recurred – she had tried to present the unknown face of Hitler as charming, funny, loyal, visionary, etc., and not everyone found this acceptable. Some of the 'contrasts' – between the luxury of her life and the fate of Hitler's victims, for instance – were shocking, and her class assumptions were offensive. If Mosley had achieved the rank of historical curiosity, she had achieved that of sacred monster. The book sold extremely well.

Diana's views were always sought. Throughout the 1960s she reviewed for *Books and Bookmen* under the editorship of Philip Dossé; she continued reviewing books for the *Evening Standard* and other publications into the late 1990s. After her memoirs, she produced two more books. *The Duchess of Windsor*, in 1980, was commissioned by her girlhood friend Lord Longford for Sidgwick and Jackson, to the annoyance of Diana's previous publisher Jamie (Hamish) Hamilton. The idea began as extended captions to a set of photographs, but ended up as a full book, and Diana was tempted to do it, she said, because so many lies were being told about Wallis. By this time the Dook was dead and Wallis was lying in a terminal coma so Diana's method was to contact everyone she had ever met at their house. The book sold 23,000 copies. No doubt encouraged by this, Sidgwick asked Diana to do another, and in 1985 she published *Loved Ones*, a series of pen portraits of some close friends who were no longer alive. There are incisive chapters on Lytton Strachey and Carrington, Evelyn Waugh, the Mitfords' old family friend Violet Hammersley, Derek Jackson, Gerald Berners, Prince and Princess Clary (friends from Venice), and finally her own version of Mosley's life.

Perhaps the whole book was designed as a vehicle for this: as her way of writing about Mosley, of continuing the campaign for his support and defence that had occupied her for the last fifty years, and of replying to some recent slights. Eventually, all Mosley's papers went to Nicholas, who produced in 1982 and 1983 a pair of remarkable books about his father – *Rules of the Game*, which covers the years up to Cimmie's death and the foundation of the BUF, and *Beyond the Pale*, which takes up the story from 1933. They are meditative books, full of revealing information and painfully honest, but Diana thought Nicholas had made unwarranted use of letters and private documents, and after the first volume was published she never spoke to him again. A number of barbed comments in *Loved Ones* about his relationship with his father constitute a token revenge.

For several years Mosley had struggled with Parkinson's disease, and in 1980 he died at the age of eighty-four, 'as we should all hope to die when the time comes', Diana said – with no long illness, doctors or nurses, just one day of restless malaise. For a time, it almost looked as though Diana's life were over, too; she could not seem to recover, and her grief and depression were extreme. Nancy, to whom she had become close again in recent years in France, had died of a painful cancer in 1973; Sydney had died at Inch-kenneth ten years earlier, in 1963. Old friends everywhere began to disappear, and her life in France – with its gentle rhythms of winter travel to South Africa and the Bahamas, visits from family, books and the perpetual task of making Mosley happy – seemed pointless without him. A year later, there was little improvement, and on holiday in Italy that summer with Lord Lambton she fainted in the cathedral at San Gimignano. Later she was staying with Max and his wife Jean in the South of France when she passed out again, in a restaurant, and this time she was taken by air ambulance to the London Hospital in Whitechapel, where brain specialists diagnosed a large tumour. Perhaps there was some connection with the fierce migraines she had suffered ever since the war. The operation to remove the brain tumour was successful, but her immediate recovery took twelve weeks. In Whitechapel she could be visited by lots of old fascists, and the hospital impressed her: *Loved Ones* is dedicated to her surgeon and the nursing staff there.

Eventually she could leave the hospital for a long convalescence at Chatsworth. She had weighed 9 st 8 lbs for most of her life (she was 5 ft 10 ins); now her weight had dropped to 7 st 7 lbs, where it stayed. But she had made the decision to live on after Mosley, surrounded by her ever-increasing family of grandchildren and great-grandchildren, and during the next two decades her life was a peaceful one. Her legend grew – with tales of her beauty, her capacity for outrageous remarks, her spirited adherence to what had mattered most to her. Never less than controversial, she could reflect on the fact that she had had the kind of life she wanted, one that was lived at a high pitch and for high stakes. Even to those who knew her reasonably well, she was enigmatic – every remark seemed to imply another, every disclosure appeared to conceal another facet. The final exchange of questions at her interrogation by Norman Birkett in 1940 was as follows:

Q: Have you ever reflected during your detention why you have been detained?

A: Yes, often.

Q: What conclusion did you come to?

A: It was because I had married Sir Oswald Mosley.

Diana's answers get to the heart of her personality, and vividly express the style she adopted all her life. On the face of it, she had been the traditional helpmeet and supporting wife – yet for all her pleasure in surfaces, and her expertise in perfecting them, she was someone who perpetually negotiated between appearances and the darker impulses which underwrote them. 'She created a garden in the present,' Nicholas wrote of her relationship with Mosley, and her ability to float above the past was one of her most striking features. Yet that 'garden' was only part of the picture. The qualities which made her charming and unforgettable to some were the very traits that made her impenetrable, disturbing, or even sinister to others. That is her great fascination. The larger significance of her life lies in the fact that these contrasts were formed by the temper of her times, and connect so powerfully with them.

Note on Sources

The quotes attributed here to Diana Mosley are all taken from my interviews and conversations with her over the course of several years, or from her letters and faxes to me, unless otherwise stated. The two main published sources from which I have quoted Diana Mosley's words are her own books *A Life of Contrasts* (London: Hamish Hamilton, 1977) and *Loved Ones* (London: Sidgwick & Jackson, 1985). I have not had access to her unpublished letters and diaries, nor to those of Oswald Mosley or of her immediate family, so all quotations from letters and diaries appear in one of the published sources mentioned here. The only exception are the letters to James Lees-Milne, for which I am grateful to the Beinecke Library at Yale. Other important sources for this text are several other books by and about Diana Mosley's family, and I am indebted to their authors:

Jonathan Guinness and Catherine Guinness, *The House of Mitford* (London: Hutchinson, 1984)

Selina Hastings, *Nancy Mitford* (London: Hutchinson, 1986)

Jessica Mitford, *Hons and Rebels* (London: Victor Gollancz 1960)

Nancy Mitford, *The Pursuit of Love* (London: Butterworth, 1945)

Nicholas Mosley, *Rules of the Game* and *Beyond the Pale* (London: Martin Secker & Warburg 1992, 1993)

Oswald Mosley, *My Life* (London: Thomas Nelson & Sons, 1968)

David Pryce-Jones, *Unity Mitford* (London: Weidenfeld & Nicolson, 1976)

Robert Skidelsky, *Oswald Mosley* (London: Papermac, third edition, 1990)

Select Bibliography

Mark Amory, *Lord Berners* (London: Chatto & Windus, 1998)

Mark Amory (ed.), *The Letters of Evelyn Waugh* (London: Weidenfeld & Nicolson, 1980: New York: Tickner & Fields, 1980)

Richard Bessel (ed.), *Life in the Third Reich* (New York & Oxford: Oxford University Press, 1987)

Horst Bergmeier & Rainer Lotz, *Hitler's Airwaves: The Inside Story of Nazi Radio Broadcasting and Propaganda Swing* (New Haven & London: Yale University Press, 1997)

Michael Burleigh, *Ethics and Extermination: Reflections on Nazi Genocide* (Cambridge: Cambridge University Press, 1997)

Lucy Butler (ed.), *Robert Byron: Letters Home* (London: John Murray, 1991)

David Cannadine, *Aspects of Aristocracy: Grandeur and Decline in Modern Britain* (New Haven & London: Yale University Press, 1994)

David Cannadine, *History in Our Time* (New Haven & London: Yale University Press, 1998)

Humphrey Carpenter, *The Brideshead Generation* (London: Weidenfeld & Nicolson, 1989)

John Charnley, *Blackshirts and Roses: An Autobiography* (London: Brocking Day Publications, 1990)

Mike Cronin (ed.), *The Failure of British Fascism* (London: Macmillan, 1996; New York: St Martin's Press, 1996)

Michael Davie (ed.), *The Diaries of Evelyn Waugh* (London: Weidenfeld & Nicolson, 1976; New York: Little, Brown, 1976)

R. F. Foster, *Modern Ireland 1600–1972* (London: Allen Lane, 1988)

Saul Freidländer, *Nazi Germany & the Jews: Vol. I, The Years of Persecution 1933–39* (London: Weidenfeld & Nicolson, 1997)

Paul Fussell, *Wartime: Understanding and Behaviour in the Second World War* (New York & Oxford: Oxford University Press, 1989)

Pierre Galante and Eugene Silianoff, *Last Witnesses in the Bunker* (London: Sidgwick & Jackson, 1989)

Martha Gellhorn, *The Face of War* (revised edition: London: Virago, 1986)

Gretchen Gerzina, *Carrington* (London: John Murray, 1989)

David Gilmour, *Curzon* (London: John Murray, 1994)

Roger Griffin, *The Nature of Fascism* (London: Pinter Publishers, 1991)

Richard Griffiths, *Fellow Travellers of the Right: British Enthusiasts for Nazi Germany 1933–39* (London: Constable, 1980)

Trevor Grundy, *Memoir of a Fascist Childhood* (London: William Heinemann, 1998)

Ernst ('Putzi') Hanfstaengl, *Hitler: The Missing Years* (London: Eyre & Spottiswode, 1957)

Selina Hastings, *Evelyn Waugh* (London: Sinclair-Stevenson, 1994)

Ronald Hayman, *Hitler & Geli* (London: Bloomsbury Publishing, 1997)

John Heygate, *These Germans* (London: Hutchinson, 1940)

Bevis Hillier, *Young Betjeman* (London: John Murray, 1988)

Michael Holroyd, *Lytton Strachey* (London: Heinemann, 1968)

David Irving, *Goebbels: Mastermind of the Third Reich* (London: Focal Point, 1996)

Robert Rhodes James (ed.), *'Chips': The Diaries of Sir Henry Channon* (London: Weidenfeld & Nicolson, 1967)

Miles Jebb (ed.), *The Diaries of Cynthia Gladwyn* (London: Constable, 1995)

James Lees-Milne, *Another Self* (London: Hamish Hamilton, 1970)

John Lowe, *Edward James* (London: Collins, 1991)

Kenneth Lunn & Richard Thurlow (ed.), *British Fascism* (London: Croom Helm, 1980)

Denis Mack Smith, *Mussolini* (London: Weidenfeld & Nicolson, 1981)

Nancy Mitford, *Pudding and Pie* (London: Thornton Butterworth, 1931)

Nancy Mitford, *Wigs on the Green* (London: Thornton Butterworth, 1935)

Charlotte Mosley (ed.), *The Letters of Nancy Mitford* (London: Hodder & Stoughton, 1993)

Charlotte Mosley (ed.), *The Letters of Nancy Mitford & Evelyn Waugh* (London: Hodder & Stoughton, 1996)

Diana Mosley, *The Duchess of Windsor* (London: Sidgwick & Jackson, 1980)

Diana Mosley, *The Writings of Rebecca West* (Francestown, New Hampshire, USA: Typographeum, 1986)

Oswald Mosley, *The Greater Britain* (London: BUF Publications, 1932)

Oswald Mosely, *Tomorrow We Live* (London: Greater Britain Publications, 1938)

Oswald Mosley, *My Answer* (London: Mosley Publications, 1946)

Oswald Mosley, *The Alternative* (Mosley Publications, 1947)

Oswald Mosley, *Europe, Faith and Plan* (Dublin: Euphorion Books, 1958)

Harold Nicolson, *Diaries and Letters 1930–39* (London: Collins, 1966)

Stanley Payne, *A History of Fascism 1914–45* (Wisconsin: University of Wisconsin Press, 1995; London: UCL Press, 1995)

Irene Ravensdale, *In Many Rhythms: An Autobiography* (London: Weidenfeld & Nicolson, 1953)

Audrey Salkeld, *A Portrait of Leni Riefenstahl* (London: Jonathan Cape, 1996)

Francis Selwyn, *Hitler's Englishman: The Crime of Lord Haw-Haw* (London: Routledge & Kegan Paul, 1987)

William L. Shirer, *Berlin Diary* (London: Hamish Hamilton, 1941)

A. W. Brian Simpson, *In the Highest Degree Odious: Detention without Trial in Wartime Britain* (Oxford: Clarendon Press, 1992)

Susan Sontag, 'Fascinating Fascism' in *Under the Sign of Saturn* (London: Vintage, 1996)

Albert Speer, *Inside the Third Reich* (London: Weidenfeld & Nicolson, 1970)

John Strawson, *Churchill and Hitler* (London: Constable, 1997)

J. P. Stern, *Hitler: The Führer and the People* (London: Fontana, revised edition, 1990)

Richard Thurlow, *Fascism in Britain 1918–1985* (New York & Oxford: Basil Blackwell, 1987)

Dan van der Vat, *The Good Nazi: The Life and Lies of Albert Speer* (London: Weidenfeld & Nicolson, 1997)

Evelyn Waugh, *Vile Bodies* (London: Chapman & Hall 1930)

Evelyn Waugh, *Work Suspended and other stories* (London: Chapman & Hall, 1943)

Beatrice Webb, *Diaries Vols I & II* (London: 1952, 1965)

Anne Williamson, *Henry Williamson: Tarka and the Last Romantic* (Stroud, Gloucestershire: Sutton Publishing, 1995)

Thomas Wilson, *Churchill and the Prof* (London: Cassell, 1995)

Philip Ziegler, *Edward VIII* (London: Weidenfeld & Nicolson, 1990)

Index

British Fascists Ltd, 130–1
British League of ex-Servicemen, 274
British Non-Sectarian Anti-Nazi Council, 198
British Union, 188
    internment of members, 242, 243–4
British Union of Fascists, 82, 85, 131–7,
    139–43, 188, 234, 274–5
    Defence Force (Blackshirts), 133–7, 141–2,
    145–6, 164, 166, 212–13, 215; Women's
    Section, 134, 144; marching songs,
    135–7; Black House, 153–4, 156–7, 199;
    funding, 154–5, 184–5, 215–22; rallies,
    163–4, 166–70; January Club, 165;
    organization, 198–9; East End of
    London, 199–200; commercial radio
    station, 216–22
British Union of Fascists and National
    Socialists see British Union
Brittain, Sir Harry, 210
Brittain, Vera, 166
Brunswick, Duchess of, 182
Buchanan, Meriel, 211
10 Buckingham Street, 64–5, 79
Burn, Michael, 175
Burton, Richard, 5
Byron, Robert, 36, 54, 58, 60, 78, 232

Cable Street, 211–13, 215
Calder, Ritchie, 166
Carrington, Dora, 73–81, 284
Castellane, Comte Jean de, 210
Castlerosse, Doris, 120, 134, 161
Cecil, Lords Hugh and Robert, 99–100
Chamberlain, Houston Stewart, 7–9
    The Foundations of the Nineteenth
    Century, 7; Life of Wagner, 7
Chamberlain, Neville, 105, 233–6
Channon, Chips, 205–8, 224–5
Chesterton, A. K., 131, 139–40, 165, 198
Chesterton, G. K., 99–100
96 Cheyne Walk, 81–3, 116–17, 137–8
Churchill, Clementine, 34, 51, 258
Churchill, Diana, 34, 41, 51–3, 63
Churchill, Randolph, 34, 41, 51, 69, 78,
    119–21, 227
Churchill, Winston, 41, 51–3, 63, 82, 112,
    225–6, 2578
Clarke, Mick, 199
Clary, Prince and Princess, 284
Clerk, Sir George, 252
Clonfert Palace, 276–7, 280
Cockburn, Claud, 166
Collins, Michael, 99, 101
Congress of Nazi Groups Abroad, 197
Cook, Arthur, 111
Cook, Sir Thomas, 255
Corrigan, Laura, 205
Courtaulds, 154

Cresswell, Billa, 180
Crossman, Richard, 169
Crowood farm, 264–5, 267–70, 277
Crux Easton house, 263–4
Cummins, A. J., 166
Cunard, Lady (Emerald), 66, 93, 120, 205,
    227
Curzon, Alexandra, Lady see Metcalfe,
    Alexandra, Lady
Curzon, Cynthia, Lady see Mosley, Cynthia,
    Lady
Curzon, Irene, Lady Ravensdale, 98, 127,
    134, 137–8, 210
    guardian of Mosley children, 144–6, 163,
    224, 245
Curzon, Lord, 95–8

Dachau, 175
de Janzé, Phyllis, 122, 161
de Laessoe, Major and Mrs, 257
Decca see Mitford, Jessica
Defence Regulation 18b, 241
Devonshire, Duchess of see Mitford, Deborah
Dicks, Laura ('Blor') (Nanny), 14–15, 22, 33,
    38
Dietrich, Otto, 172
Dodd, William E., 206
Dolphin Square flat, 241
Domville, Sir Harry, 210, 244, 257
Douglas, Alfred, Lord, 162
Downe, Vicountess, 244
The Duchess of Windsor, 226
Dundas, Ian Hope, 139, 199
Dunn, Mary, Lady, 249

Eaton Square flat (the 'Eatonry'), 107, 137–8,
    145, 161, 200–1, 230
Ebury Street flat, 107, 200–1, 230
Eckersley, Peter, 217–18
Edward VIII see Windsor, Duke of
Erskine, Hamish St Clair, 57, 126, 145
Euphorion Books, 269
Europe a Nation campaign, 275
The European (periodical), 281–3
Evans-Gordon, Jessica, 2

Farrer, Joan, 118
Farve see Mitford, David, 2nd Baron
    Redesdale
Faucigny-Lucinge, Prince Jean-Louis de, 210
Fellowes, Daisy, 270, 272
Forgan, Robert, 110, 131–3, 165
Francis-Hawkins, Neil, 141
Fuller, J. F. C., Major General, 244
Fyfe, Hamilton, 169

Game, Sir Philip, 212–13
Garibaldi, 5

marriage to Oswald Mosley, 95–9; political
interests, 104–14; husband's affairs,
106–7, 117–27; and British Union of
Fascists, 133–4; death, 143

Mosley, Diana
birth, 10; childhood, 11–23; education at
home, 29–37; schooling at Hatherop
Castle, 30, 35; Girl Guides, 35; in Paris
aged sixteen 38–44; education at Cours
Fénélon, 39–4; punishment over diary
entries, 44–5; debutante, 53–9; wedding
to Bryan Guinness, 62–4; social set
during marriage to Bryan Guinness,
65–75, 76–8, 117–22; meeting with
Oswald Mosley, 82–4; affair with
Oswald Mosley, 119–22, 137–9, 143–6;
in Venice, 119–20; leaves Bryan
Guinness, 122–7, 137–9; divorce from
Bryan Guinness, 126–7, 144–5; visits to
Germany, 146–52, 160, 171–93, 197,
203–14, 231; meeting with Hitler,
179–80; car accident, 194–6; marriage to
Oswald Mosley, 201–2, 209, 213–14,
232–3; imprisonment in Holloway,
246–50, 255–59; interrogation by the
Advisory Committee, 252–5; release
from prison, 259–61; war years under
house arrest, 262–73; publishing
activities, 269, 281–2; *The Duchess of
Windsor*, 226, 284; *A Life of Contrasts*,
12, 284; *Loved Ones*, 73, 158–9, 284–5;
see also Mitford family
Mosley, Edward, 86
Mosley, Maud (née Heathcote), 88–90
Mosley, Max, 241–2, 246, 256, 258, 263–4
schooling, 270, 279–80; hunting, 277,
279–80
Mosley Memorandum, 108–9
Mosley, Michael, 99, 119, 264–5
Mosley, Nicholas, 99, 195–6, 233, 245, 258,
264, 284–5
Mosley, Sir Oswald (father), 88
Mosley, Sir Oswald (grandfather), 87–90, 92
Mosley, Sir Oswald ('Tom', 'Kit'), 163–70,
211–13, 284–6
meeting with Diana Guinness, 82–4, 118;
forebears, 85–90; childhood, 88–90;
education, 90–1; First World War service,
91–3; Royal Flying Corps, 91–3; MP for
Harrow, 94–103; Unionist affiliation,
94–100; ideals, 95; and League of
Nations, 95; marriage to Lady Cynthia
Curzon, 95–8; children of first marriage,
98–9, 144, 236, 245; and Irish politics,
99–103; leaves Conservatives, 100;
Independent MP for Harrow, 102–3;
joins Labour Party, 104; Birmingham
Proposals, 105; Labour MP for

Smethwick, 105–10; stands for
Ladywood, 105; Chancellor of the
Duchy of Lancaster, 107; and
unemployment problems, 107–10, 115;
resigns from cabinet, 109; expelled from
Labour Party, 110; move towards
fascism, 111–16; affair with Diana
Guinness, 119–27, 137–9, 143–6; and
fascism in Britain, 128–32; and British
Union of Fascists, 153–7; meeting with
Hitler, 182–6, 213–14; marriage to
Diana Guinness, 201–2, 209, 213–14,
232–3; imprisonment, 241–2, 255–9;
interrogation by the Advisory
Committee, 250–2; litigation while in
prison, 255–6; release from prison,
259–61; war years under house arrest,
262–73; parliamentary candidate for
Notting Hill, 283; death, 285; *The
Alternative*, 268, 274, 278; *The Greater
Britain*, 121–2, 133, 139; *My Answer*,
268; *My Life*, 283; *A National Policy for
National Emergency* (Mosley
Manifesto), 110–11; *Revolution by
Reason*, 105; *Tomorrow We Live*, 230;
see also British Union of Fascists
Mosley, Vivien, 98–9, 224, 264
Mount Temple, Lord, 205, 210
Moyne, Lord *see* Guinness, Walter
Munich agreement, 233–5
Museum Investment Trust, 218
Mussolini, 128–9, 136, 139, 154–5, 195, 216
Muv *see* Mitford, Sydney, Lady Redesdale
My Answer, 268
My Life, 283

National Government (coalition), 113
Nazi Party Congress, 210–11
New Epoch Products Ltd, 216
New Party, 82, 85, 110–16, 128
Newens, Stan, 250–1
Newnes, Sir Frank and Lady, 210
Nichols, Beverley, 211
nicknames, 25–7
Nicolson, Harold, 110, 128, 135–6, 148, 188
diaries, 112–15
Night of the Long Knives, 168, 170
non-white immigration, 275–6, 283
Nuffield, Lord *see* Morris, Sir William
Nuremberg Parteitage, 150–2, 171–5, 197,
232

O'Connor, T. P., 102
Ogilvie-Grant, Mark, 36, 54, 56, 78, 162
Ohnesorge, Wilhelm, 219, 230
The Old Ladies, 162
Old Mill Cottage (High Wycombe), 15, 17,
239–40